THE BEAR AND HIS SONS

The Bear and His Sons

MASCULINITY IN SPANISH AND MEXICAN FOLKTALES

JAMES M. TAGGART

DRAWINGS BY BEATRICE TAGGART

UNIVERSITY OF TEXAS PRESS
AUSTIN

Requests for permission to reproduce material from this work should be
sent to Permissions, University of Texas Press, Box 7819, Austin, TX
78713-7819.

⊗ The paper used in this publication meets the minimum requirements of
American National Standard for Information Sciences—Permanence of Paper
for Printed Library Materials, ANSI Z39.48-1984.

Drawings © Beatrice Taggart.

LIBRARY OF CONGRESS CATALOGING-IN-PUBLICATION DATA

Taggart, James M., 1941 –
    The bear and his sons : masculinity in Spanish and Mexican folktales /
James M. Taggart.— 1st University of Texas ed.
    p.   cm.
    Includes bibliographical references (p.   ) and index.
    ISBN 0-292-78144-x (cloth : alk. paper). —ISBN 0-292-78145-8
(paper : alk. paper)
    1. Tales—Mexico.   2. Tales—Spain.   3. Nahuas—Folklore.
4. Mexicans—Folklore.   5. Masculinity (Psychology)—Mexico—
Folklore.   6. Machismo—Mexico—Folklore.   7. Communication in
folklore—Mexico.   I. Title.
GR115.T34   1997
398'.353—dc20   96-30194

For Ben, Willie, and Julian

CONTENTS

Preface ix

1. Introduction 1

2. "The Bear's Son" in Spain 23

3. "The Bear's Son" in Mexico 46

4. Tricksters in Spain 71

5. Tricksters in Mexico 96

6. "Blood Brothers" 119

7. "The Two Travelers" 144

8. Florencio's "Blancaflor" 173

9. Nacho's "Blancaflor" 196

10. "Orpheus" 223

11. Conclusions 242

Appendix: "The Bear's Son"
in Spanish and Nahuat 248

Notes 297

References 323

Index 335

PREFACE

I BENEFITED FROM MANY SOURCES OF INSPIRATION AND SUP-
port that helped me write this book. Storytellers in Mexico, Spain,
and recently the Hispanic Southwest of the United States generously
told me their stories and gave me their friendship. My training in cultural anthropology taught me to listen to the words of others in an
attempt to bridge the gap between my culture and theirs. The meticu-
lous scholarship by which folklorists classify folktales has enabled
me to place all stories I collected in a broad historical perspective. I
owe a great debt of intellectual gratitude to Alan Dundes, who invited
me to teach courses on the oral narrative at the University of California at Berkeley. Dundes generously read an earlier draft of this book
and encouraged me to continue combining folklore and anthropology
in an effort to gain broader insight into the human condition.

My family has been a consistent source of help for understanding
more fully the folktales heard in different parts of the Hispanic world.
My loving wife Carole Counihan, who is the "Blancaflor" in my life,
read two earlier drafts of this manuscript and urged me to write with
clarity of purpose. She is the mother of our two sons, Ben and Willie,
whom we are raising as equally involved parents in an effort to develop fully their human potential. The third "bear's son" came into
our family circle when my daughter Marisela, who was born in Mexico and went with me to Spain, gave birth to Julian. My relationship
with my sons and grandson made me feel much closer to the characters in stories about bears and their sons.

Many foundations generously supported my fieldwork in Mexico
and Spain from 1968 to 1984. The Andrew Mellon Foundation, the
Wenner-Gren Foundation, the American Philosophical Society, and
the National Science Foundation (BNS7706660) funded my fieldwork
in Mexico from 1968 to 1978. The American Philosophical Society,
Franklin and Marshall College, and the National Science Foundation
(BNS8201874) also supported fieldwork in Spain from 1980 to 1984. I
also benefited from the help of many people. Theresa May guided this

book through the review process with a very skilled hand; Alan Sandstrom, who has an unsurpassed understanding of the Nahua, served as one of the readers for the University of Texas Press and offered excellent suggestions for revision; a second, anonymous reader, with unparalleled knowledge of folklore scholarship, provided superb suggestions for interpreting as well as classifying folktales; Alison Tartt meticulously copyedited this book in preparation for its publication; and my sister Beatrice Taggart, who has been a very important person in my life, created and drew the illustrations.

—Lancaster, Pennsylvania
April 1996

THE BEAR AND HIS SONS

Chapter 1

INTRODUCTION

THIS BOOK TAKES A JOURNEY THROUGH THE POETIC IMAGI-
nations of Spanish and Mexican men to discover how they represent
and reproduce models of masculinity when telling popular Hispanic
folktales. It focuses on two storytellers who depicted a man's relationship with other men and with women in stories they told in Spanish
and Nahuat, an Aztec language spoken in central Mexico.[1] It sets out
on the difficult and risky course of translating their stories and life
experiences from their own languages and cultures into readable English for an audience that may already have its own images of the Hispanic man from a variety of sources. He lives in our communities, he
appears in popular culture, and he is anyone who speaks Spanish and
has a Latino-sounding name.

Oscar Lewis provided English readers with some of their most accessible and startling verbal portraits of the Hispanic man in Mexico.
He is Jesús Sánchez, the urban migrant from Veracruz desperately
contending with poverty in Mexico City.[2] He is also Pedro Martínez,
the village peasant, proud of speaking Nahuatl but "uninterested in
his 'Indian' background," struggling with landlessness in Tepoztlán.[3]
Lewis translated and interpreted their stories to represent the Mexican man as close to his mother, cruel and unconnected to his wife and
children, and proving his masculinity with violence and sexual conquest.[4] The spellbinding narratives of Jesús' daughters Consuelo and
Marta and Pedro's wife Esperanza complemented and reinforced this
picture. Village studies in Mexico and Spain added more images of the
Hispanic man as ambivalent toward women, distant from his father,
and alienated from his sons.[5]

The Spanish and Mexican storytellers described here will present
their pictures of the Hispanic man as a character in their folktales,
which are regional variants of stories popular in many parts of Europe.

He is John the Bear, who proves his masculinity in acts of strength and courage; he is Juan the cardplayer, who leaves his mother, travels to the underworld, and meets Blancaflor, who gives him her love and takes care of him by using her supernatural power, only to be abandoned when Juan marries another woman; and he is the devil who appears as a well-dressed gentleman and seduces maidens and married women, carrying them off to his cave in the bowels of the earth. The storytellers have shaped the Hispanic man as a story character to fit their own conceptions of masculinity as they molded folktales of Spanish origin to their own cultures and expressed their personal experiences.

The two narrators are Florencio Ramos, a Spaniard who lives in the village of Navaconcejo in the province of Cáceres in northern Extremadura, and Nacho Ángel Hernández, a Mexican who lives in Huitzilan de Serdán in the northern Sierra de Puebla. They are extraordinarily gifted storytellers and very accessible men who wove autobiographical elements into their folktales, which colonialists brought to the Americas after the Spanish Conquest of Mexico. In some ways, Florencio and Nacho are like other men I knew in their cultures and, in other interesting respects, they are different. Florencio lived in a culture with a high value on male autonomy, and he consequently represented male relationships with an assumption of economic independence. However, he had an unusually close and nurturing connection with his sons that affected the way he told all of his stories. Nacho lived in a culture with a value on male connection, but his family had an unusually high level of cohesiveness, and he represented masculine family relationships with more interdependence and communality relative to other Nahuat who told similar stories. Florencio's and Nacho's specific presentations of masculinity become apparent by comparing their folktales with variants of the same stories told by many narrators in their villages and cultures. The folktale comparative method can help make an ethnography multivocal by revealing the plurality of voices of different storytellers who make popular tales their own narratives.[6]

MEETING NACHO

Nacho was twenty-four and I was twenty-seven when we met soon after I settled in Huitzilan de Serdán. At Hugo Nutini's urging, I did a survey of other villages in the northern Sierra de Puebla to find the most appropriate place to do a study of Nahuat kinship and family life. Other villages did not seem right to me; the people living in them dressed like "Indians" in white cotton trousers and flowing skirts but they spoke too much Spanish. In Huitzilan, they spoke only Nahuat. They could not understand me, and I certainly could not understand them, and so they looked like the perfect ethnographic other.

Huitzilan was far from roads traveled by car, bus, or truck when I first went there in 1968. It lies in a small valley crossed by one of the main mule and horse paths extending into the heart of the most isolated part of the northern Sierra de Puebla. Lush green cattle pastures interspersed with coffee orchards covered the slopes extending up from the valley floor. Large white houses with tile roofs lined the stone-paved main road and were the homes and stores of about fifty families who speak excellent Spanish. Many referred to themselves as *gente de razón* ("the people of reason") and told me they and their families had originally come from Tetela de Ocampo, twenty kilometers to the south on the highlands. Along the paths meandering away from the main road were over 400 small houses hidden under *chalahuite* trees planted to protect the delicate coffee plants. Here lived most of the people, who preferred speaking *mexicano* (Nahuat) and called themselves mācēhualmeh (speakers of Nahuat).[7]

Nacho was a prayer leader at the novenas (nine nightly prayers) held for Victorio Cruz, an eighteen-year-old boy who had died of a mysterious illness. Church bells constantly tolled and coffins regularly passed my window on their way to the cemetery. Usually they contained mācēhualmeh whose families welcomed anyone willing to pray for their recently dead relatives. I attended many novenas in an effort to get to know the Nahuat in Huitzilan. Years later, with the help of Nacho's Orpheus tales (Chapter 10), I discovered what the living at the novena were probably feeling about the dead who were the subjects of their prayers. After kneeling while Nacho said the rosary, we sat on small benches, talked, drank coffee, and ate sweet bread. One of those present was a *razón*, and he asked me a question in Nahuat that I could not understand. I replied "quēmah," or "yes," nodding my head to make sure everyone knew I was an agreeable person. The next day, the dead boy's brother appeared nervously at my door and offered to work with me, peering over his shoulder to make sure he was not seen.

I did not understand what happened until Nacho and I became good friends some time later. Nacho explained that the *razón* had asked me if I worked with the ahmō cualli ("he who is not good"), the preferred name for the devil. He said my questioner was a sorcerer who claimed to work with the ahmō cualli himself and earlier had gone to Nacho and his brothers and demanded turkeys or chickens in return for saving their sick mother. He told them she would die if they denied him. However, Nacho's brothers, Nicolás and Miguel, refused his demand, and their mother recovered. Nacho explained that the dead boy's brother was nervous because he feared being seen by the *razón* at the novena, who was my neighbor and probably extorted other Nahuat with threats of sorcery. His practice of sorcery by diabolical intervention and his question to me at the novena are different examples of behavior that the Nahuat in Huitzilan call īlihuiz, an adverb translated into English as "inconsiderately."[8] Our common experience permitted me to gain rapport with Nacho and other Nahuat who now trusted me more than otherwise, despite my limited ability to speak their language during the early stages of fieldwork. The avoidance of īlihuiz gradually emerged as a crucially important component of Nahuat masculinity.

Nacho helped me in many ways figure out Nahuat kinship and family life, which at that time I had decided was the expression of Nahuat identity. I became aware of storytelling near the end of my two-and-a-half-year stay when Antonio Veracruz told a folktale to a group of children during an all-night vigil following the death of yet another mācēhual. Without my tape recorder and pencil and paper, I listened to Antonio's story and watched the rapt attention of his audience. Later I asked Nacho if he knew any tales that I could record, and he told a story folklorists call "The Two Travelers" (Tale Type 613), which probably came from Spain because it appears in the medieval manuscript known as the *Libro de los Gatos* (Chapter 7).[9]

By this time, I had collected many family histories to discover the "realities" of domestic life. When I transcribed and carefully examined the words in Nacho's story, I discovered that he represented in economical and poetic language the pattern of family dynamics others reported when they described their "real" family histories. Moreover, he and other storytellers tended to reveal more about family life when telling a story that took place in a different time and place than when describing their "real" experiences in ordinary discourse. With my categories of reality and fantasy seriously challenged, I learned two things. First, Nacho and other storytellers were serious when they said their stories describe things that actually happened. Second, the categories of "fact," "fiction," and "allegory," as Ruth Behar mentions,[10] are part of the baggage of Euro-American culture. The distinction between fiction and reality has troubled me ever since because it relegates folktales to the realm of fantasy and makes them easily dismissed. A fictional narrative is somehow more trivial than a real one, despite Freud's contention that the images in our dreams, which rise out of our fantastic imaginations, are to be taken seriously.[11] The persistent trivialization of folk narratives is one of the reasons Alan Dundes turned to Freudian theory to argue that folklore is important.[12]

Folktales and Nahuat Identity

With thoughts like these in mind, I turned to folktales to find Nahuat cultural identity in the poetic imagination. I went to Antonio Veracruz and others in Huitzilan and Yaonáhuac, a Nahuat village to the east, and recorded and transcribed the folktales of fifteen narrators during four summers and another extended field stay of a year and a half in 1977 and 1978. Undaunted by Franz Boas's bold pronouncement that nothing remains of the native Mexican storytelling tradition,[13] I expected to find Nahuat cultural identity expressed in stories derived from ancient native Mexican narratives written down in the sixteenth century by Bernardino de Sahagún and the other chroniclers:[14] myths of the origin of the sun and the moon and the origin of corn; tales about the opossum, which Alfredo López Austin later noted is a New World animal that appeared in pre-Hispanic iconography; sixteenth-century myths; and contemporary Mexican folktales.[15] A few storytellers I met along the way told variants of the ancient stories that they adapted to fit contemporary conditions, but they also told many more folktales of Spanish origin. Their stories of the sun and the moon, corn, and opossums represented only a small part of their experience.

Nacho did not tell tales that are the usual markers of a surviving indigenous ethnic identity, although he grew up speaking a native Mexican language. He spent very little time outside of the community where he was born, and he grew up in a large extended family, which seems like a quintessential Nahuat institution. He is related by kinship to nearly half of the people in his village. He is a gifted storyteller with an astounding memory, a vast knowledge of Nahuat, and an extraordinary ability to turn a phrase to bring his characters to life. He is not the true native Mexican I as an anthropologist thought I would find at the beginning of my search. Rather, Nacho is more like the folklorist's typical storyteller, who usually tells a tale that originated from somewhere else. A careful examination of the way he used words in his stories reveals how he expressed his native Mexican masculine identity in more subtle ways than I originally expected.

Learning and Telling Stories

Storytelling can take place any time and is not an activity for which anyone is paid. There are no storytelling competitions, and it is my impression that in Huitzilan storytellers usually learn their tales from members of their own families. Nacho learned his stories from his older brother Nicolás, with whom he had a particularly close relationship. The major exceptions are narrators in both villages who have long histories of working in migrant labor camps on the coastal plantations. Migrant laborers come from all over the northern Sierra de Puebla and include speakers of Nahuat and Totonac, another but quite different native Mexican language, as well as Spanish. They sleep together in large sheds and tell stories as they relax in the evening. Nacho spent very little time in the migrant labor camps of the hot country; he made one trip and never returned because he found the food and working conditions so poor.

Nacho reported that the most frequent storytelling setting outside of a family is in sugarcane processing groups. Sugarcane is processed in small presses turned by horses. Nacho's neighbor and cousin, Domingo Hernández, had a press in his small sugarcane field to the north of the village. Workers harvest and process sugarcane in a single operation that takes place over a two-day period. Work goes on all day and all night as harvesters place the cane into the press as it squeezes out the juice that flows down a canal into a huge cauldron heated by a wood fire. The heated juice is boiled and then poured into molds to cool, becoming brown sugar. Workers wrap the molded sugar in palm leaves and carry it back with tumplines to the village, where they store it in the loft above the kitchen so it will be preserved with smoke from the hearth. Men usually harvest and process the sugarcane, one or two women prepare meals for the workers, and many women help transport the loaves of brown sugar back to the village. Storytelling can easily take place during the day or night while several workers are waiting for the cauldron to fill and the juice to boil.

Other settings for telling stories I have actually witnessed in Huitzilan are all-night vigils preceding the burial of the dead as well as gatherings of men drinking in stores. Storytellers reported that they tell long narratives when walking to market or when performing any group task such as husking corn. Most of the storytellers, who vol-

untarily and spontaneously performed stories in Huitzilan and Yaonáhuac, were men. Nahuat gatherings, where storytelling takes place,
were strictly segregated along gender lines, and I would have acted
with īlihuiz had I invaded the spaces of women on those occasions.
The women who told me stories in Huitzilan and Yaonáhuac were
recruited by their brothers or sons, leading me to suspect that there is
an important feminine storytelling tradition in both communities.

MEETING FLORENCIO

To place into perspective how Nacho and other narrators adapted
Spanish folktales to fit their culture and experience, I went to Spain
to find out how storytellers represented themselves in a different,
Castilian Spanish narrative style. Published collections of folktales
would not do for this purpose because they provide almost no information about the narrators. I went to Cáceres because it is the region
that probably contributed the first colonialists to settle in the northern Sierra de Puebla and introduce their stories into the Nahuat oral
tradition.[16] Following the generous advice of Stanley Brandes, I began
working in 1980 on the southern slopes of the Gredos mountains and
selected El Guijo de Santa Bárbara as the first village. There I ran into
Leandro Jiménez, who coincidentally told a version of "The Two
Travelers," the first folktale recorded from Nacho. The following
summers I went to Garganta la Olla and Piornal, the highest village
in the province of Cáceres. During 1983 and 1984, I spent a year looking for more storytellers in Navaconcejo, Cabezuela, Tornavacas, Serradilla, and again in Garganta la Olla.

Florencio was one of forty-two women and men in Cáceres who told
me their folktales, many of which resemble the tales I heard from
Nahuat-speaking narrators in Mexico. He was sixty and I was forty-
two when I met him one evening in 1983 as he put his horses away in
a stable inside a very large, old house he called "la fábrica" ("the factory"). Here, he explained, he lived as a child and learned all of the
folktales in his repertoire. Later on, after telling his version of "Blancaflor" (Tale Type 313C), he offered a glimpse of growing up living in
the "factory." Living quarters were on the second floor, which had a
huge hall and the doors to many apartments. Florencio explained: "In
that big hall above there were no fewer than seven or eight kitchen
hearths. People used to gather at one of them, and the old women
would tell stories and that's how we passed the nights. Those nights
were long during the winter."

Florencio's nickname is "Remoliniego" because his father was from Arroyomolinos, another town below Piornal on the slopes of the Gredos mountains. His father followed an older brother to Navaconcejo to find work and eventually married a woman from the village. Florencio was born in a small house in front of the church in the central plaza of Navaconcejo, and then went with his parents to live at the "factory" when he was two years old. After paying rent, his parents bought a sixth of the building. Florencio spent his childhood there except for a brief period at the outbreak of the civil war when his father ran into trouble with the "Falangistas" and took his family to live in Arroyomolinos for two months and eight days. Florencio started attending school but soon left just as he began learning block letters because his father needed him to care for some calves he was raising for their owners in return for half the selling price. Florencio eventually learned how to read when he went into the military in 1944. He married his wife and the mother of his five children soon after being discharged and began married life in his wife's parents' home. He remained in Navaconcejo until 1955 when he took his family to sharecrop in Murcia for a year and a half. Florencio explained that he left Navaconcejo because he got into a dispute when he grazed his goats on land a neighbor claimed was private property.

Learning and Telling Stories

Florencio is like many storytellers in Cáceres who said they learned their tales in a family setting. Most declared that they first heard their tales from parents and grandparents who told them stories at bedtime. Several unusually skilled storytellers, like Julio López Curiel of Garganta la Olla, reported that they learned their tales from grandparents with whom they slept as young children. Some, like Mercedes Zamoro Monroy of Cabezuela, learned their stories from books: Mercedes said her aunt read her stories that she committed to memory and told to her daughters when working in the kitchen. Cáceres narrators often mentioned learning tales while sitting in small intimate family gatherings next to the kitchen hearth or sitting around the circular kitchen table (*camilla*) with a brazier in its base. Felisa Sánchez Martín from Serradilla said: "When we were young, since there was no television, people gathered, men the same as the women, sitting at the fire, and there everyone told us what they knew."

One of the main differences between storytelling in Cáceres and the Nahuat villages of Mexico is that Spanish women were much more accessible storytellers. Of the forty-two narrators I knew, twenty-five were women and only seventeen were men. Moreover, many male narrators, including Florencio, reported that they learned their stories from older women. In some respects, the patterns of storytelling in the two cultures coincide with the different configurations of family loyalties. Cáceres women have particularly strong ties to parents and children while men are reputed to be estranged from fathers and sons. The strong filial ties of women and the weak ones of men are manifest in a higher frequency of matrilocality among newly married couples who, like Florencio and his wife, live with the wife's parents during their early marital years. Women also express their filial loyalties by exclusively caring for their young children, who are consequently more likely to learn stories from the mother than the father.

In Nacho's village of Huitzilan, young couples often begin married life with the family of the husband. Patrilocality clusters fathers, sons, and brothers, who are consequently more likely to be the source of a story learned in a family setting. Moreover, fathers regularly sleep on a separate mat with young children, from the time they are weaned, and work with their young sons on their corn and bean plots. Nacho, who reported he learned his stories from his older brother Nicolás, appears to have described a typical family experience.

THE LINK BETWEEN FLORENCIO AND NACHO

Nacho probably acquired folktales like those told by Florencio and other Spanish narrators from an intermediary category of Spanish-speaking Mexicans. Most were originally descendants of Spanish men and native Mexican women. They now live in Tetela de Ocampo and other communities throughout the northern Sierra de Puebla, they moved into Huitzilan, and they work in the migrant labor camps on the coastal plain. Nacho and his brother may have learned some stories from the *gente de razón* who originated in Tetela, although none I knew told any of the folktales I heard from Nacho and other Nahuat in Huitzilan. Nacho went only once to the hot country, but he and his brother Nicolás could easily have heard stories, originally told by Spanish-speaking Mexican storytellers, when they worked with other Nahuat of their community, who spent more time in the migrant labor camps and who helped Domingo Hernández, Nacho's neighbor and cousin, process sugarcane.

It is difficult to find the best word to describe the Spanish-speaking settlers from Tetela de Ocampo and migrant workers on the hot country plantations. They are a diverse group, and they refer to themselves

Fig. 1. Sugar cane press of Domingo Hernández.

with a variety of terms depending on where they are and with whom they are speaking. They call themselves *gente de razón* in Huitzilan, but in Tetela they say they are residents of their village, their state, or their nation. They have a Hispanic culture, but the word "Hispanic" has a loaded meaning for an English-reading audience. Eric Wolf used the term "mestizos" for the non-Indian population in Mexico that rose to power following the Mexican Revolution that toppled the regime of Porfirio Díaz and his European-oriented advisors, known as *los científicos* ("the scientists").[17] I prefer to identify this category of storytellers linking Florencio and Nacho as Spanish-speaking Mexicans to emphasize the important relationship between language and cultural identity.

THE COMPARISON OF COGNATE FOLKTALES

As the tellers of cognate folktales or stories from a common historical source, Florencio and Nacho lend themselves to the comparative method in folklore and anthropology. The method, argues Alan Dundes, has fallen into disfavor, particularly in anthropology, which embraced cultural relativism.[18] According to that doctrine, societies develop distinctive cultural forms that are products of particular historical experiences and must be understood in their own terms rather than in terms of the constructs that are part of the culture of the observers. The doctrine of cultural relativism was embraced in reaction to the excesses of nineteenth-century comparative studies conducted within the framework of unilinear evolutionary theory.

The concept of cultural relativism has, if anything, grown in importance with the increasing conviction that ethnographers are often unaware of the extent to which their own hidden cultural assumptions color their perceptions and representations of the ethnographic other. James Clifford contends that Malinowski, renowned for his extensive fieldwork, actually spent less time in the field than many missionaries but was nevertheless convinced of the power of his observations because he focused on specific aspects of culture through the lens of theory. He wrote with an "ethnographic authority" that is unjustified given the actually chaotic nature of his field experience revealed in his posthumously published diary. A close reading of that diary and his accounts of the Trobriands, written years after he made his field observations, leave many unanswered questions and lead to the skeptical conclusion that his ethnographic writing is really a fictional representation. What is true of Malinowski, contends Clifford, is true of other ethnographers who were committed to making objective observations but produced ethnographic descriptions that are products of "a predicament of culture" or being in one culture while observing another.[19]

Nevertheless, Dundes notes that the assumption of cultural uniqueness, which is a corollary of the general premise of cultural relativism, can lead one seriously astray when interpreting folktales.[20] For example, Thomas Beidelman offered an interpretation of a Kaguru trickster tale as a reflection of matrilineal kinship without realizing that the story he considered is one variant of a very popular tale told in various societies, some of which could have a social organization very different from that of the Kaguru. Dundes notes that "Beidelman's remarks on the Kaguru version of a standard tale type are not necessarily wrong, but if the same tale were found in a patrilineal society, it would tend to weaken his overall argument that the tale exists as a peculiar response to the pressures of interpersonal relations caused by Kaguru matrilineality."[21]

While anthropologists sometimes overemphasize the uniqueness of a particular product of cultural expression (such as a folktale), folklorists embracing the comparative method have completely removed folktales from their social and cultural context. Dundes traced the nineteenth-century antecedents of the comparative method in folklore to the efforts to reconstruct the past. The brothers Grimm observed that "folktales and other forms of folklore could be shown to demonstrate genetically/historically common traits."[22] The comparative method in folklore, known as the Finnish method, was used to reconstruct the historical process by which a story originated and spread throughout human societies. Archer Taylor and Stith Thompson promoted the use of the method in the United States, and Thompson eventually applied it in his study of folktales in the oral tradition from around the world. Thompson's use of the comparative method is built around the concept of the cognate folktale, stories in the oral tradition that originate from the same historical source and have spread to different storytelling communities.

The centrality of the concept of the cognate folktale in Thompson's use of the comparative method runs counter to the tendency in anthropology to see cultural expression as unique to a particular individual or society. Dundes argues that anthropologists would profit by knowing more about the cognate forms of cultural expression they observe and describe in particular ethnographic situations.[23] Likewise, folklorists would profit by placing particular items of folklore in their social and cultural settings. To remove the tales from the tellers would ignore how much Florencio and Nacho made the stories their own by using narrative styles and imagery that fit their cultures and personal histories. To examine Nacho's or Florencio's stories alone and without regard to variants of the same tales told by other narrators would serve only to isolate the two men from the currents of history that have affected them.

THE STORIES COMPARED

I shall first apply this comparative method to the stories of Spanish origin that Florencio and Nacho told in common. Their cognate stories depicting a man's relationship with other men are "The Bear's Son" (Tale Type 301), which resembles the Grendel episode of *Beowulf* but probably derives from a European oral source,[24] and "The Rich and the Poor Peasant" (Tale Type 1535), which is similar to the tenth-century Latin poem *Unibos*.[25] A comparison of these tales in Chapters 2 through 5 reveals how the two men used distinctive narratives styles to represent and reproduce masculinity according to their cultures and their personal histories.

Florencio and Nacho also told other stories, not included in their common folktale repertoires, which nevertheless revealed a great deal about their views of male family relationships. Florencio told "The Three Magic Objects and the Wonderful Fruits" (Tale Type 566) and "Blood Brothers" (Tale Type 303), in which he expressed his conception of fathers, sons, and brothers. Nacho did not include these folktales in his repertoire and expressed his view of male family relationships in "The Two Travelers" (Tale Type 613), a story that appeared in a collection of fourteenth-century Spanish folklore but not among Florencio's tales.[26] The cognate folktale comparative method cannot be applied to Florencio's and Nacho's images in these particular cases. Nevertheless, others in Spain and Mexico told two of these folktales, permitting one to see how each man represented masculine family relationships relative to other men in the two cultures. Several Nahuat in Nacho's village of Huitzilan and in Santiago Yaonáhuac told "Blood Brothers," allowing comparisons with Florencio's version of this important folktale (Chapter 6). Likewise, Spaniards in Cáceres told "The Two Travelers," enabling one to see how Nacho represented brothers with unusual cohesiveness relative to storytellers in Florencio's culture as well as narrators in different parts of Mexico. I shall explain Nacho's version of "The Two Travelers" by describing his actual relationship with his brothers, who pooled their labor to fill a common granary and purse (Chapter 7).

Florencio's and Nacho's most important cognate story about man's relationship with woman is "The Girl as Helper in the Hero's Flight" or "Blancaflor" (Tale Type 313C), which resembles the Greek tragedy "Jason and Medea."[27] Comparison of their versions of this fascinating folktale (Chapters 8 and 9) indicates how the two men developed their views of gender relations as part of their general vision of all human relationships, including, of course, man's relationship with other men. Nacho also expressed his conception of a man's relationship with woman in two Orpheus stories that have as their central feature "The Man on a Search for His Lost Wife" (Tale Type 400). I did not hear this tale from any of the forty-two storytellers I met in the eight Cáceres villages where I collected folktales. Although Tale Type 400 does appear in other parts of Europe, it is rare in Spain except as the final episode in some variants of "The Bear's Son," which is also known as "The Three Stolen Princesses." Nacho's two stories seem to be part of an independent native North American Orpheus tradition.[28] His Orpheus tales (Chapter 10) represent his conception of a man's relationship with his dead wife, which is an extension of his general view of living human relations that he expressed in all his stories.

To place more fully Florencio and Nacho in their cultural contexts and the currents of history that have affected them, I shall compare throughout this book their folktales with variants of the same stories told by three different categories of storytellers. First, Florencio's stories will be examined together with similar tales I heard from the forty-one other Cáceres narrators and Spanish folklorists collected from storytellers in other parts of Spain. Comparison of the Spanish stories reveals how Florencio represented and reproduced masculinity through storytelling relative to other male and female narrators in his culture.

Second, variants of the same folktales told by Spanish-speaking Mexicans are considered to reveal how this intermediate category of storytellers adapted tales of Spanish origin to new conditions before passing them on to the Nahuat and other speakers of indigenous languages in Mexico. No one has done a study of Spanish-speaking Mexican storytelling in the northern Sierra de Puebla to describe the folktales of Spanish origin that members of this intermediary category may have introduced into Nahuat oral tradition. However, one can guess about their stories by examining other tales collected from apparently similar groups in different parts of Mexico. The largest and most reliable collections come from Jalisco,[29] which I shall utilize to guess at the earlier form of the stories Nacho and his brother Nicolás now tell in Nahuat oral tradition.

Third, I shall consider how Nacho and fourteen other Nahuat storytellers in Huitzilan and Yaonáhuac adapted stories of Spanish origin to fit their own culture and social experience. To place Nacho's folktales in a broader context within Mexico, his tales will also be examined together with variants told by other native Mexicans within and outside the Nahua-speaking region of Central Mexico.[30] The category of native Mexican folktales is very uneven and poorly defined. The quality ranges from the meticulously transcribed and translated texts in Robert Laughlin's collection of Tzotzil Mayan stories from Zinacantán in southeastern Mexico to stories that appear in English unaccompanied by the original language texts and lacking in information about the narrators.[31] The native Mexican tales nevertheless represent masculinity in some interesting ways that differ from tales told by Spanish-speaking narrators in Mexico and Spain.

INTERPRETING FLORENCIO'S AND NACHO'S STORIES

Géza Róheim suggested an eclectic approach toward oral narrative interpretation drawing on folklore, social anthropology, and psychoanalysis. The comparative method in folklore provides, first of all, a story's pedigree. Social anthropology yields the cultural materials out of which stories are constructed. Seeing similarities between a folk-tale and a house, Róheim asserted that psychoanalysis permits one to descend from "attic to cellar" and locate the "unconscious tendencies which take hold of" cultural materials and "make use of them for their own purposes."[32] I shall take Róheim's suggestion, recognizing that telling a folktale is above all a discursive act bringing together language, culture, and social and psychological experience.[33] The comparative method reveals how Florencio and Nacho told stories derived from a common historical source and draws into relief how the two men built their stories out of their languages and their cultures. I shall begin with how the two men used words differently to represent and reproduce masculinity through storytelling.

The Use of Language

When Florencio and Nacho told a folktale, they communicated with others in a dialogue that involved words and images that are extremely complex and subtle. I can only imagine what took place in the minds of the children listening so intently to Antonio Veracruz when he told his story on the night of that wake long ago in Huitzilan. Although I can offer no convincing proof, it seems reasonable to conclude that Antonio, Nacho, and Florencio were actually reproducing masculinity when they told their stories because they presented to their listeners models of manliness that justified and perhaps encouraged behaviors appropriate for their cultures. Their stories offered distinct models of masculine behavior, represented by the way they used words differently. When spoken words are converted to type on a page, they lose a great deal of meaning. So one of my tasks in the following chapters is to put the meaning back into their words by paying close attention to how they used language to set the tone for the action that took place in their stories.[34] Transcriptions of their actual words are found in the appendix of this book.[35]

Florencio modeled his masculinity by using words assertively to describe aggressive male characters. He also employed narrative techniques of plot invention and hyperbole that expressed his close identification with heroes who acted aggressively and autonomously. I shall draw heavily on what Florencio told me about himself and his relationships with other men and with women to interpret his language and his story images. After comparing his stories with those of Nacho, it became apparent that Florencio represented and reproduced

an image of men who are comparatively but not absolutely disconnected from other men and heavily dependent on women.

Florencio spoke and his story characters acted with an assertiveness
that Nacho might regard as īlihuiz and thus to be avoided. Nacho
avoided īlihuiz by using a narrative style that did not contain strong
words and distanced him from the powerful and assertive characters
with whom Florencio so closely identified. The contrast in their styles
was most evident in their versions of "The Bear's Son" (Tale Type 301).
Nacho's avoidance of īlihuiz is related to his growing up in a large and
unusually cohesive extended family where he and his married brothers pooled their labor to fill a common granary and purse from which
each family member could draw according to need. The avoidance of
īlihuiz is a cultural construction of masculinity that developed according to a highly interconnected family system and extended to Nacho's
view of the universe (his cosmology). I shall use what Nacho told me
about his family and his cosmology to interpret the language and the
images of his stories.

Florencio and Nacho inherited their languages and cultures and,
thus, represented well-established gender images that appeared in the
tales told by other men in their villages. They are subjects in what
Jacques Lacan called a "signifying chain," his term for language and
culture, which imposes a gender identity on a man or woman by as-
signed meaning to their biology.[36] Lacan represented the dominance
of language (and culture) with the Saussurean algorithm S/s, in which
S stands for the signifier and s the thing signified.[37] The dominance of
the signifier represents the power of language and culture to alienate
an individual from himself in a process that is like castration.[38]

Lacan illustrated his own point by using language in a very alienat-
ing way, and his inaccessible texts are subject to a variety of interpretations. Jane Gallop offers a reading of Lacan that applies to the ways
Florencio and Nacho used language to represent and reproduce their
masculinities. According to Gallop, Lacan sees the subject as not
simply "inserted into his position of blindness within" language and
culture but also "placing himself" in his signifying chain.[39] A close
examination of Florencio's and Nacho's stories, relative to variants of
the same tales told by others in their villages and cultures, reveals
that the two men not only repeated what they heard before, but also
invented words and images to create their ideas about manliness
based on their particular family histories. A highly relativistic perspective on masculinity consequently emerges by using the comparative method for Florencio and Nacho.

Unconscious Meanings and Psychoanalytic Theory

When interpreting Florencio's and Nacho's stories, I make the assumption that some of their gender identity is under the surface because they were required to handle prohibited urges in culturally acceptable ways. Managing prohibited urges sometimes involves their repression, and to acknowledge openly a repressed urge is, as Róheim noted, a contradiction in terms.[40] To get to the "cellar" of their folktale "houses," I resort to a method of interpretation that allows me to guess at the underlying meaning of their story symbols by turning to psychoanalytic theory, which is particularly suited for reading the unconscious.

Freud made a distinction among psychical materials that are conscious, preconscious, and unconscious based on an individual's willingness and ability to express them in language. Using dreaming as his example, he illustrated the difference among the three categories of psychical materials by referring to the dreamer's ability to recall and describe in language the dream's content. He theorized that suppressed impulses make themselves felt during sleep and are expressed in language by the dreamer after awakening. The dreamer consciously describes the manifest content of a dream in language. The unconscious or latent content of the dream may be entirely different from its conscious or manifest content because of the mechanism of censorship or dreamwork.[41]

Using Freud's reasoning and Róheim's assumption that folktales are like dreams, the manifest content of Florencio's and Nacho's stories consequently consists of self-explanatory images or symbols that both men could explicate to me when I asked about their intended meanings.[42] Florencio and Nacho patiently explained many aspects of their stories which they considered obvious but I did not understand because I was of another culture. When explaining their tales, they frequently referred to their own family experiences. After I examined their stories and discovered how they presented and explained them to me, I realized that they represented their masculinity according to different social and cultural expectations. What I knew about their families enabled me to follow Róheim's recommendation and descend from the attic to the cellar of their folktale houses to discover how the mechanisms of repression might operate differently in their cultures to affect story content.[43] When I opened their cellar doors, I found the ghost of Sigmund Freud still mulling over his controversial theory of masculinity and femininity.

Freud's Theory of Gender

Many have criticized Freud's theory of gender for resting too heavily on a foundation of biological determinism and incorporating hidden cultural assumptions of his historical moment.[44] Nevertheless, his theory of gender is a useful point of departure for placing into context subsequent revisions that make psychoanalytic theory more useful for cross-cultural application. Freud considered gender on three levels: the biological presence of spermatozoa or ova, the inclination toward masculine activity or feminine passivity that derives from biology, and the actual social behavior of men and women.[45] He regarded the second level (masculine activity and feminine passivity) as the most useful for psychoanalysis. Freud hypothesized that women and men are innately bisexual because their personalities have two symmetrical halves: one that is actively masculine and the other that is passively feminine. The innate bisexuality of men and women colors many aspects of sexual development and means that adult gender identity requires that one of the halves becomes dominant.[46]

Freud believed that one's masculine or feminine half becomes dominant as one makes the choice of sexual object during the period of the Oedipus complex, which is unconscious or at the most preconscious. Dominant masculinity is less problematic for a man because he does not have to change the gender of his love object; he converts his love for his mother into love for another woman. His conversion ordinarily comes about because of castration threats, causing him to repress his sexual love for his mother and redirect his masculine sexual activity outside of his nuclear family.[47]

Freud was less certain about femininity.[48] He originally believed that the girl abandoned her mother as her original love object because the mother regulates the daughter's active sexuality, and the daughter perceives the mother as a sexual rival for the father.[49] However, Jeanne Lampl-de Groot and Helen Deutch discovered evidence of a girl's longer and deeper pre-Oedipal attachment to the mother, and their discovery caused Freud to explain more fully how a woman moves from her mother to her father as she enters her Oedipal period.[50] The girl has an insatiable need for the mother's love, which turns to ambivalence toward the mother when the girl perceives that she has not received enough maternal love. Some women, with very prolonged pre-Oedipal attachment to the mother, may develop a fear of being consumed by the mother.[51] However, boys as well as girls share many of the same experiences, so Freud turned to his famous and highly criticized concept of "penis envy" to explain why a girl shifts her love object from the mother to the father. He hypothesized that a woman develops her adult feminine identity when she converts her desire for a penis into a desire to have her father's baby, ceases to regard her clitoris as a phallus, and accepts her vagina and her passive femininity.[52]

According to this line of reasoning, Florencio manifested his masculine activity in his bold and assertive narrative style because his masculine half became dominant as he went through normal stages of his gender's development. Nacho was somehow inverted because, in his effort to avoid īlihuiz, he represented masculine identity with a "feminine" passivity and thus failed to pass through the ordinary psychological stages for his gender. Nacho is Freud's primitive, who is like the neurotic because his development is somehow arrested.

Abram Kardiner

To make psychoanalytic theory more useful for anthropology, Abram Kardiner declared that Freudian theory had to abandon "phylogenetic-ontogenic parallelism" by which primitives are equated with neurotics.[53] Kardiner incorporated cultural relativism into Freudian theory by arguing that individuals are subjected to different social and cultural demands depending on the organization of their society.[54] The demands may vary from one culture to the next, affecting the way individuals are required to repress or control their impulses. Kardiner consequently argued that Freudian theory must abandon a second assumption—that repression "always falls in the same place in all cultures"—and recommended placing the emphasis "on those forces concealed in institutions which compel the individual to repress a given impulse, and to those tendencies or conditions in the individual that make him yield to those pressures contained in or derived from institutions."[55] Kardiner contended that different group pressures on individuals produce a distinct, basic personality structure or traits of character that become expressed in folklore, which he regarded as the projective system of a culture.[56] Aware of individual variation within a particular group, he observed that "a group can no more have a common character than it can have a common soul or pair of lungs."[57] Nevertheless, certain similar traits of character can develop among individuals who project them as a pattern in folklore and religion. Such a pattern can appear when the members of a storytelling community give their folktales a particular form. C. W. von Sydow suggested the term "oicotype" to refer to the specific form a story takes when told by the members of a storytelling community.[58]

Following Kardiner's line of reasoning, I shall identify some of the group influences on Florencio and Nacho that explain their different ways of representing and reproducing masculinity in their stories. However, it is first necessary to consider more recent neo-Freudian revisions of gender theory because Kardiner, who contributed in inestimable ways to laying the foundation of psychological anthropology, nevertheless adopted uncritically some of Freud's ideas about sexuality and gender rooted in biological determinism. For example, when Kardiner interpreted Ralph Linton's ethnographic description of the Tanala, he focused on the plight of younger sons who "make up the bulk of the community."[59] His interpretation of the younger Tanala sons applies in some ways to Nacho, who is the youngest of three sons in a large patrilineally extended family household where authority was delegated along the lines of age. Like Nacho, the Tanala younger son occupies a fixed social position and acquiesces to a father who has considerable power. Kardiner believed that the younger Tanala son develops attitudes of dependency and turns to homosexuality because "homosexuality is a method of ingratiation with his father, whom he hates; but in proportion to his hatred, he inflates his father's image and humbles his own. His initial powerful and precocious heterosexuality was no match for the resources he could command as a child, and hence he threw his most valuable attribute away to guarantee for himself other more basic values of survival, support, and hope of unlimited help from his father."[60] Freud considered male homosexuality a form of inversion by which a man's masculine half does not become dominant as he passes through puberty and enters the stage of adult sexuality.[61] Kardiner concluded that Tanala folklore, which probably expresses the masculine identities of younger sons, who form the bulk of the community, "showed a typical father-son relationship in which jealousy was repressed and a passive feminine attitude appeared in its place."[62]

The notion that men are active and women are passive appears to be a cultural assumption as well as a proposition in Freud's theory of gender as applied by Kardiner to the Tanala. The *razón*, who owned the house where I lived in Huitzilan, remarked to me that he considered Nacho, then twenty-four and single, a gay man because he did not pursue women. Nacho was an anomaly because he was noticeably unlike the archetypal Hispanic man as aggressive progenitor in the mind of my Spanish-speaking Mexican neighbor. My retrospective conclusion from this experience is that theoretical and folk definitions of masculinity can exclude a broad range of behaviors found among men. Their narrowness becomes dramatically apparent when one man interprets or translates the deportment of another man who speaks a different language and has a different culture and family history.

Robert Stoller and Nancy Chodorow

Revisions after Kardiner's pioneering studies have moved Freud's theory of gender farther away from biological determinism and toward cultural relativism. The revisions help explain why Florencio differed from and Nacho resembled Spanish women when representing and reproducing masculinity in storytelling. Margaret Mead and many other anthropologists reported a wide range of gender identities in many different parts of the world, laying the foundation for less biologically determined or less essentialistic theories of gender.[63] Robert Stoller incorporated the insights from cultural anthropology and revised Freud's argument by defining gender identity not as an "eternal truth" but as a personal conviction that varies from one culture to the next and shifts when culture changes.[64] Working with transsexual men, he concluded that masculinity is actually more problematic than femininity because a man must break his symbiotic relationship with the mother and identify with the father in order to become masculine, according to the prevailing cultural construction of manliness. Transsexual boys, who biologically are males but who do not adopt a masculine gender identity, have an extraordinarily close symbiotic relationship with the mother that is not disrupted by the father. The mother regards her son as the completion of her own gender identity, which is incomplete because her parents devalued her femininity. The transsexual boy's father is too passive to break the symbiotic relationship between the mother and son, and consequently the son lives in a world where he perceives little of value in masculinity.[65] The essential point for my purposes is that Stoller stressed the importance of the father who helps his son make the transition from the feminine world of the mother to the masculine world of the father. Stoller applied his revision of Freud's theory of gender to several Native American cultures and collaborated with Gilbert H. Herdt to interpret the development of masculinity among the Sambia of New Guinea.[66]

Stoller's revision of Freud's theory of gender and sexuality set the stage for other approaches to masculinity and femininity emphasizing the role of social conditioning and culture. Nancy Chodorow placed Freudian theory in a Marxist perspective, contending that Freud incorporated the gender roles of his historical moment by assuming the women always parent small children.[67] However, Chodorow observed that women primarily cared for young children when "production" was distinguished from "reproduction" in modern capitalism.[68] Women, who assume the care of young children, reproduce in their daughters greater relational capacities required for parenting. Relational capacities are created out of the early infant's relationship with the mother and include the development of empathy, reciprocal primary love, and a sense of oneness with or connection to another.[69] Relational capacities, which permit mothers to empathize with their children, develop in daughters because they remain attached to the mother longer than sons during the pre-Oedipal period. Girls experience Electra rivalry differently than boys experience Oedipal rivalry under these conditions because daughters never entirely give the mother up as the object for their libidinal attachment and add the father as a new object. Boys, on the other hand, experience a shorter period of pre-Oedipal attachment; they separate from the mother earlier and identify with a father who is less involved in their nurturing care. The remoteness of the father does not permit the same relational capacities to develop in boys that Chodorow found in girls, and thus boys are less psychologically prepared for parenting and presumably nurturing others.

Chodorow's concept of relational capacities is helpful for understanding why Florencio differs from and Nacho resembles Spanish women when representing and reproducing masculinity through storytelling. Florencio's assertive narrative style is related to his representation of male characters as disconnected from other men. Nacho's avoidance of ilihuiz is part of his view of a man's connections with other men, which he shares with Spanish women who told the same stories. I shall identify some of the reasons why Florencio and Nacho manifested different relational masculinities in their variants of the same folktales, focusing on the father in their stories and their families.[70]

Chapter 2

"THE BEAR'S SON" IN SPAIN

"THE BEAR'S SON" IS A GOOD PLACE TO BEGIN A JOURNEY THROUGH Spanish and Mexican Nahuat oral tradition because it is a popular folktale in both cultures about a strong and fearless hero. The tale's popularity permits the comparison of many variants to reveal how particular storytellers represent masculinity in a folktale according to their culture, their community, and their personal history. Some oral versions are remarkably similar to the Grendel episode of the Old English epic *Beowulf*.[1] J. Michael Stitt demonstrated that both the folktales and the medieval text are "rooted in an Indo-European dragonslayer tradition."[2] Stith Thompson considers "The Bear's Son" or "John the Bear" (Tale Type 301) one of the most popular dragonslayer stories in the world. It appears in the repertoires of storytellers from all over Europe, the Near East and North Africa, and India.[3] The tale circulates widely in Spain, appearing in collections of folktales from many provinces of the country.[4]

I shall introduce "The Bear's Son" with Florencio Ramos's version of the story to illustrate how a particular narrator personalizes his hero. Through comparison with other Spanish variants, I shall show how Florencio told the tale similarly to other men in other parts of Spain but differently from Spanish women. Florencio told this tale in his home in Navaconcejo in the presence of two of his sons and my then eight-year-old daughter Marisela. He narrated the story in a high-spirited style that accords with the fantastic feats of strength and courage of the hero.

"T*he* Bear's Son"
by Florencio Ramos

Well, one time there was a man who was very rich and he had a daughter. She was single, of course. And the daughter, well, as for what happened, maybe she was the fiancée of someone or other. The thing was the daughter's belly started getting bigger. And people said, "Well this and that."

"Well nothing," said her father. "I shit on ten!"

The daughter, in effect, after some time passed, had a son. And since her father had made her so afraid of what he was going to do—what was going to happen to her, so on and so forth—he gave him to a hunter and told him, "Look, I'll give you so much to lose him or take him into the forest. That is, do what you want just so I never see him again."

The maiden's father told him this. The hunter went; he took the child, and didn't kill him, of course. It grieved him to kill an infant. He took off, leaving him in the forest. So then a mother bear, who was also raising some little bears, passed by there. And when she saw the child, who was very small, well, the mother bear picked him up very carefully and took the little boy to her cave where her other bears were. So then the boy—of course there were little bears who grabbed on to the mother bear to nurse—the little boy also grabbed on to nurse at the mother bear. And they all went with their mouths open to the mother bear. The bears and the boy did. Then, after he was a little bigger, he frolicked with the little bears, and the little bears frolicked with him. And they fought frolicking like boys, you see. Then the boy was getting bigger. And he started tussling with the mother bear. Some days they were frolicking. And the boy could almost hold his own with the mother bear. And when the mother bear left to find them some food, she put a very big rock over the entrance so they would not go out. But one day, John the Bear—I shit on ten!—took off and gave a shove to the mother bear and knocked her down. Now the boy was getting taller. He knocked down the door—I shit on ten—the rock, that is, and took off and went to town: the town that was thereabouts. And—I'll be damned!—the boy showed up there in the town. And there they picked him up; a married couple did. Bah! The boy was now six or seven years old. They put him in school. They named him "Little John." And because the mother bear had raised him, they nicknamed him "Little John the Bear." Bah! Well, the boy went to school. And the teacher called him "John." But the boys had the habit of calling him "Little John the Bear" instead of calling him just "John." When the boys called him "Little John the Bear," he gave them a punch in the face. With the punch he gave them, those boys were flattened. I shit on ten! You know, when the teacher got angry with him, Little John hit him with his fist. And he split the teacher in two. I shit on ten! They tried to control that boy and see what would happen. And when he was confronted, he retaliated. He had a lot of endurance. Since he had nursed on the mother bear's milk, the boy was very strong. The result was they tried to do something.

Someone said, "This boy, it would be better if he left town. And this way there won't be any danger. This boy is going to kill fifty people, or the entire town is going to be terrorized by him."

And they told him, "Look John, we've thought it over. You hit the teacher. You hit a few boys. That Guardia Civil, you also hit him, and we decided you ought to leave town because, if not, we are going to have to take you to jail and so on and so forth."

"Oh, well yes. Bah! Fine."

The boy swallowed it. He said, "Good. It is going to be on one condition."

They said, "You tell us what."

He said, "You're going to make me an iron club that weighs one hundred *quintales* [one *quintal* is 100 kilograms]."

"Oh yeah! Well, sure."

The blacksmiths got together. I shit on ten! They started pounding the iron. Pin pan, pin pan. I shit on ten! They made a fat club. But a fat one! Like one that goes inside a bell but much fatter: out of iron. Good. Well now, they finished the club. They told him, "Look, Little John, there you have the club."

"Ah, well yes. A thing like that is what I wanted. Fine. Good. Give it to me. Tomorrow I'll leave town."

The boy left. He was getting bigger, of course. Now he was sixteen or eighteen years old. He left town with his club. I shit on ten! And he went some distance from the town. It was probably four leagues [one league is 3.5 miles] or so. And he came upon a man who was pulling out pine trees.

"I shit on ten! How he pulls out pine trees!"

He grabbed the crown. He gave it a twist like so. Pum! The pine tree was out.

"I shit on the Host! That man buzzes one's balls pulling out pine trees. He pulls them out with one tug!"

He got closer. "What are you doing, friend?"

"Look! They hired me to pull out all these pine trees here."

And Little John asked, "How do you pull them out?"

He answered, "I give a twist—Look here!—I use a little force as if pulling a molar: like a dentist."

He said, "Fuck! Well, I shit on ten! How much do you earn?"

"They give me little. They give me two *duros* [one *duro* is ten *pesetas*] every day."

"I'll give you three. Come with me."

"Well, there it is. Allah!"

Now there were two. When those two had gone farther, they saw a fellow who was playing *caras* [*cara y cruz*, or pitch-and-toss] with two millstones. He grabbed the two rocks together, as we play with a *perra gorda* [old coin], and he threw them up.

"I shit on the mother who gave birth to him!" he said. "Look at him! Don't you see him?"

He grabbed those rocks. "I shit on ten! He is stronger than we are!"

They got closer.

"What are you doing, friend?"

"I am here entertaining myself tossing these coins. All day playing *caras* with these rocks."

"I shit on ten!"

"I get paid to watch cattle but I throw the millstones up high and they fall down again."

And Little John the Bear asked, "How long do they take to come down?"

He replied, "They usually take five minutes, seven minutes, depending on how high I throw them, of course."

Little John the Bear said, "Bring them here so that I can throw them."

He grabbed them and vooshhh . . . . They still have not come down.

Little John asked, "How much do you earn taking care of the cattle?"

He replied, "Ha! Five *pesetas*."

"I'll give you ten. Come with me."

"It's a deal!"

I shit on ten! Those three took to the road. They were happier than anything because they were three scary men, those three were, because they did scary work. Night was falling. They saw a building.

One of them said, "Hey, you old fucker, there is something that looks like a house. It looks like a light. We have to look and see if we can arrange to spend the night there."

The result was, they arrived there. There was no one. But there was plenty to eat. They went into a house. Do you know what it was?

Little John the Bear said, "We are going to do something here because we are all hungry. There is a lot to eat here!"

They ate well.

"Good, well, now that we have eaten, we're going to bed."

And because they were not afraid, no one closed the door. They left the door open. So they went to sleep. No one said anything to them. And nothing happened. The three of them got up in the morning.

"How are you? How are you?"

"I am better than ever."

"Look, no one bothered me last night. I am better than ever and so on."

Good. One of them said, "Well look, we're going to take a stroll and look at the countryside over there. You stay here. You stay here and prepare dinner. When you have dinner prepared, put a flag up on top of the roof."

He said that to "Pull Out Pine Trees." Well then, the others took off. It was getting to be midday. I shit on ten! He did not raise the flag. Nothing. I shit on ten! It was time to raise the flag. They went there to eat. They arrived. Neither dinner nor the host. They went over to "Pull Out Pine Trees."

One of them asked, "How did it go here?"

"God damn! What happened to me! I was making dinner. A man appeared from over there. He hit me all he wanted."

"Where is he?"

"Uh. He hit me and went away again. I shit on ten! Well, I tell you the man left me bruised."

He of the millstones said, "I shit on ten! Tomorrow I'll stay. Let's see if he hits me as well."

He stayed. In effect, when he was making dinner, he appeared. He was the devil! The devil appeared again. I shit on ten! He gave him another whipping. All that he wanted and more. Those others came and saw what happened to him. The man was spread out on the ground.

"I shit on ten! There he came. And he gave me a fight. But nothing. I couldn't with him. He hit me. He left me the same or more bruised."

Good. Little John the Bear said, "Well, tomorrow I am going to stay. Let's see if he also hits me."

In effect, those others prepared him in the morning.

One of them said, "Good, we're going over there. You raise the flag soon."

He was making dinner.

The devil said, "I'm coming down."

Little John the Bear asked, "What did you say?"

The devil replied, "I'm coming down."

"Wait a minute."

He went to grab his club. Little John said, "Come down when you want."

He came down. He threw himself on top of Little John the Bear.

He could do thus with the club. Pum! He hit him in the chest with the club. I shit on ten! The other one fell with the cudgeling. The man, the devil, was left half bruised. They wrestled, pin pan, pin pan. I shit on ten! It was torture coming and torture going. Little John the Bear saw how he left the devil, let's say, just like when a dog kills a snake. With all its bones broken. He hung him up behind the door.

He said, "I showed you a thing or two." Little John the Bear said to him.

He cut off an ear. I shit on ten! He put it into his jacket pocket. Then he went and flew the flag.

That was when one of the others said, "God damn! Now Little John has raised the flag."

They went there right away.

"How are you? How are you?"

"Fine. Dinner is ready. That is, if you want to eat and all."

One of them said, "But did anything happen?"

He replied, "God damn! We had a small fight. You two said the man fights like hell. With me he was left all black and blue. I have him over there, behind the door. I hit him all I wanted."

They went to look behind the door and . . . vooshhh. He had escaped.

One of the others said, "I shit on ten! It's a lie, and I do not know what . . . ."

Little John said, "Look." He took out the ear and said, "Look here. I have a memento. Here is his ear. That's how you know. You'll see as time passes."

So it was that Little John the Bear, because he was more manly, said, "I shit on ten! Well, I must go hunt for that man!"

In effect, he left the door and spotted a stream of blood that had dripped every so often from the ear he had cut. And they followed the blood. They followed the blood. They arrived at a well. And one of them said, "He threw himself down here. He got to here. He threw himself down this well."

The well was dry.

One of the companions said, "I shit on ten! Well, so it's probably true."

Little John asserted, "Of course! This isn't a trap. The trail of blood ends here. It means he threw himself in here."

Little John the Bear got into action. "I shit on ten! Give me the rope. I am going down below. I have got to see this guy."

In effect, they tied the rope to Little John the Bear. Tan, tan, tan, tan, tan, tan. To the bottom. He reached the bottom and found a maiden more beautiful than the sacramental chalice. And she said, "Oh! How did you come here?" So on and so forth.

He replied, "Oh. Don't you worry. Don't you worry." He said to her, to the maiden.

She said, "Oh! This one kills everything that comes here. This man, this man is the devil. This man kills everything in the world. This man, when someone comes, he'll smell that you are here. He's going to try to kill you, of course. He's going to ask what you want to drink. Tell him nothing. Because what he drinks is poison. What he eats is poison. And he smokes poison. Then if he doesn't kill you, he's going to ask if you want to fight with swords, to kill you of course. There at the entrance, to the left is a sword that is ruined. Ugly. And that room over there is full of shining, beautiful swords. And he is going to tell you to pick the one you want. But you go in to the left; in a corner there is one that is ruined, ugly. You pick that one. You fight with that one. The others are made out of tin and they all bend."

The maiden told him what was what. In effect, the man arrived after a little while. The maiden had prepared his dinner for him.

He said, "Rrrr. I smell human flesh here."

She replied, "Oh, well look there is a man who has come." And so forth.

He said, "Uhhhh. Where is that man? Come out!"

With that, Little John appeared.

The devil said, "Very good. You old fucker! Friend! I shit on ten! Man, how have you been?"

The devil was happy to be with Little John. And Little John with him, of course.

The devil said, "Well, great. Have a cigarette, man."

"I don't smoke," he replied.

"Come, eat something."

He replied, "No. I've eaten a lot. That is, I don't eat."

"Well, drink something. Take it. Have a drink."

"No. I don't drink."

"Good gracious! The man is satisfied. He does not eat or drink, or smoke, or anything. Well, good."

The man was eating and so on and so forth.

"Well, would you like to fence a little? Do you like to?"

He replied, "It isn't that I like to fight but let's go. If that's the way it is." And so on. That's what Little John the Bear said.

The devil said, "Well, let's fight over there with swords and so forth. You pick the one you want."

The devil placed himself in front of the ruined one.

"You pick the one that you want in that room. There are many there. Look at them."

The devil glanced back [over his shoulder].

Little John said, "I see one here."

The devil replied, "Bah! This one, well, this one is dumped here. No one . . . . It is so . . . . It isn't good for anything." Little John insisted, "Bah! I'll go with this one." And so on . . . .

The devil replied, "Well, over there, look there are shiny ones that are better than anything."

"Oh, you do me a bad turn. I'll make do with this one."

I shit on ten! He took the one from there. Of course, the devil had to take one of the shining ones. They mixed it up there. The one of the devil doubled over the first time he struck a blow. The other one—I shit on ten!—worked fine to hunt the man down. He hit him with the ruined one—I shit on ten!—until he beat him. He beat the devil.

And then, once he was left defeated, the maiden said, "And what do we do now?"

Little John replied, "Well, that's easy. Whatever you want."

"I am the king's daughter."

He said, "Whatever you want."

She replied, "Man, what I want is to get out of here," said the maiden.

So then Little John the Bear said, "Well, that is what I'll do. That's what we are going to do. I think we'll get out."

The others were up above. And he went. He called. He tied the maiden. And the maiden went up. The others pulled the maiden up. They threw the rope down again. Instead of tying himself, he tied his club. The others pulled it up halfway. They let go and pum! Down it went.

One of the others said, "He won't come up."

Good. He stayed down below alone without the maiden or the others. I shit on ten! He got hungry.

"I shit on ten! How does one manage here? I shit on the mother who gave birth to him! I shit on ten! Yes, I have an ear that I put here in my jacket pocket the other day."

He stuck in his hand. The other one appeared as he shook the ear.

"What do you want of me? What do you command of me? I'm at your disposal."

He said, "Look, I am just going to ask you for one thing. Get me out of here and place me in the king's palace."

The devil replied, "Yes. Done."

He went on. Pum! He took him out, him and the club. Pum! At the king's palace. He put Little John the Bear there. So then the others had the maiden stupefied into thinking they, they had been the ones who had removed the maiden. The king. Bua! The man had been delighted to see his daughter. But then Little John the Bear appeared.

And the maiden said, "Father, this is the one who saved me. This one."

He replied, "Well, didn't you tell me it was the other one?"

She replied, "No. No. This one, this one was the one who saved me. It's this man who was down there."

So then her father said, "Well then, you say whom you want to marry."

She said, "This one."

And then the maiden said, she said to Little John . . . . No, Little John said to the maiden, "What do you want to do with these two?"

She replied, "Well, these two, we have to punish them."

And Little John the Bear replied, "Whatever you say."

She said, "But because I am a good person, I don't want anyone to suffer on my account."

Little John said to the maiden, "Well then, you say what is to be done with them."

She replied, "I think what ought to happen to them is put them here in the palace. Not to marry me but also I don't want those men mistreated."

So it was that Little John married her and they held a wedding. Bua! It was up there in the clouds. And of course, if I had been there too, they would have given me something, even if it were just a bone, for example. But I am thankful that my nose is very straight. They never throw their bones in my nose. Do you know what I mean? And *colorín colorado, cuento terminado* [little red linnet, this story is over].

Florencio's lively narrative style is typical of all his stories and includes blasphemous and scatological expressions found in many tales I heard from other Cáceres men. Florencio frequently exclaimed "I shit on ten" to express astonishment or surprise. The phrase in Spanish is *"Me cago en diez,"* a euphemism for the scatological and blasphemous *"Me cago en Dios"* ("I shit on God"), common among many men in Cáceres and other provinces in Spain. Florencio occasionally used the word "host" (*hostia*), also to express surprise or astonishment, and the word has a similarly blasphemous meaning because it stands for the scatological phrase "I shit on the sacramental host" (*Me cago en la hostia*). Other blasphemies that appear in Florencio's tale include "I shit on the mother who gave birth to him!" (*Me cago en la madre que le parió*), which can refer to anyone's mother, including the mother of Christ, or even a factory, which is the "mother" of machinery.

Some of Florencio's blasphemies make associations that are not scatological. For example, when Little John the Bear discovered the beautiful maiden at the bottom of the well, Florencio declares that he "found himself with a maiden who was more beautiful than the sacramental chalice" (*se encontró con una moza más guapa del copón*). The use of the sacramental chalice (*copón*) suggests the common expression "*más cojonudo del copón*" ("more big-balled than the sacramental chalice"). Florencio's use of blasphemy is part of his masculine style of recounting this tale and seldom, if ever, appears in feminine speech and in the feminine variants of Cáceres folktales.

Blasphemy in masculine speech has many possible explanations. Cáceres women and men I knew considered blasphemy an honest expression of feelings and distrusted men who avoided blasphemy in an effort to appear virtuous. The hypocrisy of some clean-speaking men is the theme of Cáceres versions of "The Two Ploughmen," regional variants of a story folklorists call "God's Justice Vindicated" (Tale Type 759).[5] Esperanza Cozas and Casiano Miranda from Garganta la Olla and Alvino Bravo Sánchez from Serradilla told this story, which dramatically represents the difference between appearance and reality in a man's character; a man, whose appearance is blasphemous, is in reality virtuous. All three of their tales tell of two men, one of whom has a good pair of mules and the other a very bad pair because he is poor. The one with the bad pair repeatedly uses the expression "*Me cago en Dios*" and the related obscenity "*Me cago en la hostia*" to express his frustration as he attempts to plow his field. Along come Christ and Saint Peter, who are very hungry, and they decide to ask one of the ploughmen for a bite to eat. They avoid the humble but rough-speaking ploughman and go directly to the one with the very good pair of mules whose speech is entirely free of blasphemous and scatological expressions. However, the clean speaker refuses their request for a piece of bread, saying: "No, the lunch I bring from home is for me." They walk over to the one with the very poor pair of mules, who gladly offers them food. The storyteller Casiano explained that the scatological expressions of the poor ploughman are really not blasphemous because no man can actually shit on God, who is in heaven high above mortal men and women. He added, however, that God can defecate on a man. Esperanza further illustrated the moral superiority of the humble, blasphemous man when she described in her tale how he refuses to harm a crucifix that his clean-speaking counterpart is only too willing to destroy.

Florencio's blasphemous and scatological speech also represents a stance toward authority, particularly religious authority. William Christian, Julian Pitt-Rivers, and many other observers of Spanish village life report that Spanish men rarely confess and are critical of the religious authority of priests.[6] Christian considered men in the Nansa Valley of Santander to be profane or at the margins of religious authority.[7] Florencio's blasphemous and scatological speech also expresses powerful feelings toward the wealthy, who are represented as stingy religious hypocrites, as the narrators of "The Two Ploughmen" make clear. Thus, to say "I shit on God" or "I shit on the Host" or "I shit on the Virgin Mary" conveys strong feelings against the authority of priests and the wealthy, who had a great deal of power and control in Cáceres villages during much of Florencio's own lifetime. Florencio, born in 1923, was thirteen at the outbreak of the Spanish Civil War in 1936, and fifty-two when Franco died in 1975. Franco had very strong support among large property owners, who were allied with priests in many villages in Spain, and his supporters found the blasphemous and scatological expressions that abound in Florencio's stories so offensive that they jailed their users or forced them to kneel in penance at the front of the church during mass.[8]

Perhaps because of the power of the wealthy in communities like Navaconcejo, a man needs to establish his independence from the economic domination of other men by working on his own estate rather than working for a wage on the estate of another. A man with comparatively few resources, like Florencio and his father before him, can establish relative economic independence by sharecropping or raising animals by halves. Florencio and his father did both, and Florencio sharecropped with his father until he inherited his share of the family estate. Navaconcejo, Florencio's community, is filled with families from the adjacent but poorer community of Piornal who have moved to Navaconcejo to sharecrop the fertile lands along the banks of the Jerte River. The worst option for a man is to work for a wage on the landed estate of another because such a man has very little personal autonomy (*autonomía*).[9] A man who lacks personal autonomy because he works as a wage laborer on the estate of another is in a very weak position to resist domination and may even have trouble defending his moral reputation by keeping other men from seducing his wife, daughter, and sister.

Florencio expressed his ideas about personal autonomy when he described the values he learned from his father, using metaphors of elimination and food symbolism to make his points.

Well, my father always worked a lot more in the countryside. And he was a very hard worker. My father was a very hard worker. But he always preferred to work on his own. He did not like working

33

for anyone else because I heard my father say many times, "It is very bad to clean oneself in front of another." Do you know what I mean? And he was that way, he was, even though he was poor. The rich ones in this town, well they tried a few times to dominate him. But they couldn't. He, when he was right, he didn't even consider the Virgin Mary. And he always went forward. And he knocked down a few, in the matter of them not making fun of him. And he made money. He made some money. He lived on his capital. And never worked for a wage. A few times he hired a worker, but not often. And he was very honest. My father did not like eating anything off of anyone, but they did not eat off of him either. Then, of course, he told me several times, "Look son, it's better that you take care of a pig because it's yours than go work for anyone else."

Florencio patterned his own life after his father and supported himself by sharecropping, raising animals by halves or sharing the profit with the owners, and by herding his own goats and cattle and selling their milk products.

Within the family, sons prefer to escape from the authority of the father by setting up an independent household or, if necessary, living with the wife's parents. When Florencio married, he went to live in his wife's parents' house, where I found him in 1983. Michael D. Murphy explains a man's preference for matrilocality over patrilocality by referring to the concept of honor requiring that a man establish his domination over other men or resist the attempts of other men to dominate him.[10] In the family, honor requires that a father establish his authority over his son and his son to establish his independence from his father. The son's desire for independence requires that he move to a new domicile, if money permits, or at least live somewhere other than in his father's home. It is preferable to live under the authority of a father-in-law than one's own father.[11] The emotional power of scatological speech probably derives from experiences within the family, as Alan Dundes pointed out when explaining references to feces and urine in folklore.[12] The frequent mention of excrement may evoke memories of hostile parental reactions to a child's products of elimination. Evoking those reactions supports the value of personal autonomy by justifying a son's separation from his parents when he makes the transition to adulthood at marriage. The desire for personal autonomy is one reason the Hispanic man in Spain is so isolated from his father, his sons, his brothers, and men in his peer group.

Florencio's assertive style of narration is evident in other ways, which are partially concealed when an oral tale is turned into print. He is an animated narrator whose voice inflection, facial expressions, and gestures add energy to his stories. He exclaimed rather than pronounced much of his tale in a style represented in print with many exclamation marks. One can nevertheless feel some of his energy from the enthusiasm of his characters even when acting hypocritically. "Very good. You old fucker! Friend! I shit on ten! Man! How have you been?" blurts the devil when he meets the hero, who has bludgeoned him with a club weighing 10,000 kilograms and cut off his ear. The original Spanish is even more colorful (*"¡Muy bien! ¡Coño! ¡Amigo! ¡Me cago en diez! Hombre. Tal y que se yo. Tal."*). A great deal is nevertheless lost in translation, particularly with words like *coño* (female genitalia), which has no direct equivalent in American English.

Florencio's language and animated style of narration serve to convey the image of Little John the Bear as an assertive character who establishes his position among men by using his enormous strength and courage. Little John, the hero, is obviously a symbol of manliness, and his story is a metaphor for the transformation of an unruly boy into a controlled man who is ready for marriage. The plot represents three stages in a man's life: childhood, when little John lives with his bear mother and his adoptive parents, who send him to school; bachelorhood (*la mocedad*), when the hero leaves home and joins a peer group of other similarly strong boys (*mozos*); and adulthood, when Little John defeats the devil and marries the king's daughter.

Florencio represents the three stages by projecting his own personal history onto the hero in accord with the construction of manliness in the culture of his community. The particular as well as shared representation of the hero becomes apparent when Florencio's story is placed side by side other variants of the same tale circulating in Spanish oral tradition. I shall examine first how Florencio told his story relative to other male narrators in Cáceres and other Spanish provinces and then compare masculine and feminine variants to reveal how men tell the story differently from women. Men and women narrators generally include five parallel episodes in their versions of "The Bear's Son," which they develop with different details. The five episodes are (1) the hero's origins and his relationship with his father and mother, (2) the hero's problems in school, (3) his leaving town and meeting his companions, (4) their stay in the haunted house, and (5) the hero's discovery of one or more enchanted maidens and the changing relationship among the hero and his companions.

MASCULINE VARIANTS

Most narrators in Spain and Mexico describe the hero's origins by recounting how a bear abducts a woman and takes her to his cave where he holds her prisoner. After a period of time, the woman gives birth to a son who is half bear and half human. The son grows quickly and becomes incredibly strong. He helps his mother escape from the cave by removing the rock the bear has placed over the entrance and by confronting the bear if he attempts to block their escape. However, individual narrators develop their picture of the hero's origins in many ways that sometimes depart radically from the composite account of the story. How each teller departs from the composite account can be very revealing.

Florencio as well as the other men I knew in Cáceres provided very little or no details on the hero's father and the father-and-son relationship. Relative to other narrators, Cáceres men *deny the father* in their accounts of this story. Florencio made only a vague reference to the hero's father, whom he identified as an unnamed suitor who seduced a rich man's daughter. While most Spanish and Mexican narrators describe the hero's bearlike strength deriving from his father, Florencio attributes Little John's physical power to the milk he drank from his adoptive bear mother. Julio López Curiel of Garganta said nothing about the hero's origins while Juan Julián Recuero of Serradilla noted that the hero's father was a bear but said little else about him.

Other masculine narrators, whose tales appear in published collections, generally provide few details on the hero's father in their accounts of the hero's origins. Isidro Lurengo Porras, who lived in Trujillo in southern Cáceres, mentioned the father in passing as a member of a band of thieves who apparently conceived a son with the band's servant girl. He is silent on the hero's relationship with his father.[13] Rafael Currillo of Saucelle, in Salamanca to the north, is more typical of all Spanish and Mexican narrators taken as a whole because he described how the hero's father abducted the mother and took her to his cave and how the hero won an Oedipal struggle by killing his father and by helping his mother escape. Rafael, nevertheless, provided only a sketchy picture of the father, who is a distant figure in the hero's life.[14]

The hero, in most Spanish and Mexican variants, arrives with his mother at her natal village where he attends school. He usually strikes and sometimes kills the schoolchildren and must leave the village. He acquires a heavy iron club or walking stick and sets out into the world. Florencio's description of the hero's experience in school parallels very closely his account of his father, who, he said, "knocked down a few, in the matter of them not making fun of him." Little John in Florencio's story similarly uses his incredible strength to knock down his school chums when they tease him by calling him Little John the Bear.

The hero's *violent reaction* to being made fun of is a characteristic found in all masculine variants of the story, where narrators develop the episode of John's experience in school. Juan Julián Recuero similarly has the hero knocking down his schoolmates when they taunt him by calling him Little John the Bear, and Julio López Curiel has the hero killing not only the school chums but also the teacher. Isidro Luengo Porras of Trujillo also recounted how the hero killed school-children in response to their teasing.[15] To be teased in Cáceres village culture is to be made less of and results in a reduction in manliness necessary to protect one's autonomy and one's women. Florencio's recollection of his father and his recounting of "The Bear's Son" make clear that men need their strength and courage because they live in an antagonistic and sometimes cruel world of men inclined to prey on each other's weaknesses.

Florencio established his hero's *relative position* in the peer group of three strong and scary men by a poetic device that represents Little John as underestimating his own position, only to emerge as truly the strongest and the most courageous. At first, Little John thinks he is weaker than Millstones. "I shit on ten! He is stronger than we are!" Soon Little John emerges as the stronger when he tries his hand at the game and tosses the millstones so high they "still have not come down." Julio López Curiel of Garganta and Juan Julián Recuero of Serradilla similarly describe their hero comparing himself unfavorably with his companions to set up a situation where the hero can prove his superiority in a subsequent episode.[16]

The need for a man to establish his relative position among other men is part of a hierarchical view of social relations according to which men struggle to dominate or avoid domination by other men. Florencio characterized the struggle in many ways, one of which was to recall his father's words: "It's very bad to clean oneself in front of another!" The reluctance to expose one's backside to another man expresses one's vulnerability and could derive from what Stanley Brandes called a fear of anal penetration, which is actually a fear of being feminized by assuming the "female position" in sex. To become feminized is tantamount to losing one's hard-earned assertive masculinity.[17]

The hero and his companions spend their first night together in a house haunted by a demon or the devil. The companions take turns staying in the house to prepare a meal while the others go out to their fields or the forest, or simply take a stroll through town. The demon or devil appears, beats up the companion, and ruins the food. When the hero takes his turn, he strikes the demon with his club, sometimes knocking off his ear and tucking it in his pocket, and the companions come home to eat a delicious meal. At this point, Little John the Bear emerges as the truly strongest and most courageous. The encounter with the demon or the devil in the haunted house defines the hero's maturity because, for the first time, he uses his strength for a moral and socially constructive purpose: to defeat the devil, a symbol of evil, and feed his companions. The use of strength for a moral and socially constructive purpose makes Little John the Bear a *gallant* man whose power is now under some control.[18]

The expression of man's need for woman sets the stage for the subsequent episode, in which the hero establishes further his strength and fearlessness when he pursues the devil or demon into the underworld and removes a maiden from her enchantment. All male narrators I know of emphasize Little John's superior valor by describing him as the only one who goes down into the well (Florencio Ramos) or as the only one who has the courage to descend all the way to the bottom.[19] Florencio and other men develop the theme of *sexual rivalry* with the introduction of the enchanted maiden. Sexual rivalry appears in many forms; the hero fights the devil a second time in order to remove her from her enchantment, as in the case of the version recounted by Florencio. The companions steal the maiden, as Florencio and Julio López Curiel of Garganta la Olla recounted in their stories, and sometimes try to kill the hero, as in Florencio's tale, or the hero kills his companions for stealing the maiden, as in the story related by Julio López Curiel. The hero disenchants three maidens in other variants and will not let his companions marry any of them.[20] To be sure, men develop sexual rivalry to different degrees, and Florencio presented a comparatively mild form of it when he ended his story by describing how the hero acquiesces to his wife's request that no harm come to his companions.

The theme of male sexual rivalry recalls that a man must establish and maintain his honor as virtue by preventing other men from seducing his wife, daughter, or sister.[21] The fear of being a cuckold is so strong that men who came of age in Florencio's generation were reluctant to court women who had experienced previous courtships that did not turn into marriage. According to Julian Pitt-Rivers, a man who courted a woman already courted by another feared that she might have lost her virginity with her first sweetheart, making her second suitor a cuckold in retrospect.[22] Florencio expressed his ideas about his own and other courtships in the following way:

> My woman, that is to say the one to whom I was married, well, I don't think that she ever had a fiancé. A fiancé that one could call a real fiancé. To dance at a dance, well, she would have danced with fifty thousand. Do you understand? But a fiancé, I think that she probably never had one ever. No one other than me. Do you understand? So then those who are like her marry just fine. That is to say, very well. We are talking about women who are good. On the other hand, if the one who has been the sweetheart of this one for half a year and has left her, then she has been the sweetheart of another for another half year, and he has left her, well, she is going to be losing her reputation. Do you know what I mean?

The importance of female chastity was perhaps extreme during the period of Spanish history between the fall of the Second Republic, which took place from 1936 to 1939, and the collapse of the land-based and labor-intensive economy in the early 1960s. Jane and George Collier report that women of one village in southern Spain during that period had to guard their moral reputation, particularly their pre-marital and marital chastity, in order to guarantee legitimacy and the right of inheritance of family property, thus ensuring the economic future of their children.[23] With the fall of the Second Republic, an un-contested reign of private property supported a particularly strong form of the chastity code precisely during the period when Florencio courted and married his first wife. Florencio initiated the courtship with his wife soon after he left the military on March 2, 1946.

FEMININE VARIANTS

A look at how women tell "The Bear's Son" differently from men pro-vides a fuller picture of men's representation of manliness. Although I did not happen to hear a Cáceres woman tell it, feminine variants appear in published collections of Spanish folktales. Sixty-six-year-old Manuela Hoyos from La Alberca, twenty-one-year-old Manuela Martín Cuadrado from Vilvestre, an unnamed twelve-year-old girl from Cádiz, and Ángela Cuadrado of undetermined age from Trujillo told published versions of the story.[24] Vilvestre and La Alberca are in the province of Salamanca to the immediate north of Cáceres, Cádiz is in the extreme south of Spain, and Trujillo is in southern Cáceres. It would be ideal to compare Angela Cuadrado's and Florencio's stories were Angela's age known, as speech and story imagery are likely to vary by region. However, stories also differ markedly with the age as well as the gender of storytellers, and so I shall examine how Florencio told his tale relative to Manuela Hoyos, a woman close in age to Florencio at the time she gave her version to Luis Cortés Vázquez.

Manuela Hoyos and Florencio used language differently in their versions of "The Bear's Son."[25] Gone are the blasphemous and scatological expressions in Manuela's tale. Luis Cortés Vázquez may have edited them out because they do not appear in the masculine variants of the same tale he collected from men. However, I never heard a Cáceres woman say "I shit on ten," "Host!" or "more big-balled than the sacramental chalice" when telling a tale. Women do occasionally use scatology, as when exclaiming "I shit on the sea!" (*Me cago en la mar*), a euphemism for "I shit on the mother who gave birth to him" (*Me cago en la madre que le parió*), which becomes blasphemy when the mother is the Virgin Mary. However, scatological and blasphemous expressions are rare in women's stories, probably because women do not react in the same way as men to figures of authority. Cáceres women, like those in other parts of Spain, more regularly go to confession and are involved in carrying out devotions to Mary. To be sure, some expressed resentment about the practice of taking new mothers to church, ostensibly to bless them but actually to remove the traces of sin that come from participating in sexual reproduction. Women in Cáceres have a much closer relationship with their mother than men have with their father. Women express a strong desire to live near their mother and prefer matrilocality over patrilocality. Many women I knew in Cáceres villages said they needed their mother for support and for help in child care, and they cared for their elderly parents who were unable to care for themselves.

Manuela Hoyos and the women narrators I knew in Cáceres did not embellish their stories to the same degree as Florencio and other men. Florencio, for example, appears to have invented more radically new plot elements and poetic language, leaving his personal stamp on his stories. Florencio's inclination to invent story elements appears in the first episode when he described the hero's origins. No other Spanish narrator I know of described Little John the Bear being adopted by a mother bear, nursing on her milk to become strong, and establishing his strength while tussling with his bear cub brothers and sisters and eventually his bear mother. Florencio liberally sprinkled his story with his own figures of speech by making analogies between the hero's club and the ringer of a bell, depicting a companion twisting out pine trees like a dentist yanks out a molar, and describing the hero leaving the devil as a dog kills a snake by breaking all of its bones. He more liberally used hyperbole, as he told how the millstones his hero tossed into the air have yet to return, and understatement, as he had his hero saying "We had a small fight" to describe his first battle with the devil.

Manuela Hoyos, who appears to be a gifted storyteller, embellished her story by making more subtle changes to the plot and by using fewer invented or personal figures of speech and less hyperbole and understatement. Narrators usually performed stories in front of family or neighbors, and I often heard members of their audience loudly exclaim, after a tale's conclusion, that they heard the same tale differently. I saw Florencio take the microphone to finish a tale started by his son Bernardo because he disapproved of Bernardo's way of storytelling. Men and women storytellers frequently reacted to audience criticism by declaring they were telling tales exactly as they had heard them. Manuela Hoyos could be among those storytellers who are more sensitive to criticism by members of an audience and attempt to conform to audience expectations by making more subtle story changes. Whatever the reason, embellishments are one way a narrator can project himself or herself into the story, and the projection of self could be a gender difference in narrative style. Florencio's tendency to make greater changes to his story is one way he projected more of himself into his tales, and Manuela's more subtle story changes could mean she projected less of herself into hers.

More differences emerge with a comparison of the specific ways that women and men develop the parallel episodes of the story. *Denial of the father*, a feature of masculine variants, is not a characteristic of the feminine accounts of the hero's origins. Manuela Hoyos contrasts dramatically with Florencio when opening her tale because she focuses on the hero's father rather than on his mother. To be sure, the father may not be a biological parent because Manuela begins her tale by mocking masculine ideals of manliness that require a man to defend his honor by guarding his wife's marital chastity. She tells of a husband who banishes his wife for barrenness, ordering her not to return until she has a child. The wife goes into the wilderness and comes back with a son who is obviously half animal because he has a tail. Manuela nevertheless identifies the husband as the hero's father and develops a clear picture of his relationship with his son. For example, she tells how the teacher complains to the father, not to the mother, because the hero injures other children in school. It is the father, in Manuela's account, who makes the iron club for the hero and gives him money to help him make his way in the world when he must leave town. The hero eventually uses the money to form his peer group by offering payment to his companions.

Manuela Hoyos is not alone among Spanish women in her development of the father. Other feminine narrators also develop their picture of the father, to whom they attribute human qualities. Manuela Martín Cuadrado from Vilvestre in Salamanca and the unnamed girl from Cádiz specify that the hero's father is a powerful animal—a bear in Manuela Martín's story and an orangutan in the girl's tale—who takes a woman to his cave, has a son with her, and shows human emotion (anger) when his wife and son leave home.[26] The tendency for women to identify the hero's father and develop more fully than Florencio and other men the hero's relationship with his father accords with the actually strong filial orientation of women to both their parents.

Women include *less violence* when representing the hero's difficulties in school. To be sure, Manuela Martín Cuadrado describes the hero disobeying and striking the teacher, Manuela Hoyos has him hitting other children, and the girl from Cádiz says he slapped other children and the Civil Guard.[27] However, no woman depicts the hero killing anyone in school. The comparative lack of violence in feminine variants is part of a less hyperbolic style and accords with a less confrontational stance toward figures of authority. It fits women's strong filial orientation in families and their fuller participation in religion.

Violence is the exercise of physical strength, and feminine narrators seldom make comparisons of strength and thus do not attempt to establish the hero's *relative position* when describing the formation of the peer group. As mentioned earlier, Florencio, Julio López Curiel, and Juan Julián Recuero compared their hero's physical strength unfavorably with that of his companions to dramatize the hero's eventual emergence as the strongest and the bravest. Manuela Hoyos and Manuela Martín Cuadrado from Salamanca, and Angela Cuadrado from Trujillo, however, make no such explicit comparisons, and the girl from Cádiz does not include companions in her story.[28] Manuela Hoyos uses a subtle but very effective device to illustrate that the companion, Blows Windmills (*Soplamolinos*) is strong by describing how his wind prevents the hero and Pulls Out Pine Trees (*Arrancapinos*) from ascending a hill. No companion declares himself the weaker or the stronger, and all three work out a peaceful solution to what could have been a confrontation by having Blows Windmills simply stop blowing his wind upon request from the other companions.[29]

All Spanish storytellers describe the companions' stay in the haunted house to make the point that the hero now uses his superior strength for a moral and socially constructive purpose. However, Manuela Hoyos and Manuela Martín Cuadrado make two very subtle but important points about food when they tell how a demon attacks the companions when they are preparing a meal.[30] The first point is that there is enough food for everyone; the demon never destroys or eats all the food. Using dramatic example, Manuela Hoyos makes a second point—that food is to be shared—when she describes the witch beating up a companion when he denies her request for food.[31]

Food is a symbol of a woman's love in the culture because women express their love of others by nurturing them with food. A woman is, of course, food when she nurses her infant, and, according to the gender division of labor, she prepares and gives food to her children, her husband, and her parents. Women narrators in several Cáceres villages represent the giving of food as an expression of love when telling "Cinderella" tales (Tale Types 510 and 510B), in which the heroine, in disguise, feeds an ailing prince puddings and soups containing the tokens he gave her at the ball so he might recognize her in other than beautiful form.[32] If food represents love, then Manuela Hoyos and Manuela Martín Cuadrado are delivering the message, in the episode of the haunted house, that a woman's love is plentiful and to be shared. Their messages contrast dramatically with those of Florencio and other Cáceres men, who represent a male demon taking or destroying all the food. The fear that another man will take away or destroy all the food could represent a man's fear that other men will take away a woman's love. A man's anxiety over the loss of women's love finds expression in many aspects of culture, including haunting poetry recited to David Gilmore and Sarah Uhl in southern Spain.[33]

When women describe the hero descending the well and removing the maiden from her enchantment, they play down male *sexual competition*, perhaps because they view women's nurturing love as plentiful and something to be shared and their sexual love as exclusive and belonging to their chosen husband. To be sure, sexual competition does occur in feminine stories; Manuela Hoyos and Manuela Martín Cuadrado represent men's competition for women by telling how the hero must kill the guardians who keep the maidens in the underworld,[34] and Manuela Hoyos has the companions steal the maidens as they wonder what four men will do with three women.[35] However, they tone down sexual competition by expanding the number of maidens from one to three, and Manuela Martín Cuadrado tells how the hero is left in the underworld unintentionally[36]—rather than intentionally, as in Florencio's story, when the rope lowered by the companions to pull the hero up to the surface breaks from the weight of his club. Moreover, both Manuela Martín Cuadrado and Manuela Hoyos do not describe the companions trying to kill the hero or the hero harming his companions for taking the maidens. In this detail, their ending is the same as that of Florencio Ramos, who, relative to other men, played down sexual rivalry in the closing episode of his story by eliminating any punishment for the companions.

All Spanish women I know of express a much greater concern with the hero's efforts to establish his position in the maiden's family, perhaps expressing a woman's generally strong ties to parents. Disenchanting maidens, through strength and valor, is not enough in itself for a man to marry a woman. Manuela Hoyos told how the hero, after disenchanting the maidens and then confronting their loss, must contend with a stubborn king who is determined that his three daughters marry the companions. The hero must struggle to find the means that will enable the maiden to convince her father that it was the hero who rescued her.[37] Manuela Martín Cuadrado has the hero win a tournament and create a valuable object—half of an orange made of gold—to win a maiden's hand in marriage. He must also struggle to win her father's love by establishing that he, not his companions, provided the cure for the father's illness. The hero also appears first in ugly and then in handsome form and experiences first rejection and then the love of the maiden's father's family.[38] Manuela Martín Cuadrado's ending of "The Bear's Son" reminds one of "Cinderella" stories told by Cáceres women, in which the heroine alternates between appearing beautiful and ugly and receives the love and the scorn of the prince and his family.[39] However, the maiden in Manuela Martín Cuadrado's tale, unlike the prince in the "Cinderella" stories, always recognizes the hero even when he appears in disguise.[40]

SUMMARY

At this point in our journey, Florencio appears to be a classic example of his gender. He and his hero have many things in common with the Hispanic man in Spain and with Freud's active man. Florencio narrated his story with an assertive style to portray his hero, with whom he closely identified, as denying his father, establishing his position in a group of peers by showing his superior strength and courage, using his masculine power to remove a maiden from her enchantment, and defending his honor by tracking down his companions who left him underground after stealing the maiden. This hero's disconnection from other men is based on a man's fear of recapitulating the Oedipal triangle. Florencio's main departure from the stereotypical picture of the Hispanic man in Spain is his hero's willingness to leave sexual rivals unpunished. Other departures will emerge in the stories considered later. Florencio's relative isolation from other men becomes particularly apparent when his story is examined next to those told by Spanish women. Manuela Hoyos and other women expressed their "relational capacities" in a subtle style of narration and in their depiction of the hero as more connected to other men, less fearful of sexual rivalry, and more devoted to establishing his place in his wife's family.

Chapter 3

"THE BEAR'S SON"
IN MEXICO

NACHO PRESENTED HIS MASCULINE IDENTITY WHEN TELLING his version of "The Bear's Son," which he learned from his older brother Nicolás. Spanish and French storytellers probably brought the tale to the Americas,[1] where it became firmly established in the repertoires of Spanish-speaking Mexicans and many Native Americans on both sides of the Mexican-U.S. border.[2] The tale is well known among Nahuat narrators in Huitzilan and Yaonáhuac,[3] and it circulates among speakers of many native Mexican languages outside of the Nahuat area.[4]

I recorded Nacho's story after he moved out of his cohesive extended family household and established his own home with Victoria Bonilla. He told me his version of "The Bear's Son" in his home with Victoria and their two small children. Nacho included all five episodes found in Florencio's version of the same tale: (1) Nacho's hero originates from a union between a human mother and an animal father, who in this case is a monkey; (2) he grows up to be incredibly strong and injures his school chums; (3) he is banished from town, goes out into the wilderness, and meets two other male companions; (4) the companions spend the night in a haunted house where they take turns preparing meals and are beaten by the devil; and (5) the hero bludgeons the devil and recovers maidens from the underworld.

Nacho's story also has episodes that do not appear in any versions of "The Bear's Son" that I heard or read in collections of folktales from Spain. He included parts of another story that folklorists call "Strong John" (Tale Type 650), which Stith Thompson considered closely related to "The Bear's Son" because the hero in both has similar origins and grows up to be incredibly strong.[5] The tales usually diverge when the hero in "The Bear's Son" leaves home, joins his incredible companions, descends into the underworld, and releases maidens from their enchantment. The hero in "Strong John" goes to work for a man who gives him incredible and often very dangerous tasks to get rid of him because he has an enormous appetite and consumes all of his employer's livestock. Both stories appear as distinct tales in Spanish and Mexican oral tradition. In Spain, Aurelio Espinosa collected two "Strong John" tales by unnamed narrators from Extremadura and Asturias,[6] and I heard a third from Juan Julián Recuero in Serradilla. "Strong John" appears as a separate tale among Spanish-speaking Mexicans in Jalisco and Tzotzil Mayas in Chiapas,[7] and I heard one from the Nahuat narrator Antonio Veracruz in Huitzilan. Because of the close relationship between "Strong John" and "John the Bear," is it not surprising that some narrators in the Hispanic world would include episodes from one when telling the other. However, no Spanish narrator I know of mixed "Strong John" with "John the Bear," while Spanish-speaking Mexican and native Mexican storytellers frequently combined the two stories. "The Bear's Son" with "Strong John" episodes appears in the repertoires of Spanish-speaking Mexicans, Zapotecs, and, of course, the Nahuat.[8] In addition to Nacho Ángel from Huitzilan, I heard "The Bear's Son" with "Strong John" episodes told by the Nahuat-speaking Mariano Isidro of Santiago Yaonáhuac.

Nacho and other Nahuat narrators told "The Bear's Son" with a second change that occurs only in Huitzilan de Serdán and may consequently be an "oicotype" of this particular village.[9] They turned the main protagonist into Nānāhuatzin, a culture hero who was originally Nānāhuatl, the sixteenth-century Nahua god who jumped into the pyre at Teotihuacán to become the fifth sun and who broke open Sustenance Mountain to provide corn for starving humans who appeared in the fifth and last era of creation.[10] In contemporary Nahuat narratives from Huitzilan and Santiago Yaonáhuac, Nānāhuatzin is an anthropomorphized lightning bolt who, like Nānāhuatl, broke open Sustenance Mountain and taught corn-planting knowledge to his lightning-bolt children, with whose help he brings water from the sea to make plants grow. Nānāhuatzin is baptized John and his saint's day is June 24, a date that falls at the beginning of the rainy season. The association between Nānāhuatzin and John the Baptist is based on their common connection with water. Nacho and Juan Hernández ended their "Bear's Son" stories with an account of how the lightning bolts or rain gods (quiyahteōmeh) trick the hero into moving away from the top of a mountain (Cozōltepēt) that towers above Huitzilan to the south. The rain gods feared that Nānāhuatzin might destroy Huitzilan with a flood, using the water in a spring on Cozōltepēt's summit. A flood had brought an end to an earlier era, according to a number of mythic accounts of creation that circulate in Huitzilan and Yaonáhuac. The Nahuat tell of two eras in human history: the first was an era of darkness peopled by giants who grew tall because they did not have to endure heat; this was followed by the present era of light, which began with the appearance of the sun. The first era ended when many of the giants, representing Spaniards, drowned in a flood.[11] Accounts of the rain gods tricking the hero into moving from Cozōltepēt to the edge of the sea occur only in Huitzilan variants of "John the Bear," although narrators from at least three different Nahuat communities tell other narratives locating Nānāhuatzin's home at the edge of the sea and identifying him as the father or captain of the lightning-bolt rain gods.[12]

Nacho's casting of the hero in his "The Bear's Son" as Nānāhuatzin is key to understanding his presentation of masculinity. The hero personifies īlihuiz, and his strength, courage, and assertiveness are not qualities with which Nacho can easily identify. Consequently, Nacho used a style of narration by which he distanced himself from his main character.

"The Bear's Son"
by Nacho Ángel Hernández

One day there was a man who worked in his corn and bean plot. And every day his wife went to feed him. And she passed through a wood. The wood through which she passed was very big. And forest animals lived in that wood. Every day, every day that little man worked. And every day his wife went to feed him. And the day came when that woman went at noon to feed her husband. And they say a monkey grabbed her. And he took her to a mountain. There, in a cave, he slept with her. He did not do anything to her. He did not bite her. She could do whatever she wanted. It was as if she were his wife. He kept her there. She stayed there a long time. That is how it was. He saw that the woman had brought clothes. To be sure, she had just one set. So it was that every day, every day, he brought her food. Yes, he brought her bread and meat, which they ate raw. Where would they get fire? Every day the beast went somewhere. Every day he went to find them something to eat. He brought her whatever he found. But he really did make her eat the meat raw. It was not cooked. He brought bread that was baked, but the meat was not cooked. And so it was until they had a child. The child they had was half beast and half smooth as Christians are. And half of him was furry as an animal. So that child started to grow. The woman had a son. The boy was high-spirited. And so it was, they say, that he grew quickly like an animal. Not slowly as Christians do. So it was that he started growing and growing and growing. Then that boy reasoned and spoke.

"Well now, go with me to where our house is," he said to his mother. "I want to take you to where you came from."

"But how will you take me?" his mother asked.

"We are very high up here. We are up on the side of a mountain. No," she said. "Your father closed us in with a big rock."

"Yes, but I am strong enough to move the rock," the boy replied. He started lifting a big rock.

The monkey had covered her up when he went away. Well, the boy was strong; he lifted the rock.

"You are not strong enough to do more," his mother said to him.

"No. I shall take you," he insisted. "Let's see you go with me to the place you came from."

And so it was that the days passed. His mother did not believe him.

"No," she said. "You are still a child who won't be able to move the rock. And you won't last carrying me," she added. "We have come to a faraway place."

"No," he insisted. "I am strong enough to take you. You'll see," he said.

So it was that the days passed. And the boy thought some more.

"It won't work for you to take me. Your father will be angry and he'll hit us. He'll hit you."

"No," the boy replied. "I'll face my father. I'll hit him. He won't hit me."

The boy was inspired. He said he'd hit that animal even though he was his father.

"I'll hit him if he gets angry and comes after us. Don't be afraid of him."

And then the day came. That monkey went out from where he was up there, from his house. He went away looking for food. That monkey left. And the little boy was alert along with his mother.

"Well yes. Now he's gone," he said after the monkey had left. "Let's go."

That boy decided to move the rock. He turned it over on its face.

"Now, yes. Climb up on my back. Let's go. I'm going to carry you."

All of that little woman's clothing had ended. She worked hard to cover herself. She worked very hard pulling together the shreds of her clothing. Her clothes had ended. She had been in that cave for a long time.

"I'm going to carry you. Don't worry about anything," he said.

Her child carried her. He lowered her down the face of the mountain. He took her. From there, yes, they came to that town. And then the little woman went right away to see a priest. She took her son there. She went to tell the priest what had happened. She was taken care of.

"Well, I say you ought to accompany me to baptize your child," the priest said.

Then that priest became the boy's godfather. That boy was named John. And so that child grew and grew. He started playing. He started playing with those children. He played with the children in school. His godfather, the priest, sent him to school. John was going to learn. Now the boy went to school.

And the day came when John said to his godfather, "I want a ball. Have one made for me. Have them make me my ball and my club."

"Why the two things, godson?"

"I ask for them because I don't like the ones the children play with because they are not heavy enough. I want my ball and my club each to weigh one *arroba* [about 25 pounds]," he explained.

"Well, I'll order them," the priest agreed.

They say that his godfather really did place an order to have them make a ball weighing one *arroba*. They brought it to him. And yes, that boy started playing with them. He threw the ball. And he was indeed strong enough. But the other children were not strong enough. John killed them when he threw the ball to them. So his godfather got angry.

"Now what am I going to do with my godson? He doesn't listen very well," the priest, who was that animal's godfather, thought.

"Well now," he said to his godson, "I'm going over there. Someone asked me to hold mass. You sleep in my bed. Take care that no one comes around. I'm going. I'll arrive home when I arrive. I'll arrive drunk when they get me drunk. I don't know when I'll arrive home. But I'm going."

As for what that priest did, he really did not go anywhere. He went under the bed. He went in. He gave his godson a knife.

"Well now, I give you this knife and I'm going," he said.

And at midday, the boy went outside. He didn't know if his godfather had gone or not. Then the priest went under the bed. Night fell, and the boy went to lie down on the priest's bed. And from there, yes, that night the priest started groaning. He intended to frighten his godson. So he started groaning. The boy woke up.

"You son of the fucked mother!" the boy declared. "What are you doing? Who are you? I don't play around. My godfather left me here to take care of things."

He groaned some more.

"I told you, son of the fucked mother, tell me who you are!"

John lifted up the bedsheet and put the knife to the priest's throat.

"Oh godson, I've fallen here. I'm drunk. I don't know when I got here. Forgive me. I'm drunk. I don't know."

"Well, get out right now because I would have killed you. Why did you come in here? You told me to take care of this place. Well, I am taking care of it."

"But I got drunk. I didn't know."

So then he removed his godfather. From there, yes, that priest continued thinking about what to do with his godson. They say he decided what to do.

"Well now, there is a well-known forest with a lot of human-eating beasts. May the beasts eat him. Let him go into the forest. Now, I'll tell him to go into the forest to bring me firewood," the priest said to himself.

"Take those donkeys. Be sure to bring me some firewood," the priest told John.

So then that boy left with the donkeys. He went to bring the firewood. While the boy started cutting the firewood, something grabbed his donkeys. When he went to find his donkeys, he found out that the beasts had eaten them. That boy shook with anger. He started looking for those beasts—where they had gone after they ate the donkeys. He found them. They say he loaded them with firewood. He loaded them. Then his godfather saw the beasts coming. They flung themselves to and fro, complaining as they came loaded with the firewood.

"Godson, why did you bring those human-eating beasts? They're very bad. They bite. You shouldn't have brought them."

"But, godfather, I didn't bring them. My donkeys brought them to me. That's why I went to get them. They don't bite. They're very tame. They don't bite. Why do you say they bite?"

"Yes they do! It won't work because they'll just eat people," the priest explained.

"But they didn't do anything to me."

"But yes, unload them. Go leave them now where you went to get them," the priest insisted.

He unloaded the firewood and went to leave the beasts in the forest. From there, yes.

"What am I going to do with him? And he still doesn't understand anything! Well now, I'm going to handle him this way," his godfather said to himself.

"Now," he tells his godson, "I'll hold mass early in the morning."

The priest decided to fetch some empty skulls. So he went to gather some of those bones and placed one on every other step in the belltower. He put one all the way up to the top. He did not tell his godson about them.

"Godson, you're going to ring the bell early."

So then the boy went early in the morning to ring the bell. The priest thought he was going to frighten him with the skulls of the dead. When the boy went there, he saw the skulls as he passed to go up the stairs. He rang the bell. From there, yes, he came down gathering up the skulls in his clothes. He went to where his godfather was.

"Godfather, won't you eat some squash I brought? Have them prepared for you to eat. That's why I brought them."

"Oh godson, those are not squash [*calabazas*]. They're skulls [*calaveras*]."

"I know them to be squash."

"No, they're skulls. Where did you get them?"

"Well, over there, where the stairs are."

From there, yes.

"What am I going to do with my godson? And he's never going to listen. I can't complain to him. I'm thinking and I don't know what to do. It isn't possible to scare him."

Then he remembered a house that was far away. The house was in a lonely place. It frightened him a lot.

"I have a house over there. No one can go near it. And there I'm taking care of some . . . I want you to take care of it."

"Sure, godfather. I'll go."

He went that same afternoon. His godfather gave him some tortillas, and he went. He went there to sleep. He spread himself out on the floor that evening. He lay down. That night, he heard something fall from the rafters. He didn't know what it was. He heard it fall again. And so it continued to fall.

"Son of the fucked mother, who are you?" he demanded. "Nothing here frightens me. My godfather sent me here to watch over this house of his. No one can frighten me."

More fell from whatever was happening in the rafters. He heard more and it became alive.

"I say! Who are you, son of the fucked mother? Answer me!"

It did not answer him. Then one of the whoever was doing it said, "Do I fall or don't I?"

And so it was.

"That's why I tell you to come down. Who are you?"

It really was a dead man. So he lowered himself.

"Here I am. This place is not your godfather's house. It's my house," the dead man said.

"No it's not. It's his house!"

"No, this is my house. Do you want to know why I'm here? Not to scare anyone. It hurts me to look for some money. I have some money here and I can't pass in front of God."

"Where is it?"

"It's here inside the house. That's why I am like this. But this is not your godfather's house. It's my house." From there, yes. "Now go tell you godfather to show me where the money is. And you go call your godfather, and you two remove the money. Take it out of here. There is a lot."

He said there were twelve barrels of money. They say he had a lot of money. From there, yes, that boy came back during the night. His godfather heard him return soon.

"Godfather, I've come."

His godfather didn't answer him.

"You said you were sending me to your house. It isn't your house. The one whose house it is spoke to me. He said it's not your house. It's his. And he said you must remove some money that's there. He said for you to go remove it right away. There's a lot of money."

"Well, really?"

"Yes! So he told me. Let's go right now."

He got up to get those donkeys again to carry the money. They removed it and returned. As they were returning, his godfather said to himself, "I'm never going to teach my godson a lesson. It would be better if he took to the road."

From there, yes. They returned, and the sun came up.

"It would be better if you went away now. Go far," the priest said to his godson.

As for what that boy did, well, he went away after hearing what his godfather said. He followed the road. He took his ball and club. He found a friend. They were getting drunk. They say he invited John the Bear so that he might ask him a question.

"And you, friend, how much does it take to get you drunk?"

"Well, I get drunk on a tubfull."

And that boy said it was the same for him.

"We're companions."

"Yes, we're companions."

"So then, let's go."

Those two friends left together. They went on. And they went on until they found another one. They went up to him. They were getting drunk. So then again they invited him to have a little drink, and one of them asked again, "For you, how much does it take to get you drunk?"

"Well, I get drunk on one tub."

He lasted for one tub.

"We also get drunk on a tub."

He, the new friend, also could drink one tub full.

"Good. Well then, we're companions."

"Yes. So then, let's go. We're companions."

He took those two companions with him.

"Let's go," he said.

They went on. They came to someone's house.

"Now, now we have to work. We work. And how can we when we don't have a woman? We're alone. We must work. We didn't think about that."

So then John the Bear decided; he told one of his companions, "Now, you stay here. We'll go to work, and you stay here. You make dinner for us and go feed us."

That companion stayed there for a day. They say he made the meal. Noon came, and the one whose house it was came out of his cave. The one who is not good [the devil] came out. He ate all the food the companion had prepared, and peed on it for him. From there, yes. After he did that, they say, he fought with [the companion]. But since the companion had no strength, he couldn't defeat him. So the companion made another meal and went to feed the others.

"Why do you come in the afternoon?" his companions asked.

"And what did I do? Someone came and ate the food and peed on it for me. I made another meal to bring you."

"Son of the . . . . Well."

The other companion said, "Well now, tomorrow I'll stay."

The three companions spent the night and slept and, the next morning, one of them stayed.

"I'll stay now."

Again, the others had to go work. They went off. And John the Bear was the first in command. So it happened again. Noon came, and the companion who stayed made the meal. And he put on the tortillas, and the devil appeared. He ate the meal again, and peed on it for him and went away again. They fought, and he went away again. So then the companion went to feed the others in the afternoon.

"Well, it was after noon and what could I do? It was true. The man came. He came to fight for sure. That's why I come in the afternoon."

"Son of the . . ." said John the Bear. "Now I'll stay."

So the next morning, he said to his companions, "Now, go work, and I'm going to stay here."

Noon came, and he saw that the man had not yet appeared.

"Come here right now! I'm by myself. Is it really true the man, whoever he is, comes?"

So he roused him. Noon came, and the devil appeared. He tried to eat the meal, but John the Bear didn't let him. They called each other names. They started pounding each other. It was past noon, and the companions saw that John the Bear did not come. They came from where they were working. They saw him when they arrived. They went to find him. They say he was really fighting with the devil. John the Bear fought, laying him out with his club. They were lying on their stomachs. John the Bear hit him with his club. They grappled as they fought and tried to cut each other. John the Bear hit him and hit him until he chased him out of that house. He drove him far into that cave. He chased after him. And the devil had three maidens whom John the Bear went to bring. He took them out of the cave and brought them.

"Now, I brought these maidens. I'm going to give one to each of you, and there is one for me. And now each one of you can go work."

From there, they say, they took John the Bear to Cozōltepēt. He wanted to live there. He stayed there for a while. But the rain gods decided, "He can't be there because he'll wash us away."

They decided it would be better to take him to the river. They told him they were going to take him to adorn thereabouts, down below. They say it was down the Cempōhuala River. They took him to adorn the river with arches of flowers. They were going to adorn it.

"Now, let's go. Let's go have a fiesta."

He didn't want to go. He didn't want to go.

"No. I'm fine here."

"No. Let's go. We must hold a fiesta."

They say they decorated the Cempōhuala River with arches of flowers. They adorned them beautifully. He was gazing at them from there. The flower arches were rainbows. They placed them from one side of the mountain to the other.

"Good," said John the Bear. "Let's go. But I'm not going to return to this place. I'm going to take one of my pillows."

So then he went to tie up a piece of the mountain to carry. So it was. And they say the piece of mountain cut the rope. He passed below Zoquiapan leaving that mountain. It is like Cozōlin [Cozōltepēt]. It's a small mountain. So then he couldn't take it any farther. So he left it. Then they reached the sea. John the Bear did not see where he had come and didn't go back anymore. From there, they say, he wanted to know when it was going to be a fiesta and rain. He wanted to know when the day of St. John was. But they wouldn't tell him.

"It's still coming. We'll tell you when the fiesta comes. We'll tell you," one of the rain gods said.

He had to tell him because John the Bear did not know how to read. He did not read. So they could hide the fiesta from him. He did not know when it was. One of the rain gods told him each time the fiesta came. But they did not say when. He had to ask.

"It's still a long time coming."

They didn't tell him when the fiesta passed. And that's how it was. And there it ended.

Nacho's and Florencio's use of language is very revealing for understanding how they represent masculine power. Florencio spoke Spanish rapidly and with many exclamatory words, phrases, and expressions, whereas Nacho spoke Nahuat evenly and with few exclamations. The slow and measured words of a Nahuat storyteller might give a Spaniard the impression of a phlegmatic style of narration unless the listener knew the images suggested by Nacho's narrative style. The inclination to speak Nahuat slowly and evenly is part of a general preference for doing all things slowly and in measured ways. One should eat by taking measured bites, dipping pieces of tortilla into a bowl of bean soup with a smooth and even motion. One should walk in smooth and measured steps and avoid jumping to prevent slipping and falling on the paths criss-crossing Huitzilan, which become very treacherous during the long rainy season. One avoids jerky ways of speaking, walking, and eating to prevent dislocating the parts of any ordered structure ranging from the human body to the cosmos. To slip and fall could mean breaking a bone and bringing about an actual state of bodily disorder.[13] The Nahuat use the adverb īlihuiz ("inconsiderately")[14] when talking about especially disruptive or dislocating behavior which, if unchecked, can bring about the destruction of the universe, as when a flood brought an end to the prior era of darkness. Nacho's hero personifies īlihuiz and threatened to destroy Huitzilan with a flood.

The art of telling "The Bear's Son" for Nacho is to use language representing the hero's power without actually mimicking the hero or employing words that are themselves so powerful that no one should utter them. Nacho did not rely on blasphemous and scatological expressions, like those that appeared so often in Florencio's version of the same story, because they are too strong. When Nacho occasionally uttered the obscenity "Son of the fucked mother"—to express his hero's reaction to the priest groaning under his bed and the dead man searching for the money he left in his house—he used the Spanish phrase *Hijo de la chingada*. Like all narrators I knew in his community, he never named the devil, who is the personification of disorder and dislocation; instead, he employed the euphemism ahmō cualli ("he who is not good") when referring to the devil in his story. The Nahuat word for devil is tācatecolōt, literally translated as "owl man,"[15] the pronunciation of which is itself an act of īlihuiz. To engage in disorderly speech is tantamount to bringing disorder into one's own life and the lives of others within earshot of the utterance. The way Nacho explained it, to pronounce the name of the devil is a way of calling him, and to call the devil is actually to bring him and, by implication, to invite disorder.

To create vivid images and make his story compelling to his listeners, Nacho employed several narrative devices that are appropriate to his culture. One device is the *difrasismo* (diaphrasis), a term Ángel Garibay used for placing two words together to "give a symbolic meaning of expression to a single thought."[16] In Nahua languages, the words placed together to form a new meaning appear as separate words or as compounds. For example, the concept of "the town" consists of two separate nouns with their articles: in ātl, in tepētl (the water, the hill) as well as the compound noun in āltepētl.[17] Miguel León-Portilla explains that combining words to create new metaphors makes Nahua languages "rich in meaning, fresh, vigorous, and dynamic."[18] Nacho generally used many compound nouns and verbs to add color to his story. An example of a compound noun is tzontecomameh, consisting of tzonti ("head of hair") and tecomat ("clay pot") to make "dead human skulls." A compound verb in Nacho's story is the word cualāncamiqui ("he is furious"), used to describe the hero's rage upon discovering that human-eating beasts had devoured the donkeys he planned to use to bring firewood from the forest. The word cualāncamiqui consists of cualāni ("he is angry"), the infix -ca-, and miqui ("he dies"). Frances Karttunen notes that miqui is used in a number of compound verbs that "do not have the literal sense of 'to die.'"[19] Death is an extreme form of disorder, so cualāncamiqui suggests that the hero is so enraged that he is in a very disorderly state approaching death. The most equivalent meaning in idiomatic English is "scared to death."

To emphasize important story elements, Nacho employed repetition rather than exclamatory words and phrases. Repetition may involve doubling syllables within a word, using the same word twice in

THE BEAR AND HIS SONS

a sentence, or repeating the same idea in successive phrases. For example, to emphasize the length of time the hero's mother spent with the monkey, Nacho drew attention to the deterioration of her clothing by describing her struggle to cover herself and guard her modesty. The repetition of key syllables in the following passage emphasizes her struggle:

> (Ī)ca tetepitzintzin zā nitilman, quemeh nohon, pos tēl tequitzān (tequitzayān) (ī)ca tzitzicāutoc nohon tilmantzin.
> With only the little tiny bit of her clothing, like that, well, she works very hard struggling to fasten that little bit of torn clothing of hers.

The word tetepitzitzin is an expansion of tepitzin ("little"), with the first and last syllables repeated to indicate "little tiny bit." Similarly, Nacho doubled the first syllable of the gerund form of the verb "to fasten" (tzicoā) to create "she (works very hard) struggling to fasten" (tzitzicāutoc), conveying the picture of a woman making a great effort to cover herself. The result is an image of a woman struggling to guard her sexual modesty in a culture where a woman is reluctant to show her sexuality even to her husband.

Nacho repeated words within sentences to draw attention to other aspects of his tale. For example, he indicated the length of time the hero's father and mother lived together by repeating the word "every day" (mōztah) in the following passage.

> Ihcon, mōztah, mōztah, ōmpa nē, quitquiliah, mā yā quitequipanoā non.
> So it is, every day, every day, in that place there, they say, he goes hunting to serve her.

The effect of the repetition is to draw attention to the continuity in the relationship between the hero's father and mother and make the listener aware of the father's relationship to hero.

Repetition of phrases, with slight changes in words and alterations in word order, has a similar effect of emphasizing important story images. When explaining how the hero's mother ended up in the cave of a monkey, Nacho described how she passed by a large wood on her way to feed her husband, who is working in his milpa:

> Huān panōhuaya cē cuauhtah, nohon huēi cuauhtah cāmpa panōhuaya.

And she passed through a wood, that wood was big through which she passed.

The effect of the repetition is to give importance to the wood (cuauh-tah) where forest animals (cuauhtahocuilimeh) like monkeys live.

Less obvious, but nevertheless important, is the repetition of key images throughout the tale, one of which is food symbolism. References to food, eating, and feeding occur frequently in Nacho's tale, appearing first in the opening lines when the wife goes to feed her husband, who is working in his corn and bean plot. Food symbolism shows up again when the monkey provisions his family with food. Repetition in a raw versus cooked food metaphor emphasizes the plight of the hero's mother when living with the monkey. Nacho repeats the words "raw" (xoxōhuic) and "cooked" (yoccic), drawing attention to the monkey's lack of human culture as represented by fire and cooking.[20] He also identifies the hero's father with the eating-related verbal noun tēcuāni ("wild beast"), derived from tēcuā ("he/she bites or devours someone"). Eating appears again when the human-eating beasts (tēcuānimeh) devour the donkeys that the hero planned to use to bring firewood from the forest. References to food appear elsewhere: the hero brings what he thinks are squash but actually are skulls; the priest gives the hero tortillas as he sends him to the haunted house; and the hero meets his companions, who are drinking rather than performing feats of strength. As in most "Bear's Son" stories, the companions prepare food in the devil's house, but Nacho describes each companion taking meals to the others, much as the wife took meals to her husband while he worked on his milpa.

The repeated mention of food is related to the Nahuat concern with disorder in many ways. The forest and forest animals (cuauhtahocuilimeh) are presented as powerful and disorderly because they consume raw (xoxōhuic) meat and, as tēcuānimeh, they devour humans. The domain of humans is represented by fire (tit) that converts raw into cooked (yoccic) food. Fire has heat and light, which the Nahuat associate with the sun, regarded as the most important order-creating force in the universe. Death, which is the ultimate state of disorder for the human body, results from the loss of heat and light derived ultimately from the sun. Mictān, one of the Nahuat lands of the dead, is a dark place where the devil (ahmōcualli), the personification of disorder, devours the unfortunate dead who reside there, much as the human-eating beasts devour the living. The use of food symbolism to represent order and disorder may be related to food and eating as markers of Nahuat ethnic identity, which Alan Sandstrom so effectively demonstrated for another contemporary Nahua group in Mexico.[21] The Nahuat tell a number of myths distinguishing themselves as tortilla-eaters and identifying Spanish-speaking Mexicans as beef-eaters. The Nahuat of Huitzilan serve pork but never beef at the harvest banquet because they associate beef with the Spanish-speaking Mexicans who converted milpas into cattle pastures. Spanish-speaking Mexicans, in many narratives from Huitzilan and Yaonáhuac, are identified with the devil and appear as agents of disorder who sometimes devour their victims.

Repetition itself is related to Nahuat concerns with order and disorder because duplication in ritual is one way of creating order. For example, the climactic ritual performed in wedding ceremonies is "the dance of four" (nānāhuin), in which the bride, groom, and godfather and godmother of marriage circle each other and rotate in a clockwise and then counterclockwise direction as the intermediary (cihuātanqueh), an old and respected woman, surrounds them with incense. The participants must perform the "dance of four" with exactitude to get the married couple off to a propitious start. If they make a mistake, another four must repeat the dance until done correctly.

Nacho's avoidance of strong words has the effect of distancing him from the masculine power of his main character, who personifies īlihuiz. Other stylistic devices have the same effect. Nacho frequently inserted the syllable quit- several times in the same sentence throughout his story, and he explained that quit- actually stands for quitquiliah ("they say that"). The numerous insertions of "they say that" have the effect of constantly reminding the listener that Nacho is telling a story he heard from someone else and is not recounting events that he witnessed.

As mentioned in the previous chapter, Florencio's willingness to invent story images and figures of speech expressed his identification with the masculine power of his character. Nacho, on the other hand, was reluctant to depart from customary narrative style and less willing to invent his own images, keeping himself more remote from his character. Instead, he employed stylized images that appear in many other narratives circulating in his community. For example, he located the hero's father's home high on the face of a mountain (tepēīxco), a location connoting a slippery and dangerous surface. The hero's mother repeatedly alludes to danger when she tells her son that they are very high up—to discourage him from taking her back to her home. Danger and disorder are often represented by slipping and particularly falling; in contemporary Nahuat myths, falling into an abyss represents passing from the ordered state of life into the disordered state of death. Louise Burkhart observed that slipping and falling are among the most common metaphors for disorder in ancient Nahua moral discourse. Moreover, the image of the steep side of a mountain is a common feature of the Nahua view of the universe, in which the earth (tālticpac) is thought of as the summit of a tall mountain. The steep sides of the mountain represent the edges or the periphery of the world and are associated with disorder.[22]

Nacho and Florencio drew their stories to a close in different ways that accord with their respective stances toward masculine power. Florencio presented his hero as going through the stages of maturation and using his power for a morally and socially constructive purpose. His John the Bear becomes a gallant and manly man who is a model for other men. The turning point in John the Bear's life is his defeat of the devil, the personification of evil, preparing him for marriage and adulthood. The hero's defeat of the devil is a redemptive experience that allows him to return to the human community. Juanito's redemption is the critical event that makes the plot of Florencio's tale linear, and a linear plot structure is a common feature of many folktales from Judeo-Christian Europe. Max Lüthi characterizes the plots of many European folktales as beginning with unpromising heroes or heroines who become isolated, face adversity, experience a transformation, and marry a handsome man or beautiful woman in a culture where beauty stands for divine perfection.[23] Nacho's tale is not a story of redemption because his hero is not transformed by vanquishing the devil or by any other experience. The hero is not a model for other men because he is too powerful and disorderly from the beginning to the end, when the rain gods take him from his first home on Cozōltepēt, towering above Huitzilan, to his final home at the edge of the sea.

In their concluding sentences to "John the Bear," Florencio expressed his proximity to and Nacho his distance from the hero and the masculine power represented. Florencio ended his story by conveying that he could have attended his hero's wedding.

De modo que ya Juanito se casó con ella y tuvon [tuvieron] una boda. ¡Bua! Allá por las nubes. Y claro, yo si hubiera estado también, me había tocado algo, a que se hubiera sido un hueso por ejemplo. Pero yo hago gracia que allí la tengo bien derecha. A mi no me manda nunca con los huesos en las narices. ¿Entiende usted? Y colorín colorado, cuento terminado.

So it was that Juanito married her and they had a wedding. Bua! It was in the clouds. And, of course, if I had been there too, they would have given me something, even if it had been a bone for example. But I am grateful that my [nose] is perfectly straight. They never throw their bones in my nose. Do you know what I mean? And little red linnet, this story is over.

Florencio played with the formulaic ending to folktales in his community according to which narrators frequently close their tales by saying that bones from a wedding banquet are thrown in their noses. He departed from custom by saying he did not attend the wedding but implied he could have attended and, thus, could have witnessed the events in his story.

Nacho ended his tale with "And that is how it was, and there it ended" (Huān ihcon, huān ōmpa tamic), which does not convey the impression that he witnessed the events in his story, a stance consistent with a general narrative style representing his distance from the main character. The phrase "And there it ended" is formulaic for narrators in Nacho's community but not necessarily for other Nahuat and Spanish-speaking Mexican storytellers, some of whom adopted closing formulae representing proximity rather than distance from their story characters. A number of Nahuat from Santiago Yaonáhuac concluded their tales by saying "I came from there" (Ōmpa nihuāllā), implying they were witnesses, although Mariano from Yaonáhuac did not end his version of "The Bear's Son" this way. The Nahuat of Santiago Yaonáhuac are more bilingual and mix more Spanish into their stories and their everyday speech. They tell more folktales of Spanish origin and may have adopted from Spanish-speaking Mexicans a formulaic ending suggesting they were witnesses. No one has yet done a good study of the Mexican folktale tradition among Spanish speakers in the northern Sierra de Puebla, but some Spanish-speaking Mexicans from elsewhere concluded their versions of "The Bear's Son" with formulae indicating they were present.[24]

COMPARISON OF PARALLEL EPISODES

Florencio and Nacho's distinctive styles of narration are related to the ways they developed the details of the parallel episodes of their "Bear's Son" stories. Florencio's assertive style, sprinkled liberally with scatological and blasphemous expressions, and his identification with his hero are related to his comparatively disconnected view of the hero's relationship with other men. Nacho's narrative style, in which he avoided speaking with īlihuiz, is related to his more connected view of his hero's relationship with other men.

Florencio's and Nacho's different representations of a man's relationship with other men are evident in how they depicted the bear and his son. Florencio presented a completely disconnected picture of the hero's relationship with his father. He said nothing about the father and attributed the hero's strength to the milk of the adoptive bear mother. Nacho, on the other hand, presented a fuller picture of his hero's relationship with his father, which he described with ambivalence. He used repetition to emphasize the hero's father as the provisioner of his household, giving him a conspicuous place in his family like that occupied by many fathers in the patrilineally extended families of Huitzilan. Like many Spanish-speaking narrators in Spain and Mexico, Nacho described his hero's willingness to confront his father as he allies himself with his mother in an obvious Oedipal triangle. However, Nacho also represented the conflict between father and son in the context of īlihuiz as used in Nahuat moral discourse. Both father and son act inconsiderately, just as both have bodies covered partially or completely with hair. The potential confrontation between father and son is inevitable because each acts inconsiderately with respect to the other. The hero's father set the stage for his relationship with his son by abducting the mother while on her way to feed her husband in the forest. This initial act of inconsiderate behavior set into motion a chain of events that ultimately unravels the father-son relationship. Nacho, as will become apparent, told several stories describing scenarios of disaster triggered by some form of inconsiderate behavior.

The characterization of the hero's father as someone acting with īlihuiz and consequently seriously disrupting the father-son relationship appeared in another variant of "The Bear's Son," told by Nahuat narrator Juan Hernández, also of Huitzilan de Serdán. This father brutally punishes his son and drives him out of the house, something most Nahuat fathers I knew tried to avoid at all costs unless, of course, they were out of control and acted with īlihuiz. The portion of Juan's story that deals with the father-son relationship appears below.

Before the sun rose and it was dark, our ancestors perished in the flood. There were big mountains then, and the water drilled holes into the canyons, making the caves. The sun appeared and dried up the water. A bear appeared along with the sun to plant and make people again. After the bear came a woman. The bear and the woman had a child whom we know as Nāhuēhueht

63

Fig. 2. "The bear and the woman had a child whom we know as
Nāhuēhueht (Nānāhuatzin)."

(Nānāhuatzin). When he was just a boy eight years old, he was already big. He grew quickly because he was a god.

When Nāhuēhueht had feeling, his parents sent him to school. He went to school for a long time, but he struck other children and threw rocks at them and hit them with his hand and kicked them. He even talked back to the teacher, saying, "Don't hit me. You're not my father. You're just here because you're lazy. What do you teach me? We can choose to fight or not to fight, and it isn't any of your business." Nāhuēhueht hit the children with stones and he hit little girls. One day a man came to the bear's house and told him that Juanito hit his boy with a rock and split his head open. The bear said he would hit Juanito without any warning. Martha, Juanito's mother, told the bear that Juanito would come home soon and he, the father, could thrash him. The bear wondered, "How shall I beat him to teach him a lesson? You've seen that he never obeys and gets very angry when I punish him." The bear decided to hang Juanito from the rafters to punish him, but Martha pleaded with him not to hang him by the neck lest he kill him. She told him to just beat him with a rope until he no longer cried out. Juanito came home from school, and his mother asked him what he had done the day before. She told him about the man who had come and asked him if he had hit his child. Juanito denied everything, and then the bear chased Juanito, he grabbed a rope and tied it around Juanito's waist and hung him from the rafters and beat him until he was tired of thrashing him. He threatened next time to put the rope around Juanito's neck until he died. Martha was angry and complained that the bear had almost killed him. She said Juanito could not go to school.

When Juanito was ten or twelve, he was a big man. His father sent him into the forest for some firewood, but Juanito told his father he would not return. He said it would be better for him to make his own house and live alone. Juanito went into the forest to find a site and returned to tell his mother where he would be living. He made his house on Cozōlin [Cozōltepēt]. Juanito, or Nāhuēhueht, never learned to read and write and this made his father angry. Juanito stayed a long time at Cozōlin, where a spring flows at the summit. One day the bear went there and told Juanito, "You've built a fine house. I see that you're better off here." Juanito replied, "Yes, because you beat me so badly at your house. You [plural] got very angry with me."

Several other native Mexican narrators provided more detail on the father and his relationship with the hero than men from Cáceres.

The Nahuat storyteller Mariano Isidro of Yaonáhuac identified the hero's father as a bear to whom he attributed the hero's strength and also described an Oedipal struggle in which the hero escapes with his mother and kills his father. Other native Mexican men depicted a bear or a tiger taking a woman to his cave, they told how the woman has a son, and they represented the son helping his mother escape from the cave and return to her community.[25] The son many threaten his father or kill him in the escape, and sometimes other agents kill the father.[26] Some native Mexicans, however, resemble Spanish men when telling this tale as they provide no information about the hero's father. Two Nahua storytellers from Durango are like Florencio in mentioning only the hero's mother and attributing the source of his incredible strength to milk drunk in infancy, but in this case the mother cannot make her own milk and has the hero nurse from a she-donkey.[27]

Nacho and some other native Mexican men represented the hero's father and his relationship with his son more fully than Spanish men for several reasons. Native Mexican narrators may have heard "The Bear's Son" from Spanish-speaking Mexicans who described more fully than Spanish men the hero's father. Despite the assertion that Spanish-speaking Mexican men have a strong Oedipus complex,[28] narrators represented a lack of father-son tension when telling "The Bear's Son." In only one variant does the hero talk about killing his father,[29] and in no case does patricide occur. The hero's father is, in some versions, very anthropomorphized and appears as a sympathetic character who lives as a human male might live with his wife.[30]

J. Frank Dobie collected a "Bear's Son" tale from a Spanish-speaking Mexican man identified as Ismael, a vaquero on a ranch in northern Mexico, who devoted a great deal of his attention to describing the bear-father as a husband-provider.[31] The bear is a sympathetic character in a variant Barakat heard from another Spanish-speaking Mexican man from northern Mexico.[32] When this bear discovers his wife and son have fled their cave, he is so anguished that he cannot pursue them and is unable to block their escape, leaving the impression of a father who loves his wife and son more than they love him. A slightly more developed account of the father-son relationship appears in a variant of "The Bear's Son" by an unknown or Spanish-speaking Mexican narrator from Jalisco.[33] This criollo narrator mentions the hero's father but not his mother; he brings the father into the picture when the hero is about to leave town and the father helps him by giving him a lot of money. Among Spanish-speaking women from Jalisco, one provided no information about the father, and the other mentioned a father but not a mother, attributing the hero's unusual animal identity to his mother by calling him "Juan the son of a she-donkey."[34]

Denial of the father in the Spanish male versions of "The Bear's Son" and the father's more fully developed image in the Spanish-speaking and native Mexican tales could be related to different configurations of family life. As mentioned earlier, the father's absence and the comparatively sparse details about the father-son relationship in the Cáceres male variants are consistent with Michael D. Murphy's contention that many Spanish fathers and sons have an avoidance relationship and with ethnographic descriptions of fathers uninvolved in the care of their infant children.[35] The tendency for Spanish female narrators to identify fathers and develop more fully the father-son relationship accords with their strong filial orientation to both parents. Men's and women's representations of Juanito as closer to his mother also fits father-son avoidance and accords with many ethnographers' description of women as the primary parents of small children.[36]

Descriptions of the actual Spanish-speaking Mexican father are variable and sometimes inconsistent. Rarely nurturant, often authoritarian, and frequently a harsh critic of his sons, the Spanish-speaking Mexican father of urban, working, and underclass Mexico was a central figure in the Sánchez family described by Oscar Lewis.[37] However, Matthew Gutmann recently observed the Spanish-speaking Mexican father's parenting role in a similar setting in Mexico City and discovered that he is much more involved in the nurturant care of his infant children than previously thought, particularly when economic conditions favor women working outside the home.[38] The father–infant son relationship is very important for understanding the father's image in masculine oral narratives because, as Alan Dundes points out, folktales contain material flowing from the unconscious or subconscious memories of early childhood.[39]

Among some native Mexicans, the father-son relationship is a major axis of family life. Nahuat sons reside patrilocally much more than matrilocally after marriage and form patrilineally extended family households where father and son work together on a common milpa to fill the family granary and purse.[40] Nutini reported preference for patrilocality in other native Mexican villages in his survey of the ethnographic literature.[41] While many ethnographers describe the native Mexican father as a figure of authority demanding respect from his sons, Nacho presented a story image of the father concordant with his close and complex relationship with sons in the patrilineally extended family.

Nacho expressed his strong relational consciousness in other episodes of his story. Like other native Mexican and Spanish-speaking Mexican narrators, he stressed the companions' equality, rather than relative strength, and depicted their interdependence. He told how each companion has the ability to drink exactly the same amount (one tub full) of *aguardiente*. He represented the companions' interdependence by presenting them in a division of labor like that between husband and wife; each of the companions takes a meal to the other two, exactly as the hero's mother took meals to her husband. To be sure, he eventually demonstrated the superior valor of his hero when describing him as the only one capable of vanquishing the devil.

A majority of other native Mexicans also presented the hero and his companions in an egalitarian relationship when describing their first meeting. Mariano Isidro, a Nahuat narrator from Santiago Yaonáhuac, made no comparisons of the companions' relative strength, and he referred to them as "brothers." Tzotzil, Popolucan, Tepecano, Tepehua, and some Zapotec narrators similarly depicted initial equality among the companions.[42] A minority of native Mexicans presented hierarchical and competitive views of male peer relations reminiscent of Spanish men. In one Zapotec story, the companions attempt but fail to vanquish the hero on their first meeting.[43] In a Nahua tale from Durango, the hero initially admires the strength of his companions, who immediately identify him as the strongest of them all, firmly establishing his superiority from the moment of their first meeting.[44]

Spanish-speaking Mexicans, who may be the source of the Spanish folktales adopted into native Mexican oral tradition, similarly described the hero and his companions starting out with siblinglike solidarity and interdependence. Few Spanish-speaking Mexican men or women made comparisons of relative strength when depicting the companions' first meeting. One from northern Mexico represented the hero and his companions as half-brothers, and another from the same area described the companions as having complementary abilities and acting interdependently and cooperatively.[45] One northern Mexican man described the hero as lacking abilities possessed by the other companions on their first meeting; the hero must perform tasks to acquire the same abilities (run as fast as a deer, leap over mountains, shoot very accurately, move mountains, and change the course of rivers), which enable him to perform heroic feats later on.[46] Mestiza women from Jalisco, like their counterparts in Spain, did not emphasize the relative strength of the companions when describing their first meeting. One simply said that the hero joins up with some sharecroppers, and the other depicted the hero and his companions as actual brothers.[47] Howard T. Wheeler's unidentified criollo storytellers from Jalisco, who may be men or women, represented the companions as equal in age to the hero, as capable of great physical feats but not necessarily stronger or weaker than the hero, and as unable to vanquish the hero in a fight.[48]

Each narrator leaves a particular stamp on a story, which becomes evident when parallel episodes of different variants are placed side by side and subjected to careful comparison. Nacho's particular stamp is the elimination of any trace of male sexual competition, a conspicuous theme in other native Mexican, Spanish-speaking Mexican, and Spanish male variants of "John the Bear." In Nacho's tale, the hero removes three maidens from the devil's cave—one for each companion—and there is no treachery; each companion ends up with a maiden, enabling him to work his corn and bean plot.

Mariano and other native Mexicans generally represented more sexual competition than found in Nacho's tale, and some described levels of sexual rivalry approaching those found in stories told by Spanish men. Mariano recounted how the companions steal the maidens and abandon the hero in the underworld, although he concluded his story with the hero forgiving his "brothers" and threatening the devil for harming them when they attempted to prepare meals in the haunted house. The companions abandon the hero in the underworld and steal the maidens in other native Mexican variants; Popolucan and Tzotzil storytellers recounted how the companions try to kill the hero, and Popolucan and Zapotecs described how the companions are punished for their treachery.[49] It is interesting that Rito Villa, a Nahua from Durango, also described the companions stealing the maiden from the hero, but unlike other narrators, he told how the companions kill the hero when he tries to recover the maiden.[50] The Popolucan and Zapotec narrators, whose image of sexual competition resembles that of Spanish men, also expressed a strong filial orientation.[51] They described the hero struggling to establish his position in the king's family by winning the hand in marriage of one of the princesses he rescued in the underworld. Their filial orientation as well as sexual rivalry could develop in families where the father is more involved in the lives of his children relative to fathers in Cáceres and other parts of Spain.

Spanish-speaking Mexicans also depicted male sexual competition when maidens appear in the plot. Three of Howard T. Wheeler's unidentified storytellers described the hero finding three princesses and taking them from guardian animals or demons.[52] He loses the princesses to the companions, who try to kill him while he is in the underworld, and struggles to gain his rightful place in the king's family. The hero kills two of his companions and remains allied with the other two in one variant.[53] Among Spanish-speaking Mexicans who are identified, one did not include maidens, and another did not include companions at the point in the plot when the maidens appear in the story.[54] One Spanish-speaking man from northern Mexico represented mild sexual competition; the companions take the princesses for themselves and abandon the hero in the underworld, but they also help the hero escape, and the hero does not avenge them for treachery.[55] Two known mestiza women, who tell "John the Bear," combined sexual competition with a strong filial orientation, weaving "Cinderella" elements into their story. Sexual competition is apparent when the hero disenchants the maidens by killing their husbands, when he takes the maidens away from another man who is guarding them, and when the companions steal the maidens and try to kill the hero.[56] The two women also represented the hero and his companions as rivals for a place in the king's family; the hero vanquishes his rivals by producing valuable jewelry that the princesses gave him when he removed them from their enchantment.

SUMMARY

The journey from Florencio to Nacho has led farther away from the assertive Hispanic man who is Freud's active male. It also raises some questions about who the Hispanic man in Mexico really is when he is a Spanish-speaking Mexican. Particularly enigmatic is the Mexican man as father, whose image in stories by Spanish-speaking Mexican men and women is developed and sometimes very humane. Often locked in an Oedipal struggle with his son, he nevertheless is a conspicuous presence who can grieve when he faces the prospect of losing his family. By the time we come to Nacho, we find a man who represented his masculine identity with a reluctance to act assertively lest he set into motion a chain of disastrous events by which fathers become unraveled from sons and men become estranged from each other. Nacho is in some respects like a Spanish woman because his reluctance to act assertively is based on strong filial loyalties and an interconnected or relational view of the human condition. Nacho's connected and Florencio's comparatively disconnected views of a man's relationship with other men become particularly apparent from a comparison of all thirty-six variants of the Spanish and Mexican "Bear's Son" stories. The following chapters will take us further into Florencio's and Nacho's poetic imaginations, where we shall discover there is more to both men.

Chapter 4

TRICKSTERS IN SPAIN

A MAN LIKE FLORENCIO, WHO WISHES TO FOLLOW HIS FATH-er's advice and avoid "cleaning himself in front of another," tries to live on his own capital rather than work for a daily wage, submit to the domination of another, and lose his personal autonomy in the process. However, Florencio, like his father before him, is a member of the agrarian working class of Navaconcejo and inherited little family property. He would have to acquire his capital by making shrewd transactions. Florencio and other narrators in Cáceres told many folktales about men whose transactions are particularly profitable. Their heroes are often poor and unpromising tricksters who use their cunning to outsmart those who are greedy and too willing to strike a good bargain. I shall examine two of Florencio's trickster tales to reveal how one narrator shaped stories told by others in his culture to express his particular vision of a man's relationship with other men in a world where the bargain is necessary to achieve personal autonomy.

Florencio's first trickster tale is a variant of a very popular story that circulates widely in Spanish oral tradition. The tale in Spain is actually a composite of several stories that exist as independent tales in other parts of Europe: "The Rich and the Poor Peasant" (Tale Type 1535), "Cleverness and Gullibility" (1539), and "The Parson in the Sack to Heaven" (1737).[1] "The Rich and the Poor Peasant" appeared in literature as the tenth-century Latin poem *Unibos* and the nineteenth-century Hans Christian Andersen story "Big Claus and Little Claus."[2] It is also a very popular folktale existing in at least 1,397 variants.[3] Generally, the hero of the oral tales is a poor man who blackmails and strikes handsome bargains with a richer man. In many variants, he sells ashes or lime as gold, a cowhide or bird with miraculous powers, and a flute that brings the dead back to life. The rich man, angered by the deceptions, tries to kill the trickster by placing him in a sack and throwing him into the river. However, the trickster trades places with a shepherd, claiming he is being taken to marry a princess, and returns home with a herd of sheep. He explains to his astounded adversary that he found the sheep in the river, and the rich man persuades the trickster to throw him into the same river so he can obtain more of the animals for himself. The final episode is sometimes an independent tale folklorists call "The Parson in the Sack to Heaven" (1737).[4]

In Spain, episodes from "The Rich and the Poor Peasant" are frequently combined with "Cleverness and Gullibility," a particularly popular oral narrative in Finland, the Baltic region, and Russia.[5] The hero is also a trickster who strikes good bargains by selling a messenger rabbit, a donkey or horse that produces gold in its dung, and other allegedly miraculous animals. Narrators in many parts of the world easily combine "The Rich and the Poor Peasant" and "Cleverness and Gullibility" because their episodes stand alone and are strung together in different ways without affecting the structure of the plot.[6]

Particular Spanish narrators give their stories a variety of titles, and Florencio called his tale "The Three Brothers." His is one of at least seventeen variants folklorists have collected in Spain since Aurelio Espinosa and Aurelio de Llano Roza de Ampudia carried out their projects between 1919 and 1923.[7] The variants come from unidentified narrators in Burgos, Santander (where Aurelio Espinosa reported two versions), and Granada, from Mercedes Morán and Serafín Pérez in Asturias, and from Victoria Coca and Magdalena Frutos in Salamanca.[8] I heard nine versions from Román Santo as well as Florencio in Navaconcejo, Santos López and Maximina Castaño in Garganta la Olla, Victoria Díaz and Zacaria Iglesias in Piornal, Leandro Jiménez and his daughter-in-law Felipa Sánchez in El Guijo de Santa Bárbara, and Felisa Sánchez Martín in Serradilla.

The variants circulating in Spain are of two types. The first type features a hero who takes money from gypsies, innkeepers, oil sellers, thieves, and compadres by selling donkeys that drop coins, rabbits that appear to carry messages, and flutes, bellows, and whistles that are supposed to revive the dead. The victim discovers he has been fooled and tries unsuccessfully to get revenge on the trickster.[9] The second type features a hero who obtains money from blackmail and by selling hoes that dig up loaves of bread, cowhides and crows with the alleged power to divine, messenger rabbits and pack animals that drop coins, and human excrement. The hero broadcasts his newly found wealth, causing others—usually brothers or neighbors—to act on their greed and attempt to repeat the trick with disastrous results.[10]

In both cases, the would-be tricksters often try to kill the hero by putting him into a sack and throwing him into the river. However, the trickster changes places with a goatherd, cowherd, or shepherd and then meets his envious and greedy brothers and neighbors, who beg him to throw them into the same river so they too can repeat the transaction. The results are always the annihilation of the greedy and envious. Narrators in Cáceres villages tell both types of stories: Román Santo and Florencio Ramos are from Navaconcejo; Román told the first type and Florencio the second.

I shall examine first Florencio's tale of "The Three Brothers," in which the hero obtains wealth by selling human excrement mixed with sugar. His envious younger brothers try to repeat the trick with disastrous results and then attempt unsuccessfully to get revenge on their older brother by throwing him into the river. The interpretation following the story will focus on how Florencio has apparently changed the tale to represent his particular view of a man's relationship with other men in a world where the transaction has so much importance for establishing personal autonomy. The story elements, which are the focus of the interpretation, are Florencio's narrative style, the significance of excrement, the importance of capital in family relations, and the representation of relations among three brothers.

"The Three Brothers"
by Florencio Ramos

Well, once there was a father and he had three sons. And among those three sons was one who was a little stupid. And the father died. He told them, he said, "Look, as long as the oldest is unmarried—because he is this way, the poor thing—as long as he doesn't marry," he said, "the capital is not to be divided."

The other two, even though they had a lot to lose, agreed. And, of course, the oldest was shackling the capital, and the others, those other two poor things, well, naturally, more whores passed them than anything after the other one didn't release the capital. Because their father left it that way in writing.

And one brother said to the other, he said, "I shit on ten! As for Brother, we must look for a trick to pull if we're not going to die of old age without getting anything from Father." And so on and so forth.

"You're telling *me.*"

73

And [the stupid one] put up a banner saying that whoever wanted to shit at his house—he put the banner up in the town— he would give a *perra gorda* [an old coin] to whomever would go to his house to shit. At once he filled two copper kettles. I shit on ten! And he tossed in a huge amount of sugar. And he said it was honey water. The entire town said, "I shit on ten! This uncle is stupid, he's a lost fool."

"And he'll turn Father's capital into dust for us. Now he gives a *perra gorda* to anyone who goes there."

And in those days!

"That so and so and this and that," said his brothers.

Well, nothing. The stupid one went and said to one of his brothers, he said, "Listen, Martín."

That uncle was called, he was called Martín. He said, "Martín, would you let me take the donkey?"

"Where are you going to take the donkey?" he replied. "Heh, *now* what with the donkey? The donkey?"

"Those who went there to the house said I was stupid and so on and so forth," he said. "Look here, I have here two big loads of honey water. I'm going to sell it."

"But where are you going to sell this? This won't bring you anything. Oh my and I don't know what. Bah! There is the donkey. Take it."

He gave him the donkey, his black donkey, a very fine one. He took the donkey with the two kettles. I shit on ten!

Honey water! Bah! The women tried it. It was sweeter than the sacramental host.

"You know, it's big-balled," the women said. "Eh, well give me so much."

"How much is it?" asked another.

And so on. So he exhausted his supply. He arrived in the afternoon.

"See. See. You said I was stupid. Stupid. Look at the money I've earned! And there's more. I have more here. Go look."

"I shit on ten! Well, he who's dumber than the sacramental host struck a big-balled blow."

"I shit on ten! Do you know what we are going to do? He paid two *perras*. We'll pay four. I shit on ten! Fuck! He took out more money than the mother who gave birth to him."

And they said he was stupid. The result was, his brother went calling out four *perras*. Well, the town went to their house rather than to the house of another. He had prepared some big loads. I shit on ten! They threw in a big load of sugar. I shit on ten! Allah! They arrived there.

"Honey water!"

It was the same donkey his brother had taken a few days or a week earlier, whatever. The people—the town—had gotten sick with the honey water.

"I shit on ten! That's the uncle with the honey water!"

They gave those brothers a caning.

"This is the uncle with the honey water the other day, this so and so."

They gave them what they wanted to, of course. I shit on ten! Those brothers came from there without selling the honey water. They were paid a good caning.

"I shit on ten! We have to kill him. I shit on ten!" said the two brothers.

"I've thought of something, Brother."

"Tell me."

"I shit on ten! We're going to tell him he's going to marry the king's daughter. Let's see if he takes the bait. I shit on ten!"

"Tell me, how are you going to get him out of the house?"

"Very simple. We're going to tell him the king's daughter wants to get married and—listen to this—she loves him. She loves him. We'll put him into a sack. I have one of those big sacks, and we'll load him onto the donkey. I shit on ten! We'll trick him and take him. And that pond over there, down below, we're going to go and throw him into the pond and let's see if we don't get his ass. I shit on ten! Didn't you see the caning they gave us, which was his fault?"

"Well yes, you're right. I shit on ten!"

Well, it turned out they loaded their sack on the donkey—I shit on ten!—and they walked behind the donkey, of course. They went down the lower road. They were roads then, not highways. Soon they were hungry and had to eat a piece of bread. Well, then, they left the donkey there in the road, and the donkey was eating by the roadside. They stopped there at the fountain to eat a piece of bread. And the donkey went a little farther down. There was a herd of sheep there. From inside the sack the other one says, "They take me to be a king, and I don't want to be one. They take me to be a king. I don't want to be one."

The shepherd came closer. "What did you say?" he asked.

"They're taking me to marry the king's daughter, and I don't want to," he repeated.

"But what is this?"

"They take me to be a king, and I don't want to."

"I shit on ten!"

He let him out, and the other one put the shepherd into the sack. He tied him approximately how he was tied, and there went the shepherd. And the stupid one stayed with the sheep. Well, he drove not just a few sheep down the road. When his brothers had eaten their piece of bread, the donkey had gone farther on down.

"Burros."

They continued on down. They walked for a while. And then they arrived at the pond. It was one of those lakes around here that are almost round. They arrived and removed and untied the sack and grabbed it—one at one end and the other at the other. Viish. I shit on ten! Into the middle of the pond. And when they saw the sack had sunk, "We took him by the ass. Let's go."

They took their donkey and went back up to the town. When they were coming back up, they saw some sheep and someone with the sheep, and one said to the other, he said, "Brother, it looks like Narciso."

The stupid one was named Narciso.

"No," said the other one.

They went closer. "I shit on ten! Yes, he is just like little Narciso."

"Well yes, he looks just like him," replied the other.

"Well, you tell me. Fuck, we were there until he sank. I shit on ten!"

And they got closer.

"Narciso? It's Narciso."

"Cillo, well how are you doing here?" those two asked him when they had gotten closer.

"Huh? How am I here? How am I here? Well, fine."

"I shit on ten! Look at the sheep here with him! Whose are they?"

"Mine."

"Fuck! How?"

"Well, when you threw me into the pond, I could stick out my hand. The sack was ripped a little."

"Well yes, it's true the sack was torn," said the other.

"As I was sinking, I stuck out my hand. I did this. I brought all of these. If I had stuck out two—I shit on ten!—I would have brought twice as many as these. There were a lot of sheep in the pond," he explained.

"I shit on the mother who gave birth to him! Fine."

When the other two brothers were a little farther up, one said to the other, "Brother—I shit on ten!—this is what I am thinking. I shit on God! You and I are going to throw ourselves in and we'll take out, of course, a lot more than he has!"

"I shit on God!"

"Well, you old fucker, it's true."

"You know, you're right. I shit on ten! Let's go back!"

They went back. I shit on ten! They came to that pond. One

said to the other, he said, "Look, I'm going to jump in first. If you see me do this with my hands, jump in. It means I can't get them all out."

So it was that one—splash—went into the pond. It was touch and go as to whether he would stick up his hands. I shit on ten! He stuck up his hands. The other one saw him. Splash! Down into the water. I shit on ten! Of course, there those two stayed. And the stupid one stayed with the herd of sheep, and his two brothers disappeared. The dumb one said, "Uh-huh. They called me dumb. There are those who are stupid because they were born stupid, there are those who are stupid because they are stupid, and there are those who are stupid because they become stupid thinking they are not stupid."

El cuento terminado y punto colorado.

Perhaps the most obvious feature of Florencio's story is the importance of human excrement in both his narrative style and the story plot. Florencio's narrative style is filled with scatological and blasphemous expressions, which, as mentioned earlier, represent a man's stance toward authority in a culture with a high value on personal autonomy. The use of human excrement in the trickster's principal transaction is rare but not entirely unknown. The sale of human excrement appears in "Juan Bobo," which Aurelio Espinosa heard from an unidentified narrator in Hoznayo, Santander.[11] Juan Bobo collects excrement that his neighbors drop in his house when they cannot repeat his trick of converting animal hides into great quantities of cash. Juan takes the excrement to Madrid where he uses it in a blackmail scheme; pigs eat it, and Juan Bobo demands and receives compensation on the grounds the pigs have eaten something very valuable. Excrement and money are associated in many variants of the same story I heard from Cáceres narrators. Usually the trickster feeds gold or coins to a donkey, collects the precious objects from its dung, and sells the animal as a gold-dropping ass.[12]

A transaction in which excrement becomes money is a very interesting image if one takes into consideration the possible early childhood associations with excrement and the importance of the transaction in modern capitalism. Freud observed that excrement and money are symbolically connected.[13] Florencio builds on the association to make a particularly bitter comment about a world where one must acquire personal autonomy by making shrewd transactions, which are the functional equivalent of turning excrement into money to acquire capital if one does not have a particularly good inheritance. Florencio's symbolism also conveys the impression that money is shit, expressing another side of his critique of capitalism.

The importance of the transaction, the difficulty of making good ones, and the ease of making bad ones are apparent in Florencio's and his son's Bernardo's accounts of their own personal histories. Florencio explained that his father was a relatively poor man who moved from Arroyomolinos de la Vera to Navaconcejo to work in the vineyards. He was eighteen or nineteen years old at the time and followed his brother, who married a woman from Navaconcejo. Eventually he and his brother inherited from their father a few small plots of land in Arroyomolinos; they sold the plots to buy others in Navaconcejo, which eventually became part of the inheritance Florencio divided with his sister and younger brother.

To establish his own economic autonomy, Florencio carried out a series of transactions, some successful, and others unsuccessful. When he returned from two years of military service in 1946, he married the woman who became the mother of his five children. They lived in her mother's house, and Florencio managed to buy four goats and live reasonably well. Two years later, he traded his herd of goats for a small piece of land and acquired a milk cow. However, his wife became mentally ill and was unable to sell milk and make and sell cheese. Florencio sold the milk cow and bought another small herd of goats, but was still unable to make a go of selling their products. He inherited small plots of land from his father, which he sold to start a "cafeteria," a small house of prostitution. The house did well for a while until a neighbor woman complained to the Civil Guard that the car doors of the clients kept her awake at night. The Civil Guard discovered that Florencio was not paying social security taxes on his employees, closed the "cafeteria," and fined Florencio 250,000 pesetas, forcing him to sell much of his remaining property.

The difficulty of making even simple transactions is apparent in the economic history of Florencio's son Bernardo. After working for wages in Barcelona and Madrid, Bernardo decided to return to his hometown of Navaconcejo. He had inherited small plots of land from his mother and needed some horses to work the land. He bought two mares, one from a man in the neighboring town of Cabezuela and the other from a man in Tornavacas, a town to the north of Navaconcejo. However, the mares continually returned to their towns of origin, and Bernardo tired of bringing them back every single evening. One of them died, and Bernardo traded the surviving mare for a colt, carrying out the transaction with a neighbor in Navaconcejo. Bernardo explained the rest as follows:

The neighbor told me, "Well look, this colt is new. The thing is, the colt won't plow but it's gentle."

And since he was from the town, and so on, since he was someone I trusted, I said to myself, "Well, it'll be true."

We appraised the mare at 30,000. I said, "Well, we'll appraise the colt for half because it was very thin."

I said to myself, "Well, you geld this colt and it'll turn out that, in about one year or the following year, he'll be more grown and you can plow with him even though he isn't for plowing now. He'll probably be worth 20,000 or 22,000 pesetas."

It turned out the animal wouldn't fatten up for anything. It was of one of those thin breeds. And then it was bad, really bad because, as it turned out, we went to geld it and I told the geldor, "Watch out, because this colt kicks."

He said, "Bah! I've seen beasts worse than this one."

So true enough, he grabbed it, and Zas! The kick. I said to him, "Didn't I tell you!"

"I shit on the diola," he says, "If it were my colt, I'd put a bullet in him."

"Fine, but it's your fault. I told you," I said.

Well, they gelded him. Then I took him up there by the Albardillo [a locality in the hills above Navaconcejo] and came down, and it turned out I was riding him along the road and I was about to make him gallop, right? As he started to gallop, he put his head down between his legs and threw me. And after throwing me, he wanted to kick me. And since he couldn't kick me—because I slid out of there—well, it turned out afterwards, since I was behind him, he tried to kick me. At least he didn't connect because I lay down flat on the ground. No? But come on, he was bad. Then I traded him. I sold him to the gypsies. They were very happy because they said he was real cheap. But then the next day, they wanted to go back on the deal."

"But why?" I asked.

"Oh. It's because what you sold us isn't a colt."

"What is it?" I asked.

"A murderer."

In his story, Florencio represented the brothers as locked together by the provision in their father's will that the family capital is not to be divided until their older brother marries. The will's provision, of course, places the family property in trust and shackles the capital. Wills with provisions restricting the division of family property after the death of a parent are rare in Navaconcejo, where family land and other assets are usually divided immediately after the death of the property owner. Florencio's father and uncle immediately acquired their father's plots of land in Arroyomolinos de la Vera after his death, and Florencio likewise acquired his share of the patrimonial land soon after his father's death.

However, the grain of truth in Florencio's story is that young men, usually sons, in this narrator's generation faced hard times while waiting for their patrimony. Many married long before acquiring any inheritance and made do by sharecropping and raising animals on shares. Florencio and his sister and younger brother, like many in the Cáceres villages I knew, sharecropped their father's plots, giving him half of the yield and dividing the rest among themselves. Florencio emphasized, in his folktale, how the brothers quarrel for two reasons. First, the younger brothers must postpone their marriages and defer their sexual gratification until their older brother marries. Florencio used the expression *Pues les pasaban más putas que nada* ("Well, more whores passed them than anything"), meaning the brothers visited prostitutes because they could not marry. Second, the younger brothers strongly disapprove of their older brother's transaction with their father's capital—paying a *perra gorda* to anyone who will defecate in the family home. A *perra gorda* is an old coin with little value in today's world, but the word *perra* refers to money in general. The absurd image of a man paying money to buy human excrement may capture the powerful feelings of young men who must rely on the wisdom of older men who are not necessarily their brothers, but who make transactions with family money that younger men might inherit. To be sure, the plight of the three brothers in Florencio's tale is a rare occurrence in Cáceres, where the norm is for brothers to establish their economic independence immediately upon marriage. However, one can take the older brother as a symbolic recasting of the father and consider the younger brothers as sons. By such substitutions, Florencio's story becomes an autobiographical expression of his effort to convert the family property, which his four children stood to inherit, into a fortune by starting the "cafeteria."

In Florencio's tale of "The Three Brothers," the transaction that looked so unpromising actually leads to huge profits when the older brother successfully sells his honey water in the next town, perhaps as Florencio hoped his cafeteria would turn into a very profitable venture benefiting his sons. The reaction of the two younger brothers to their older brother's success is very interesting because it reveals a great deal about how family life is represented in folktales. First, the younger brothers might have decided their older brother could actually do what a man like Florencio and others in the agrarian working class of his generation aspired to do—turn nothing into something—

and trust him with managing their family estate. However, the younger brothers take a different course, which accords with the actual expectation of economic independence among the men of a family. Acting out of envy and greed and in fidelity to the norms of their culture, they go out on their own and attempt to repeat their older brother's transaction, setting into a motion a chain of events that results in their annihilation.

In general, brothers in trickster tales of this type circulating in Spanish oral tradition seldom enjoy the fruits of another brother's profitable transactions. I heard four other variants of the same tale from narrators in Cáceres in which the central protagonists are brothers. Two brothers are the victims of unrelated tricksters in stories by Leandro Jiménez of El Guijo de Santa Bárbara and Santos López of Garganta la Olla. One faces annihilation when he fails to revive his wife with bellows he buys from a trickster (a variant by Santos López). Others are annihilated when they persuade the trickster to throw them into the river so they might acquire a herd of goats (a variant by Leandro Jiménez).

A closer parallel to Florencio's story is the tale told by Felisa Sánchez Martín of Serradilla in which a younger brother acquires wealth through blackmail and cunning and his older brother perishes as he, consumed with envy, tries without success to repeat his brother's transaction. The main protagonists are Nicolasillo and his older brother Nicolasón. Nicolasillo is poor because he has only one mule, and Nicolasón is rich because he has five mules. Nicolasillo's mother-in-law dies in a fall, and he takes her body to a town where he leaves her in an inn while he runs an errand. He instructs the innkeeper to speak to his mother-in-law in a loud voice. The innkeeper takes her a glass and milk, and after shouting and getting no response, throws the milk into her face in a fit of bad temper. The innkeeper pleads with Nicolasillo not to let anyone know, they bury the woman, and the innkeeper pays Nicolasillo a lot of money. Nicolasón learns of the money and tries to repeat the trick by killing and selling his own mother-in-law, ending up in prison for his efforts. Meanwhile, Nicolasillo makes another successful transaction when his mule dies and he prepares the muleskin with tar so it squeaks when rubbed together. He goes to another inn, and the innkeeper's wife lets him into a straw loft from where Nicolasillo can see into the kitchen. He spots the wife preparing a meal for a priest just as her husband returns home. The woman quickly puts the supper into the cupboard and the priest into a chest. The husband hears Nicolasillo in the straw loft and tells his wife to have him come down. Nicolasillo squeaks his mule-hide, and the husband asks him what the squeak means. Nicolasillo explains that the hide says there is a fine supper in the cupboard (*Que en la almacena hay una buena cena*) and a priest in the chest (*En el arca hay una cura metido*). The husband buys the hide for a lot of money, and Nicolasillo returns home.[14] Soon Nicolasón gets out of jail and skins his five mules to repeat the transaction of his younger brother, earning very little for his efforts. He decides to kill Nicolasillo by putting him into a sack and throwing him into the river, but the hero trades places with a cowherd, and Nicolasón perishes when he persuades his younger brother to throw him into the same river so he can obtain more for himself. Felisa follows a pattern very familiar in many other Cáceres narratives—"The Two Travelers" (Tale Type 613), "Open Sesame" (676), and "The Table, the Ass, and the Stick" (563)—discussed in Chapter 7. According to that pattern, one brother is rich, another poor; the poor one becomes wealthy and the rich one envious and greedy. The rich one perishes when he tries to become even richer by following in his brother's footsteps.

The only instance of one brother enjoying the wealth another brother acquires by making a cunning transaction appears in a variant of "The Rich and the Poor Peasant" (1535) from Asturias. In a story told by Serafín Pérez, two brothers have only one calf. The younger brother decides to kill it, angering the older brother. They calm down after eating the meat, and the younger brother takes the hide to sell. After crows eat the hide, the hero catches one of the crows and heads for lodging in the home of a woman whose husband is temporarily away. She places the boy in a room from where he can see the kitchen, and he watches the woman prepare a delicious tortilla for her lover. As in the tale by Felisa Sánchez Martín, the boy sees the woman hide the supper and her lover as her husband returns home. The boy pretends the crow divines the presence of the supper and his wife's lover and sells the bird to the husband. Unlike other variants of "The Rich and the Poor Peasant" in Spain, the younger brother's transaction does not make the older brother envious and greedy. Rather, the hero returns to his brother and uses the profits from his transaction to buy calves for them both.[15]

Despite the frequent representations of envy and greed among brothers, male sibling rivalry has its limits in stories circulating in Cáceres and other provinces of Spain. No brother in any Cáceres variant of "The Rich and the Poor Peasant" and "Cleverness and Gullibility" makes his brother the target of his transactions. Florencio did not describe the older brother selling excrement to his younger brothers, and other Cáceres narrators did not represent brothers carrying out transactions with each other. Narrators usually told of the trickster carrying out a profitable transaction with someone who is not a member of his family.[16]

Florencio's tale is distinctive because it focuses on the relations among three brothers from the beginning to the end of the plot. The only other tale with three brothers is the one just described by Mercedes Morán. However, in Mercedes' tale, the one brother (Manuel) drops out of the plot when Juan and Pedro head out into the world, and Juan disappears after the two brothers return home with the money they obtain from the thieves. Pedro single-handedly sells ashes for gold and acquires pack animals when angry and envious neighbors try to throw him down into a well in the subsequent episodes.[17]

Florencio's focus on three brothers is one example of his relatively strong orientation to male relationships in the family, which could have something to do with his own circumstance. At the time he told me the tale of "The Three Brothers," he had a close, although sometimes complicated, relationship with his three grown and unmarried sons, which I suspect is attributable to a combination of particular circumstances. Florencio probably took over some of the parenting roles ordinarily assumed by the mother when his wife became mentally ill and their children were quite young. Frequently a grandmother, particularly the mother's own mother, steps in and takes care of children when their mother cannot. However, Florencio's mother-in-law died eight years after his marriage when his children were still quite little. From what Florencio told me about the gender division of labor during his early marital years, his wife was the primary parent of their children during infancy and early childhood. Florencio appears to have become the primary parent in later years and is an especially important nurturant figure for his adult sons, who have yet to marry. A sister may provide meals for her unmarried adult brothers who cannot turn to a mother or grandmother. Bernardo lived with his married sister when he give up his unpromising job in Madrid and returned to Navaconcejo to earn some money during the cherry harvest. However, she and her husband had a family of their own to support, and she quarreled with Bernardo over the 3,000 pesetas he paid her for his monthly room and board. The quarrel was one of the reasons Bernardo gave for leaving Navaconcejo to work in Barcelona, where for six years he installed sheet metal roofing material on factory buildings, a job that required working at great height, something to which Bernardo was accustomed after climbing high into cherry trees during the harvest. Bernardo returned to Navaconcejo and set up his own home. Still unmarried, he frequently visits his father, who seems to enjoy cooking for his sons.

My visits to Florencio's home are among my fondest memories of fieldwork in Spain. I particularly remember one evening when I showed up uninvited at his house in Navaconcejo when two of his sons were home and Florencio was preparing a dish of potatoes and milk. He stirred the pot slowly and gently until the potatoes were thoroughly cooked. I brought a bottle of what I thought was good wine, which Florencio and his sons tasted and summarily rejected as undrinkable. They pulled out their own locally produced wine, and we sat down at the table and scraped the pot clean, enjoying with particular relish the browned part at the bottom. Perhaps on this or possibly another occasion—I visited Florencio many times during fieldwork in Cáceres—he told me the story he called "The Two Eggs," which one of his sons considered his favorite.

"THE TWO EGGS"

Florencio's story is a variant of the Fortunatus legend, which exists as an oral narrative folklorists call "The Three Magic Objects and the Wonderful Fruits" (Tale Type 566).[18] The oral tale usually features the acquisition, loss, and recovery of three magic objects: a money- or gold-filling purse, a magic carpet, and a flute, horn, or whistle that provides military support.[19] The transaction by which the hero acquires the magic objects does not necessarily involve trickery. For example, the hero sometimes obtains the objects by removing the grateful donor from enchantment, and two of the seven Spanish oral variants are of this type.[20] In one, told by Ángel García of Madroñera in southern Cáceres, a gypsy, a peddler, and a deserter receive the objects from maidens they remove from their enchantment by enduring three horrible nights of dripping hot oil.[21] In another by Pilar Díaz from Villanueva in Asturias, a hero receives the objects from a man he removes from his enchantment by staying three nights in a house filled with frightening noises.[22] However, most of the Spanish stories, including Florencio's tale of "The Three Eggs," feature heroes who acquire the objects by trickery. The hero usually meets three brothers who are quarreling over the division of their inheritance, consisting of the purse, the carpet, and the horn, trumpet, or whistle. The hero offers to mediate, as an uninterested party, in their dispute and sends them off to distant hills. He tells them he will shout for them to run or call out for each object. When the brothers are sufficiently far away, the hero grabs the objects, steps on the carpet, and whisks away. Trickery is particularly popular in Cáceres, where narrators told four closely related variants of the same story.[23]

Usually the hero loses the magic objects when he courts the daughter of a king; she or her father takes them when the hero visits her at the palace. The hero often recovers the objects with the help of an intermediary agent—an old man or woman—who introduces him to the wonderful fruits that have the power to grow and remove horns on the heads of those who eat them. The hero sells the horn-producing fruit to the king and his family and then, dressed as the doctor, cures their illness with the horn-removing fruit on the condition they return the objects to him. In most variants, the hero marries the princess and becomes a king.[24]

Despite the popularity of the story as a folktale in Europe, Stith Thompson believed it has some "unsatisfactory motivations." When the hero obtains the magic objects by removing maidens from their enchantment, the "hearer wants to know more about these women and vainly imagines they are going to end as wives for the companions." Moreover, the hero often starts out with several companions who "drop out of sight."[25] Both problems exist in the Spanish folktales; the enchanted maidens do not marry the hero in the tale by Ángel García of Madroñera,[26] and the hero inexplicably separates from his companions, who disappear in most of the narratives I know of in Spain.[27]

Florencio, however, solved both problems in his story and, in so doing, represented a less alienated picture of a man's relationship with other men. As in many Cáceres variants, the hero begins his adventures with his brother, who, in Florencio's tale, remains more connected to the hero than in stories told by other narrators in Cáceres and other provinces in Spain. Below is an English translation of Florencio's story, followed by a discussion of the hero's relative isolation from his companions in other variants of the same tale.

"The Two Eggs"
by Florencio Ramos

Once there was a married couple who had two sons. One was named Pedro and the other Javier. And the husband, well, he died. The woman was left a widow, of course. And the little boys were small. One was about eight and other about ten or so. And since the woman was left a widow, well, of course, she walked about. And the little boys went for bundles of firewood. They had to go to the countryside for bundles of firewood for the kitchen hearth. Well, one day, the two brothers went, and one said to the other, "Brother . . . ."

I think Pedro says to Javier, he says, "Javier, look, there is a nest."

"Well, you're right. I shit on ten!"

"Climb up."

Pedro went over to the tree and climbed up. There was a vine, a vine attached to the pine tree where the nest was. He climbed up.

"What does it have?" Javier asks.

"Two eggs. But you'll see how beautiful they are. They have writing," he declares.

"But how and what? Come down so we can take a look."

He brought those eggs down. He showed them to his brother. "Fuck! I shit on ten!"

The older one, who climbed the tree, says, "Fuck! 'He who eats this egg will be the Pope in Rome.' And 'He who eats this one will be King of Spain.' I shit on ten!"

Of course, it made a big impression that those eggs had writing when the bird laid them. Well, nothing. He took them to their mother.

"Mother, we saw a nest with two eggs. Look here. Take a look."

"What is this and so on and so forth?" she says to them. "Oh yes. Imagine that. Well, how come they're like this?"

Their mother took the eggs. She kept them in a certain place. And the mother immediately let it be known in the town there was a woman who had two eggs and she was in charge of them and so on. I shit on ten! Soon, the next day, a widower, who was young enough to marry her, appeared. And the little boys—I shit on ten!—didn't swallow well the idea of their mother remarrying. But in the end, their mother was determined, and the boys let her do it. And when their mother was about to marry and her husband was about to be her husband, Javier says to Pedro, "Pedro, what am I thinking?"

"I know what you're thinking."

"Well, I'm thinking he is going to marry Mother only for the eggs. I know I'm right. Well, that's a fine thing. Do you know what we're going to do? You eat one, and I'll eat the other."

It turned out Pedro ate one, and Javier ate the other. And one of the boys says, "When it comes down to it, if he knows we've eaten the eggs, he'll probably give us a bad time."

So it was better to get out of there. Well, the other one says, "Yes, you're right."

"Come."

They grabbed their clothes. I shit on ten! Those boys left town. It turned out they came to a place where there were two roads, and one says to the other, he says, "Brother, I'm thinking something."

"Say what it is."

"The two of us together will make our way worse than if we're apart. Wherever it is, they're more likely to give a piece of bread to one of us than the two of us together."

"You're right."

Well, nothing. They drew lots and one went one way and the other the other. The little boys were walking along separately, each one going to his own place. And one came to a place where there was a fountain and there were three or four brothers. It was touch and go if they were going to fight each other. The brothers were arguing.

"I shit on ten!" says Pedro, who was the oldest. "What's going on with you? Why do you fight?"

"Huh! Why fight! What do *you* know?"

"Fuck, maybe I can mediate something because I see you're getting into a fight."

"My father died. We are dividing the inheritance."

"But what are you dividing?"

"What! Well, this."

"What is it?"

"This—look here—this carpet, this flute, this hat."

The hat was torn!

"And this purse."

They had a purse made of material for holding coins.

"I shit on ten! This isn't worth the trouble. It's nothing. There isn't any money. They aren't worth anything. The piece of carpet is worthless. The hat is torn. The purse doesn't have anything in it. The flute? What's the flute worth? It's worthless."

"Huh. If you knew what they are."

Those men told him.

"Look, this flute will put everyone on your side in a quarrel. You are arguing with whomever; all of the others will be against him."

The boy remained silent.

"And this purse. You see it doesn't have anything. Each time you put in your hand, one *duro* [ten pesetas]."

"Well, I'll be. Host!"

"This carpet, you see it as a worthless rag. You put it down like this and step on it and say, 'Carpet, from here to France,' and there it'll be."

"Host! You're right. I shit on ten!"

"Good, now be quiet. Well, fine."

The boy, who was a rogue, said, "I shit on ten! Well, fine. This is very good. Look here, I'll do the dividing. You go over to where that little hill is, a little farther, and when I say to you, 'Whose is this?' then one says, 'Mine.' And then I'll say to you, 'Whose is this?' Another says, 'Mine.' And that way, since you'll see me divide this up for you, you won't argue anymore because I'll divide it up without being partial."

"Fuck! I shit on ten! Well, you know, the boy is right. Well, it's much better that way. It's better this way because, of course, everyone will want the carpet or something else."

So just as the boy said, each one would take whatever.

"Well, you're right. Come, Brothers, let's go forward."

The four brothers went over to the hill and, of course, since they went slowly, when they had gone over there to hide behind the hill, the boy says, "This is simple."

He put the hat, the flute, and the thing to put in a hand to get the coins [the purse] on the carpet. And he stepped on the carpet and said, "Carpet, from here to France."

Those poor brothers were behind the hill. Of course, he didn't ask them whose each thing is. He just went to France on the carpet. In an instant—Pum!—he was in France.

"Bah! Well, this is going well."

That's what the boy said. Now the goat bucked. Soon the boy, who of course was getting older, was now a man, probably was twenty years old. That is to say, he was already a grown man. That's when he heard it was touch and go whether the Pope died or not. And they were talking about whether the bishop or I don't know whom they were going to make Pope if the other one died. And the man says, "Fuck! Now is the chance to place myself there."

So he says, "Carpet, from here to Rome."

I shit on ten! When they went in the morning, there he was placed on the dead Pope's throne. So then all the priests and bishops and those people said, "I shit on ten! But how did this happen? This has come from God. This has come from God. This one is the true Pope."

All of the people lifted that man up, because he had placed himself on the throne, and no one had seen him before.

"This has come from God. This one is the true Pope." And so on and so forth.

And they convinced themselves.

"Well yes, it's true. Yes, it's true."

Bah! People came to see him. The man was lifted up as if he had come from Heaven. Well, nothing. He was seated as the Pope and he alone was Pope. And Pope he remained. Well then, the Pope they had before went after mass to the poorest of the poor, who were gathered at the palace, and gave them alms. And the Pope who was there before gave one peseta every day to each one of the poor. This one gave two pesetas.

"Bah! Notice he is a good one. And look, the one before was good. But this one is much better. He gives two pesetas to every single one of the poor every day."

So then word of "two pesetas" traveled far and wide. Bah! Well, nothing. Everyone was happy with him as Pope. They were happier with him as Pope than anything. Well, he went and said one day, to the one who was the Pope's helper—someone who was like a monk or something—he says, "Look."

He appeared and told him, he says, "Look, that poor man over there who has the tattered shoes and trousers. Skip him. Don't give him alms."

"What do you have against him? How can we give out pesetas without giving them to everyone the same?"

"I tell you not to give alms to him."

Just as the Pope had said, so it was. The monk started giving out two pesetas to each one. And the one with the tattered clothing, who was there so he would be given pesetas too, the monk came to him and nothing.

"Fuck! You didn't give me anything."

"They aren't giving alms to you," the man informed him.

"I shit on ten! Why?"

"Because that's how it is."

"Aren't I poor just like all of the others? I don't understand."

"Yes, you are, but I have orders not to give to you today, and I won't give them to you."

"I shit on ten! Well, give me a peseta. I don't know what and which. Bah! Look over there where they are paying them what they want."

"Well, nothing."

He didn't give any pesetas to him. The man stayed there. The poor left as soon as they were given the two pesetas. He just stayed there complaining loudly to himself, growling so they might give him two pesetas. When the public had left and he remained there alone, the Pope told his assistant, "Tell him to come into my office."

"Bah! Well, he's going to be killed," said the assistant.

He went in.

"Let's see. How are you?"

"What! Well, look here, I came for the alms because he gave me two pesetas every day."

"He didn't give you anything?"

"What! Nothing." And so on and so forth.

And the man was crying and complaining, he growled because he didn't . . . .

"Do you have a brother named Pedro?"

"Uh! My poor brother Pedro. Yes, I had a brother. Who knows where the poor thing might be?"

"Would you know him if you were to see him?"

"What! If I were to see him, yes. I would probably know him. But where is the poor thing?"

"Were you there when your brother once burned himself on the leg, when he was roasting chestnuts one time in the forest?"

"Oh yes. Yes. We were frolicking. I threw him into the fire."

"Yes. Look."

He lifted up his leg, which had the scar from the burn.

"I shit on ten! Perico! Perico!"

"Shhhh. Be quiet."

Well, he stayed there. The Pope told him to be there as a sexton.

"Look, put him over there as a sweeper."

He placed Javier there as a sweeper. And, of course, he immediately removed all of his clothes. He made new clothes for him that were the right things for him to wear. Now the man was well dressed.

"Fuck! Well, the Pope has taken up with that poor man, the one to whom he didn't want to give alms that day. But he is better off now he's there with him."

"Good. Good."

He had him there for a while. And he went along better than ever; he had him in the shadow of the Pope. One day Pedro says to Javier, he says, "Javier, you're not looking for a wife or anything. Aren't you trying to get married?"

"Bah! Me?"

He was a little dumb.

"Huh, no one wants me."

"How come they're not going to want you, man? You have to look and see."

"Yes, they don't want me. Women don't want me."

"Of course they do, man. You have to look and see. How come you haven't gone to the king's daughter?"

"Huh! The king's daughter? Fuck man, you're giving me *good* advice. If women don't want me, and I don't know what."

"Yes, man. You have to go there one of these days. Go to the palace and do nothing more than talk to her and you probably will hook up with her."

"Huh! No one wants me. How is she going to want me? What's different about her?"

"Well, nothing. Tomorrow you have to go there."

He went there and asked permission to go into the king's palace.

"What do you want?"

"I've come to marry the king's daughter."

"But man! Get out of here!"

They pushed the man out of there.

"But man!"

He came back.

"What happened?" his brother asks him.

"They almost hit me. They almost hit me. They told me not to go there anymore. That . . . ."

"You must go, man. In two or three days, you go there again." After two or three days, he went there. He was well dressed. He went much better dressed than before.

"Look, you're going to take this carpet. And you ask her to play cards."

"Yes, but I don't have any money."

"Well, you take this purse. Even though she wins one *duro*, two, three, twenty from you, it doesn't matter. Each time you put your hand in—one *duro*. You tell her one *duro* each time you play." Bah! He went in, being a man who was well dressed. He asked permission again. He went in to where the maiden was. And he asked, "Do you want to play cards?"

"Bah! Well, let's play cards," she replies.

The worthless piece of carpet was there.

"Well, come on, yes. Play cards. How much a hand?"

"One *duro*."

The maiden, of course, was the smarter one because he was a little dumb. He was stupid. The maiden beat him. She won each hand she played. He put his hand in the purse, and there was the *duro*. Then they played another hand. Another hand she won. He put his hand in. Pum! Another *duro*. I shit on ten! She played twenty hands. Well, the maiden won twenty *duros*. They were becoming friends a little bit. Bah! He came back.

"How was it? How was it?" his brother asks.

"Heh. How was it? How was it? She won every time; every time we played, she beat me. And so on and so forth. And here and there and so on."

"Good. Good. Well, go back another day."

Another day back there.

"And you take the hat," his brother tells him.

He went taking the hat and the carpet, of course.

"And never let go of the carpet," his brother warns him.

He arrived there. And he asked permission again. He went to where the maiden was. Now the maiden knew him.

"Huh! Today I bring something else and it's a very good thing."

"What did you bring?"

"Yes, it's torn, see. I can squeeze into a room just like an ant with this."

"Maybe."

"Sure! Maybe you'd like to see."

Tan! He went into a room.

"Now, I'll come out. You'll see."

He put it on. Zas! Out of the room. I shit on ten!

"Let me put it on," she says to him.

He was stupid and let her have it.

"Now I'm going to put it on."

Well, she put it on. Pum! Inside. I shit on ten!

"Now you can go," she says to him.

I shit on ten!

"I'm not coming out."

But they were becoming friends. Well then, it turned out she didn't come out, and he had to go, of course, on the carpet, to where his brother was.

"How was it? How was it?"

"Huh! How was it! How was it! How was it! She took the hat from me."

"But fuck—I shit on ten!—I told you not to let her take it from you."

"Sure! Don't you see she took it and went into a room and then she didn't want to come out? I shit on ten! Well, what do I do now?"

"I shit on ten! You go there again tomorrow. Tomorrow you go again and see if you can hook up with her again. When she puts her feet on the carpet, you just put your feet on it too and come back here."

It turned out the young man went there and asked her, "Do you want to play cards?"

"Bah! Let's play some cards."

"But you have to give me the hat."

"Fuck! To me . . . ."

So they started to play and—Puh!—she won a *duro* from him. She won two. She won ten and then all she wanted because the man didn't know how to play or anything. Javier was a little stupid. So when it looked right to him, he said, "Carpet, from here to the Pope's palace."

Do you know what I mean? So they arrived there. And his brother asked, "Well, very good. What is going on with you two? What is going on with you two?"

"Oh, look here, my father." So on and so forth and I don't know what.

"Damn! I shit on ten!" says the king whose daughter they stole.

And they figured out where the daughter was. That they had stolen her.

"Nothing," says the king.

The king gave the order that if Javier did not return his daughter—he determined Javier had her—then he would do nothing less than kill him. They would shoot him, and that would be the end of it. Because he was the king. Who would contradict the king? "I shit on ten!" says Javier.

"This is nothing. This is a very simple thing. You go there with her. You arrive at the palace door. But don't go in. Then you say you want to marry the king's daughter. Then the king is going to say no. And he is going to get the troops ready to threaten you if you don't go. But don't go."

So, it turned out, Javier went there with his two balls and said, "Look, here is your daughter."

"Oh, it's you who has her."

"Yes."

"Nothing. Arrest him immediately," says the king to the troops he had there, the guards and so on.

"No. I'm not going to turn her over because I'm going to marry your daughter."

"She neither marries nor anything else. And if you don't turn her over, they'll put some bullets into you and you'll be out of here," declares the king. "I have a lot of men, and they'll shoot you a couple of times and it'll be all over."

When the situation was getting difficult, as they were about to shoot the man—I shit on ten!—he took out his flute. Tiriti, tiriti, tiriti. I shit on ten! They all pointed their guns at the king. Do you know what I mean? They point them at the king.

I shit on ten! That man just about died. So then Javier tells him, he says, "This is a very simple matter. Sign. Here are the papers giving me permission to marry your daughter. And if you don't sign them, you know what will happen."

So, of course, the man, since Javier had him in a bind—I shit on ten!—went to sign. He signed that his daughter would marry Javier. Do you know what I mean? So then their wedding resounded very loudly. The wedding of the king's daughter was when they brought up a lot of pigeons and partridges. And they started eating and throwing their bones over their shoulders. Those in back of them were hit in the snout. And they ate pigeons and partridges and threw their bones in the people's noses. *Colorín colorado, cuento terminado.*

Florencio presented a more integrated story by developing the connections between the two brothers and by explaining, in more plausible terms, key turns of events in the plot. The brothers are connected by their common discovery of the eggs, on which it is written that he who eats one will become the Pope in Rome and he who eats the other will become King of Spain. They are united in their opposition to their mother's remarriage. Their destinies are interlocked by their decision to eat the eggs rather than let them pass into the hands of their new stepfather. They separate temporarily for the plausible reason that they will have an easier time begging for food separately. They are linked by a common experience—frolicking and roasting chestnuts in the woods—which permits, after many years, one brother to recognize the other by the burn on his leg, caused when one accidentally pushed the other into the fire. Florencio gives a plausible picture of a man courting a woman; at one brother's urging, the other brother repeatedly visits the princess in her castle, gallantly losing in cards and developing a friendship that eventually turns into marriage. At the cost of eliminating the episode of "The Wonderful Fruits," Florencio tells a more satisfying story because one brother does not drop out of sight; the two brothers act interdependently, with one helping the other achieve his destiny as King of Spain.

By including these changes, Florencio represented the two brothers as more connected relative to other Spanish narrators who have told the same tale. The hero has brothers in six out of seven variants of "The Magic Objects and the Wonderful Fruits" circulating in Spanish oral tradition.[28] Leandro Jiménez of El Guijo de Santa Bárbara represented the hero as most disconnected from his brother; this hero acts entirely alone in acquiring, losing, and recovering the magic objects with the help of the wonderful fruits provided by an old man as helpful intermediary agent. An unidentified narrator from Rio Tuerto in Santander included three brothers, but they often act against the hero, who ultimately separates from his brothers and single-handedly courts a princess but loses the magic objects despite his use of the wonderful fruits.[29] Pilar Díaz from Villanueva, Asturias, featured two brothers, one of whom shares his wealth with his brothers after obtaining the self-filling purse. However, the hero also acts alone in losing and regaining the objects with the wonderful fruits, and the story concludes with an episode of male sibling rivalry.[30] The school-age boy Juan Antonio Sánchez Ávila and María Alfonsa García Gil from Madroñera, in southern Cáceres, told variants closely related to Florencio's story of "The Two Eggs." However, both included "The Wonderful Fruits" episodes and made old women the helpful intermediary agents who enable the hero to recover the magic objects.[31] Florencio is the only narrator who represented one brother enabling the other to recover the fruits and marry the princess.

SUMMARY

The tour through the Spanish versions of "The Rich and Poor Peasant" and "The Magic Objects and the Wonderful Fruits" reveals that there is more to Florencio's representation of masculinity than was apparent from examining just one of his folktales. On the first leg of our journey, Florencio resembled other men and differed from Spanish women when he told his version of "The Bear's Son." He represented his hero as disconnected from his father, allied to his mother, bent on establishing his position in his masculine peer group, and the victim of male sexual competition. Florencio's disconnected picture of other men contrasted with the one presented by women narrators, who represented their hero as more connected with his father, less concerned about establishing his position in the male peer group, less engaged in male sexual rivalry, and more concerned about finding his place in his wife's family. Florencio seemed to be a good representative of his gender because he exhibited weak relational capacities that are more developed in women when telling "The Bear's Son." However, his depiction of brothers, showing an unusually strong orientation to male family relations and brotherly interdependence, revealed hints of relational capacities not apparent in his first story. Florencio is a complicated man; he is like other men in his culture because he embraces the value of male economic autonomy, but he sees male characters in stories as unusually connected, perhaps because he actually has a closer relationship to his own sons than other men in his village. Differences between Florencio and Nacho change shape when one compares the patterns running through their storytelling repertoires.

Chapter 5

TRICKSTERS IN MEXICO

NACHO GAVE THE TRICKSTER A DIFFERENT IMAGE IN HIS story of "Relajo" ("Troublemaker"), a retelling of "The Rich and the Poor Peasant" (1535).[1] His narrative breaks from the pattern in Florencio's trickster tales, in which the main protagonist is an unpromising hero who carries out a profitable transaction and dupes someone who is richer and more powerful. Relajo is an antihero with supernatural power who dupes his comparatively powerless compadre and sets into motion a disastrous chain of disorderly events. Relajo is another personification of īlihuiz (acting inconsiderately) and is no model for other men to follow.

Nacho's tale follows a formula that I found only in stories circulating in the Nahuat oral tradition of Huitzilan de Serdán. According to that formula, two characters love each other at the tale's beginning, and one of the loving pair is dead at the tale's conclusion. Nacho began "Relajo" with two compadres who "loved each other a great deal" (motazohtayah cimi), using the verb tazohta ("he or she loves someone"), which refers to platonic as well as carnal love. Love with respect should prevail between two compadres, but Relajo and his compadre have excessive love, which is one form of disorder bound to bring about other forms. Nacho's trickster is a sinister character who takes advantage of a gullible man who loves him as a compadre.

I shall examine closely how Relajo carries out his transactions in the first two episodes of Nacho's story, which are retellings of two very popular motifs that folklorists call "The hat that pays everything" (K111.2) and "The resuscitating horn" (K113.7).[2] Both motifs appear in Spanish and Mexican variants of "The Rich and the Poor Peasant" (1535). "The hat that pays everything" appears in a story that Luis Cortés Vázquez heard from Victoria Coca in Salamanca, Spain, and Stanley Robe collected from Augustina Gómez in Jalisco,

Mexico.[3] "The resuscitating horn" is more popular, found in tales from Santander, Burgos, Granada, and Salamanca,[4] as well as from Cáceres, where I heard it in stories by Santos López and Maximina Castaño in Garganta la Olla, Román Santo in Navaconcejo, Felipa Sánchez and Leandro Jiménez in El Guijo de Santa Bárbara, and Zacaria Iglesias in Pironal. The motif also appears in Mexican stories that Stanley Robe heard from Augustina Gómez in Jalisco[5] and that I recorded from Fernando Vega in Santiago Yaonáhuac and Nacho in Huitzilan. In most stories by Spanish and Spanish-speaking Mexican narrators, the trickster only pretends to buy food and drink without paying his bill because he wears an allegedly bill-paying hat and he feigns resuscitating his play-acting dead wife with a horn, whistle, flute, or bellows. In Nacho's story, the trickster actually obtains food and drink without having to pay his bill, and he really does resuscitate his dead and dismembered wife because he is born with a supernatural power his compadre will never possess.

"Relajo"
by Nacho Ángel Hernández

One day there was a man called "Relajo." And he had a compadre, and they really loved each other. And they decided to go get drunk together. And they got drunk in a store. They got very, very drunk. Relajo really asked for his drinks. He asked for a lot of them. And then he said to the person who sold them, "Well boss, it's all taken care of. We're even. I'm paid up."

"Yes," replied the bartender. "Everything is all paid up. It's a fine thing you paid your bill."

But it wasn't true. It was just Relajo's luck. He didn't pay. So his compadre was tricked. And his compadre went on being tricked. Yet another time, tomorrow, the next day he reached with his hand for a drink. Yet another time they went to get drunk together. And yet another time Relajo asked for the drinks, and after they finished drinking a great deal, he said again, "Well boss, now it's taken care of. It's all paid up."

"Yes, we're even," replied the bartender.

Afterwards, his compadre says, "I saw you ask for drinks, my dear compadre. You ask for them, and he doesn't charge you. You ask for a lot of drinks, and he doesn't charge you."

"Yes, that's the way I am. I don't pay."

"I couldn't do that."

"Why not? Be sure to go there tomorrow and ask for the drinks."

"Well, good."

They went the next day. The other compadre started asking for the drinks. He asked for everything. They drank a lot and took several things to eat, since the other one was asking. Afterwards he asked the one who was selling, "Now we're even?"

"Even with what? You drank a thousand pesos worth of drinks!"

And so he took out one thousand pesos, and afterwards he says to his compadre, "Oh compadre, why did I have to pay a thousand pesos? I saw that you didn't."

"No! I'm that way. Tomorrow you'll see us go again and you'll see me ask for the drinks again."

They went the next day. Relajo took him again. He started to ask again. He asked and he asked for the drinks. Again they drank and took what they wanted. Afterwards the bill was added up, and Relajo said to the bartender, "It's all paid up."

"Yes. We're all even. You're paid up."

That man, his compadre, saw him do it again. "My dear compadre, what did you do? I can't say what you said to him. I had to pay."

"But I'm that way."

"Well, tomorrow I'm going to ask again, and you'll see if I don't do it again."

"Well, let's see you try it again."

The next day, he asked again. That compadre asked for the drinks. He asked again, he asked for a lot. Plenty. They got drunk. And they ate what they wanted. He said to the bartender, "And now we're even."

"Even with what? It'll take a thousand pesos to pay the bill."

"Son of the . . . ."

Well, he paid the thousand pesos. Afterwards, his dear "turkey" [ilamatzin = wife] scolded him, "Where do you get the money? You *only* took two thousand pesos! And you didn't bring back anything. You just got drunk."

Later he got angry with his compadre, Relajo. "Right now I'm going to kill that compadre of mine. He tricked me, and my wife just scolded me. I'm going to kill my compadre. Twice he tricked me. He did what I couldn't do."

He came to Relajo's house and his compadre greeted him, "Dear compadre, compadre, sit down."

"I've come to kill you right now because you tricked me. My wife scolded me for the money. I spent it, and she got angry."

"No. I was just leaving. You're delaying me. I have this little flute," says Relajo.

Relajo blew a note on the flute.

"Well, right now I want you to give me back the money I lost. Your dear comadre scolded me."

"Well, fine. But don't bother me or else I'll also decide to get angry!" warns Relajo.

"But I want you to give me my money. My dear turkey is angry right now."

"I'm telling you right now, don't get me any angrier or you'll see me get mad, and I'm telling you, I'll kill my [own] dear 'turkey.' I'll kill her," declares Relajo.

"But I want the money I lost."

"Don't make me any angrier. You'll see right now how I am going to give it to her," says Relajo.

Relajo went over and grabbed that dear "turkey" of his. He started cutting her head off to kill her. He cut her all up.

"You saw how you got me so afraid and angry I killed my wife."

Then he started walking around her, playing his flute. He started playing his flute to her. He walked around her again and again, until she started to become whole again, until he made her into a person again.

"Dear compadre, you saw this little flute of mine is very good. Look how I killed her and woke her up again."

"Really, dear compadre, won't you let me buy it from you?"

"I won't sell it. I won't sell this little flute of mine because it's worth thousands of pesos."

"You must let me buy it from you."

"No. I won't sell it because it is very useful."

"I'll buy it from you. How much do you want for it?"

"Yes, compadre, but I won't sell it. You saw what I did and how I brought my wife back to life."

"No. I must buy it from you."

"Well, give me a thousand pesos. I'll sell it to you for that much because you wanted something that's very good."

"Well, then, let's do it."

He gave his compadre a thousand pesos and went home. His wife began scolding him again. "Well, why do you do this with the money? You spent three thousand pesos. What did you get for it? You just got tricked."

"Don't make me angry because I bought this flute. My dear compadre gave it to me because it's a very good thing. I can help myself with this little flute."

And so his dear "turkey" scolded him, and he grabbed her and cut her up. He killed her. Then he took the flute and played it, walking all around her. But how could she come back to life? He couldn't wake her up after walking around her playing the flute. Then he was sorry he quarreled with her.

"Dear me, you've really tricked me this time," he says to Relajo. "I also wanted to kill my wife, but I couldn't wake her up again."

Fig. 3. "He started playing his flute to her. He walked around her again and again, until she started to become whole again."

"Why not?"

"I couldn't do it."

"Why not? You saw me do it."

"Yes, but I couldn't do it. Give me back my money or else I'll kill you."

"No, dear compadre. Why should I?"

"I gave you my money for something that didn't work."

"No. It's a very good thing because I woke up my wife with it."

"Now there is nothing you can do to help yourself. I'm going to take you."

He put him into a sack and put him on top of a pack animal and took him to the bridge to throw him off so he'd die. He started on his way and became hungry. He went to eat something. The pack animal just stood in the road. And Relajo, whom he was taking, saw a boy come up to him. The boy was an orphan, but he was very, very rich. He had a lot of animals, much money; he had plenty. Relajo let himself be known.

"Don't touch me because I'm going to get married and I don't want to go because I can't drink. He's taking me to a dinner, and I don't want to go because I can't drink and I can't eat meat. I know you can, and so get in here so I can get out. That's why he's taking me. I don't want anyone to see me."

"Really?"

"Really! That's why I'm going in here. If you want, come up here right away, and I'll tie you in."

That silly boy, he decided he would be better climbing up into that sack. He climbed into it quickly, and Relajo climbed down and fled. He tied him up and left him on that pack animal and didn't let himself be seen. Meanwhile, his compadre came back from where he had gone to eat. He came and took that animal. He reached the high point on the bridge. He untied the sack and dropped it off. Meanwhile, Relajo went to that rich boy's house. He removed his money, taking out a lot. The boy had many pack animals, and Relajo started to load those animals with the money. He removed plenty of money. There were many bags of money. Then he met his dear compadre.

"Oh, dear compadre, you're still around!"

"Yes, didn't you see? Where you dropped me was not the exact middle of the bridge. If it had been in the exact middle, I would have found a little bit more money. It would have been more had you thrown me off the middle. I just found this much. But if you had thrown me off the exact middle of the bridge, I would have found more money. You saw what I brought."

"Son of the . . . , and I thought I left you there. I went to kill you."

"How could that be? Look what I found."

His compadre decided, he says to him, "Well now, I'm going there tomorrow. Let's see if I find a lot of money."

"Well, let's go. You jump off the exact middle of the bridge, and I'll see what luck you have. If you hadn't dropped me off the bridge, I wouldn't have found this money. But there will be more because you didn't drop me from the very middle."

"Good, now you drop me off tomorrow."

"Fine."

The next day, Relajo tied his compadre in a sack and took him on a pack animal. He dropped him off the exact middle of the bridge, but he was watching him, knowing his compadre went to die. It wasn't true he found money under the bridge. He tricked his dear compadre. There the story ends.

Relajo, as the personification of īlihuiz (inconsiderate behavior) in the *compadrazgo* relationship, sets into motion a disastrous chain of events; his compadre spends money on food and drink that he cannot afford, he quarrels with and eventually kills his wife, and he perishes when thrown off a bridge. Similarly disastrous events take place in Spanish and Spanish-speaking Mexican variants of the same story but with a major difference: the trickster is an unpromising hero who dupes an unsympathetic character. He is unpromising usually because he is poor and he gains the upper hand by turning the tables on someone who has an initial advantage. The situation is turned around in Nacho's story because Relajo has power his compadre can never possess since he has a different destiny. Moreover, Relajo is unsympathetic because he takes advantage of a comparatively powerless character who loves him as a compadre and is consequently vulnerable to his manipulative transactions. The powerlessness of Relajo's compadre is evident from an examination of how the motifs of "The hat that pays everything" and "The resuscitating horn" are reworked in Nacho's story.

Spanish and Mexican narrators, who include the motif of "The hat that pays everything," explain the trickster's deception in different ways. Victoria Coca, from Miranda del Castañar in Salamanca, Spain, described the trickster talking his compadre into believing his cap pays all the bills. The trickster does not demonstrate his cap's alleged power, and, in reality, the trickster never pays any of his bills, whether wearing his cap or not. His greedy compadre buys the hat, believing the cap actually works when merchants do not immediately demand that the trickster pay for what he eats and drinks (they know he is rich). He is shocked, however, when eventually presented with his unpaid bills.[6] Augustina Gómez from Tepatítlan in Jalisco, Mexico, represented the trickster paying the restaurant owner in advance and then pretending to eat without paying his bill because he wears a red cap. He so impresses his compadre that he sells the hat for a great deal of money.[7] Nacho's trickster operates differently; he is someone who never pays his bills, and he does not pay in advance. In fact, there is no cap at all. Relajo does not have to pay for what he eats and drinks because he has different luck than his compadre. Nacho offers no explanation because none is needed for an audience who realizes that some possess supernatural power and others do not.

Relajo's supernatural power is further evident in the next episode of "The resuscitating horn," which is more widespread in Spanish and Mexican versions of "The Rich and the Poor Peasant." In most stories, the trickster tells his wife to tie an animal intestine filled with animal blood around her waist. When his compadre comes to demand his money back because he was duped, the trickster stabs his wife, she bleeds and falls down as if dead, and the trickster uses the instrument to bring her back to life.[8] The events are different in Nacho's tale; Relajo's wife ties nothing around her waist, he actually cuts her into pieces, and he revives her by circling her dismembered body while playing his flute. Nacho used the verb quitmomahmahxītiā ("he makes her make herself whole") to describe her resuscitation. Although Nacho was clear about Relajo's magic, he nevertheless emphasized that deception is taking place by using the verb cahcayāhua ("to mock or deceive someone") in several places in his story.[9] Deception takes on a different meaning because it is based not on Relajo's compadre's confusion between semblance and reality, the theme in the stories of Spanish and Spanish-speaking Mexican narrators. Rather, it occurs because the compadre refuses to understand and accept that he does not and cannot possess Relajo's supernatural power.

One poetic effect of attributing Relajo's possession of supernatural power to luck is to emphasize the importance of fatalism in human relationships. The unusual degree of fatalism in Nacho's version of "The Rich and the Poor Peasant" becomes apparent when his story is compared with another variant I heard from a narrator living in a different Nahuat village. Fernando Vega of Santiago Yaonáhuac told the same story with the motif of "The resuscitating horn," and his trickster deceives his compadre the same way as in the Spanish and Spanish-speaking Mexican sources; he tells his wife to tie an animal intestine filled with animal blood around her waist, he pretends to stab her, she feigns death, and he revives her with an allegedly resuscitating whistle. This trickster used conscious deception, which Fernando explained fully in his tale. As mentioned earlier, Fernando and other narrators from Santiago Yaonáhuac told more tales of Spanish origin and used a narrative style more like that of Spanish-speaking Mexicans.

The imagery in "Relajo," which combines a message about emotional excess with fatalism, appears connected to the place of the transaction in Nacho's life, which differs from those of Fernando Vega in Santiago Yaonáhuac and Florencio Ramos in Navaconcejo. To be sure, all three live in communities where men and women make similar exchanges. The transaction has a long and remarkably well understood history in Nahua culture. James Lockhart discovered, in colonial Mexican documents "done by Nahuas for Nahua eyes," evidence of land transactions in the sixteenth century.[10] The term for a purchased field (tlāllocōhualli) appears in the Cuernavacan census of around 1544 and other early (1558) records of land transactions. Purchased land increased, relative to other categories of land, as the Nahuas adopted Spanish rituals of property possession along with the European distinction between public and private property.[11] The changing use of language is one basis for concluding that Nahua culture altered in profound and important ways from the 1500s to the 1700s. One of the most compelling examples is the changing use of the verb -piya, which originally had a custodial meaning, as in "take care of (animals)" or "guard (a home)," coinciding with a corporate social organization. Eventually -piya acquired a possessive meaning, like that of the Spanish verb *tener* ("to have"), because the corporate social organization broke down and the Nahuas adopted Spanish notions of private property and developed an economy based on the acquisition rather than the reciprocal exchange of valuables.[12]

Despite the convergence in meaning for -piya and *tener*, Florencio and Nacho represented exchange very differently in their versions of "The Rich and the Poor Peasant." Florencio emphasized the importance of taking possession of material wealth when carrying out a transaction, and Nacho stressed the importance of the relationship between exchange partners who are linked by their human bond of love (tazohtaliz). Moreover, Nacho represented the transaction with the assumption of permanent power asymmetry between the exchange partners. Relative to other narrators even in his own culture, Nacho's image of exchange is unusual and could be an expression of his particular position in his community and his family.

NACHO'S POSITION IN HIS COMMUNITY

Nacho's story of "Relajo" is a cautionary tale that makes a great deal of sense to a Nahuat living in a biethnic community where Spanish-speaking Mexicans own the bulk of the arable land and operate the largest stores. The permanent power asymmetry between exchange partners in Nacho's story fits with actually rigid power asymmetry between ethnic groups in Huitzilan. Nacho represented exchange with a fatalism which, in the words of Abram Kardiner and Lionel Ovesey, is the mark of his oppression.[13]

Nacho's repeated mention in his story of heavy consumption of food and especially drink is related to several actual problems in inter- as well as intra-ethnic relations in his community. Many Nahuat reported that they lost their land when they charged food and drink in stores established by Spanish-speaking Mexicans, who had moved into the community after the turn of the century. Some ran up large bills in order to meet their heavy ritual kinship obligations, which require that godparents spend money they often cannot afford on clothes for their godchildren. The children's parents must honor the godparents, who become their compadres, with lavish turkey *mole* banquets accompanied with abundant supplies of *aguardiente*. Nahuat in Huitzilan usually select other Nahuat in their village to be their godparents of marriage and baptism of their first children. However, a number select Spanish-speaking Mexicans to be baptismal godparents for later children. Nacho's godfather is Ignacio Bonilla, a Spanish-speaking Mexican who owns considerable land and employs many Nahuat to work on his estate. Nacho, following community custom, took his godfather's name; Nacho is a form of endearment of Ignacio. Inter-ethnic *compadrazgo* is like the relationship between Relajo and his compadre because Spanish-speaking Mexicans have economic power their Nahuat compadres do not and cannot easily possess. In this respect, the fatalism Nacho expressed in "Relajo" is a metaphor for his fixed position relative to Spanish-speaking Mexicans like Ignacio.

Nacho's story, which he and his brother Nicolás told to their nephews, nieces, and children in their extended family, has the didactic function of warning the next generation that they cannot spend money they do not have in Spanish-speaking Mexican stores without disastrous consequences. It reminds listeners of the bitter experiences of Nahuat who earlier pawned and eventually lost their land. The didactic message of Nacho's tale becomes even more meaningful if one considers that the compadre is vulnerable to Relajo's manipulations because he excessively loves another man more powerful than he. Some Nahuat in Huitzilan have very warm and loving relationships with Spanish-speaking Mexicans in their community, and their friendship can blossom into *compadrazgo*. Nacho spoke very warmly of Ignacio Bonilla, who had an unusually close relationship with Nacho and other Nahuat. Ignacio actually preferred the company of Nahuat over his fellow Spanish-speaking Mexicans, something Ignacio's brothers mentioned to me many times. Platonic love between a Nahuat and a Spanish-speaking Mexican, who is wealthier, makes a Nahuat man vulnerable, particularly if he wants to express his devotion through conspicuous consumption when fulfilling his ceremonial obligations.

Nacho made clear, by dramatic example, how the compadre's excessive love for Relajo causes bad reverberations in his other relationships. He told how his wife scolded him for spending so much money so many times and recounted how the compadre, duped by Relajo, kills and fails to revive his wife with the resuscitating flute. The compadre is sorry he quarreled with his wife, but the damage is done. Nacho made the point that the compadre's love for Relajo, which is excessive and consequently disorderly, results in other forms of disorder. Nacho presented the quarrel between the compadre and his wife with a great deal of verisimilitude to give his story more impact on his listeners. Women understandably become upset when their husbands squander money on drink in Spanish-speaking Mexican stores. I have seen many wives march into stores and angrily snatch their husband's money out of his shirt pocket during episodes of heavy drinking.

Nacho's resuscitating flute episode is a particularly dramatic expression of his feelings of economic powerlessness, which draws on a man's deepest fears of sexual inadequacy. If one takes Relajo as a Spanish-speaking Mexican, his compadre as a Nahuat, and the flute as a phallus, then the phallus only has potency in Nacho's story when in the hands of a *razón*. When it passes into the hands of a Nahuat man, then it loses its potency, just as a man becomes impotent when threatened by castration or Oedipal anxieties.[14] Nacho's particular expression of a Nahuat man's sexual inadequacy resonates with other images of Spanish-speaking men taking women from Nahuat men in tales we shall encounter later in our journey through Nacho's poetic imagination (Chapter 10).

The importance of power asymmetry between Nahuat and Spanish-speaking Mexicans in Huitzilan is apparent when one considers Nacho's version of "The Rich and the Poor Peasant" next to variants of the same tale told by Fernando Vega in Santiago Yaonáhuac, Mexico, and Florencio Ramos in Navaconcejo, Spain. Fernando Vega, who represented in "The resuscitating horn" the trickster-hero deliberately deceiving another man more powerful than he, lives in a monoethnic community where the Nahuat own most of the land and control the local economy. Florencio Ramos, who represented the trickster as an unpromising hero who proves his worth to his critical younger brothers who doubted his ability to manage the family capital, lives in Navaconcejo, where many have successfully made transactions to improve their economic position during the post–World War II boom. As mentioned earlier, Navaconcejo has many residents, including Florencio's father, who immigrated from other neighboring communities and made successful transactions by raising animals and sharecropping. Many, including Florencio and his father, eventually acquired plots of their own on which they grow cherries, a very important and profitable cash crop. Despite the collapse of the labor-intensive agrarian economy in the early 1960s, Florencio's community of Navaconcejo remains quite prosperous because of the demand for cherries in the markets of Madrid. To be sure, not everyone is a success story; Florencio's "cafeteria" turned out to be a financial disaster, and his son Bernardo lost a lot of money buying and selling horses. However, the hope of making transactions to acquire economic independence and remove one from the domination of another is a realistic possibility in Navaconcejo.

Nacho and his brother faced very different conditions; they had little hope of making transactions within their community to improve their economic position because of the dominant Spanish-speaking minority, who moved into Huitzilan after the turn of the century. Spanish-speaking Mexicans control trade because they own most of the land; they are the local creditors and bankers; they export all of the coffee and import corn, beans, staples, cloth, and manufactured goods, which they sell to the Nahuat. Nacho's older brother Miguel rented land in their neighboring community of Zapotitlán for growing corn and beans to fill the extended family household granary. The three brothers—Nacho, Nicolás, and Miguel—grow coffee and chilies on a small piece of land held by their mother and acquired from their father, who died many years ago. Nicolás and Miguel earn wages by cutting coffee on Spanish-speaking Mexicans' orchards in Zapotitlán, and all three have made a few trips to the coast where they worked as migrant laborers. In short, Nacho, Nicolás, and Miguel lack the opportunities for making profitable transactions like those that occur occasionally in Yaonáhuac and frequently in Navaconcejo.

NACHO'S POSITION IN HIS FAMILY

Fatalism and emotional restraint also make sense if one considers Nacho's position in his family. At the time he told "Relajo," he was the youngest of three brothers in a large and unusually stable extended family. As the youngest (taxocoyot), he had to accept that his oldest brother Miguel was the tayacānqueh ("the boss"). When the father died when Nacho was ten years old, Miguel became the ostensible head of the extended family, although considerable control remained in the hands of their mother, María Gabriela Hernández. By virtue of being the youngest, Nacho's position in a group of three brothers was determined by the luck of his birth order, much as Relajo's compadre's relative powerlessness was a function of his luck.

The connection between fatalism and the avoidance of emotional excess becomes apparent if one considers what it means to occupy a fixed position in a large extended family. It is my impression that Nacho and everyone else in his household maintained considerable emotional restraint because they subordinated their individual identities to the family group. They could not act in a self-centered way without disrupting the complex and sometimes delicate working relationships among all members of the household, who contributed their productive labor to fill a common granary and purse from which all could draw according to need. The emphasis was on the sharing of the fruits of communal family labor rather than on the productivity of individual members. Most of the characters in Nacho's stories, who act out of excessive love, behave inconsiderately with respect to those with whom they are connected. Were Nacho and his brothers to place their love for their wives and children before their love for each other, they might act inconsiderately and disrupt the cohesion of their extended family.

"THE ASH-SELLER"

Most of Nacho's stories describe scenarios in which characters behave with īlihuiz and end up banished from the human community or they set into motion a chain of events ending in someone's annihilation. Other Nahuat of Huitzilan told tales illustrating how characters avoid banishment and annihilation by resisting their impulse to act inconsiderately. Miguel Ahuata's variant of "The Rich and the Poor Peasant" is such a tale; one of his characters resists the impulse to be greedy and consequently avoids the annihilation of similar characters in the Spanish and Spanish-speaking Mexican variants of the same story. Miguel's main protagonist is an ash-seller who appears in several folktales told in Spain and other parts of Mexico. Following Miguel's story, I shall examine how he represents human behavior relative to other narrators who told similar variants of this story.

"The Ash-Seller"
by Miguel Ahuata

There lived a man. He looked for work. He didn't find any. He looked. He had a friend and he says . . . . He met him and asked, "Where have you been?"

"I went looking for work."

"Did you find any?"

"I didn't."

"There is some. Look for it."

"But where? There isn't any anywhere. Well, I'm going to look for it again."

He went looking for it. He met his friend again, and his friend asked him, "And did you find it?"

"I didn't."

"Well, go to Mexico City."

"What am I going to take?"

"Take some things to sell."

"What?"

"Take ashes. They really buy them."

"Honest?"

"Honest."

"They don't buy ashes."

"Yes, they do buy them. I went to see for myself. I come from there. Trash, you take a lot of it. It's an item that's purchased."

He went to Mexico City.

"Well, honest?"

"Honest. I took them to sell," his friend tells him.

"Oh, so then I'm going to collect them and take them."

"Collect them and take a bag of them."

He really did fill up a bag. He spent a lot of time collecting the ashes and he took the bag to Mexico City. He came to the plaza. He checked it out. He put his bag down. There wasn't any of it anywhere.

"Sit down in the plaza, and they'll ask for it," his friend told him.

He reached the plaza, and there wasn't any of what he brought.

He said to himself, "They'll buy this and no one has put down anywhere what I brought. There isn't any anywhere."

He was the only one who brought it. He said to himself, "Well, now it's very late, it's late already, and they haven't asked for it."

Everything else was gone. Only he was there. He decided, "Now I'm going to speak to that man. Maybe he'll buy it."

He went over and spoke to him, "Perhaps you'll buy some ashes?"

"No. What for? I won't buy any."

Again, he went on alone.

"Maybe you'll buy ashes?"

"No, I also have some. You brought them?"

"Yes."

"Well, I don't buy them. But if I buy them, put your sack down there. Scatter the ashes over there."

He didn't [really want to] buy them.

"Go leave them over there, and I'll give you your money."

He just gave him twelve cents. Just those little pennies that look like buttons.

"I'll give you twelve cents."

"Well, all right, even if that's what it'll be."

Then he left the plaza. He went to the edge of town. He found someone selling tamales. He bought a tamale for himself.

"Give me tamales; six cents' worth."

"Yes."

There were a lot of tamales. He left and went over to the edge of town and started to eat. He ate and went on again. He came to a store and gazed from afar at nothing but masks. There wasn't anything else: just masks.

"Well, good, fine. Now I'll take one."

He bought a mask; it was also six cents. He spent all of his money. He bought it and headed for home. It got dark. He went on and on and on. He got caught in a rainstorm. It was plenty dark. Nowhere was dry.

"Now, I'll just keep going," he said to himself.

A little light appeared ahead. He went into a wood; he came to a mountain. He was gazing at a fire.

"Perhaps I'll go over there. There is a fire."

He came closer and closer. He looked at the fire. Things were piled.

"But what is it? There are a lot of things. I'll ask them to please let me dry myself over there."

He was all dripping with water. He had been going. It rained. The weather had not cleared. He went over there. No one appeared. They had all gone. They were thieves. That was where they went to sleep. He just wanted to warm himself where the fire was burning that night.

"Good, they've gone," he said to himself. "They won't scold me for warming myself."

Right away he wrung out his clothes. Water dripped from everything. He warmed himself by the fire. He warmed himself that way; he started getting warm. No one appeared. They had all gone. He was getting a little dry. He was next to the fire for a long time. He was a little dry now. He was fine after he dried off a little. He stood up. He walked around there. No one appeared.

"Well now, let me warm myself even more." He went to sit down again and decided to take the mask out of his pack. He gazed at it. He gazed at it. He decided to put it on. It was better to sit and warm himself that way. He was warming himself that way. And the thieves came. They came and gazed at him from afar. Many came and gazed at him. They wanted to warm themselves. They came and saw him standing.

"Oh! Mary! Who knows what he is? Maybe he's the devil warming himself."

Now they were frightened. They ran furiously [īlihuiz]. They didn't go over to where he was. They left suddenly [īlihuiz]. So then the sun came up. Now the sun had come up; there he was. He was nice and dry. Yes, he was all dry. He was dry just like this.

"Now, they all live here where I've been."

It was getting late. They had fled, they fled leaving all of their pack animals and everything. He saw the pack animals. The sun came up. There were things they brought after taking them. They killed or they stole and they killed. The sun came up. They had a lot of money.

"Well now, there are pack animals. I'm going to load them with this money."

He realized there were many boxes of money. He loaded them all; he loaded the pack animals and left. He went down the road and met his friend, who told him to go where he had gone.

"You've returned already."

"Yes."

"They really do buy ashes?"

"I won a lot. Now you gather ashes and go."

He wasn't going to trick him into also going.

"No, I realize that you came out fine. Always a little bit."

Many pack animals brought the money. Son of the . . .

"Well, I have to go because I'm still coming."

He went to bring more things and, after three trips, who is to say how much money he collected?

He brought many things. Who knows how much? He won it.

Greed as a driving force in economic transactions appears in all published Spanish and Mexican variants of "The Rich and the Poor Peasant" with ash- or manure-selling episodes I know of. At least two variants appear in Spanish oral tradition, and they feature a trickster who sells ashes in a deceptive bargain by playing on the greed of his compadre or his neighbors. In a tale by an unidentified narrator from Santander, the trickster as hero sells his bag of ashes by placing a few pieces of jewelry on top of his bag and claiming that other pieces are to be found inside.[15] In a story by Mercedes Morán from Asturias, the hero trickster merely claims his ashes are actually gold.[16] Their deliberate deceptions closely resemble that of the unpromising older brother who sold human excrement mixed with sugar as honey water in Florencio Ramos's version of the same tale.

The Mexican "Rich and Poor Peasant" stories with ash-selling episodes also assume greed to be a basic human emotion. Most Mexican narrators represented the hero as a poor compadre who takes his rich compadre's deceitful and belittling advice to become similarly rich by taking ashes to sell in the marketplace. The hero finds that no one will buy his ashes and receives a small sum of money to throw them away. He buys a mask, heads home through the wilderness, stops at the camp of thieves, warms himself by their fire wearing his mask, scares the thieves (who think he is the devil), and takes their loot home. His success inspires his greedy companion, who unsuccessfully tries to retrace the hero's steps and become even richer. Mexican narrators frequently offer their own scathing critique of entrepreneurial capitalism when they tell how the greedy rich compadre dies a brutal death at the hands of the thieves.[17]

Miguel Ahuata departed from the formula by eliminating greed as the motivating emotion of the hero's companion; like Nacho, he emphasized the importance of luck or fatalism. He concluded his story with the hero meeting his companion and telling him of his good fortune. He told how the companion knows better than to retrace the hero's steps because he recognizes that he has a different destiny. I suspect that Miguel's emphasis on destiny is also attributable to his position in his biethnic and rigidly stratified community and his own extended family experience. When I first met Miguel, he was fifty-eight years old and lived in Huitzilan with his wife Augustina Pasión (age fifty-two) and their five children. Their oldest son, de la Cruz (age twenty-seven) was married and had a family of his own. Miguel was very interested in keeping his patrilineally extended family together and was in the process of constructing a new house for de la Cruz twenty-five meters from his own house on the same plot of land. Telling "The Ash-Seller" to his sons has the didactic effect of reinforcing a relational conception of masculinity by playing down the importance of a supremely egocentric emotion like greed, which could tear an extended family apart by focusing attention on individual productivity rather than on the sharing of the fruits of community labor.

"THE MASTER THIEF"

Nacho and other Nahua narrators represented a relational masculine identity in another trickster tale folklorists call "The Master Thief" (1525).[18] Stith Thompson considers this "the chief of all folktales concerning robbers" and notes that "in one form or another it appears in nearly every collection of tales from Europe and Asia."[19] Nacho's story begins with a very popular nucleus of three brothers who learn trades: one becomes a priest, the other a lawyer, and the youngest a thief. They are orphans adopted by a king who puts the thief to a test and challenges him to steal a well-guarded horse and the sheet on the bed where his wife sleeps.

Nacho's story probably came into his repertoire by way of Spanish-speaking Mexicans who originally acquired it from colonialists who brought the story from Spain. The tale appears in Renaissance literature and is popular in contemporary Spanish oral tradition.[20] Narrators appear to have embellished the story as they retold it in the Spanish-speaking Caribbean, South America, and Mexico. Boggs found three subtypes in Spanish oral tradition, Hansen identified six in the Spanish-speaking Caribbean and South America, and Robe reported ten types in Mexico.[21] The tale is quite popular in Cáceres and adjacent provinces in Spain: Curiel Merchán heard one from a man in Madroñera in southern Cáceres, I recorded another from Abundio Sánchez Sánchez in Cabezuela, to the immediate north of Florencio Ramos's village of Navaconcejo, and Luis Cortés Vázquez heard a third from a woman in La Alberca in southern Salamanca.[22] The tale has passed through the lips of Spanish-speaking narrators in Jalisco and Oaxaca and from several narrators in the Nahua-speaking region of Mexico.[23] Américo Paredes recorded a very interesting variant in Spanish from a man in the Nahuatl-speaking village of San Miguel Canoa in the Tlaxcalan-Puebla Valley,[24] and I heard three from Nahuat narrators in the northern Sierra de Puebla: Luciano Vega in Santiago Yaonáhuac, and Juan Peréz and Nacho in Huitzilan de Serdán.

Nacho told "The Master Thief" to express two dimensions of his view of a man's relationship with other men. First, he expressed his connected view of masculine relationships by depicting his hero collaborating with his brother when stealing a closely guarded object. Second, he represented, with the surprise ending to his story, the incompatibility between īlihuiz and living in society.

"The Master Thief"
by Nacho Ángel Hernández

Once there were three orphaned boys, and the oldest decided that they should see the king, a very rich man, so that he might feed them. So they went to see the king and asked for work. The king gave them work and decided to send the boys to school so that they might learn a trade. After a while, the king asked the boys what they had learned. One was studying to become a priest, the other a lawyer, and the youngest did not want to say what he was studying because he was ashamed. However, the youngest finally confessed that he chose to become a thief. The king decided to put him to a test and said, "I am going to leave a horse over there . . . You take it . . . . I left some watchmen . . . . I'll see if you are a bandit."

So the youngest went to see his brother, the priest, and asked, "Well, how do I do it?"

The priest replied, "I'm going to lend you my clothes, and you take a liter of this wine, and you trick them . . . You're going to make them get drunk . . . and they will sleep . . . and you take what they are supposed to be guarding."

That is just what the youngest brother did. He went to where the watchmen were watching the horse and told them, "Aren't you offended that he left you out here to be cold? It is a punishment . . . putting you here. Won't you drink just one glass of what I drink?"

"Sure, if you invite us," they replied.

So he poured drinks, they drank, they slept, and the boy took the horse back to the king.

"So you really are a bandit," the king said.

The king decided to put the boy to one more test. "Go inside the house . . . . Go take my first sheet."

The king was waiting in the floor above for the boy to appear. But the boy was smart and he made a doll in his image. He went into the house, and the king shot the doll, thinking that he shot the boy. The doll fell down below, and king went down after it, taking the doll out of the house to dispose of the "body." Meanwhile, the boy circled around to the back of the house, and reentered and went into the bedroom.

"Give me that first sheet so that I can clean my hands," he said to the king's wife. "I really soiled my hands. I shot that youngest brother."

He removed the sheet and went out of the house. The king returned and asked his wife for the first sheet so that he could clean his hands, but she replied, "What sheet? You took it already. Didn't you just come to take it?"

Well, the sun rose the next day, and the king ran the boy off because he did not know what to do with him.

Nacho's relational masculine identity becomes apparent when his story is placed next to variants of the same story from Spanish and Spanish-speaking Mexican narrators. The hero has a solitary masculine identity in "The Master Thief" told by Spanish-speaking narrators, who depict him acting alone. A woman from La Alberca in Salamanca featured two main characters who are unrelated by any kinship. The characters act in serial episodes, and one takes over after the death of the other. The well-guarded object in this case is the decapitated body of the thief's companion. This narrator described how the hero as thief steals the body single-handedly by going to a convent, buying a donkey, some bread, a sack of wine, a ham, sausages, and several friar habits, and dresses as a friar himself. He goes to the outskirts of town where the governor's guards are on the lookout for the thief. He successfully gets the guards drunk, dresses them in the habits, and steals the body of his companion.[25] More interdependence sometimes occurs in Spanish-speaking Mexican variants of "The Master Thief" told outside of the Nahua-speaking region. Stanley Robe heard a version in Amapa in which the hero has helpers, but they are associates who work for him as a client works for a patron.[26] Most Spanish-speaking Mexicans generally follow the Spanish pattern of beginning their stories with brothers but representing the hero acting alone.[27]

Nacho, of course, described his hero as the youngest of three brothers who gains the help of his brother the priest to steal the well-guarded object. The priest-brother tells him how to perform the task and lends him his frock so he can deceive the guards. Fraternal interdependence is a common feature of "The Master Thief" when told by several Nahuat- and Nahuatl-speaking narrators in Huitzilan and other parts of Mexico. Nahuat Juan Peréz, also of Huitzilan, repre-

sented fraternal interdependence by describing the master thief sharing his wealth with his brothers. Juan opened his tale with a popular
image, appearing in other stories circulating in Nahuat oral tradition,
of brothers quarreling because one refuses to work and eats food produced by the other. Juan's story performs the didactic function of
shifting the focus from the productivity of individual labor to the
sharing of the fruits of family labor. There are two brothers in his
story, and the hard-working one decides to go out on his own. He
heads down to the hot country, but his lazy brother catches up with
him. The hard worker insists that his lazy brother go to another town,
and they agree to meet "in so many days." The lazy one runs into the
bad one (ahmō cualli), who helps him steal a lot of money that he
brings home to his mother. Meanwhile, the hard worker returns with
a tiny sum of his earnings, and the brothers decide to work together;
the hard worker plants with the money provided by the lazy one
turned thief.

Luciano Vega, a Nahuat-speaking narrator from Santiago Yaonáhuac, and a Nahuatl-speaking man from San Miguel Canoa also represented a relational masculine identity by depicting fraternal interdependence in "The Master Thief." Their stories contain episodes of
thieves who steal animals by putting shoes in the road, which folklorists identify as subtype 1525D.[28] Where this subtype appears in Spanish and Spanish-speaking Mexican oral tradition, the hero usually
acts alone by placing one shoe in the road, enticing the animal's
owner to tie up his animal and look for the other—this provides an
opportunity for the trickster to make his theft.[29] However, in Luciano's tale, two brothers use a different technique, which requires
that they work together to steal a pig. They buy a pair of shoes, tossing
one before and the other after a bend in the road. The shepherd spots
one shoe, continues on until he finds the other, then ties up his pig to
fetch the first shoe. Meanwhile, one brother snatches the first shoe
and the other brother snatches the pig. The two brothers cooperate to
steal a calf: one hides in the forest and bleats like a sheep to distract
the cowherd and to provide the opportunity for the other brother to
steal his animal. In the variant Américo Paredes collected from a narrator in San Miguel Canoa,[30] four brothers cooperate with each other
to steal three teams of mules loaded with money, using techniques
found in the stories by Nacho and Luciano Vega. One brother becomes
a shoemaker and provides boots with which the thief steals the first
group of mules loaded with money. Another becomes a tailor and
makes the vestments that his brother wears to trick soldiers into getting drunk on liquor disguised as holy water. The third becomes a

carpenter and makes a dummy that the hero uses to steal a blanket from inside a rich man's house.

Despite the sympathy a Nahuat might feel for a thief who steals from a wealthy Spanish-speaking Mexican, Nacho developed his concluding episode according to the notion he expressed in other tales—that īlihuiz is incompatible with living in society. The hero successfully responds to his wealthy patron's second test by stealing the bedsheet. It is possible to read an Oedipal meaning into the second episode of Nacho's story if one regards the patron as a symbolic casting of the father and one considers how the hero comes dangerously close to his wealthy patron's (or father's) wife. The hero's bold behavior, which could represent acting on an Oedipal impulse, is nevertheless īlihuiz, so Nacho concluded his tale by having him sent away.

"The Master Thief" is the second story by Nacho in which a character personifying īlihuiz is banished to the periphery of the world. Banishing heroes who are unusually strong or bold occurs frequently in Nahuat stories circulating among narrators in Huitzilan. Antonio Veracruz, also of Nacho's community, told a version of "Strong John" (Tale Type 650) in which the hero, who has an enormous appetite and performs many dangerous tasks for his wealthy and powerful patron, disappears into the periphery not because he is evil but simply because he represents īlihuiz and cannot live in human society. I did not find similar endings to similar stories in Yaonáhuac or Cáceres, so banished heroes may be a feature of oicotypes in Nacho's community.

SUMMARY

By the end of the last chapter, Florencio began to appear more like Nacho because he displayed a relational masculinity in his trickster tales. By the end of this chapter, it is apparent that Florencio and Nacho are separated by their ideas about economic exchange. Florencio's tricksters are individualists who carry out amoral transactions and emerge as the unpromising heroes of entrepreneurial capitalism. Nacho's tricksters personify īlihuiz and threaten the interconnected human order because they act individually and without consideration for others. Relajo destroys love (tazohtaliz), the bond of human connection, and the Master Thief, a more sympathetic character, cannot remain in the human community.

Florencio and Nacho appear to present their masculinity according to their respective models of community relations, which are also models of family relations. The next chapter will take a close look at

Florencio's view of fathers, sons, and brothers to identify the ways in which he is similar to and different from other men in his culture and the Nahuat of Mexico. Nacho will temporarily drop out of the picture but will return in the following chapter when he presents his vision of male family relationships in a story of Spanish origin not in Florencio's repertoire.

Chapter 6

"BLOOD BROTHERS"

FLORENCIO EXPRESSED HIS PARTICULAR VIEW OF MASCULINE family relationships when he told a story about three brothers, one of whom rescues the others from enchantment in "The Castle Where You Will Go and Will Not Return." Known among folklorists as "Blood Brothers," Florencio's tale has a long pedigree and enjoys widespread popularity beyond the Hispanic world.[1] His story may have a historical connection to an ancient Egyptian narrative about two brothers, which Susan Hollis considers the oldest fairytale in the world.[2] Kurt Ranke compared many variants of "Blood Brothers" in contemporary European oral tradition and concluded that the story probably developed in France from "The Dragon Slayer" (AT 300) because one brother kills a hydra-headed dragon and earns the right to marry a princess in the former tale.[3] Folklorists have offered a number of interpretations of the story's meaning. Heino Gehrts argued that "Blood Brothers" contains vestiges of an ancient ritual in which one brother is sacrificed so the other can achieve victory in battle.[4] Donald Ward believed the story expresses the widespread belief in divine twins.[5]

French storytellers undoubtedly took "Blood Brothers" across the Pyrenees to Spain, where it has become a very well known folktale. The story is popular among the narrators I knew, particularly in the village of Navaconcejo, where it was told by Florencio Ramos, his son Bernardo Ramos, Miguel Chorro Hernández, and Estrella Iglesia. Julio López Curiel in Garganta and José Díaz Sánchez and Julia Lobato Gil in Serradilla also told me this story. I shall focus on Florencio's version of "Blood Brothers" to explore how he represented fathers, sons, and brothers according to his culture and personal family history. I shall then compare the Cáceres and Nahuat variants to reveal how Florencio and other men in the two cultures told this tale according to their conceptions of a man's relationship with other men in the family. Nacho did not tell "Blood Brothers," so I shall present a variant by Nicolás Cabrera, who also lived in Huitzilan de Serdán.

FLORENCIO'S VERSION OF "BLOOD BROTHERS"

Florencio characteristically introduced many plot changes to express his own family history, in accord with the norms of masculinity in his culture, when he told the story he called "The Castle Where You Will Go and Will Not Return" and which folklorists call "Blood Brothers." Florencio's autobiographical inventions are apparent when his variant is compared with those told by other narrators in Cáceres and different parts of Spain. In many respects, Florencio is not a representative Cáceres man because of his unusual personal history and his close relationship with his children, particularly his three sons. Despite denying the father when telling "The Bear's Son" (301), he made the father a pivotal figure in the relationship among the blood brothers. He also continued the pattern, observed in his earlier stories, of representing brothers with more connection by toning down episodes of male sibling sexual rivalry that appeared in the "Blood Brothers" stories told by other Cáceres men. It was mentioned that Florencio also represented less fraternal sexual rivalry in his variant of "The Bear and His Son" (301) and more male sibling interdependence in "The Magic Objects and the Wonderful Fruits" (566) relative to other men in Spain. Florencio nevertheless bore the stamp of his culture because his plot of "Blood Brothers" also expresses male economic autonomy.

"The Castle Where You Will Go and Will Not Return"
by Florencio Ramos

Well, this is about the time there was a father who was very rich. But he was corrupt. He was dedicated to gambling. And, well, the father spent a lot of money. And he had three sons. And he told those sons, he says, "Look, I've lost all the capital tonight in a game. The only thing you can do is each take a horse and get away because, if you don't, they're going to come tomorrow for the things that are left."

"Ah, well fine. Well, fine," those young bachelors said.

They were young bachelors. Each one took a horse, a dog, and a lance. And the three brothers left riding the horses. And they came to where there were three roads. And one of them said, "Now this is what I think we ought to do. It's better to earn our living each on his own than the three of us going together."

"That's right. Well said! Yes."

And when they left home, each left a bottle full of water with his name.

"When it turns into blood, then we're dead," they told their father.

Each one went down his own road. The oldest went walking, walking, walking, and stopped at a village. And a maiden was there, a young woman, and he became betrothed to her. The result was, he married her. And when he was going to bed at night, he stood at the window and said, "Listen, Fulana, that light out there, what is that light?"

"Oh. It can't be told what that light is."

"Why?"

"I won't tell you about it."

"You have to tell me."

And so on and he obligated her to tell him as a husband to a wife, and she told him, "That is the castle of 'You Will Go and You Will Not Return.'"

"Oh wow! I shit on ten! Tomorrow I'm going to see what it is."

He was very brave. So it turned out that in the morning he took his horse, his dog, and his lance. I shit on ten! Tin tan, tin tan, tin tan. And he arrived there about when it was getting dark. And he came close to the castle. It had a wall.

"I shit on ten! How does a person go in through here? How does anyone go in through there?"

He couldn't see an entrance. And he kicked the wall, because the wall couldn't be strong. Tan! He knocked a hole in the wall and then—zas!—out came a rabbit.

"Sic 'em, dog."

And the dog—tan!—caught it.

"I shit on the sacramental host! We have something for supper."

Bah! He approached the house. He knocked.

"Who is it?"

"A man passing through to see if you'll give me lodging."

"Ah, well yes, yes, yes, yes. Very good." And so on and so forth.

And that woman was a witch. She was a witch living in the castle.

"Very good and so on. Well then . . ."

"Look here, I brought a rabbit. Let's see if you will prepare it for supper and so on."

"Yes, yes, yes, very well. Very well."

She made him supper, and he started eating the supper, and the witch says to that man, "Take this strand of hair, tie up your horse so it doesn't kick me."

And he tied it up.

"Take another strand of hair, tie up your lance so it does not prick me."

And he tied it up. Good, the man was involved in eating supper, and the woman says to him, "Give me a leg."

"Sure, take it."

She was eating it and says, "Give me another leg."

"Take it."

In a little while she says, "Give me another leg."

"But, what the hell, how many legs does a rabbit have? I shit on this! I shit on that!"

So it was the man who was now worked up. He says . . . . Those two lit into each other. The man and the woman were grappling with each other. And the man says, he says, "Come here, my dog, my horse, my lance."

"May everything turn into chain."

It turned out, of course, they could have given him the advantage, but the witch killed that man. She killed him. What she did was kill him. Good, very well. The man stayed there. And that woman put him into a room where she put all whom she killed or vanquished.

Well, the brother, the second one, I don't know how he came back again and went by his brother's house as he passed through the town. When . . . . Fuck! He saw from the bottle his brother was now dead.

"I shit on ten! Now my brother is dead. I shit on ten! I'm going right now to see if I can verify my brother's death."

He took the road where his brother had gone and, it turned out, he came to where his brother had been with the woman he married. Since he took his dog, his lance, and his horse and they were brothers . . . they looked a lot alike . . . well, upon seeing him, she says, "Fuck! I shit on ten! You've come back! My husband! I don't know what, I don't know where."

And the brother was pretending. He said yes, he was her husband. He didn't leave the bottle at home. They each took three bottles. Then it turned out that he, well, he made out as if he were his brother. They had supper. They went to bed. And he saw the light. And he said to her, he said, "Well, that light shining over there?"

"Oh, stupid! That's the castle of 'You Will Go and You Will Not Return.' Well, weren't you there the other day?"

"Yes, but I didn't quite get there." And so on and so forth . . . .

Well, of course, he made an excuse and so on. He says, "And I'm going to see what it is and so on."

"Don't go. That's the castle of 'You Will Go and You Won't Return.'"

She told him the same thing she had told the other one.

"Well yes, tomorrow I'm going to look for him," he said to himself.

He took off. Traca, traca, traca, traca. And it turned out the same thing happened to him as to the other one. He knocked out an entrance. The rabbit came out, his dog caught it, and the woman cooked it for him.

"Look at this little rabbit," he says.

"Well yes, yes. Very well," the woman says.

She cooked it for him and so forth. He sat down to eat supper. "You take a hair, you tie your horse so it won't kick me. You take a hair, you tie your dog so it won't bite me. You take a hair, you tie your lance so it won't spear me."

They sat down to eat supper and the same thing. "Give me a leg."

"Take it."

"Give me another leg."

"Take it."

"Give me another leg."

"Fuck! How many legs does a rabbit have? I shit on this! I shit on that!"

The man became agitated, and she hurled herself at him.

"Come here, my dog and my horse."

"Everything turn into chain."

She hit him all she wanted. So much so she killed him or vanquished him, of course. Well then, nothing. The man stayed there, now vanquished.

In a little while the brother, the youngest, goes by his oldest brother's house again. He says, "I shit on ten! Now my two brothers are dead. First the oldest died, and now the second has died. The situation is, I must go to find out how those men have died."

He took the route taken by the oldest. And he came to where the oldest was with the woman he married. When she saw him, she said he was her husband because he took the same things and he looked just like her husband. But he was the youngest. Just like the one I have in the military.

"Oh! Now he comes and so on."

They were kissing and so on and so forth. Good, well fine. They agreed to go to bed. They were going to bed when he looked out of the window just like the other one.

"Oh, that little light over there . . . . What is that light so far away?"

"That's the castle. Weren't you there the other day?" And so on and so forth.

"Yes, but I have to go there more carefully and so on and I don't know what."

"That's the castle where 'You Will Go and You Will Not Return.' I already told you the other day and I don't know what and I don't know which. And what do I know?"

Good, well so it rested. The result was, in the morning, he took the same route as the others. He arrived there just as it was about to dawn.

"And do I go in here or do I go in there?"

The entrance wasn't visible. And he kicked the wall, and the rabbit came out.

"Get it, dog."

The dog caught the rabbit. Fine. The supper. He arrived and said to the woman, "Look here, I have the rabbit and so on."

"Good, well yes, yes. Very well."

They started to eat supper, and she says to him, she says, "Take this hair, tie up your horse so it won't kick me."

Usss. Through the flame of the kerosene lamp. "Take another hair, tie up your dog so it won't bite me."

Usss. Through the kerosene lamp.

"Take another hair, tie up your lance so it won't spear me." Usss. Through the kerosene lamp. They sat down to eat supper, and the woman says, "Give me a leg."

"Take it."

"Give me another leg."

"Take it."

"Give me another leg."

"Fuck, how many legs does a rabbit have?"

And so on and I don't know what. Then the two of them started in on each other.

"My dog, my horse, my lance."

"May everything turn into chain."

Of course, because they were not tied—he had burned the hairs—well, it turned out they all threw themselves on the witch. I shit on ten! They left her black and blue. They hit her all he wanted them to. And then he said to her afterwards, he says, "You were the one who killed my brothers. I want to see them here exactly as they were."

So then she had them there in a room and she had a little ointment, like a paper and a hen's feather. Then she anointed them, perhaps in the asshole, and the result was they were revived and they became again exactly as they had been before. Do you understand? And then those three brothers went away. Now they were together. And they came to where the woman was, the woman the oldest had married.

"But man, how is this possible?" she said.

"Well, I have slept with her," one of the brothers said.

"Of course, me too."

The three brothers were embroiled, the one with the other, now that they knew they had slept with their brother's wife. And then . . . as one says, *"Colorín colorado, cuento terminado."*

Florencio was an unusual narrator because he located agency in the father when explaining why the blood brothers leave home. He told how the father gave each of his sons a horse, a dog, and a lance because he had lost the family capital in a card game and expected his creditors to seize all of his property the following morning. Florencio, of course, actually lost a great deal of his own family capital in the failed "cafeteria," which cost his sons a good part of their inheritance. Most other narrators located agency for the brothers' departure in the brothers themselves and provided other reasons for their leaving home that also make sense given the norm of male autonomy in a culture where betrothal rituals have, as their ostensible purpose, the provisioning of a household to enable a married couple to live separately from their parents. Miguel Chorro, who is also from Navaconcejo, referred to the honor and shame code when he told how the blood brothers decided to leave home because their peers taunted them for having suspect parentage. Their peers called them "sons of a fish" and thus raised doubts about their parents' honor (*honra*) by implying the mother did not maintain her marital chastity. Bernardo Ramos, Florencio's son, and José Díaz Sánchez of Serradilla expressed a son's desire to be independent of his father, saying that the brothers decided to leave home to find their destiny. Julio López Curiel of Garganta la Olla said the brothers wanted to leave home because they were the focus of envy and others wanted to kill them.

Women expressed their more connected view of family relationships by representing the brothers leaving serially rather than in a group. Serial departures emphasize sibling solidarity because the younger brothers leave home for the purpose of rescuing their older brothers who are lost in the castle where "You Will Go and Will Not Return." Estrella Iglesias of Navaconcejo, for example, told how the first brother leaves home to find his fortune and deposits, with his brother, a bottle filled with a special liquid that turns black if he dies. When the younger brother sees the liquid change color, he leaves home to rescue his older brother. Serial departures also appear in feminine variants of "Blood Brothers" by other women from Trujillo, in southern Cáceres, and two villages in Salamanca.[6] To be sure, there are some exceptions; Manuela Martín Cuadrado in Salamanca described the brothers leaving home in a group and separating without explanation, presumably because she regarded male independence as the norm.[7]

Women provided interesting reasons, not mentioned by men, for the brothers' departure from home, and the reasons they gave in their stories accord with the actual experiences of many narrators I knew in Cáceres villages. Julia Lobato Gil of Serradilla and Francisca Borrallo of Trujillo specified that the brothers had to earn money to eat,[8] much as many Cáceres men have had to leave home to make the money they could not earn in their own villages. Florencio Ramos took Bernardo and the rest of his family to Murcia for a year and half; Bernardo worked on construction projects in Madrid and Barcelona; Miguel Chorro left Navaconcejo to work on construction projects in Bilbao and the Pyrenees; Julio López Curiel sharecropped land for many years in Galisteo on the plain below his native Garganta la Olla.

Florencio is nevertheless like other male Cáceres narrators because he expressed the norm of male autonomy when representing the brothers separating from each other after they have left home. He told how the brothers decided to travel down different roads because it was better for each to earn his living separately. Florencio's son Bernardo, Julio López Curiel of Garganta la Olla, and José Díaz Sánchez of Serradilla provided no explanation for their separation, presumably because male independence is a normal fact of life. However, Julia Lobato Gil of Serradilla, who described the brothers leaving home in a group, expressed her more connected fraternal vision by drawing attention to an emotional bond existing between the brothers; she told how one twin did not want to separate from the other and did so only with reluctance.

In all variants I know of in Castilian-speaking Spain, the brothers maintain a mystical connection represented by a liquid or an object that changes if one experiences misfortune. The objects vary—they are vials containing blood or an unnamed liquid, a sword, or a fish skeleton[9]—but they all turn color or bleed when one brother becomes trapped in the castle. In most cases, the brothers hold in their possession the vial or other magical object. Florencio gave a special role to the father when he said the brothers each left a bottle with his name on it when they departed from home. They instruct their father, "When it turns into blood, then we're dead." There was tension between the way Florencio wanted to represent the father, as a strong and important figure in the lives of his sons, and the requirements of the plot, which necessitate placing the vial in the hands of the brothers as they travel down separate roads. Otherwise, they would have no way of realizing that one is in trouble without returning home to find out. To tell a seamless story, a narrator must introduce a reason why they make an about-face and return home after going down their chosen path. Florencio did not solve the problem he created by placing the bottle in the hands of the father and uncharacteristically became confused as he reached the point in his story when the second and third brothers retrace the steps of their older brother, who has become lost in the castle of the witch. "I don't know how he came back again," said Florencio when referring to the second brother. As for the third brother, he described him returning to his older brother's house, which is not the house of the woman he married, but another house, presumably that of their father. Many of Florencio's stories are brilliantly told because their plots work perfectly; he produced a beautifully woven plot in his version of "The Magic Objects and the Wonderful Fruits" (Chapter 4). I suspect Florencio's confusion in "Blood Brothers" resulted from his effort to shape the father in his own self-image in a story whose parts are intricately connected.

A universal feature of all Spanish and Mexican "Blood Brothers" tales is the youngest brother's rescue of his older brothers, usually trapped in the castle of where "You Will Go and Will Not Return." One brother rescuing another is obviously what brothers should do for each other and represents the ideal of sibling unity. However, Cáceres variants of "Blood Brothers" often include scenes of fraternal sexual rivalry in their concluding episodes; narrators frequently described one brother quarreling with or killing another upon learning that his rescuer spent the night with his wife. Stith Thompson calls this feature "The jealous brother" motif and reported it in about 20 percent of the variants worldwide.[10]

The motif of "The jealous brother" usually develops in two ways in the masculine stories from Cáceres. First, Miguel Chorro of Navaconcejo and Julio López Curiel of Garganta la Olla described one brother killing the other and then reviving him after learning that his dead brother had placed a sword in the marital bed to guard the family honor. Second, Bernardo Ramos, Florencio's son, omitted the sword detail and ended his tale with one brother ordering the other brother shot for his treachery.

Florencio was comparatively unusual among men in the way he developed the motif of "The jealous brother" in his variant of the story. He concluded his story with the brothers quarreling but eliminated fratricide, which frequently appeared in other male variants. The brothers reveal they have slept with the older brother's wife and do not mention placing their swords in the bed to guard their brother's honor, as they do in some versions. Florencio went so far as to say that one brother kissed and presumably had sex with his older brother's wife. Still, no brother lifts a hand to harm another, as happens in other Spanish variants of this story. As mentioned, Florencio played down male sexual rivalry in his version of "The Bear's Son" when he told how the hero accepts the formerly enchanted maiden's request that no harm come to his companions for stealing her from the hero.

Florencio's subdued depiction of fraternal sexual rivalry makes his version of "Blood Brothers" similar to the variants told by women in Cáceres and other provinces in Spain. Estrella Iglesias of Navaconcejo, Adela Romero Cuesta of Herrera del Duque in northern Badajoz, Magdalena Frutos of Hinojosa de Duero, and Beatríz Mancebo from La Alberca in Salamanca omitted the jealous quarrel in their variants of this popular Spanish folktale.[11] There are, of course, some notable exceptions to this generalization that women represented less sexual rivalry than did men. José Díaz Sánchez of Serradilla did not include the motif of "The jealous brother" in his story but did describe his hero placing his sword in the marital bed to guard his brother's honor. The motif of "The jealous brother" appeared in tales by Julia Lobato Gil of Serradilla and Manuela Martín Cuadrado of Vilvestre in Salamanca.[12] One Cáceres woman described the brothers competing for parental affection rather than for women. Francisca Borrallo from Trujillo in southern Cáceres described the brothers as jealous over filial rather than sexual love;[13] the brothers live with a king after the youngest helps them escape from a female dragon, and the older brothers are jealous of their younger brother because the king regards him as the wisest and loves him more than the others.

It is nevertheless difficult to escape the conclusion that a father like Florencio, who parents his children directly by nurturing them with food, will develop a comparatively less alienated view of a man's relationship with other men. Florencio consistently appeared different from many other men in his culture and resembled women by representing more solidarity and connection among brothers, possibly because he performed what ordinarily is a woman's role in caring for his sons. A comparison of Florencio's story with cognate variants by Nahuat men reveals that Florencio nevertheless took for granted male autonomy that is normal for his culture but not for the Nahuat, particularly in Nacho's village of Huitzilan de Serdán.

A NAHUAT VARIANT

James Lockhart considers sibling relations a major difference between Spanish and ancient Nahua culture.[14] The contemporary Spaniards of Cáceres and the Nahuat of Mexico continue to manifest, in sibling terminology and family life, many of the differences Lockhart observed for the earlier period. The Nahuat use one term (-cnīuh) for all blood relatives in a speaker's generation; they distinguish among brothers according to their relative age by calling the oldest tayacān-queh and the youngest taxocoyot. Spaniards in Cáceres make a terminological distinction between a brother (hermano) and a cousin (primo), and they do not customarily apply different elementary terms to brothers according to their age. The Nahuat, who classify a brother and a cousin under the same term (-cnīuh), express in kinship terminology their common practice of clustering the children of married brothers in the same household or in adjacent houses. The Cáceres distinction between brothers and cousins accords with their practice of separating the children of siblings, who generally live in independent households in different neighborhoods. Cáceres children of some sisters occasionally live in the same or neighboring households because of the preference for matrilocality over patrilocality. However, the Nahuat more frequently form extended family households, and their rates of patrilocality are higher than the Cáceres rates of matrilocality. The Nahuat distinctions among brothers by their age accord with the organization of family life whereby authority is delegated along the lines of age as well as gender. The father, who is the oldest member of the family, is the head of the household and officiates at all major rituals taking place in the home. He greets the guests and offers them cigarettes and shot glasses of *aguardiente*, and he invites them to dip the freshly made tortillas into the ceremonial *mole*. The oldest brother succeeds the father as the head of the extended family household. The Cáceres family has a more egalitarian and independent organization, where the relative age of a brother does not confer a special authority.

Differences related to kinship terminology appeared in the Cáceres and Nahuat variants of "Blood Brothers." I heard this popular folktale from four Nahuat narrators: Nicolás Cabrera and Ramírez Manzano in Huitzilan and Mariano Isidro and Luciano Vega in Yaonáhuac. The four men have long histories of working on the coastal plain with other Nahuat, Totonacs, and Spanish-speaking Mexicans from villages all over the northern Sierra de Puebla where they may have heard this tale. It is nevertheless difficult to determine the extent to which Nahuat narrators may have patterned their versions of "Blood Brothers" after the stories circulating in Spanish-speaking Mexican oral tradition because so few examples of this folktale appear in collections of this category of narrators. Paul Radin and Aurelio Espinosa included two among the tales they probably heard from Spanish speakers in Oaxaca.[15] None of the other well-known folklorists, who worked with similar narrators, reported hearing the story within the boundaries of modern Mexico. Future generations of anthropologists and folklorists working in Mexico are bound to turn up more variants because the story is popular among Spanish-speaking narrators in what used to be Mexico but is now the United States.[16]

Nicolás Cabrera, a forty-nine-year-old Nahuat man from Huitzilan, represented a markedly different picture of a man's relation to other men than did Florencio in "Blood Brothers." Nicolás' story resembles one told by Ramírez Manzano, also from Huitzilan, and differs not only from the Spanish variants of the same story but from other Nahuat versions I heard from Luciano Vega and Mariano Isidro in Santiago Yaonáhuac. An English translation of Nicolás' tale appears below, and the analysis following his narrative will focus on certain story elements to reveal how Nicolás and Ramírez represented male relations with a narrative style that fits their culture.

"The Fisherman"
by Nicolás Cabrera

Once there was a fisherman who made his living from the water. He didn't have any children of his own. He really liked children. But he didn't have a single child. So then, they say, he went every day, he went every day to cast his net. And one time it got stuck. It got stuck, they say. "Why did it get stuck?" he wonders. "I'm going to go get it."

He went to get it. And someone says to him, "Do you like catching fish?"

"Yes, I like to," he replies. "But I don't do an irritating thing inconsiderately but rather to sell them because I'm poor. I sell them to support myself."

"Well yes, you sell them," the someone says. "Now we give you just three."

"Fine."

From there, they say, they gave him three fish. He went to the edge of the water. He took three fish. "Now," the fisherman is told, "you will bury the heads. You surely have a garden. Bury those heads in the garden's corners."

"Fine," he says.

And, they say, he buried those heads in three corners of his garden and went again, they say, to the edge of the water.

"And what appeared from each head?" he is asked. "What appeared?"

"Three boys appeared. Each of their faces is the same," he replies.

"Fine."

He went again. Again he was given three fish. Again he buried each of the three heads in a corner of his garden. "Let's see what appears," he says.

Three identical swords appeared, they say.

So then again, again he went to the water's edge. Again he was given three fish. "Bury them again," he is told. "Do it the same way."

So he buried them. Again, three identical horses appeared.

Again he went another time. "What appeared?" he is asked.

"Three horses appeared."

"Fine," someone says. "Now bury them again."

Again, they say, he buried them. Then three saddles appeared. They appeared where he planted the heads. "Did they appear?" he is asked.

"Yes," the fisherman replies.

"And now bury these three again," he's told. "Who knows what will appear?"

Three identical dogs appeared. They had given him ones that were all smooth.

"Now yes. Do you like those boys?" he's asked.

"Yes, I like them. Each one has his blanket, his sword, a saddle, a horse, and a dog that are identical," he says.

"Yes. Good. Now give the road to those brothers," he is told. "Give the road to them. The road belongs to them. Those children belong on the road."

So they went away. Those children left, they say. They went, they say. They went on and on. They came to a fork in the road. There were three roads. So they decided. One of the brothers was put over there, one over there, and the middle was left to the oldest.

"Good," the oldest says. "Now we're going to cut this tree. You'll see sap running from this tree if something happens to me. You'll realize right away that something has happened to one of us," he says.

"Fine."

They cut the tree with their swords, and they took to the road again. Each one went down one road. Good. First the oldest brother went. He went until he found a little store. "Where are you going?" a person in the store asks.

"I'm going over there."

"Don't go over there because there is a big animal. No one goes there," the person in the store warns.

"It's not true," he replies.

"Yes, it has twelve heads."

"Fine, sure. I'll hit it. I have my fine dog, my fine sword, and my fine horse."

"Don't go."

"No. I'm going."

So he came to where that animal was, they say. At that moment, that animal was in the water because it had just changed its face into that of a fish. So then that boy went into the water. And since the animal—the serpent—was there in the water, the boy removed its tongues. Twelve of them. He cut them all off with his sword. He put them all into his pocket. Fine. So he went on and he went on. He came again to a little store. "Where are you going?" the person in the little store asks.

"Over there."

"Not true. No one goes there."

"Sure," he says. "I have my fine horse and sword and my dog. I come bringing these tongues here."

He removed them.

"Now yes," the person in the store says to the boy. "Because you struck that animal down, they'll give you a girl."

"I don't believe it."

"Yes," the person in the store replies. "They'll give her to you because that animal would have killed her. They would have given the girl to it. She is the general's daughter," he explains. While the boy was talking, a charcoal seller came along. He threw down his load and he picked up the animal. He took it and he reached the general first. That charcoal seller did. The general truly loved that charcoal seller because he killed the animal. So then he gave him the girl right away. The boy had not yet arrived. They took the charcoal seller to her over there. She threw her arms around his neck, they say. And she kissed him, and the charcoal seller was really pleased. And then that boy appeared.

"How are you going to get through here?" asks the general.

"I'm sure to get through," he says. "I killed that animal. I bring its tongues."

"It's not true!"

"Yes, it is. Here they are."

"But a charcoal seller appeared over there," he says. "He killed it."

"Let's see if you can show how he killed it. Let him open its mouth and have him count the tongues," he says.

He proceeded. "Well, it doesn't have any!"

And here he is holding them. "Here they are. I brought them."

They gave the girl to the boy, and the general ordered the charcoal seller, "Now stand over there, and fire five shots."

They shot the charcoal seller, and the girl went over to the boy. And she told him, they say, that there was a house far away. It was so far that it took work to see it.

"Good," he says to her.

The sun came up. "That house, what is it called?" he asks.

"That house is called 'You Go and You Won't Return,' " she says.

"It sure won't be," he says. "My horse and my dog are fine. I'm going," he announces.

So then he went. But before he went, she said, "Don't go, son. Don't go because you are going to stay there."

"No," he says. "I'm going."

He went to that place. And there was an old woman, they say. When that boy dismounted, she quickly grabbed him around his waist, and he went into a prison. He went in there and there he stayed. Then his other brother had a dream. When he came to where the tree was, tears of sap had appeared because they imprisoned his brother-companion. So he came down the same road. He came until he was with the girl.

"You came back, son!" she exclaimed.

"Yes, I've come back."

So then he went to rest. Night came, they say, and he slept with that girl. But he put his sword between them so he wouldn't sleep with her. The sun came up, and again he asked, "And what is that house?"

"Oh God, son," she says. "You forgot I told you: 'You Go and You Won't Return.' "

The boy also went. He went and was snatched the same way. He also went to stay. They also imprisoned him. Then the last of the three brothers went. He went where the others had gone. And he came and he came again. The boy came until he arrived again at the girl's house. He arrived and he went in to lie down again and saw the sun again come up.

"Good, and what, what is that?" he asks her.

"Oh, son," she says. "I've told you many times. They say it is 'You Go and You Won't Return,' " she says.

"Fine. I'll return for sure," he says.

He left on his horse. He was the solution. The boy arrived. He dismounted his horse. And since that old woman was standing there, he removed his sword from its scabbard and hit her immediately. He hit her and really turned her black and blue until she couldn't get up anymore. And she told him of the many she had imprisoned. She imprisoned many. He opened them up, and there were many troops. Many. Many. They all came out, but there were a lot. So then they started blowing their coronets. And there came the three brothers, and they reached the general again. And just as he spotted them, he said, "Good, and they are all brothers."

Well, they didn't do anything to them. One of the brothers took the girl. And the general told the other two, "Now you work here. You'll take these soldiers and you will know how to work them."

And there the story ended.

Nicolás expressed a highly connected view of male relationships by emphasizing the ties between the father and his sons and among the three brothers with narrative devices not found in Spanish versions of the same tale. He depicted a father as more connected to his sons in three ways: (1) the father wants children; (2) his role in their procreation is emphasized with an association between planting and conception; and (3) the agency for the sons' separation is taken out of the family. Nicolás described the father as a childless man who "really found children pleasing" (melāuh que cualittiaya in conēmeh) and employed the familiar narrative device of repetition by using the word "like" or "find pleasing" (cualitta) two more times in the following passage to emphasize the father's pleasure in finding three sons sprouting from his garden:

"Ticualitta," quiliā, "non oquichpil?"
"Quēmah, nicualitta . . . ."
"Do you like," he asks, "those boys?"
"Yes, I like them . . . ."

Nicolás' image of a father wanting children because he finds them pleasing is like the mother's desire for children in Spanish-narrator Julia Lobato Gil's version of the same folktale. Julia opened her story by describing a mother praying so much for children that she has twins.[17] Spanish men are generally a contrast to Nicolás because they frequently represented the birth of the blood brothers as a loss for their father. In their stories, a father trades a promise of future economic prosperity for children. He catches a talking fish that promises him prosperity if thrown back into the water. The fisherman's wife insists he bring the talking fish home if his fishbasket is empty. The fisherman agrees to the request, and his wife eats the fish and becomes pregnant with male twins or triplets. Giving up a promise of future economic prosperity for children appears in masculine "Blood Brother" stories by Bernardo Ramos and Miguel Chorro of Navaconcejo, José Díaz Sánchez of Serradilla, and Julio López Curiel of Garganta la Olla. Miguel Chorro did not mirror his own reality at the time he told his story. He lived with his unmarried son Luis (age thirty-six), who did most of the work on the family estate and provided a great deal of economic support for his parents.

Nicolás drew attention to the father's role in his sons' conception by making an association between planting and procreation, which emphasized the man's role of putting something into a woman. The fisherman plants the heads of three fish in the corners of his garden from which emerge his three sons. Nicolás used the verb tōca (to bury or plant something), which ordinarily refers to planting corn and beans in a milpa.[18] The association between planting and procreation is based on the Nahuat personification of the earth as a woman and is very widespread in Nahuat oral narratives. It appeared in Ramírez Manzano's variant of "Blood Brothers" and in a creation myth by Huitzilan narrator Miguel Ahuata, who told of two brothers planting people as well as corn in the forest that once covered the earth. The contemporary association between planting and procreation probably derives from the ancient Nahua idea of conception as seating the infant in the womb, an act closely related to the practice of placing a seed in the earth, personified as a woman.[19]

Male as well as female Spanish narrators in Cáceres and other provinces emphasized the mother's rather than the father's connection to sons by describing the fisherman's wife becoming pregnant after eating the talking fish. Eating as conception occurred in "Blood Brother" stories I heard from Bernardo Ramos and Miguel Chorro in Navaconcejo, Julio López Curiel in Garganta la Olla, and José Diáz Sánchez in Serradilla. It also appeared in feminine variants by Manuela Martín Cuadrado and Beatriz Mancebo in Salamanca.[20] The closest association between planting and procreation in a Spanish variant of "Blood Brothers" appeared in a story by Adela Romero Cuesta of Herrera del Duque in northern Badajoz.[21] Adela told how the fisherman's wife cleans the fish, throwing the entrails on the ground, from which sprout the three brothers. An association between planting and procreation is not surprising because Adela and other narrators in northern Badajoz, Cáceres, and Salamanca regularly plant fields and have occasion to witness the regenerative power of the earth, which resembles the pro-creative power of women. What is significant in Adela's tale is that she made a woman rather than a man the planter and procreator of the blood brothers.

Hispanicized narrators in Mexico, who included the Nahuat of Yao-náhuac and Spanish-speaking Mexicans, also associated eating and conception to emphasize the role of the woman in procreation. Lu-ciano Vega of Yaonáhuac explained the brothers' origins by saying the fisherman's wife became pregnant when she ate the flesh of the talk-ing fish. Luciano may have heard "Blood Brothers" from Spanish-speaking Mexicans who likewise associated eating with procreation. Paul Radin and Aurelio Espinosa heard such a variant from a narrator who probably was a Spanish speaker living in Oaxaca. He or she—the narrator's identity is unknown—told how a fisherman catches a fish of three tails in three colors. Following instructions from his *patrón*, his wife cooks the unusual fish on her *comal*, a flat clay dish or piece of iron for heating tortillas, and grinds it into dust, some of which the fisherman puts into his wife's food; this causes her to become preg-nant and give birth to three kings.[22]

The two ways of representing the brothers' origins—planting as procreation and eating as procreation—fit the gender division of labor in agriculture and in family life in the two cultures. The image of the father as planter as well as procreator builds on the Nahuat gender division of labor in Huitzilan, according to which men and only men plant a corn and bean field by rhythmically inserting a dibble into the moist earth, then taking kernels of corn or beans from a pouch worn near the groin and inserting them into the hole made by the dibble. The image of the father as planter as well as procreator makes less sense in Cáceres villages, where a woman customarily inserts pieces of potato into holes her husband makes in the ground.

The emphasis on the father's or the mother's roles in procreation also accords with other realities of family life in the two cultures. Nahuat men, who represented planting as procreation, generally at-tempted to create very strong filial loyalties in their sons to keep them in the same household after marriage or to encourage them to live close by and continue contributing their labor to the family economy. However, the relationship between a story and the personal family history of the narrator is complex because storytellers sometimes re-flected their culture but not their own personal experiences. Nicolás, who represented the father's role in procreation, illustrates how a nar-rator may use images suited to prevailing family patterns that differ from his family history. When I first met Nicolás Cabrera in 1968, he,

Fig. 4. Men planting milpa with a dibble.

like many in his village, lived right next door to his father, Manuel, and his older brother Pedro. However, I discovered later than Nicolás is among the 20 percent of married couples in Huitzilan who once lived with the wife's family during the first marital years. Nicolás remained about five years in his wife's mother's household; when she lost her rented home, Nicolás moved to a house next door to his father and brother, bringing his mother-in-law with him. Manuel owned the house site, which he probably will bequeath to both sons. Nicolás' brother Pedro had a more usual family history, which Nicolás expressed in his story by emphasizing the close tie between a father and his sons. For about ten years Pedro, his wife Guadalupe, and their children lived with Manuel in a patrilineally extended family household. The two families separated when Manuel built another dwelling on the same house site, and Pedro remained in the family home. Pedro is among the approximately 80 percent of all married sons who began marriage in their father's household. Ramírez Manzano, who told a very similar variant of "Blood Brothers"—emphasizing the father as planter and procreator of his sons—also had a more typical family, which he represented in his story. He lived with and maintained a close tie with his unmarried, adult son, who was coincidentally one of Nacho's best friends.

The Spanish association between eating and procreation, which draws attention to the role of the mother in the creation of the blood brothers, expresses the comparatively strong filial loyalties between a mother and her children in the Cáceres villages I knew in Spain. As mentioned earlier, women prefer to reside with or near their mother after marriage because they rely heavily on the mother for help in child care and for emotional support throughout life. A woman expresses her loyalty to her elderly mother and father by caring for them when they are unable to care for themselves, and she maintains a symbolic relationship with her deceased mother through her devotion to Mary.[23]

The strong filial loyalties between father and son in the Nahuat family make it difficult for sons to declare their wish to separate from parents unless the father is abusive. It was mentioned in Chapter 3 that Huitzilan narrator Juan Hernández took care to represent the father as brutally punishing in his version of "The Bear's Son," justifying his building a separate home on Cozōltepēt, far from his father. That the father in "Blood Brothers" is not abusive poses a dilemma to a Nahuat narrator like Nicolás, who must justify why the sons leave home. Yet in "Blood Brothers" the central characters leave home and separate from each other until reunited when the youngest rescues his older brothers from the castle. Nicolás and Ramírez Manzano handle the dilemma by locating agency for the decision to leave home outside of the family; Nicolás located agency in an unnamed voice whom Ramírez identified as St. Michael, the guardian of the fish. The "voice" in Nicolás' tale carries out a long dialogue with the fisherman, giving him many orders and asking him many questions. Nicolás used repetition to draw attention to the importance of the voice, which delivers six commands serially rather than one command with different parts, as usually appears in the "Blood Brothers" stories told in Spain. The first five commands in the series are orders to bury three heads of three fish five different times in the corners of the fisherman's garden. The sixth command is an order for the boys to separate from their father and take to the road.

> "Bueno, āxcān," quiliā, "āxcān," quiliā, "xiquimaca in ohti," quiliā, "nin ēyi icnīmeh," quiliā de nonhermanos. Quiliā, "Xiquimaca non ohti. Non niāxcā," quiliā, "non ohti. Tech cē ohti, non yehhăn niāxcā non pipil."
>
> "Fine, now," [the voice] says to him, "now," he says to him, "give the road," he says to him, "to these three brothers," he says to him about those three brothers. He says to him, "Give the road to them. That road is," he says to him, "their property. On the road, that is the property of those children."

The importance of removing agency from within the family will perhaps become clear with an anecdote illustrating the depth of feeling experienced by a father when his married son wants to move away. When Mariano married, he brought his wife to live with his parents, Juan Gravioto and María Antonia Santiago, as is the prevailing custom of patrilocal residence in Huitzilan among older sons. However, tension soon developed between María Antonia and her daughter-in-law when the latter registered complaints with the municipal judge about the former. Juan came to me very concerned because he did not want Mariano to move out of the household. He said that if his son did move out, then he and María would keep Pascual, Mariano's son. María was nursing Pascual as well as her infant son Eduardo at the same time to create a very strong bond between grandmother and grandson to prevent Mariano from leaving home. Juan and María worked through the crisis by building a new dwelling approximately two feet from the family home so their daughter-in-law could work in a separate kitchen.

Despite an ideal of sibling solidarity, the blood brothers separate from each other in nearly all Nahuat as well as Spanish-speaking Mexican and Spanish variants of "Blood Brothers." However, Nicolás emphasized the connections among the brothers in two ways: (1) embellishing their mystical connection, and (2) eliminating the motif of "The jealous brother." Nicolás, like many other narrators in Spain and Mexico, expressed the ideal of brotherly unity, after separation, by an object that magically changes when one of the brothers experiences a misfortune; the brothers agree to make cuts in a tree, and the cut corresponding to each bleeds if he is in trouble. A few Cáceres narrators also provided other examples of the connections among the brothers: Julio López Curiel said that one guesses what the other guesses; Julia Lobato Gil told how one feels what the other feels; and Miguel Chorro described one twin informing the other, apparently by letter, of his marriage. However, all Cáceres narrators I knew relied on the changing state of a physical object (a vial, sword, or skeleton) rather than shared emotions, divination, or letter writing when explaining how the younger brothers know that the older ones are in trouble.

Nicolás added a dimension to that mystical connection by representing one brother dreaming about the other brother when he becomes trapped in the witch's castle. Communication through dreaming is a poetic device by which Nicolás expressed an idealized state of male sibling solidarity. A connection through dreams is not an idiosyncratic feature of Nicolás' tale; it also appears in the closely related story by Ramírez Manzano, who is Nicolás' neighbor in Huitzilan. The more Hispanicized narrators I knew in Santiago Yaonáhuac, Spanish-speaking Mexicans, and Cáceres villagers in Spain did not use any psychological or parapsychological connection among the brothers to explain how one knows that the other is in trouble. They relied entirely on a supernatural device—the changing state of a physical object (a tree, liquid in a bottle, the skeleton of a fish, or a sword)—to represent the mystical connection between brothers that stands for their unity.

Male sibling unity is, of course, expressed in the plot of many "Blood Brother" stories in Mexico and Spain when the youngest brother rescues his older brothers from the castle. It was mentioned earlier that Spanish narrators mixed sibling unity with sibling rivalry in their concluding episode when they told how one brother kills his rescuer for sleeping with his wife. However, no Nahuat I knew included the motif of "The jealous brother" in his variant of the story; Nicolás and other Nahuat narrators did not describe any sexual rivalry among brothers whether or not the youngest brother spent the night with his older brother's wife and neglected to lay his sword on the marital bed to guard his sister-in-law's marital chastity. To express openly sexual rivalry among brothers is very threatening and would not be appropriate in a story like "Blood Brothers," which has a didactic function in the culture. The Nahuat call a folktale a neīxcuītīl (example, model, or pattern),[24] and they tell stories like "Blood Brothers" in the family to support the moral order, which includes the ideal of male-sibling solidarity.

An examination of the specific words and images used by Nicolás and Ramírez reveals how their stories are part of the moral discourse of their village. The men opened their stories describing a fisherman's encounter with the guardian of the fish, whom Ramírez identified as St. Michael. As is often the case with Nahuat folktales, the two men used language with rich but incompletely stated connotative meanings. They did not believe it necessary on each storytelling event to elaborate fully on important words, phrases, and passages because they used standardized images that their listeners have heard on other storytelling occasions. Nicolás referred to disorder caused by human excess when he described the fisherman wading into the water to recover his net and hearing the "voice" ask if he enjoyed catching fish. The fisherman replied: "Yes, I like to. But I don't do an irritating thing inconsiderately. . . ." Nicolás used the word niqueh(quel)īlihuizchīhua ("I do [not] do an irritating thing inconsiderately"), which is made up of quehquel ("irritation") and īlihuiz ("inconsiderately"),[25] to convey the meaning of annoying and excessive behavior that causes disorder. Ramírez provided a specific example of this excessive behavior and the resultant disorder in his version of the same story. He told how the fisherman's wife gave some of the fish to her lover, bringing illness to the fish. The excessive behavior occurred when the fisherman's wife had sex with more than one man at a time, and the resultant disorder is illness of the fish, which the Nahuat regard as the breakdown of the ordered structure of the body. The Nahuat moral discourse incorporated into the first episodes of Nicolás' and Ramírez' versions of "Blood Brothers" presupposes a highly interrelated view of the universe according to which humans are connected to animals and one form of disorder can bring about another.

Nahua moral discourse, which emphasizes the need to avoid inconsiderate behavior, developed in part to regulate relations in the patrilineally extended family that depend heavily on cooperation among brothers, fathers, and sons. It is quite possible that Nicolás, Ramírez, and other Nahuat narrators before them censored a direct expression of male sibling rivalry by removing the motif of "The jealous brother" and recasting it as rivalry between men who have no family connection in their episode of "The Dragon Slayer" (300). They recast male rivalry by telling how the first brother slays a twelve-headed serpent, rescues the general's daughter, and contends with a charcoal seller who tries to win the daughter's hand in marriage by stealing the serpent's heads and claiming that he rescued the maiden. It is quite likely that Nicolás and Ramírez retained a "Dragon Slayer" episode in the story originally acquired from Spain through the intermediate category of Spanish-speaking Mexican storytellers. Mixing the two stories is very common in Europe, as Kurt Ranke demonstrated in his monumental study of both folktales.[26] The two tales are combined by Spaniards, Spanish-speaking Mexicans, and by the Nahuat, all of whom incorporate in their versions of "Blood Brothers" a Spanish form of "The Dragon Slayer" that includes, as one of its identifying motifs, the charcoal seller as an impostor.[27]

Censoring and recasting male sibling rivalry appear related to the management of male sexual aggression in the patrilineally extended family. Sexual competition between brothers would destroy the relationships among the men on whom the unity of the family depends. It is safer to handle sexual aggression among brothers in storytelling by censoring the motif of "The jealous brother" and recasting any sexual rivalry that might originate in the family as rivalry between a man and a hydra-headed monster and a charcoal seller who is obviously not a family member. Freud originally applied the concept of censorship to interpret the manifest and latent content of dreams; he suggested that the dreamer is "sometimes like the political writer who will encounter government suppression if he tells the truth without reserve."[28] The result in both cases is distortion through the defense mechanisms of displacement and projection.[29]

The process of censorship in storytelling is very difficult to observe; it takes place with subtle changes in a plot over successive storytelling situations and can only be inferred from the available evidence. Censorship is likely to operate in storytelling according to the requirements on behavior expressed in the moral discourse of the culture. Nahuat narrators tell many stories in family settings where listeners voice their reaction to a story during and following its performance. A storyteller of renown, like Nicolás, knows how his audience is likely to react to the stories he has told many times before. It is possible that the Nahuat narrators, who originally heard "Blood Brothers" from Spanish-speaking Mexicans, censored the tale by removing the motif of "The jealous brother" and retained "The Dragon Slayer" episode to satisfy their audience.

SUMMARY

Florencio's image of brotherly relationships and his actual relationship with his three sons, who are of course brothers, are unusual among the men in his culture. His comparatively connected view of fraternal relationships resembled that of Cáceres women, who told the same story and who have very strong ties to their children. Florencio nevertheless represented brothers differently than Nahuat men in Nacho's village of Huitzilan de Serdán. Nicolás and other narrators in Nacho's village employed story images that do not exist in Florencio's culture. The images include procreation as planting (emphasizing a man's role in conception), parapsychological communication among brothers, and a highly connected view of humans and animals in which inconsiderate behavior is out of place. The next chapter will reenter Nacho's poetic imagination to discover how he represented brothers according to his own relationship with an unusually cohesive extended family.

Chapter 7

"THE TWO TRAVELERS"

NACHO REPRESENTED HIS VISION OF BROTHERS IN "THE TWO Travelers" (Tale Type 613), a story he told when still pooling his labor with his older brothers in their extended family household. His story is a variant of a famous folktale that has a very interesting history. At least 1,500 years old, the tale appeared in literary as well as oral tradition; it is found in Buddhist, Hindu, Jaina, and Hebrew literature, *Thousand and One Nights*, Basile's *Pentameron*, and the Grimms' *Kinder- und Hausmärchen* under the title "Die beiden Wanderer." It is also a popular oral narrative originating in Asia, appearing in the Middle East and then in Europe, and traveling with the colonists to the Americas.[1]

The story has a long and remarkably well known presence in the Hispanic world; it is in the medieval collection known as the *Libro de los gatos*, a manuscript discovered in the Biblioteca Nacional de Madrid and containing sixty-six pieces of folklore by anonymous authors who used language typical of the period from 1350 to 1400.[2] It is a folktale in contemporary Spanish oral tradition in several parts of Spain: Luis Cortés Vázquez heard one variant by Beatriz Mancebo of La Alberca in Salamanca,[3] and I heard another by Leandro Jiménez of El Guijo de Santa Bárbara in Cáceres. Spaniards undoubtedly brought "The Two Travelers" to the Americas, where it appears in the oral tradition of Latinos in the United States and of Spanish-speaking and native Mexicans, including the Nahuat of Huitzilan and Yaonáhuac.[4]

This chapter examines how Nacho represented an image of brothers transformed from Spanish culture, where narrators depicted a man in an alienated relationship with other men. Florencio did not tell this folktale, so I shall temporarily turn to other Spanish storytellers to discover how they represented brothers for the purposes of making comparisons with Nacho's story. Spanish narrators generally told

"The Two Travelers" with a linear plot that developed according to moral absolutes. The principal protagonists are usually two men, one of whom is good and the other bad; the good one triumphs, and the bad one perishes.

In the version appearing in the *Libro de los gatos*, the two men are companions, one of whom tells the truth and the other lies.[5] The two companions agree to tell their versions of the truth to two apes. The liar, known as Bad Truth (La Mala Verdad), tells the apes that they appear to him as a king and a famous person highly valued by others, and the apes reward the liar with silver, gold, and other riches. The honest one, known as Good Truth (La Buena Verdad), tells the apes that he has never seen such dirty and ugly beings, whom only crazy people would value. The apes blind him and leave him groping his way through the wilderness. Good Truth senses the presence of bears, wolves, and other beasts and climbs a tree to escape being eaten. He hears a vixen tell her companions she knows a king who could cure his daughter's muteness if he only knew how. On Sundays, the vixen customarily snatches some of the king's cake, and the king only has to remove the bite from the vixen's mouth to cure his daughter. The king is also blind and can cure his own blindness by bathing his eyes in the water from a fountain under a rock at the tip of his house. The following morning, Good Truth climbs down from the tree and cures the king's daughter of her muteness and the king of his blindness, restoring his own sight and earning a handsome reward. When the two companions meet again, Bad Truth learns of Good Truth's fortune and climbs the same tree in the hope of becoming richer. The animals appear; the vixen reports her plans were foiled and demands to know who revealed her secret. The animals each swear they did not tell; then they spot Bad Truth up in the tree and tear him to pieces.

The medieval variant of "The Two Travelers" in the *Libro de los gatos* conforms in many ways to Max Lüthi's description of the style of a European folk- and fairytale: characters are not particularly well delineated and represent extreme contrasts; they are moral opposites in a world of moral absolutes where good must triumph over evil (Good Truth becomes rich and Bad Truth perishes at the hands of the vixen and her animal companions). Lüthi describes the hero of many European fairytales as a man who becomes an isolated wanderer and is delivered from an inauthentic existence, achieving complete self-realization.[6] Good Truth, of course, is an isolated wanderer when blinded and left in the wilderness. He is delivered from his miserable condition and achieves his self-realization by curing the princess of her muteness and the king of his blindness. Like many heroes in European folk- and fairytales, Good Truth becomes wealthy, and wealth, according to Lüthi, represents the achievement of inward and cosmic perfection.[7]

The contemporary Spanish oral versions of "The Two Travelers" have the same linear plot featuring characters who represent extreme moral opposites in a world of moral absolutes where the good triumph and the bad perish. The principal protagonists are two brothers in the stories Luis Cortés Vázquez heard from Beatriz Mancebo in La Alberca in Salamanca[8] and in those I heard from Leandro Jiménez in El Guijo de Santa Bárbara in Cáceres. In Beatriz' tale, one is rich and the other is poor, and the rich brother is morally inferior because he is greedy. In Leandro's version, one brother believes in the church, and the other is a disbeliever who is greedy besides. Leandro's story is the first folktale I collected in Spain that is cognate with a story I heard from Nacho many years earlier.

"The Two Travelers"
by Leandro Jiménez

Once there were two brothers who were muleteers. One of them went with the beasts of burden, the mules. The other believed in the church and announced, "I'm going to mass."

He didn't go with his brother, who took the mules.

"Nothing is lost," says the one who goes to mass.

The one who went to mass didn't know where his brother had gone and he had no animals to ride. When night came, he climbed a tree because there were many wild beasts in the forest. He climbed up into the tree. Night fell. He heard a big noise. Three birds came and they were three enchanted men. They arrived and spoke as three enchanted birds, and he was up in the tree.

"Good. Let's see how we are going to use the time here. Each one will tell what is happening," says one of the birds.

"Well, I heard about this and I'm going to do it. There is a town where there is no water. And there is a handsome supply of water in the town. And they would give me so much if I were to go and give water to the town! I only have to go and lift up a slab of rock in the middle of the plaza. The water is there, and all the people in the town are dying of thirst."

[After the enchanted men leave, the brother climbs down and goes to the town that does not have any water.] There hadn't been any water anywhere until he arrived.

"Mama, water."

146

Fig. 5. "He heard a big noise. Three birds came
and they were three enchanted men."

They asked for water. He says, "But man, everyone is dying of thirst," he says, "with the water that's in the ground under the town!" He says, "Come, Mr. Mayor, come with me to the central plaza. I know where there is water."

They took some of those bars, which they call around here "turf-breakers," to move and raise the rock off the ground. And, upon raising the stone slab, the town saw a gush of water.

"How much are you going to give me for digging the water out for this town? The people are dying of thirst."

Well, they went and loaded three mules with money.

[The narrator returns to the time of the conversation between the men enchanted as birds.]

The other bird says, "Well now, I know about another one. The king's daughter," he says, "there aren't any doctors who [can] cure her." He adds, "But this is very easy. This one I'll cure myself, but quickly."

[The narrator jumps ahead to the moment when the hero goes to the second town.]

He arrives. Knock, knock.

"Who is it?"

"A foreign doctor."

"Oh, for God's sake, we're full of doctors up to here. There is no one who can cure my daughter."

"I'll cure her myself."

He went into her room.

"Leave me alone, eh. I must go in alone," he says.

And they were wary, but their daughter was sick and so forth. What were they going to do? They were wary.

"Let's see," he says. "Lift yourself up off the pillow."

She lifted herself up, and he grabbed a creature she had underneath—a toad or one of those bad things. And he grabbed it and he threw it, and, at once, the king's daughter asked for clothes so she could get up.

"That doctor has made her well."

He made her well, but really well. She immediately asked for her clothes so she could get up. Her parents were happy because the foreign doctor threw out the vermin she had underneath her and which carried the disease. Well, they loaded money on another three mules.

[The narrator returns to the point in time when the enchanted birds were talking at the foot of the tree.]

Well then, another says, "Well, I have a house in which the chickpeas don't cook."

And it was the house of a king or the son of a prince, whatever. He says, "And the husband and the wife are always about to quarrel because the chickpeas don't cook." He adds, "I just have to arrive when the stewpot is on the fire. I grab [the cat]. I hit it with a club, and the reason for the quarrel is gone. They're now cooked forever."

[The birds leave, the hero climbs down from the tree, and he goes to the house of the married couple.]

They grab [the chickpeas]. They cook them.

"Oh, what a man, but what a man is he! With those fights we've been having about the chickpeas, the husband and I. And look how they cook!"

Well, they cooked deliciously. The couple loaded coins on another three mules, and he marched home. And the rich one, who had taken the donkeys, had something called a *tamerín*, a quarter or half *fanega* [a grain measure of about 1.5 bushels] to measure the money he brought on the mules. And, of course, he gave his churchgoing brother the half *fanega* to measure the money. He had asked for it at his brother's house and his brother stuck tallow or whatever to it so the money he measured would stick, so it would stick so he might see it. And, of course, the one brother asked the other how he had made his fortune, how he came to have so much money.

"Well, I acquired this fortune after you separated from me. I went to mass and I was up in a tree. And three enchanted men came, and I learned and I came away from there."

"Oh! Brother, I must go to that tree as well! Let's see if those three men will come again."

And it turned out, he climbed the tree that very night. The three birds came again.

"And how did it go?"

"Well, as for me, the town that didn't have any water has it now."

"The king's daughter is well."

"The chickpeas cook."

"Someone was listening to us."

And the brother was there, the rich one, waiting to see if they would speak to each other so he could make another fortune. And they heard he was up in the tree.

"He is the one who heard us."

And they grabbed him. They killed him and destroyed him. His brother returned the *tamerín* to his sister-in-law in his brother's house.

"Isn't it time for him to come, for your brother to come?"

"It depends on whether those birds went there or not."

And after waiting and waiting, they went. He was dead and all cut to pieces. And that's what greed does. He was rich and he wanted to be richer because his brother had become rich. The poor one had won all of that pile of money.

Leandro, like the anonymous author of the medieval tale, begins his story with an extreme contrast; one brother is good and the other is bad. Neither brother changes and, as perhaps one would expect from such an extreme and permanent contrast, one must perish and the other must triumph because good must prevail over evil. Leandro casts his tale in terms of male sibling rivalry, a theme developed by many Cáceres narrators who told several different stories that feature two brothers, one of whom is poor and essentially good and the other is rich and primarily evil because he is greedy and selfish.

Other Cáceres stories with similar depictions of brothers develop in two directions. One is along the lines of "Open Sesame" (Tale Type 676), a folktale that probably originated from European translations of *Thousand and One Nights*.[9] In variants I heard from Julio López Curiel of Garganta, Zacaria Iglesias of Piornal, Mercedes Zamora of Cabezuela, and Julia Lobato Gil of Serradilla, the poor brother discovers a den of thieves into which one can enter by pronouncing a secret password. The hero waits until the thieves depart, enters the den, and returns home a wealthy man. In the variants by Zacaria Iglesias and Mercedes Zamora, the rich and greedy brother tries to retrace the steps of the poor one so he will become even richer; he is trapped in the den and killed by the thieves, angry because they have been robbed. In the story by Julio López Curiel, the poor brother tells the rich one that he obtained his wealth by selling a strap of flesh from his wife's back. His rich and greedy brother, who gave the poor one some meat for his starving children on the condition he take his portion to eat at the Gates of Hell, asks his wife to allow him to remove a strap of her flesh. She readily agrees, and he takes the strap to sell in Madrid. However, he arrives at the king's palace where he is given a caning, he crawls home to find his wife in agony, and both die at the same moment.

The other story line is a variant of "The Table, the Ass, and the Stick" (Tale Type 563),[10] which I heard from Florencia Herrero of Garganta la Olla. Florencia opened her tale with an episode almost identical to the one in her neighbor Julio López Curiel's version of "Open Sesame" (676): a poor brother, with many starving children, asks his rich brother for something to feed his family, and the rich brother gives him meat on the condition he take his portion to the Gates of Hell. However, in Florencia's story, the poor brother stops at the houses of the winds, who tell him how to survive his ordeal: he must knock three times on the door of Hell, throw the meat down, and get out of there. The hero passes the homes of the winds on his return journey and is given a pouch that fills with money and empties on command, a napkin that produces all good things to eat, and a club that beats but does not kill. The club comes in handy to punish thieving innkeepers who steal the pouch and the napkin. The poor brother arrives home a rich man, and his rich brother's wife decides to take some meat herself to the Gates of Hell in the hope of becoming even richer; she is told by the winds that she will find her house in flames when she arrives home.

The lone exception to the pattern of depicting brothers as enemies is Julia Lobato Gil's version of "Open Sesame," in which one brother goes back to the den of thieves and rescues his other brother, despite the envy in their relationship. Julia is an interesting but atypical narrator who represented an unusually close relationship among brothers in several of her stories. As mentioned in Chapter 6, she depicted an unusual amount of brotherly love in her variant of "Blood Brothers" (Tale Type 303).

The more usual pattern of depicting brothers as enemies personifying moral absolutes in stories with linear plots is related to several aspects of village culture in Spain. Many stories about brothers, including the trickster tales featured in Chapter 4, represent brothers as enemies because they violate a strong preference for egalitarianism among men. The brothers have vastly different amounts of wealth, and the rich one is usually evil. Nearly all Spanish folktales about brothers, including "The Two Travelers" (Tale Type 613), "Open Sesame" (Tale Type 676), "The Table, the Ass, and the Stick" (Tale Type 563), and the trickster tales present irreconcilable conflict between brothers because male economic autonomy is the norm. There are no group demands requiring brothers to repress or manage their feelings of sibling rivalry. The death of one of the brothers poetically expresses the autonomy and alienation among men in Spanish village culture.

SPANISH-SPEAKING MEXICO

Spanish speaking Mexicans also tell "The Two Travelers" with a linear plot structure based on similar contrasts between two companions who personify moral opposites. One traveler likewise has qualities ordinarily considered evil: he is rich, envious, just plain bad, an enemy, a false friend, a miserable person, and selfish.[11] Like his Spanish counterpart, he often blinds his companion, leaving him alone in the forest.[12] The good traveler triumphs by foiling the plans of witches and demons, he saves others and becomes rich, and his bad companion perishes when he follows the footsteps of the good one in an effort to become even richer.

Some Spanish-speaking Mexicans, however, have introduced interesting changes to express a different vision of a man's relationship with other men by reducing or eliminating the extreme contrasts found in the European tales. The changes are most dramatic when the Mexican narrators deal with family relationships. An unnamed narrator from Tuxcaculso, Jalisco, focused on interdependence between a father and his son that can take ironic turns during the life course.[13] The father has three sons; two of them work hard and the third is lazy. One day the father sends his sons to cut wood, but the youngest hides; when his father finds him under a fig tree, the son tells his father he is listening to birds who say his father will serve him at the table one day. The father gives him a good caning, the boy leaves home, and he spends the night in a cave where he hears devils tell of one city where people are dying because there is no sun, another where all are dying of thirst, and a third where the king's daughter is dying of a disease no one can cure. The lazy son hears that one can restore sun to the first city by knocking down a pine forest, find water for the second city by looking under a big rock in Bull's Canyon, and cure the king's daughter by removing a blood-sucking toad from under her bed. The lazy son saves the two cities, becomes rich, and cures the king's daughter, whom he takes as his wife. He returns to his father, who does not recognize him, and asks for lodging and something to eat. His father agrees to give him lodging but says he cannot give him anything to eat because he has no food. The boy gives his father the ingredients and asks his parents to prepare him a meal. When his father serves him and they are sitting at the table, the boy reveals his identity and reminds his father what the little birds told him under the fig tree. The father, who needs his son more than ever, is overjoyed to see the son returned home.

The emphasis on the father-son relationship in this variant of "The Two Travelers" is particularly interesting in light of the earlier observation that some Spanish-speaking Mexican narrators restore the lost father in other folktales of Spanish origin like "The Bear's Son" (301).[14] It is unfortunate that Wheeler, who collected "The Bear's Son," "The Two Travelers," and many other stories of Spanish origin from Spanish speakers living in Jalisco, did not report the gender of the narrators.[15] If the narrator was a man, then the Jalisco variant of "The Two Travelers" from Tuxcaculso represents a much less alienated view of a man's relationship with other men than that found in masculine variants of the same story in Spain. If the narrator was a woman, then she, like her Spanish sisters, may represent the father-son relationship in accord with her own strong filial loyalties.

NATIVE MEXICAN VARIANTS

Some native Mexicans tell "The Two Travelers" with linear plots based on extreme contrasts between a good and a bad companion, but others depart in interesting and different ways from the Spanish models in the medieval *Libro de los gatos* and contemporary Salamanca and Cáceres oral tradition. I know of at least five variants told by different native Mexicans: a Tepecano man (Felipe Aguilar), a Zapotec woman (Isidora), a Nahuatl-speaking man from Matlapa in San Luis Potosí,[16] and the Nahuat Mariano Isidro from Santiago Yaonáhuac and Nacho from Huitzilan de Serdán. The story by the Tepecano Felipe Aguilar most closely resembles the linear plots of the Spanish stories: one brother is poor and the other is rich and envious; the rich brother perishes as he retraces the steps of his poor brother in an effort to become even richer because devils (*chamucos*) beat him so severely he dies from magical fright.[17]

Other native Mexicans depart from the Spanish model in different ways. Isidora, the Zapotec narrator from Mitla in Oaxaca, focused on the animal-human relationship in a story that combined elements from "The Two Travelers" with another folktale known as "The Claw in Split Tree" (AT 38).[18] Isidora told her story from the perspective of a lioness and her cub-son to make the point that humans are bad to animals. By taking the point of view of the lioness and her cub-son, Isidora expressed her identification with animals.

In her tale, the cub asks his mother to tell him a story as they are walking along, and the lioness tells of a town where the people are suffering from thirst but where one can find water by touching a large rock. The cub asks his mother why they do not recover the water for the town, and the lioness explains they cannot approach the town because humans fear them. A woodcutter overhears the lioness's tale and recovers the water supply of the town, earning a fine reward for his efforts. Meanwhile, the cub is curious about humans; disobeying his mother, who tells him men will kill him, he sets out into the wood to find one. He meets a donkey, who declares he is not a man but suffers at the hands of one. He comes upon a bull, who says he is not a man but is dominated by one. He finally meets a woodcutter and declares he is going to eat him for man's cruelty to animals. The woodcutter asks the cub to help him cut wood and tricks him into putting his paw into a crack in a piece of wood, which closes when the woodcutter removes his ax. The cub, in great pain, pleads for the woodcutter's pardon and returns to his mother. He meets the woodcutter again but turns down his invitation to help him cut wood. When the cub asks his mother for a drink of water, she tells him not to drink any water lest he become bad like man.

Stith Thompson observed that, from a European point of view, there is "confusion between men and animals" in many Native American folktales.[19] However, native Mexican narrators actually express a more interconnected view of humans and animals, as is evident in several Nahuat stories considered earlier. In Nacho's "Bear's Son" (Tale Type 301), Nānāhuatzin, or Nāhuēhueht, is the captain of the rain gods, who appear as lightning bolts, serpents, and humans. The multiple and shape-changing form of the rain gods is based on the belief that all humans have animal companions (tōnalmeh) whose fate is linked directly to their human counterparts. Ramírez Manzano's fisherman in "Blood Brothers" (Tale Type 303) discovered the connection between humans and animals when his wife, who was committing adultery, fed fish to her lover and made all the fish ill. The interconnected view of the universe is one reason that Nacho and other Nahuat narrators avoided "inconsiderate" or strong words when telling their stories and kept their distance from characters who personify īlihuiz. As will become apparent below, Nacho's concern with inconsiderate behavior developed in a family where he and his brothers had an unusually cohesive, interdependent relationship.

NAHUA VARIANTS

Nacho is among several Nahua-speaking narrators who departed from the linear Spanish model when telling their versions of "The Two Travelers" (613) by introducing different degrees of communality between brothers. The Nahua variant with the least amount of communality and the greatest resemblance to the Spanish tales is the story by a Nahuatl-speaking man from Matlapa in San Luis Potosí.[20] Two brothers are working on a common milpa, and the older brother is envious of the younger because he has a many-colored bird. The older demands the eyes of the younger in return for some of the tortillas their mother packed for them both. However, the younger succeeds in restoring his sight with the leaves of a miraculous tree in which he spends the night. He hears two devils, who have hidden the water supply of one town and made a princess incurably ill in another. He saves both, with the help of the miraculous multicolored bird, and returns home after being treated like a god. The most obvious departure from the linear Spanish model is the removal of any punishment for the envious brother. The Matlapa narrator implies, but does not specifically state, that the younger brother shares his wealth with everyone in his family.

Mariano Isidro, a Nahuat from Santiago Yaonáhuac, told a version of "The Two Travelers" in which the central protagonists are two orphaned brothers, one of whom is selfish and envious. While Mariano retains the contrast of moral opposites found in the Spanish and some Spanish-speaking Mexican stories, he represents that contrast differently by representing moral inferiority as the refusal to share food and moral superiority as sharing wealth with the members of one's family. In Mariano's tale, the brothers are living with their uncle and aunt and decide to leave home to work in order to live. They enter a wood, and the older tells his younger brother to wait for him while he looks for work. He finds an employer who tells him he has two jobs: one taking care of turkeys and the other caring for pigs. The employer gives him some tortillas, and the older brother returns to his starving younger brother; he refuses to share his tortillas and claims he found only one job. The younger brother is left alone, and, like many heroes in other variants of "The Two Travelers," he climbs a tree to spend the night and hears three devils tell how they will destroy a married couple, a king, and a town—by turning into a cat and shedding fur in the couple's food, by becoming a toad and sucking the blood out of the king, and by hiding the water supply of the town. The hero saves the couple, the king, and the town and returns home a rich man. His now envious older brother climbs the same tree so he can become as rich as his younger brother. However, the devils, angry because someone must have heard their plans, find the older brother in the tree and devour him. The younger brother shares his wealth with his uncle and aunt.

The most developed communal vision appears in Nacho's version of "The Two Travelers," which coincidentally begins with three brothers who live in an extended family. The interpretation following the story focuses on the reasons for the hero's temporary isolation from his brothers and their relationship after recovering the water supply of one town and curing a plague caused by blood-sucking toads in another.

"The Two Travelers"

by Nacho Ángel Hernández

One day there were three brothers. The two older ones worked very hard, and the youngest one did no work at all. Every day the older brothers took their younger brother to work, but he just ate tortillas. Every day he carried the tortillas but did no work. His older brothers were angry. They had wives. They pondered, "What does our brother think he is doing? Our wives give him tortillas, and he doesn't work. He goes with us every day and doesn't work. What do we do now?"

They put their heads together and wondered, "What'll we do with our brother?"

They thought about it, and one asked, "What'll we do? Shall we kill him? Shall we talk to him?"

"Who knows what we're going to do?" replied the other.

"So things will turn out well, we'll take him into the woods. That boy doesn't like planting [tatōcaliz]. He does go hunting [tatocaliz]."

"This is what we're going to do now. Let's go," they say to their brother, the lazy one. "Let's go."

They took tortillas and all their firearms, their guns, and they went. They took their dogs, their guns, and rope, whatever they needed for what they did, and went into the forest and started to go and go.

They went on and on. They left in the morning and had gone far by afternoon. That lazy one, his brothers took him and their tortillas and went on and on and on into the wood. They arrived at a place. His brothers made sure they had gone far; since they were far into the forest by noon, they had gone too far to return home. There wasn't time; it would be dark soon.

"We bring him to this wood," they say to themselves. "It'd be better for a wild beast [tēcuāni] to devour him so no one will be angry with us."

They brought him far. "Now wait for us here. Take this gun, and we'll take the dogs to flush out the animals," they tell him.

"Fine."

Those brothers of his left him and went away. Because they went off just to trick their brother, they left him pretending to circle around, but they didn't circle around and return to where they left him. They went home. That lazy one was waiting for them, but they took a long time. He paid close attention. He saw they didn't arrive.

"What are they doing and why don't they make any noise? The dogs don't make any noise anywhere," he says.

What are his brothers doing?

"The dogs don't make any noise anywhere."

He was figuring there wasn't time to return home because it was getting dark already.

"It's better to stay here because I won't make it back in time," he says.

He climbed up into a beautiful mamey tree to sleep.

"Where shall I go from here? Let the sun come up, and I'll go in the morning. My brothers have gone and haven't come back looking for me," he says.

He climbed the tree, but he didn't sleep that night. "I'm going to sleep here and nothing will scare me. I'll tie myself to the tree with this rope. And where shall I go? I won't make it back home. I won't fall," he says.

It was night, and he heard old men talking as they came. "Surely they could be my brothers. Perhaps I'll call out to them," he says.

He heard the old men talking more. He saw the road. The road passed by the tree he had climbed. It passed right by that tree.

"Maybe my brothers are coming."

The old men came and stood at the tree and started to talk. He listened. The man, the lazy one, realized he felt like relieving himself. And he started to pee down the trunk of the tree. His pee fell on one of the old men, who noticed the water.

"What's this that fell on me?" he asks his companion.

The other one took it into his hand and smelled it.

"That's blessed water from heaven," he replies.

And the lazy one started shitting his shit just then, and it fell down. And it found those men. One of them reached and grabbed it.

"What is this I have here?" he asks.

"Ah, this is blessed bread from heaven," replies the other.

"Yes."

Those old men started talking. That man listened from above.

"Fine, and you, what are you going to do to lose them?" one of the old men asks the other.

"For my part, I am not seeing it as difficult. I'm going to lose them with thirst. And I'm going to bury the water under the middle of the town. The water will go in there, and they won't see it to find it, and there will be just one sign. Every day at about ten o'clock, an eagle will come and show where the water is. But the town won't realize. Yes, that's the way I'm figuring it won't be hard to finish them," he explains.

"Well fine," says the other.

"And you? Who are the ones you are going to lose?" asks the first.

"I'm going to lose them with this plan. I'm seeing that it won't be hard to finish them off. I'm going to finish them with toads. I'm going to bury a toad one meter deep under each of their heads. With that, even though there is a doctor, no matter what the doctor does, he can't cure them," he explains.

"Ah yes."

"Yes, it'll be that way for me. I'm considering that plan."

"Well, that's fine."

That's the way they talked.

"Yes, I think I can do it this way."

"That's fine. We'll talk again. We must go. The meat screams early [The rooster crows early]."

Those old men heard the rooster crow and said good-bye to each other. They left. The boy heard them from above.

"Now I heard what they are planning. Let the sun rise, and I'll pass by my house and go see them where they're perishing. I want to be sure to cure them where they'll be dying," he resolves.

The sun rose, and that boy climbed down and arrived home.

"Those brothers of mine?" he asks his sisters-in-law.

"They went to work."

"Well, that's fine. Thanks. They abandoned me in the forest so a wild beast would devour me. But it didn't devour me. I helped myself. Now it's better for me to go without consideration for my brothers. Give me some tortillas. Surely you'll share some with me and let me take to the road."

Those women gave him tortillas with great pleasure. Yes, half a bag full. They had a big gourd jug [tīcomat]. He took the gourd jug.

"Now I'm heading to where they're going to die. I helped myself where my honored brothers abandoned me. It's really better for me to go."

That lazy one left. So it was he went on and on. He took his tortillas and that gourd jug and went on and on. He went asking where they are perishing with thirst. He went on and on until he had gone far. He went on and met a man, a muleteer, who asks him, "Where are you going?"

"I'm going to walk over to that town."

"What are you going to get?"

"Nothing. I'm just going there," he replies.

"Well, don't go."

"Why?"

"Don't go because what are you going to get from way over there? They're dying of thirst way over there."

"Where?"

"There," explains the muleteer. "Stay away."

"No. That's where I'm going."

"I'm telling you, don't go because that's where there's thirst. There's no water. Don't go."

"Yes."

"Well, there isn't any more water way over there. There isn't any. There's still water but only over here. But there's no water way over there," adds the muleteer.

"Good. Thanks," replies the lazy one. "I'm going to get some water."

And he resolved to take his jug where the muleteer told him there was water. He filled his jug and went on.

"I tell you not to go there because of the thirst. There isn't any water. Don't go."

"Yes."

"Well, there isn't any water over there anymore. There isn't any. There is just some water over here. There isn't any water way over there," insists the muleteer.

"Good. Thanks. I'm going to get the water out."

He resolved to take his jug to where the muleteer told him there was water. He took his jug and filled it and went on. He arrived at the town. He arrived there asking, "What is going on here?"

"What! We're being crushed with thirst. There isn't any water. Everything is dried up."

"Yes. And don't you know where the water is?"

"Don't we know? Well, there isn't any! I don't know where it is."

"But it's here. You must look for it."

"Not true. Where will you get it? Do you know where it is? It's no more because it dried up. And there is water somewhere? There isn't any anywhere."

"But there is water even though it isn't found."

"Not true. Where will you get it?"

"It's true. Look for it. I'll look for where it is."

"Not true."

"Yes. Get a lot of townspeople together, and we'll look for it. Doesn't a sign appear?"

"Well, yes."

"Haven't you seen a bird come over there?"

"Sure."

"About what time does it come?"

"It comes sometime around ten o'clock."

"Good. Now we'll wait for it."

The townsperson resolved to take him to the authority and consult with him.

"This man came saying he found the water."

"You're not telling the truth," the official says. "Where will you get it? It's not true. Someday you'll give us water?"

"Yes. The water is found."

"That's not true."

The official didn't believe him.

"Yes, it is. Help me. Get the men together."

The town president collected the men.

"Now tomorrow, we'll wait for that bird to come."

The next day, the entire town gathered and waited for that bird. And the bird appeared, it landed, and the lazy one asks, "Is that the bird which comes over and over again?"

"Yes, yes."

"Well, right now we're going to watch it."

He watched that bird land and grab at something it stood over. It was on top, looking where the water was. That man went over to stand in that spot; he checked out where they could dig for water. He stood for a long time.

"Now here! Get up! Dig here!"

The men started to dig. They dug and dug, and their faces paid close attention.

"It's not true," someone says. "It doesn't appear. It isn't so."

"Dig, dig, because you'll find it."

And so they dug and dug. They went down deep and found the water. That water exploded. But water! A lot of water started coming out; it flooded half of the town. Yes, there, yes, the water began, but there was a lot of it.

"Now are you pleased?"

"Yes. You tell us the truth. Now who knows what to do? How much did you earn?" asks the president.

"I don't know. I don't know how much you'll pay me. Think it over with your town. Who knows what to do?"

"The gift will have to be a big one because, if it weren't for this man, everything would have ended."

They started to collect the money. The president started collecting it. They told him, they say, there were thirty beasts of burden. They told him, sixty sacks of money. And after collecting the sixty sacks of money and the thirty beasts of burden along with the muleteers, three of them, the president says, "Here is your payment."

"Lock it up over there. Put it away for me. I'm going walking again because they are also perishing in another place."

"Good. We'll lock it up over there. Whatever you leave, there it'll be."

That money was put into a house along with the beasts of burden, and the man went on. And so it was he went on and on for a long time. He went on and asked questions.

"Well, what is going on here?"

"What do you know? Here we're dying. Many are being crushed, and there isn't any cure."

"What have they given you?"

"Nothing. An illness begins and there is no cure."

"Yes? And there is nothing?"

"What! They didn't give me anything. No, nothing has been found. Nothing. What do you have to offer?"

"No. It's true. I've come to cure you."

They resolved to gather the people of the town and see the authority.

"A man came who says he'll give us something to cure us."

"Well, if it's true, let him see us because everyone here has not recovered since the illness began."

"Good. Let's go see who is sick."

They resolved to take that man to where the sick were. Well, that man gave orders. He came to where the sick were.

"Dig, dig here under his head. Dig one meter deep."

They started digging one meter and, when they reached a meter, they saw a huge toad. It was full. It was sucking out of that sick man. That's why he wouldn't recover even with what doctors were doing. So the lazy one began walking over to where each one was sick. They started digging where everyone sleeps, even where no one is sick. But everyone had a toad. The toad was finishing them off. And so it was he went around removing the toads. Then they started doing it themselves. They dug where there was a sick person because he had told them what to do. He gave them the cure for the toads. And afterwards the people gathered to go where the authority was.

"And now you must pay this man."

"Yes. How much did you earn?"

"Well, who knows?"

"No. You tell us. We're going to give you however much you want."

"Well, on my way here, I passed by where others were also perishing. They gave me a bit already. They gave me thirty beasts of burden with sixty bags of money."

"No. That's what we'll give you."

They started to collect the money and showed him the money and the thirty beasts of burden.

"Here it is."

"Good."

They handed over those thirty beasts of burden and the three muleteers, and he brought them to where he had passed to cure the others before. He removed everything the first town had given him and loaded on the beasts of burden led by the muleteers, and he came home. He arrived, and his brothers saw him.

"Son of the . . . Our brother!" they say to each other. "Who knows where he went to steal the money he's bringing?"

He brought sixty beasts of burden, all loaded with money, and six muleteers.

"Son of the . . . Let's see how our brother got that money."

Those older brothers started to wonder. Yes, that boy, the one who used to be lazy, started working with the money. He built a house and set up a store, but one so big that three women were selling in it. Afterwards his brothers, who were working, ran into difficulty. They found everything hard.

"Well, let's go see our brother so he might lend us a little money," they resolve. "Do us a favor, brother. We don't have anything. We're in bad straits."

"Yes? How is it you're in such a bad way? You work. I'm the lazy one. I don't have money."

"No. You do have it. Lend it to us."

"Wasn't it so that you abandoned me in the forest for the beasts to devour me? When would you have given me money? It won't be for that reason that I'm going to give it to you."

He gave money, one hundred pesos, to each brother, and they left.

"Work," he says.

But they didn't ever see where they left that money. They just ate it.

"We didn't do anything. What shall we do?"

They couldn't do it anymore. They couldn't work. Everything they had passed into the hands of their brother.

"Who knows what to do?" they wonder. "Will you please do us the favor of lending us money again? We lost it and can't work."

"Ah yes?"

He told them the same thing he had said to them the first time.

"What if you had abandoned me in the forest and the beasts had eaten me? There would be no one to give you money again."

"Yes, now pardon us and give us money. We lost it. Lend it to us."

And he gave each brother about four hundred.

"Well, don't give this money back to me. Don't return it. I'm giving it to you. But work. I'm not lending it to you. I'm giving it to you."

The younger brother was charitable to them because they were abandoned by God. They didn't have anything. He gave his brothers money, and they went. But they did not even see the money again. They spent it. They didn't even see how it ended.

"What shall we do? Our brother works, but we can't. He turned out well since we left him in the forest. He had good luck. What shall we do? We can't anymore."

The story ends here.

The social vision of a man's relationship with other men in Nacho's version of "The Two Travelers" departs from the one represented in the medieval and contemporary oral versions of the same tale told in Spain because Nacho does not represent the three brothers with an extreme contrast based on absolute moral values. To be sure, the two older brothers, who abandon their younger brother in the forest to be eaten by wild beasts, act badly from a Nahuat point of view. However, the younger brother also acts badly by eating the tortillas prepared by their wives and by refusing to work on the family milpa, the yields from which fill the family granary. None of the three brothers is intrinsically bad; none is like Bad Truth or the nonbelieving brother who steals the pack animals in the Spanish stories. Rather, the older brothers act badly because they focus on their productive contribution to the family granary, forgetting to place sufficient emphasis on the sharing of the fruits of communal labor in their fraternally extended family household. Nacho's exact words represent how focusing narrowly on one's own particular interest ultimately results in the destruction of an extended family. When describing the hero leaving home, Nacho uses the word īlihuiz in the hero's speech to his sisters-in-law in which he explains how he intends to go away because his brothers abandoned him in the forest:

"Āxcān," quitquiliā, "mejor nyo īlihuiz."
"Now," he says to them, "it's better for me to go without consideration [for my brothers]."

The adverb īlihuiz refers to behavior disruptive to an ordered structure, in this case a fraternally extended family, and consequently is "inconsiderate" of the people who make up that structure. It is clear in Nacho's story that the hero's inconsiderate behavior is the consequence of a chain of events he helped to put into motion himself by refusing to work on the family milpa. In this respect, Nacho's story of "The Two Travelers" is like many tales I heard from Nacho and other narrators in Huitzuilan who described one character setting into motion a long chain of disorderly behaviors involving other characters.

That disorderly behavior should arise among male siblings is not surprising to many Nahuat I knew, who frequently blamed the breakup of patrilineally extended family households on poor working and sharing arrangements among brothers. Very few Nahuat in Huitzilan live in fraternally extended family households like the one Nacho described in his story because, as many in his community explained, brothers quarrel over the productive contribution of individual members and are similarly unable to keep in mind the advantages of sharing the fruits of community labor in their family.[21] Nacho makes clear what those advantages are when he described the youngest brother's return from saving one town from thirst and the other from the plague. The older brothers are no longer able to work effectively, and they need the wealth of their younger brother to survive. Nacho presented, in the poetic language of his story, the most compelling reason for living in an extended family household where members contribute their labor to fill a common granary and purse from which each can draw according to need, regardless of their individual contribution to the contents. The reason simply stated is that one's productivity may vary because of sickness, accident, or bad luck. Many imponderables also affect agricultural production: pests, the weather, one's energy and will to work on the milpa, unforeseen demands on one's time (which get in the way of performing milpa tasks according to an optimum schedule), and the ability to find productive land on which to grow crops.

Nacho's story plays with the reality and the perception of life in an extended family household. The reality is that labor produces variable results, and the perception is that one may actually produce more to fill the family granary and purse than one draws out. However, a close examination of the details of Nacho's story reveals that the older brothers are too self-centered and fail to consider that, although their younger brother eats tortillas and does no work, they have wives and presumably children who also consume the granary's contents. Women most assuredly do contribute substantially to the contents of a granary and purse by earning wages from cutting coffee, cooking for sugarcane processing groups, harvesting milpa crops and transporting them from the field to the home with a tumpline, husking corn, marketing produce in local and neighboring markets, weaving cloth on the backstrap loom, curing disease, and serving as midwives. However, the Nahuat I knew expressed the view that the economy of a household improves substantially with an increase in the number of

men able to work in milpa agriculture and earn wages on the estates
of Spanish-speaking Mexicans in Huitzilan, neighboring communities, and the coastal plain. So a listener sharing such a perception
could easily conclude that the contents of the family granary depend
more on the productive labor of the brothers and not on all family
members, including the brothers' wives. One reason for such a conclusion is that women spend a lot of their time on tasks related to food
processing and child care: fetching water from springs, boiling husked
corn with lime to make *nixtamal*, grinding the *nixtamal* on the *me-
tate* to make tortilla dough, preparing bean soups and sauces, feeding
and caring for domesticated animals (pigs, turkeys, and chickens), and
caring for young children. An examination of birth and death records
for a thirty-year period in Huitzilan revealed that women give birth
approximately every twenty-four months and often have very young
children under their care during all their reproductive years. The
value placed on male labor is one of the reasons that some Nahuat
express a desire to have sons, although they love their daughters, and
they strongly encourage their married sons to remain members of the
same household. Of course, women, who clearly value their sons, also
express tremendous loss when their daughters leave home to live with
their husband's family. Women express anger toward their future son-
in-law and his family during the betrothal ritual when the intermediary (cihuātanqueh) invites the future bride to dance with her husband-
to-be so they can embrace in front of the bride's family altar while
surrounded in a web of incense.

Because of a desired cooperative relationship among brothers, Nacho ended his story differently than the Spanish and Spanish-speaking
Mexican storytellers, who brought their "Two Travelers" to a conclusion with the death of the bad brother. The bad brother's death fits the
norm of male autonomy and expresses Christian dualism, where God
is the personification of all that is good and is counterposed with the
devil, who represents all that is bad.[22]

Nacho and other Nahuat in Huitzilan are well aware of Christian
dualism, which they see enacted during their patron saint celebration in August when the St. Michael dancers repeatedly slay the
devil, represented as a Chichimeco.[23] They have also heard the vision
expressed in many folktales in which the devil is personified as a
Spanish-speaking Mexican (coyōt). However, dualism based on extreme moral contrasts between male characters appears primarily in
folktales from Nacho's community in which narrators are representing inter-ethnic relations rather than relations among Nahuat. The
brothers in Nacho's version of "The Two Travelers" are like the mem-

bers of Nacho's own family; at the time he told me the story, he lived in a fraternally extended family with his older married brothers Nicolás and Miguel. Nacho was the youngest brother and frankly admitted that he did not like to work in the milpa and ate tortillas made by his mother and sisters-in-law.

Linear plots based on an extreme moral contrast are comparatively rare in all of Nacho's stories about characters who are Nahuat rather than Spanish-speaking Mexicans. Nacho did not incorporate other related Christian themes into his stories. His version of "The Bear's Son" (301) did not include the idea of Christian redemption found in Spanish and some Spanish-speaking Mexican variants of the same tale. Christian redemption, of course, depends on a system of moral absolutes because redemption means being saved from a state of sinfulness. With respect to Nacho's telling of "The Two Travelers," no brother is permanently and intrinsically so bad that he must perish, so the older brothers do not retrace their younger brother's steps by climbing the tree in the wilderness and dying a terrible death at the hands of the demons.

Instead, Nacho ended his story with brothers working through their relationships. The older brothers recognize they can no longer work and ask their younger brother for money; their younger brother reminds them of their unwillingness to give him money and tells them that he would not be around to help them if a wild beast had eaten him in the forest; the older brothers ask for his pardon; and he decides to give rather than lend them money. Nacho used the verb quīnicnēliāya, based on (i)cnēliā, which has a variety of meanings—to look after someone's welfare, to do a favor for someone, to be charitable to someone[24]—and conveys the sentiment that should prevail in an extended family household where the emphasis is on the sharing of the fruits of community labor rather than on the productivity of individual labor.

The personal stamp of Nacho's story becomes particularly evident after examining all other known variants of "The Two Travelers" told by Spaniards, Spanish speakers, and native Mexican narrators. Relative to others, Nacho represents a more communalistic vision of brotherly relations. To be sure, communality is not entirely absent in other similar tales; a wayward and coincidentally lazy son shares food with his grateful father in a story by the unknown Spanish-speaking Mexican narrator in Jalisco.[25] A younger brother may share his wealth with his older brother, who blinded him in the tale by the Nahuatl-speaking man in Matlapa.[26] And a nephew takes his money to his aunt and uncle in the narrative by Mariano Isidro in Yaonáhuac. Only Nacho, however, actually described the brothers working through their past wrongs and told how the younger brother gives money to his older brothers because they are abandoned by God. If one takes "The Two Travelers" together with his "John the Bear," it is possible to see a consistent social vision in which a man is connected to other men who are peers or brothers.

NACHO'S FAMILY

Nacho's particular vision of a man's connected relationship with brothers in "The Two Travelers" accords with the unusually stable communal organization of labor among his actual brothers at the time he narrated the story. Then Nacho was an unmarried twenty-four-year-old man who lived with his widowed mother María Gabriela Hernández (age sixty-five), his older married brothers Miguel (age thirty-nine) and Nicolás (age thirty-five), their wives and children, his widowed maternal cousin María Josefa Santiago (age thirty-two), and her son Edmundo (age fourteen). Nacho's father had died about fifteen years earlier, just after Miguel's marriage to his wife María Agustina Ayance (age thirty-five). Altogether, there were eighteen adults and children sharing a common granary and purse and living in three rooms in two neighboring houses separated by a narrow passage. María Gabriela Hernández, Nacho's mother, had inherited the house site from her father and consequently lived in a neighborhood where she had many close family members.

The household economy was partially based on the labor Nacho and his brothers performed on two small plots of land, acquired from Nacho's father; at the time, Nacho and his two brothers had not yet divided the land into three separate parcels. The three brothers used one plot for growing corn and coffee trees and the other for growing chilies. They also grew corn and beans on land rented in the neighboring *municipio* of Zapotitlán. The oldest brother, Miguel, made the rental contract with the landowner, and all three brothers, together with Miguel's and Nicolás's older sons, pooled their labor to grow corn and beans to fill the common granary. Miguel's and Nicolás's wives contributed their labor by helping to harvest the corn and transport it to the house site. No member of the household earned a wage for working on the family estate, but the brothers made contracts with other workers who helped plant or harvest the corn crop. On some occasions, the brothers paid the workers a wage and on others they entered into labor-sharing agreements whereby they contributed an equal number of man-days to help the workers who helped them.

The household granary was not a single structure but consisted of recently harvested corn placed behind the household altar table and dried corn normally placed in an attic. The women of the household drew from the granary to prepare meals for their families according to need and without paying for what they used. The money in the household purse primarily came from the sale of coffee beans grown on the family-owned land. Nacho's mother María, like many widows in Huitzilan, held the purse, which she divided to make purchases the brothers were unable to make with the money they earned working as wage laborers in the neighboring town of Zapotitlán. When I met Nacho, Miguel and his brother Nicolás regularly worked for a wage in Zapotitlán for about two weeks a year. Miguel and Nacho had worked farther away from home as migrant wage laborers; twelve or thirteen years earlier, Miguel had made a couple of trips to find work in the lowland communities of Huehuetla and Limas, and four years earlier Nacho had made a trip to Martínez de la Torre, a frequent point of destination on the coastal plain for many migrant workers from the communities in the northern Sierra de Puebla.

The members of the family had some independent sources of income: María Agustina Ayance (Miguel's wife) had recently inherited a plot of land that she rented out, and the rent income was not placed in the family purse. With the first year's rent, Miguel bought a pig to fatten and sell, and Nacho said that Miguel and María Agustina Ayance would be entitled to keep the money even though the pig was fed from the family granary. Miguel and María Agustina had some turkeys, and Nicolás and María Gabriela Sánchez had some hens, and each couple was entitled, according to Nacho, to keep the money from the sale of the birds or their eggs, even though the turkeys and hens ate granary corn. María Gabriela Hernández, Nacho's mother, had other hens that she used to feed all the members of her household.

The organization of work changed in Nacho's extended family household, and the changes become particularly apparent if one understands how the family altered their houses as well as their activities. The houses occupied by Nacho's family were constructed with a frame of timbers supporting plank walls and a roof of thatch (*zacate*) or corrugated tar paper. The houses had attics consisting of planks placed on top of the square or rectangular house frame, creating a storage space under the roof. Nacho's family lived in several houses on the same house site, and most had one room where family members slept and ate. The kitchen hearth was a hole in the ground lined by an earthen pot and surrounded by three stones that supported clay cooking pots for boiling beans and a comāl for heating tortillas. Kitchen implements consisted of a metal bucket for boiling corn with lime, a metat and metlapīl for grinding the boiled corn to make tortillas, a mortar and pestle (chīltecaxit) for making chili sauces, clay pots of various sizes for cooking, clay cups and bowls for eating meals, a large clay jar for storing water, and a smaller clay jar for fetching water from springs. Tools, usually a machete and a wooden frame (huahcal) for carrying heavy loads with a tumpline, hung on the walls. The houses had altars consisting of tables with images of saints decorated with arches of flowers and candles. Altar tables had drawers where the family stored money and other valuables. Reed mats were spread out on the floor for sleeping at night and were rolled up during the day. Furniture consisted of small tables, low benches, and a few chairs.

Wood rots quickly in the humid climate of Huitzilan, so the brothers had rebuilt the original family dwelling and added other structures to create their three rooms.[27] Miguel's wife (María Agustina Ayance) and Nicolás's wife (María Gabriela Sánchez) eventually decided to split their kitchens and work over different hearths. Miguel's wife and mother worked over one hearth, and Nicolás's wife worked over the other. The change in the organization of women's work meant that María Agustina and María Gabriela now fetched their own water and purchased any provisions not available in the household granary or produced by their mother-in-law's hens. The women washed their own, their husband's, and their children's clothes, as they had done before the separation of the kitchens. María Gabriela Hernández and her granddaughter, Manuela Ángel Ayance (Miguel and María Agustina's oldest daughter), prepared Nacho's meals and washed his clothes when I first knew the family. The members of this large and complex household eventually created two altars out of the single family altar, placing one in the quarters now occupied by Nicolás, his wife María Gabriela Sánchez, and their children and the other in the room now used by Nacho, his mother, Miguel, his wife, and their children. The granaries changed their locations during the alterations in the physical dwellings. Recently harvested corn was once placed behind the altar and dried corn in the attic of the room occupied by Nicolás and his family. When the corn ran out, Nicolás pushed his altar flush to the wall, and the brothers placed the next harvest of corn behind the second altar, where Nacho, his mother, and other members of the household now slept.

Nacho had a very clear idea of the organization of work that de-

Fig. 6. A Nahuat kitchen.

fined a person's membership in a household when he explained how work relations changed when Matiana Hernández (Nacho's mother's sister's daughter) and her husband (Mariano Gregorio) left this large family to establish their own independent household a year and a half before I arrived in Huitzilan. Matiana and Mariano's separation involved a physical move and a change in the organization of their labor. The couple moved to a small dwelling on the same house site—about twenty meters from the other houses. Matiana and Mariano changed their working relations with the rest of the household because Mariano no longer pooled his labor with Miguel, Nicolás, and Nacho, and the couple lost their right to take corn out of the granaries and use any of the money from the sale of coffee on the extended family's orchards. Mariano started earning a wage, paid in money or in corn, when he worked on Nacho's family estate. He continued to grow corn on land that Miguel rented in Zapotitlán, but after the separation, he had to pay a portion of the rent to Miguel for the land he used to grow corn and beans to fill his own granary. Mariano continued to help the three brothers plant their corn on the rest of the rented plot, but now he earned a wage for his labor. Before the separation, Mariano had the obligation to contribute his labor to the rented corn plot without expecting any compensation, and Matiana could draw from the family granary and purse according to need and availability.

Nacho married Victoria Bonilla in 1971 and moved to a house owned by his father-in-law; then he built his own house on a plot of land he bought in the center of town. Nacho's departure from the extended family household altered the organization of labor to such a degree that Miguel and Nicolás decided to form their own independent households. Clearly, Nacho's contribution of labor was one of the reasons that Miguel and Nicolás continued to pool their labor for so many years after their marriages. A second and equally important reason was their mother's skillful handling of family relations. María Gabriela Hernández was a very intelligent and thoughtful woman who helped maintain good relations among her three sons long after the death of her husband.

SUMMARY

The linear plot of Leandro Jiménez' "The Two Travelers," based on a contrast between moral absolutes, does not fit the multiple, overlapping, cooperative working relationships in Nacho's extended family household. Nacho, Nicolás, Miguel, their mother, their wives, and their children labored together in many ways to produce food, cook the meals, wash the clothes, care for children, and reach many decisions about how best to make purchases with the money in the family purse. Their interdependence is one reason Nacho used words carefully and kept his distance from characters who personified īlihuiz. The plot of his "Two Travelers" has undergone many transformations from the Spanish original to represent a relational view of a man's connection with his brothers.

Florencio, who has temporarily disappeared in this chapter because he did not tell "The Two Travelers," will now rejoin Nacho in telling their most important cognate story—about man's relationship with woman. Our journey into their poetic imaginations will continue to reveal how they represented gender relations in accord with the other dimensions of their masculine identities.

Chapter 8

FLORENCIO'S "BLANCAFLOR"

FLORENCIO AND NACHO PRESENTED THEIR VIEWS OF MAN'S relationship with woman in their versions of "Blancaflor"—also known among folklorists as "The Girl as Helper in the Hero's Flight" (Tale Type 313C).[1] "Blancaflor" is an extraordinarily complex folktale whose heroine comes from a supernatural realm. Florencio's and Nacho's heroine is the devil's daughter, who meets her husband when he makes a long and difficult journey to the underworld to repay a debt. She uses her supernatural power to help her husband complete impossible tasks, flee from the underworld, return to his home, and recover his memory of her just as he is about to marry another woman.

This complicated story is the subject of different interpretations, depending on one's perspective and the degree to which one takes into consideration the social and cultural context. Barbara Fass Leavy seeks universal patterns in gender relations by employing a method of folktale interpretation in which she uses stories from one culture to complete the meaning of those from another.[2] Leavy believes that "Blancaflor" (Tale Type 313C), as well as stories folklorists call "The Man on a Quest for His Lost Wife" or "The Swan Maiden" (AT 400),[3] depict the universal predicament of woman in her relationship with man. Woman in both stories is an outsider whose marriage requires her intimate involvement in a world not her own. Leavy observes that the two stories are told in many parts of the world and, when taken together, represent woman's dealings with man, who is both passive and active or aggressive. The male protagonist in "Blancaflor" is passive, clinging to woman as wife as he depends on the heroine so he can perform incredible tasks, flee from the underworld, and return to his own realm. The hero in "The Man on a Quest for His Lost Wife" is active, bringing woman back to the patriarchal order from the supernatural realm to which she has fled to escape domestic toil. Leavy traces the passive and active behavior of man vis-à-vis woman to man's universal, early childhood dependence on woman as mother.[4]

A search for universals in gender relations can easily overlook how storytellers build their particular variants of popular folktales out of linguistic and cultural materials. This and the following chapters examine how Florencio and Nacho used their words and images to construct "Blancaflor" differently. At some level of meaning for both men, the heroine and the man who becomes her husband may indeed represent the psychologically universal experience of man's dependence on woman as mother and wife. However, Florencio created his Blancaflor according to his comparatively disconnected vision of a man's relationship with other men, which makes man especially dependent on woman. He consequently depicted gender relations with a higher level of ambivalence and represented Blancaflor with a great deal of contradiction.

FLORENCIO'S STORY

Florencio is among at least sixteen storytellers, living in different Spanish provinces, who have told "Blancaflor" (Tale Types 313A and 313C) to folklorists or anthropologists.[5] Luis Cortés Vázquez considers this story the most popular and best-known folktale in western Spain,[6] although it is told all over Europe and has considerable antiquity because it shares many story elements with the ancient Greek tragedy of Jason and Medea.[7]

Florencio's story is a model for how courtship and marriage can work in a culture in which men depend heavily on women for emotional support in a marriage. The hero makes a long journey to find the heroine, much as a young man must travel a long road to maturity before he is ready to court and marry a woman. The hero runs up against the heroine's father, who demands that his future son-in-law perform many impossible tasks, just as a father has high expectations of the man who courts and wishes to marry his daughter. The tasks, which are the most developed part of Florencio's particular story, stand for the accumulation of property necessary to set up a new household and the proof of competence that a man must demonstrate to a maiden's family to win their approval. The hero performs the tasks with the essential help of the heroine, illustrating how a man depends on a woman.[8] The heroine's father acts with ambivalence because he is an intermediary as well as an obstacle to his daughter's marriage. On the one hand, he sends the hero to perform a task that symbolically represents the defloration of his daughter, setting the stage for their marriage. On the other, he attempts to kill his daughter and her husband the day after their wedding. Blancaflor consequently flees with the hero, just as a young married woman must separate from her parents and live with her husband, transferring her loyalties and affections from her parents to her spouse. A husband has his own conflict in family loyalties, and the hero temporarily forgets about Blancaflor when embraced by a member of his family. The heroine must unlock his memory to restore their marriage, just as in the gender division of labor a woman is given the task of maintaining the marital tie. The story ends happily, testifying to the faith in the conjugal bond and the power of a woman's love in Cáceres Spanish culture.[9]

Typical of his tendency to identify closely with central characters, Florencio renamed his heroine Ursula after the Swedish actress Ursula Andress, whom he greatly admired. He told his story of Ursula with his assertive style sprinkled liberally with now familiar scatological and blasphemous expressions to depict masculine power and its limits in gender relations. A man may use his physical power to establish his position in the male hierarchy, take a woman from a demon, and confront his peers when they steal the same woman from him. He can acquire economic power by making shrewd transactions and rise to the top of a society where all other men are subordinated to him and cannot possibly challenge his manliness. Florencio, nevertheless, illustrated in his "Blancaflor" that man is helplessly dependent on woman and that patriarchal authority is useless in gender relations.

Florencio's model of masculinity in gender relations unfolds in the episodes that Antti Aarne and Stith Thompson identify with conventional titles for convenient reference.[10] The principal episodes are "The Hero Comes into Ogre's Power," "The Ogre's Tasks," "The Flight," and three episodes entitled "The Forgotten Fiancée," "Waking from Magic Forgetfulness," and "The Old Bride Chosen"—which Florencio and Nacho compressed into one that I shall call simply "The Forgotten Fiancée."

"Blancaflor"
by Florencio Ramos

Well, once there was a fisherman and his name was Pedro. He went fishing and, after Pedro finished his catch, a fish appeared.

"Pedro, don't kill me," pleads the fish.

So Pedro lets it go. He goes home and tells his wife what has happened, "I shit on ten! What happened to me today!"

"What happened?" his wife asks.

"After I finished my load—I shit on ten!—a fish appeared, and it was a huge fish. It spoke to me as I was going to lay my hands on it, 'Pedro, don't kill me.' I felt sorry for it and let it go," Pedro says.

"You did well if you had finished your catch. But if you don't have any luck some other day, you don't have enough of a catch, grab it and that'll be that," replies his wife.

Well, it turns out the fish appears again the following week. The fish appears as Pedro is on his way home. It's a big fish, a beauty. He reaches out with his arm.

"Pedro, don't kill me," pleads the fish.

"Look, my wife told me the other day I should kill you if you appear again. And I've had bad luck today because I'm not bringing anything worth my while for my catch. So today I have to kill you," Pedro insists.

"Well look, I'm going to ask you a favor. The first thing that greets you at home will have to go with me in a year," says the fish.

"Man, it's a deal," agrees Pedro.

His boy's dog nearly always jumps up to meet him. "I'll give him the dog at the end of the year and that'll be that," Pedro concludes.

Pedro catches the fish. He puts it in his boat and heads for home. But as he comes home, his little boy appears. The boy's name is Joaquín. I shit on ten! He's a lad eight or nine years old, maybe ten.

"Father, this and that."

I shit on ten! His father is very sad. He doesn't say anything to his son. Nothing. He comes home and empties out the fish. The father gets sick; no one knows what ails him.

"What's wrong with you, Pedro?" they ask.

"Nothing," Pedro replies.

"I shit on ten! It's like he's upset."

Of course, the father knows about what has happened.

"Look, Joaquín, this is what happened to me. A fish told me you have to go with him at the end of the year. I don't know why, but it's bound to be for nothing good," Pedro tells his son.

"Father, don't worry about it. I'll go with whomever," Joaquín replies.

No one is a better lad than he. Now that the father has told his son, the boy takes it well, and so the father quickly begins to recover. The next year—tan!—a man comes.

"Pedro."

"What?"

"I've come so you'll make good on what I told you last year."

"Fine. Joaquín."

"What?"

"Come downstairs. Go with this man."

"Well father, fine," the boy says.

The boy goes away with the man who is the devil. They arrive where the devil has his abode.

"Look, if you're a good servant, if you take orders well, you'll be fine with me, eh," says the devil.

"Well, whatever you say," replies the boy.

The boy is bigger now, he is probably fourteen or so.

"Now you'll see what I'm going to tell you to do. I'll kill you if you don't do it well. Look, these three maidens here are my three daughters. You have to kill one of the three," commands the devil.

"I shit on ten!" says the boy, who then adds, "Nothing, nothing, eh. Whatever you say."

"You have to kill one and you have to chop her up."

"I shit on ten! I shit on ten!"

So they draw lots, and it turns out to be the youngest. Her name is Ursula.

"I shit on ten! I'm not going to kill you," Joaquín tells Ursula.

"Tell him you'll kill me. You kill me," insists the maiden.

"I shit on ten! But I don't have the heart to kill you."

"It's nothing for me. You tell him yes. If you don't, my father will kill you. You say yes. You have to ask him for a guitar and a demijohn. Kill me, chop me up, put me in the demijohn, and throw me into the sea and start playing the guitar—but don't go to sleep. If you fall asleep, I won't come out," instructs the maiden.

Well, the boy does it because the devil says he'll kill him if he doesn't. I shit on ten! The boy does it. He grabs the maiden—I shit on ten!—he kills her. He chops her up. He puts her into a demijohn.

Splash! Into the sea. He begins playing the guitar—triki triki triki triki triki triki. When the maiden in the demijohn is about to come out of the water, Joaquín is almost asleep and is just playing like this—tin tin tin.

"Play," she insists.

I shit on ten! He begins to play. The maiden appears just as beautiful as before, if not more so.

"Look, you lost a drop of my blood when you put me into the demijohn. Look how I have this finger a little shorter than the others," says the maiden.

The maiden tells him about her right hand. That's why women have their little finger smaller than men. They say they have a little finger that's thinner and more beaten up than men's.

["I didn't know that," remarks Florencio's son.]

Well, that's how it is.

"Uh. Very well. You're a great servant," says the devil, who seems delighted, but he really wants to murder the boy.

"Well, nothing. Very well. Very well. That's fine. Look, tomorrow I'm going to give you another task," the devil says.

He goes to the window.

"Come. See that hill? You have to dig up that hill, you have to plant grapevines, and I want to see a bottle of wine on the table when I go eat tomorrow. If not, you know, eh. I'll kill you," orders the devil.

"I shit on ten! And how am I going to clean up the ground, plant the vines, cut the grapes, and make the wine for tomorrow so he'll have wine by midday?" wonders the boy, who goes outside half crying. "Oh my! For God's sake," Joaquín despairs.

"What did he tell you? What did he tell you?" asks the maiden.

"You'll see what he told me. Let's see how I'm going to do it. He said I have to clean that hill and plant it with vines and cut the grapes and make the wine so that tomorrow, when your father goes to eat, he'll have a bottle of wine to drink. He said he'll kill me if he doesn't," Joaquín declares.

"Tell him yes. Don't worry. You tell him yes," instructs the maiden.

So the devil asks him that night, "Well? Have you thought it over?"

"Yes," agrees Joaquín.

"What? You're going to do it?" exclaims the devil.

"Yes man, I'll do it," declares Joaquín.

"Well, nothing. Now I've told you. I want to see the bottle here by midday," demands the devil.

The girl's name is Saint or Ursula. She goes to a little patch of abandoned grapevines and says to Joaquín, "You lie down."

But how can he just lie down? She has a needle case with a number of little devils inside. I shit on ten! Some are digging, others are planting the vines, others are cutting the grapes, and others are making the wine. Before midday—pum!—the bottle of wine is on the table for the devil.

"Good, good. You're a superior servant. Good servant. Well, we've done very well."

The next day, the devil says, "Downstairs in the stable are a she-mule and a he-mule. I want you to go bring two loads of wood that don't have a span of straight pieces, eh. I'll kill you if they have a straight span."

"I shit on ten! Well, whoever brings two loads of wood without some straight pieces?" says Joaquín to himself.

The girl appears and asks, "What did he tell you?"

"Boy! What did he tell me! About the same as yesterday. He said I have to bring two loads of wood with the she-mule and he-mule he has in the stable, and he says there can't be one span of straight pieces. It all has to be crooked. Let's see how!"

"It's nothing. It's done. This is easy. See where you planted the vines yesterday? You still have them. Go there. The little devils will cut two loads of vines for you."

In fact, she sends three little devils. They cut the wood with fury. One takes it upon himself to load up and—tras!—more crooked than the host. Plop! There are the two loads of wood.

"Now here's the wood," Joaquín tells the devil.

"Oh. I've seen it. I shit on ten! Well, you this and that," the devil declares.

The man seems happier than anything.

"Look, tomorrow I'm going to give you another task, eh," says the devil.

"Good," agrees Joaquín.

"Tomorrow you're going to go for two loads of straight pieces that don't have a palm's length of crooked pieces, eh. Straight as a candle," orders the devil.

"I shit on ten!"

The girl asks again, "What did he tell you?"

"What did he tell me! The same as yesterday. Except just the opposite. I have to bring two loads of wood that are straight, that don't have even a span of crooked pieces. As straight as a candle."

"Look, tell him yes. You go to a field of reeds and cut them," explains the maiden.

So in fact—plop!—the two loads of wood.

"I shit on ten! Well, you know you're terrific! I've never seen a servant like you. You're a man of accomplishment and so on and so forth," remarks the devil.

The man seems so happy, but he can't kill him now.

"Look, tomorrow you're going set the mules free because tomorrow is a holiday. You're going to set the mules free in a certain place. Look, when you go there tomorrow, you're going to take these iron shoes. When you came back here at midday, they have to be all broken," the devil commands.

"I shit on ten! I'm to set free the mules, the she-mule and the he-mule. And how am I going to break the shoes?" Joaquín wonders.

"What did he tell you today?" asks the maiden.

"What did he tell me today! Worse than yesterday or the same. I have to take some iron shoes and set free the he-mule and the

she-mule—I don't know what—in a certain place, and when I
come home, the shoes have to be broken. And they're iron shoes!"

"It's very simple. When you go there, the he-mule is going to
pee first. Be careful the he-mule doesn't splatter a drop on the
shoes, eh. They'll get stronger if he splatters on the shoes. The
she-mule is going to pee a little farther on. You be where the she-
mule pees and then scrub the shoes in the she-mule's pee. You'll
see how fast the shoes will break apart," explains the maiden.

Said and done. He leaves with the she-mule and the he-mule for
the place, and, in fact, the he-mule pees some distance from there.
I shit on ten! He makes sure it doesn't splatter even a little. A
little farther on—plum!—the she-mule. I shit on ten! He dis-
mounts because he rides on the she-mule. I shit on ten! And—pin
pan, pin pan—the shoes have some broken places underneath.

"It's done," says Joaquín, who returns.

"How did it go?" asks the devil.

"Fine," says Joaquín.

"And the shoes, how are they?" inquires the devil.

"Look for yourself. See how they're broken," declares Joaquín.

"Fine. It's done," declares the devil. "Look, this afternoon I'm
going to send you on another job. You have to go get those mules,
the she-mule and the he-mule, which are loose. You have to go
get them in the afternoon."

"Fine."

"Look, see this helmet?" adds the devil.

It's like one of those bronze military helmets.

"See this helmet? You take the helmet. When you come back
here, you have to have the helmet broken."

I shit on ten! He knows how to scrub and break the shoes. They
are scrubbed this way. But how will he scrub the helmet?

"What did he tell you?" asks the maiden.

"He has a metal helmet, one of those bronze ones, and he told
me he's going to give it to me. He told me to get the mules in the
afternoon, and I have to bring the helmet all broken when I come
back."

"Tell him yes," says the maiden.

"Fine. I'll look for a way to break it," declares Joaquín.

"It's nothing. He has the broken shoes," adds the maiden.

Joaquín takes the helmet. He goes to the maiden, and she says,
"Look, when you're on your way back here, you put the he-mule
in front and the she-mule in back of the halter. And there is a
little hill in a certain place. The she-mule will fart when climbing
up the hill. Put the helmet like this, and each time she farts, a
hole will appear in the helmet. But don't change the she-mule
around and put the she-mule in front because then the helmet
will get stronger."

"Good. I shit on ten!" says Joaquín, who is careful to put the he-mule in front and the halter on the she-mule. In fact, there is a little bit of a hill. As the she-mule arrives there—bam! again bam!—the helmet—bam!—is broken. Bam! Bam! She has three more farts. Bam! Bam! Bam! Another three holes in the helmet. He comes back. I shit on ten! The damn thing has holes like the sacramental chalice.

"What?" inquires the devil.

"Here is the helmet," says Joaquín.

"Very good, very good. Beautiful servant. Good. Well tomorrow, I'm going to give you another task."

"Good. Whatever you want."

"You look like a good servant. You have to be a superior servant, a dream. I've had various servants, but no one was like you," says the devil.

Joaquín is becoming a young man.

"You must really want a woman just like all men," observes the devil.

"Me? No," says Joaquín.

"How can you not like women!? You have to want one just like everyone else in the world. Now seeing I have three maiden daughters, you're going to marry one of them. The one you want, eh. I won't tell you the crooked one, or the white one, or any other one. The one you want, eh. You have to marry one, but I don't care which one. They're going into a room. Each one will put her hand through a cat hole. You'll marry the one you like the best. You'll marry that one. So you see, I don't care which one you marry," the devil tells him.

"Oh well, fine," agrees Joaquín.

"What did he tell you?" inquires Ursula.

"Oh my! Better than anything so far. He told me I have to marry one of you," explains Joaquín.

"Good. You're going to tell him to give you a few days to let you think about it a little," instructs Ursula.

"What?" asks the devil.

"Well, look, I'll marry one, but I have to think about it a little," says Joaquín.

"Very well. It seems very good to me. Yes, yes, that's how I like men," agrees the devil.

The man is happier, more content, than I don't know what.

"Well now, tomorrow you'll have another job only because you're a useful man. Look, you're going to take a little stroll to-morrow to where there is a batch of fish. You have to fry them tomorrow. We eat fish around here. Tomorrow we're eating some fried fish," commands the devil. "Fine," says Joaquín.

The devil continues, "But look, I'm going to tell you something, eh. There are a lot of cats in my house. Don't lose a single fish, eh. I'll kill you if you're missing a single fish. The cats will want some of the fish, eh."

"Fine," says Joaquín.

"What did he tell you?" asks the maiden.

"Well, nothing. He said I had to fry some fish. It isn't anything," Joaquín declares.

"This is the most dangerous thing," warns the maiden.

"Oh? Well, I don't know why," wonders Joaquín.

"Well, all of us will become the cats. There are five of us in the house. The first one you'll see appear will be a big black cat. It'll have a very fat head. That'll be my father. Then you're going to see a black cat with a little white tie, and that one will be my mother. Then there will be a yellow one, which will be my older sister. The other sister will be the red one. [Like the one we have here daubed with pineapple.] I'm going to be the white one. I'll be the smallest one. You get a pan ready to fry the batch of fish and a bowl with water to wash the fish. Don't throw out the water for washing the fish because it'll smell of fish. When the big cat gets near—it'll be the first one that goes there and it will go creeping toward you. You have to be very careful because he'll snatch the fish from you very quickly. You get the oil very hot. You get a good-size cup of oil ready and, when the oil is very hot and as soon as you see the cat appear—zas!—you throw it on him. Then a little while later it'll be my mother, and you do the same thing. Keep on going. But not as hot for my sisters because the worst ones are the other two. I'll also go see if I can take a fish away from you because I have to go. But you throw the water on me in which you wash the fish so I'll smell like fish. Throw it on me instead of oil. Throw spoonfuls of water from washing the fish and, of course, I'll run out of there. They'll think I was just like them because the water smells of fish."

"Good, well fine," says Joaquín.

He does exactly as the maiden has told him. He puts the fish on to fry. In a little while, meow, meow. A big black cat comes. I shit on ten! He grabs a spoonful of oil. Zas! It flees because he throws oil on it. A little while later the black one with the white necktie appears. Meow, meow. Joaquín grabs the oil. Zas! It flies out of there. Then the other smaller ones come. Also—zas!—he throws a little oil on them too. Those cats also run away. The last one, the white one, also comes. Meow, meow. He grabs the water. Zas! I shit on ten! The other one also flees with a little bit of water. So pum! When the devil goes to eat—plop!—there is the fried fish.

"Well? Are you missing any?" asks the devil.

"No. I don't think so. There were more cats than anything else, and—I shit on ten!—I threw a little oil on them. They all ran out of there lickety-split," Joaquín tells him.

"Very well, very well. Yes, yes, yes. Fine. Right on. Well, tomorrow I'm going to give you another task. This is going to be good for you because I see you're a real man, a brave and useful man. Downstairs in the stable is a colt, a black one. It's wild, of course. At seven o'clock in the morning you have to begin goading it. I'll go downstairs at twelve to mount the colt. It has to let itself be mounted," the devil orders.

"Well, good."

"What did he tell you?" asks the maiden.

"Nothing today. He has a colt, and I have to tame it."

"Today is a very bad day," warns Ursula.

"No, it isn't anything," insists Joaquín.

"Look, the horse will be all of us. The head will be my father. The neck and the front shoulder blades will be my mother. My two sisters will be the ribs. Each rib will be a sister. And I'll be the haunches. If you are a little careless, they'll all eat you in one bite," warns the maiden.

"I shit on the mother! The horse."

The maiden continues, "Look, you strike all the blows on its head, its neck, and on the shoulder blades. But hard, eh. You hit that part of the horse hard. The horse has to pee three times. Don't mount it until it pees three times. It'll kill you if you mount it earlier. Now hit the ribs in back, but not as hard, and hit the haunches too. I'll get a club ready for you so it'll have one thin end and one thick end. Blows to beat the band on the head with the thick end. And also on the neck and on the front shoulder blades too. Then you turn the club around. Take the thick end and hit my sisters with the thin one. And the haunches in back, hit me too, but less because it's me."

"Good, well nothing," says Joaquín.

He goes downstairs. I shit on ten! There is a colt in the stable, a colt more beautiful than the sacramental chalice. He grabs the club. Brum! The animal at first—I shit on ten!—is a wild beast. He grabs the club—I shit on ten!—which is like the handle of a hoe. Bam, bam! A blow to the head. I shit on ten! And on the neck. He strikes it with more blows, he hits it on the head more times than the sacramental chalice. And now the horse pees. Brum! Blows to the head and the neck and the shoulder blades just as the maiden has told him. He hits the ribs some but less. But he strikes blows to the head. They're strong blows, and a little while later it pees again. More blows, more blows. I shit on ten! He strikes it with more blows than the sacramental chalice. In a little while— tan!—it pees again, and he mounts it. The horse goes with its head down like this and doesn't move. It's beaten. He puts it in the stable. He goes upstairs. There is the devil.

"The horse is tamed now," says Joaquín.

"And have you mounted it? Yes, yes. I know it," declares the devil.

The man is all covered with wounds. His entire head is bandaged because of the blows.

"Very good. Now I see you've done a great piece of work. Now we have to celebrate the wedding. Have you thought all about it?" declares the devil.

"Well yes," says Joaquín.

"Nothing. It's done, eh. Now I'll tell you today what I told you the other day. I don't care which one you marry. It must be one of them, but any one. They're going to put their hands through a cat hole, and you say which one you want," the devil declares.

"Well look, I'll show you my hand that has the missing finger. You say, 'That one,'" instructs Ursula.

One shows her hand, and the devil asks, "Do you like this one?"

"No."

Another hand appears, and the devil asks him, "Do you like that one?"

"No."

The other one appears, and the devil asks, "And that one?"

"Yes, this one."

"Huh. She's the most arrogant, the youngest, the most this, the most that."

I shit on ten! Joaquín does the worst thing to the devil he can by picking her. Well, they hold the wedding. They are married. Very well, the maiden and the young man go to bed, of course, and the young man asks, "And what is that on the ceiling?"

It looks like a bomb, like one of those darts with a banderole for baiting the bulls. You know what that is, don't you? One of those very colorful round things.

"What's that?" inquires Joaquín.

"Oh! If you only knew what it is!" declares Ursula.

"But what is it?"

"It's a bomb my father put here to kill us."

"Let's get out of here," says Joaquín.

"Look, go downstairs to the wine cellar, and there are two hides. One has wine, and the other has vinegar. Bring them upstairs," instructs Ursula.

Of course, that's what he does. He goes downstairs, and he puts the two hides in the bed, and the maiden tells him, "Look, go downstairs to the stable. There are two horses. One is thin, but the other one is even thinner. You take the thinnest one. We're getting out of here. If we don't, the bomb will explode and kill us."

He goes downstairs.

"I shit on God! The thin one will fall down by itself. It's better to take the other one, which is a little healthier," says Joaquín.

There are two horses. One is called Wind and the other is Thought, and he takes Wind. The young man takes Wind, the one which is a little fatter, of course, because the other one looks like it won't be good for anything because it's so thin. So then the maiden, she is a woman now, she spits some of her spittle. You know what spittle is, don't you? She spits some of her spittle in the room. Her father is a ways away. Her parents are in bed, and her father calls, "Ursula."

"What, Father?" her spittle replies.

"Ursula," he calls again.

"What, Father?"

Each time, the maiden answers in a softer voice. It is her spittle that answers. Then it begins to dry up. He calls her, "Ursula."

"What, Father?"

He calls her a little while later, "Ursula."

Now she doesn't answer because her spittle has dried up. The devil declares to his wife, "Now they're asleep. It sounds like they're asleep."

I shit on ten! So then the man goes for the bomb. The bomb explodes. Boom! Knives and a hell of a lot of grapeshot fall—Boom!—onto the bed. I shit on God! He comes right away to see. He tastes what he thinks is their blood.

"How sweet is the blood of my daughter! Man, it's delicious," the devil declares.

He tries the other.

"Oh my! How sour! How sour is the blood of my son-in-law!" exclaims the devil.

I shit on ten! The man is happier than the sacramental chalice because he believes he has killed them. Then he uncovers the vermin. I shit on ten! There are two wine bags.

"Come on! What is this? Those two have gotten away from me. I shit on ten!"

He goes downstairs, and his wife says to him, "Go open up the stable. They've taken one of the horses."

He comes back upstairs and says, "It's not so bad. She left me Thought. They took Wind. I shit on ten! I'll catch them with this one."

He mounted Thought. I shit on ten! The others have gone a ways because they've left earlier. But now he goes on the other horse, saying, "Yes I'll catch them, no I won't catch them."

And the maiden says to Joaquín, "I shit on ten! I think that horse coming down there now is my father."

So she grabs a square comb she brings with her and throws it.

Fig. 7. "The bomb explodes. Boom! Knives and a hell of a lot of
grapeshot fall—Boom!—onto the bed."

"May one of those very thick fogs appear in which you can't see your hand in front of your face," she declares.

In fact—bum!—it turns into a thick fog. You know what fog is. It's like smoke but very thick. I shit on ten! Neither the man nor his horse can turn around. And the other horse can't be seen.

"I shit on ten!" he declares.

He goes back. He arrives, and his wife asks, "What? Did you get to them?"

"Huh! You, what do you know? A fog surrounded me in a certain place, and I couldn't see my hand in front of my face. Neither I nor the horse could see. We had to come back."

"It was them. They were nearby," says the devil woman. "You have to go out again and get them."

He goes forth on his horse again. I shit on ten! It's yes he'll catch them, no he won't catch them.

The maiden says, "That horse coming is my father."

"I shit on ten! He's going to catch us," says Joaquín.

"No, I'll turn into a chapel, and you become the monk," says Ursula.

A hermitage is built, and Joaquín is there like a friar or a priest. And the devil comes and asks, "Have you seen a woman and a man mounted on a horse pass by here?"

"What did you say? Well, they're going to ring the bell for mass. If you want to come in to mass . . . ," says Joaquín.

"That is not what I asked you. Have you seen a woman and a man mounted on a horse pass by?" insists the devil.

"This is the last time they're ringing the bell for mass. If you want to come to mass . . . ," replies Joaquín.

"Damn the devil. You'll become a serpent for seven years."

The devil curses his daughter and returns home the next day, and his daughter turns into a serpent.

"Look, my father put a curse on me. I have to complete it. He said I must be a serpent for seven years. You go home to your town. You're going to be there for seven years. But don't forget about me," explains Ursula.

"Oh my! I won't. I won't," insists Joaquín.

The young man is very happy with the maiden.

"But look, I'm going to tell you one thing. Don't let anyone kiss you. You'll forget about me if they kiss you," warns Ursula. "Well, don't worry, no one is going to kiss me," Joaquín insists.

So the lad comes home to his town. Everyone is very happy because the boy has come home.

"Man, Pedro's son is coming, it's Joaquín," declares one.

"Man, well that's who he is," observes another.

"He's come," replies the first.

Joaquín's family is all there, and they go to kiss him, but he says, "No one can kiss me."

The lad doesn't let anyone kiss him. He has gotten married with good intentions. Then his grandmother comes. I shit on ten! She is a woman more than eighty years old. The lad is asleep, lying down, and she comes saying, "Oh my! Son, where have you been? How long it's been since I've seen you!"

She gives her grandson two or three kisses. I shit on ten! Her grandson doesn't remember anything about the serpent. I shit on ten! So he's a big lad. A bride appears for him, or he goes looking for a bride, because he no longer thinks about the serpent. Well, he becomes the fiancé of another one. Now with the passing of one, two, three, or four years, he becomes the fiancé of a maiden in town, and they arrange to get married within a few years. The lad's father is rich, and so is the maiden to whom he's engaged. And so the people, who have money in that town, have the custom of giving some of those little pigs, the little tiny ones, and some goats, the small ones, to whomever they want to raise for butchering in the next year or two for the wedding. And that family also gives some calves, little ones of course. By now the serpent has completed her sentence and she knows which is the lad's town and she goes there. The maiden walks about as if she were begging and says, "I think they're giving away calves. A lad is going to get married. Yes, they're giving cattle away. I'll see if they give me something."

"What? Give you one! You have no way to take care of it!" someone says.

But the maiden insists, "I've come here to see if you'll give me some cattle."

Those fat cats say, "I shit on ten! To her! How are you going to take care of it? How is she going to care for it?"

And they say the same about the worthless ones. You know what the worthless ones are.

"Eh well, that worthless calf over there?"

"The one that no one has wanted. That's the only one we can give the poor thing. This calf is going to die, so if it dies, the poor thing won't cost anyone anything."

"Well, this is the one I want," declares Ursula.

And they give her a little calf that no one wants. It's the worst one of them all. The poor thing walks up and down with the calf. It is always at the poor thing's feet, and the calf starts to prosper. One or two years later they are going to get married, and they collect the cattle from the people and are talking about those worthless ones, "Man, don't you know one is missing? You have to go get it."

"Which one is missing?"

"*Which* one is missing! The one we gave that poor thing last year. Don't you remember? We gave her a calf no one wanted and we gave it to her because it was going to die anyway. But at least someone has to ask her if you should go get it."

"Yes, that's right."

"Well, nothing. One has to go get it."

They go there.

"Eh, we've come for the calf, the one we gave you last year. If it hasn't died on you, of course."

"No. The calf didn't die. The calf is fine. This is it," declares Ursula.

"This! Man, this is the calf!" someone exclaims. One of them puts his hand on it to take it away, and the calf won't get up.

"Grab it by the tail, let's see if it'll get up that way."

"No. Don't bother the animal, because it won't get up if I don't tell it to," declares Ursula.

She speaks to it, "Little calf, little calf, don't forget to walk [*andar*], like your master forgot the serpent in the olive grove [*olivar*]."

The lad Joaquín is there, and she says again, "Get up, little calf, get up, don't forget how to walk, like your master forgot the serpent in the olive grove."

I shit on ten! She says it again, and he answers her, "Serpent of the olive grove, I'm your Joaquín, your husband."

The two of them embrace each other. I shit on ten!

He declares, "This is my wife."

Those other worthless ones say, "But man! I shit on ten! What is this?"

Joaquín and Ursula embrace and divide up the animals for the wedding with the other one in town he was going to marry. He goes for Ursula, for the Saint. Of course, they prepare a huge wedding since they have divided up all the animals. They eat in the style of a marquís. They are very well off. Well, *punto colorado, cuento terminado.*[11]

"THE HERO COMES INTO OGRE'S POWER"

Florencio put his plot into motion by depicting a fisherman acquiescing to his wife's demand that he bring the talking fish home. Acquiescing to his wife's demand ironically sends his son to hell, where he meets Ursula. The image of this fisherman is similar to that in the Cáceres version of "Blood Brothers" (Tale Type 303) told by Florencio's son Bernardo. In both stories, a man acquiesces to his wife's demand, presumably because he depends on her and sacrifices either economic prosperity ("Blood Brothers") or his son ("Blancaflor").

Gregoria Ramos Merchán of Piornal provided a different perspective on a man's predicament in her version of "Blancaflor."[12] She directed attention away from man's dependence on woman and blamed the loss of a son on a father's love of money. A gambler who loves money sells his son to the devil for a pack of winning cards. Gamblers who make transactions with the devil appear in many Spanish and Mexican "Blancaflor" stories,[13] but no other narrator I know of represented a man selling the devil his son. Nevertheless, Florencio, Bernardo, and Gregoria pointed, in different ways, to the incompatibility between man as provider and man as father.

As mentioned in Chapter 6, the incompatibility in man's roles as provider and father in Cáceres folktales is connected to weaker filial loyalties between fathers and their children evident in other aspects of the "Blood Brothers" stories. Cáceres narrators emphasized the tie between mother and child over father and child by depicting conception as eating. The tenuous ties between father and child came into relief when Cáceres stories were compared closely with versions of the same stories told by Nahuat narrators in Nacho's village of Huitzilan de Serdán. Nahuat narrators described a different father-child relationship by (1) using the image of conception as planting to draw attention to the father's role in procreation in their versions of "Blood Brothers," and by (2) representing close connections among fathers, sons, and brothers in several folktales. Although Florencio is not a typical Cáceres man, he nevertheless bore the stamp of his culture and represented fathers, sons, and brothers as comparatively autonomous relative to Nahuat narrators who told the same stories in Huitzilan.

A man's disconnection from other men in the family means his primary family ties will probably be with a woman. Florencio consequently represented Joaquín as heavily dependent on Ursula from the moment of their first meeting. The male protagonist usually meets the heroine bathing, and he steals her clothes or jewelry to extract her promise of help.[14] Florencio took a different approach and placed their meeting in the context of the first impossible task, which sets the stage for Joaquín's complete dependence on Ursula.

"THE OGRE'S TASKS"

Joaquín meets Ursula when the devil commands him to murder and mutilate one of his three daughters, chosen by drawing straws. Joaquín has to perform this task or else the devil will kill him, and Ursula uses her power to enable him to complete the task successfully and thus avoid his own death. The initial impossible task conveys the first of several contradictory or ambivalent images of Florencio's heroine. On the one hand, Ursula appears very passive as she moves from one man to another in a marriage exchange. By her father's command, she undergoes mutilation and enters into a relationship with another man who eventually becomes her husband. On the other hand, Ursula soon emerges as extraordinarily powerful because she provides Joaquín with the supernatural means to perform the many impossible tasks that make up the bulk of Florencio's story.

Ursula's image as a powerful woman has the additional narrative effect of exposing the limits of patriarchal power when a man deals with his daughter. Like other Spanish narrators of this tale, Florencio set up the heroine's father as a patriarch who seems powerful at first. The devil is so powerful that he can command his daughters to draw straws to determine who will be killed, chopped up, and thrown into the sea. In other tales, the heroine undergoes her mutilation for a purpose—usually to recover a gold ring dropped in the middle of the sea.[15] But the devil in Florencio's story merely seems to exercise his power for no apparent reason. No other heroine's father has that kind of power over the women in his family. In contrast to her father, Ursula appears at first to have no agency and has no choice but to participate in her own mutilation. However, by the end of the impossible tasks, which Florencio expanded far more than other narrators in Spain, the tables are entirely turned. The devil appears impotent, and Ursula seems powerful. Moreover, this father, like many others, uses his power with ironical results and actually sets the stage for the marriage that he does not want to take place. Ursula, like other Blancaflors, reemerges from her death and rebirth in slightly mutilated form because Joaquín failed to follow her instructions not to shed a single drop of her blood. She is missing a piece of a finger, which permits Joaquín to select her as his bride from among her sisters when the devil orders his daughters to put their hands through a cat hole.[16]

Florencio's expansion of the number of tasks from the usual three to eight serves both poetic purposes. It exposes further the limits of a father's power by making him look repeatedly foiled by his daughter. It emphasizes a man's dependence on a woman; Joaquín must turn to Ursula for help more than other men who marry supernatural brides in Spanish "Blancaflor" stories. Florencio, like other Cáceres men, may have constructed his heroine out of material stored in his early childhood memory of an omnipotent mother.[17] However, his heroine, who helped her man more than the heroines in the same tale by other

Cáceres men, fulfilled Florencio's more immediate wishes.[18] Florencio was a widower when he told me this story. His choice of the name
Ursula for the heroine, after the popular Swedish actress, made his
Blancaflor the product of his particular fantasy. Florencio's unusual
expansion of the number of times Ursula enabled the hero to perform
incredible tasks expresses Florencio's desire to find a woman who
might help him manage his family business and parent his unmarried
sons. As mentioned earlier, for many years his now-deceased wife and
the mother of his children could not help him sell cheese produced
from his herds because she was incapacitated by a tragic mental illness. Florencio was actually courting a woman at the time I met him
and perhaps he hoped she might be the missing partner in his life,
much as Ursula was the supernatural partner in Joaquín's.

Florencio's unusual need to depend on a woman like Ursula is perhaps one reason he represented his heroine with ambivalence and contradiction. Ursula is a saint, but she derives her supernatural power
from a demonic source. She uses demons to plant the vineyard and
cut the pieces of crooked wood. She is the daughter of parents who are
devils and who use their demonic power as witches do by changing
themselves into domesticated animals. When Ursula changes into a
cat, she looks very much like a witch. According to Florencio:

> I have always heard it said that the devil does what he wants. Be-
> cause I heard once that a couple got married and were going to
> bed, and they say that a cat went there, and when the cat appeared
> it went meow, meow, meow. The cat was meowing, and the woman
> said, "Sometimes the devil sounds like a cat."
>
> "Look how fast I'll get this cat out of here," said the husband.
>
> He got up and grabbed a stick, but he didn't return. And they say
> the devil went there in the form of a cat and took him away . . . .
> The devil makes himself into a dog, he makes himself into a cat,
> he makes himself into an ox, he makes himself into a goat, he
> makes himself into whatever he wants. That's what they say. I
> haven't seen it. It's something, I think, that's like a dream. I dream
> something, and it seams real to me, but of course when I awake,
> there is nothing.[19]

Florencio's distrust of a woman's power extends to his representation
of female animals in his "Blancaflor" story. He described the urine and
flatulence of a she-mule as destroying a pair of iron shoes and putting
holes in a metal helmet. The urine and flatulence of a he-mule would
have made the same items stronger.

"THE FLIGHT"

As in many "Blancaflor" stories in Spain, Ursula and Joaquín flee from the underworld because her father intends to kill them. Also like many heroines, Ursula uses her supernatural power to block her father's pursuit. She throws her comb to make a dense fog and she transforms herself into a chapel and Joaquín into a monk to escape from the underworld. Her father nevertheless retains enough power in Florencio's tale to affect the lives of his daughter and son-in-law after their safe return to Joaquín's village; he utters a curse that makes Ursula turn into a serpent for seven years. However, this father's power is once again limited because Florencio makes clear, in the subsequent episode of "The Forgotten Fiancée," that his curse is not the reason Joaquín loses his memory of the woman who brought him safely back home.

The pursuer's curse is a relatively rare feature of "Blancaflor" stories in Spain; the father utters a curse only in variants by Leandro Jiménez of El Guijo de Santa Bárbara and an unidentified narrator from Granada.[20] Despite Florencio's representation of residual patriarchal power as a curse, he and other narrators I knew in Cáceres stressed, in descriptions of their own actual courtship, that the mother is the more influential parent in a maiden's decision to engage in a courtship with a particular man. Florencio and his son Bernardo, for example, both told how their first courtship ended because mothers persuaded their daughters against the match. The importance of the mother's influence in her daughter's courtship explains why some Spanish narrators from Cáceres and other provinces identify the mother rather than the father as the pursuing parent who utters a curse. A mother's curse appeared in "Blancaflor" stories by José Díaz Sánchez of Serradilla, who also reported to me that he failed in his first attempted courtship because a maiden's mother persuaded her daughter against the marriage, and in similar tales by Adelino Blanco of Asturias and Manuela Martín Cuadrado of Vilvestre in Salamanca.[21]

"THE FORGOTTEN FIANCÉE"

The heroine's repeated use of her supernatural power to enable a weak and passive man to complete impossible tasks and flee from her father—or, in some cases, her mother—ultimately leads to her humiliating experience of being forgotten by her husband. It is ironic but not surprising that, in so many "Blancaflor" stories from Spain, a man's devotion to his supernatural bride is much weaker than his dependence on her. A man who heavily depends on but does not trust the fundamental nature of women will be reluctant to devote himself to his Blancaflor no matter how helpful she has been. "The Forgotten Fiancée," a feature of Florencio's tale, appears in most Spanish variants of this story. The husband in many variants forgets about his supernatural bride because he breaks a prohibition that the heroine has given him.[22] Joaquín follows the pattern in other stories: he breaks the prohibition not to allow anyone to kiss him. The widespread use of the prohibition in women's as well as in men's stories could represent the common perception that men have difficulty making the transition in marriage and shifting their trust and loyalty from the mother to the wife. Some Spanish narrators specifically direct the prohibition to a show of affection by a female member of the male protagonist's family.[23]

Ursula, like many Blancaflors in Spain and Mexico, uses her supernatural power a final time to recover her lost husband as he is about to marry another woman. Ursula acts like many other women in folktales from the two cultures, who use their power to restore a broken marriage with an unusually passive husband. Cáceres and Nahuat men and women tell "Cupid and Psyche" (Tale Type 425), which also depicts wives who similarly recover their passive lost husbands.[24] Florencio is once again autobiographical when depicting Ursula as nurturing a sickly calf she raised by shares in order to unlock Joaquín's memory. Florencio and Ursula are alike because both raised animals by shares and know how to nurture with food.

SUMMARY

Florencio's representation of a man's relationship with a woman in "Blancaflor" is related to his account of a man's relationship with other men if all stories considered so far are taken into account. Although Florencio is an unusual narrator, he nevertheless was like other men in his culture because he depicted a man comparatively isolated from other men in his family. To be sure, he represented a father as involved in the lives of the sons and played down male sibling rivalry in "Blood Brothers" (Tale Type 303). He also depicted an unusual amount of brotherly interdependence in his "The Magic Objects and the Wonderful Fruits" (Tale Type 566). Relative to Nahuat men who told the same stories, he nevertheless presented his male characters as comparatively disconnected from fathers, sons, and brothers. His version of "Blancaflor" reveals how a man, isolated from other men in his family, turns to a woman on whom he becomes very dependent. Because of his heavy dependence on the woman, he mistrusts her and struggles to shift his loyalties from a mother to a wife when making the transition of marriage. Our journey will continue with a look at the heroine, who takes a different form in Nacho's story.

Chapter 9

NACHO'S "BLANCAFLOR"

NACHO PRESENTED ANOTHER PICTURE OF GENDER RELA-
tions in his version of "Blancaflor" (Tale Type 313C), which he told
according to his connected view of the family and the cosmos. There
are enough similarities in Nacho's and Florencio's stories to justify
the conclusion that they probably originated from a common historical source. Both men organized their narratives around the episodes
Antti Aarne and Stith Thompson consider essential parts of Tale Type
313C, which they call "The Girl as Helper in the Hero's Flight."[1] Nacho's and Florencio's stories are both metaphors for courtship and
marriage in which a man depends on a woman. Perhaps they constructed their heroines, who possess enormous supernatural power,
out of their early childhood memories of an omnipotent mother. Nacho was still unmarried and living with his mother and married brothers when he told me his version of this popular folktale.

Nevertheless, Nacho built his story out of different linguistic and
cultural materials to present another view of man's relationship with
woman. Perhaps the most noticeable feature of Nacho's tale is his use
of language; he respected the power of the spoken word and avoided
speaking "inconsiderately" (īlihuiz). In our journey through his poetic
imagination, we have come across many other examples of Nacho's
avoidance of īlihuiz. He maintained his distance from characters who
are its personification and described its devastating effects on human
relations. His avoidance of īlihuiz was part of his view of a precariously
ordered cosmic and human structure that came unraveled in the past
and may well do so again in the future. He expressed his anxiety about
the unraveling of that structure in many of his tales, which described
threats posed by inconsiderate behavior. The Bear's Son personified
īlihuiz and threatened to destroy Huitzilan with a flood when living
atop Cozōltepēt. Relajo, who took advantage of his devoted but gul-

lible compadre and acted inconsiderately, set into motion a disastrous and frightening chain of events resulting in the deaths of those with whom he should have shared a respectful and loving relationship. The Master Thief chose a profession in which he acted inconsiderately and was banished from his community. The three brothers who behave rashly and inconsiderately with each other in "The Two Travelers" threatened to destroy their extended family.

Nacho is one of at least sixteen narrators living within the boundaries of modern Mexico who told variants of "Blancaflor."[2] Their versions permit story comparisons that reveal how Nacho may have given his heroine her distinctive personality as she passed from Spaniards to Spanish-speaking Mexicans and eventually to Nacho and his brothers in Huitzilan.[3] One of the most obvious differences between Nacho's and Florencio's story plot is that Nacho placed more emphasis on his first episode, "The Hero Comes into Ogre's Power," and less on "The Ogre's Tasks," resulting in a shift in emphasis from gender relations to ethnic relations. Nacho's hero still depends on the heroine, but he depends on her to perform far fewer incredible tasks than does his counterpart in Florencio's tale. Nacho expressed more concern with his hero's relationship with the ogre who is the ahmō cualli, first appearing in the guise of a well-dressed man riding a horse, an unmistakable reference to a Spanish-speaking Mexican. Nacho depicted ethnic relations in terms of contrasting principles of exchange. As we discovered in his story "Relajo," Nacho's Nahuat characters placed primary importance on human relationships when carrying out their exchanges. Characters who stood for Spanish-speaking Mexicans made exchanges entirely for the purpose of acquiring wealth. Nacho made clear, in his opening episode, that his hero almost becomes annihilated because he makes an exchange in the Nahuat manner with a man who intends to devour him.

"Blancaflor"
by Nacho Ángel Hernández

Once there was a man who called himself Juan Barajero. That man didn't like doing just any kind of work. He only liked the game; he supported himself by playing cards. And the day came when he didn't have the money to feed his children. He decided to go out of his house and onto the road.

"I'm going for a walk," he says to his mother. "If I run into God, then I'll speak to him. If I run into the one who is not good, then I'll talk to him."

So he takes to the road and goes on for a while and runs into a man who asks, "Where are you going?"

"Well, I'm going somewhere to find work," Juan says. "Perhaps I'll run into somebody. I play this game. I don't do anything else except this to support myself," Juan explains. "Perhaps you'd like to play?"

"Oh, son, I don't," the man says. "I don't like that game. But you will play with someone who is coming behind me. If by chance," the man explains, "you had not mentioned me first, then," he says, "you would have met him, and he would have won from you. But because you first mentioned me," he says, "I ran into you before he did. You're going to play with him," he says, "and you'll win from him because you will," he explains. "He would have won from you if you had mentioned him before me," he adds. "For that reason, it has to be that you'll win from him."

They say the man speaking to Juan Barajero was God. That's how they took leave of each other, and, once again, Juan goes on down the road and he meets a gentleman.

"Where are you going?" the gentleman asks.

"Well, I'm going to look for work," replies Juan. "I won't do just any kind of work," he says. "No! I want to play with these. Perhaps you'd like to play with me. If you'd like, let's play."

"Why not?" replies the one who is not good. "We'll play if you want."

"Well, let's go," urges Juan.

They start playing. Juan wins from the one who is not good. They play again and again. Juan wins from the one who is not good. They play still another time. Juan wins from him. Then the one who is not good says, "We'll play again, but if I win, I'll eat you."

And Juan puts himself into the other man's hands.

"Well, let's go," says Juan.

They start to play with the deck of cards, and Juan wins still another time. They play again.

"Do you want to play once more?" asks the one who is not good. "If I win, then I'll eat you."

"Well, let's go," says Juan. "But if I win, then I'll take everything you have. I'm going to take your horse and all your money. Your clothes. You're going to be left in the street."

"Well, let's go," says the one who is not good.

They start to play; they play with the cards. Juan wins again from the one who is not good.

"Yes, now you have won from me."

Juan takes everything from him: his horse, all of his clothes, money. He takes everything. The one who is not good is left in the street. They say he stands in the middle of the road feeling sorry for himself. He is naked. And the man who looked for work, that card player, he mounts the horse and comes home.

"Don't feel sorry for yourself because I won from you," Juan says. "Just tell me your name and where you live," he adds. "I'll go work for you to pay you back."

"Well, I call myself Deodan de Oro, and, as for my house, you ask for 'Way Down Below the Earth.'"

"Good, I'll go there," says Juan.

They take leave of each other. The man, who won from the gentleman, goes home. He goes home to work; all the crops are planted. He works on everything and, a long time after he started working, he resolves, "I must go to make restitution."

"Don't leave everything now," implores Juan's mother.

"No, I must go because I told him I would go," insists Juan.

And he takes to the road and goes looking for him. He goes on and on down the road and he arrives at a town and asks, "Would you know where there is a certain man?"

"What's his name?"

"Well, he told me he calls himself Deodan de Oro," Juan explains. "He says his house is Way Down Below the Earth."

"He couldn't be *that* man. That would be the one who is not good because there isn't anyone with that name here. No one. Ask anyone, and no one goes by that name," the townsperson says. "You're not right about the name."

"Yes, that what he calls himself," Juan insists.

"But there isn't anyone with that name here. No one."

So Juan goes on again. He continues on down the road looking for him. He comes to another town and asks again, "Do you know where a man is who calls himself Deodan de Oro?"

The townspeople ask each other.

"No one calls himself that. There isn't anyone with a name like that here. Where did he tell you his house is?"

"Well, he said 'Way Down Below the Earth.'"

"Oh, then his house isn't here on earth," the townsperson replies. "He can only be the one who isn't good."

"Well, I don't know," Juan says. "But he told me to go there."

"And what are you going for?"

"Well, I'm going to help him with work."

"We don't know him, and no one here goes by that name."

So then Juan continues on down the road, he continues on down the road until he comes again to someone else's town.

"Do you know where a man is who calls himself Deodan de Oro?" Juan asks.

"We don't know him."

Even though he questions them and they question themselves, no one knows.

"Where did he tell you he is?"

"He told me he is Way Down Below the Earth."

"Then he isn't a man from here on earth. He can only be the one who is not good."

"Well, I don't know, but he told me to go to his house," explains Juan.

"What for?"

"I'm going to help with work," Juan explains.

"No one here knows anyone who goes by that name. You can only look for him somewhere else."

So he continues on down the road. He goes on and on and doesn't find him anywhere. He comes to someone else's town. It is the same thing again with another one saying he does not know him. Juan asks the same question about his house, and the townspeople give him the same reply.

"That man isn't here."

So Juan takes to the road again, he passes a town, he continues, he continues on until he comes to a land where there is no one. It's a place where one is alone. He finds a little old woman sitting by herself, and she asks, "Where are you going, son?"

"Well, nowhere," Juan says. "I'm looking for a man who says he's called Deodan de Oro."

"Where did he tell you he is?"

"Well, he says he is Way Down Below the Earth."

"Oh, son," says the old woman, "it isn't true he has work. It's not true because he is lazy. That man doesn't have any work."

"Well, I don't know. He told me to go to that place. I won some money from him, and that's why I'm going: to make restitution," Juan says.

"Yes, but you'll go to stay," she warns. "It is not true that you'll work with him because he just wants to eat you."

"Well, I don't know. But I'm going."

"Well, I'll tell you what to do so he won't eat you. You'll help yourself these ways. First," she says, "right now over there you'll cross four bodies of water: four seas. There will be a wild beast (tēcuāni) exactly where you'll cross from here, and it is lying on its back. Don't be afraid of it. You'll arrive and climb right up on its back. It is going to take you across. And you're going to come out over there and go on again. Over there you're going to come out, and there will be a water dog. You'll cross again. Don't be afraid of it. You'll arrive and climb up on its back. It will take you across. You'll arrive at another body of water. Again there will be another animal. You climb on its back and cross again. It will take you across. There will be another body of water, and there will be another animal. An eagle. Don't be afraid of it. You get there and climb up on its back, and it'll take you across."

So then that man does those things. He goes on. The animals take him across.

"And from there," the old woman continues, "the one you're going to see will not eat you. He would have eaten you, but he won't eat you. He has a daughter whom you will find washing laundry. She'll be playing in the water with her hands. And you'll come upon her playing with her hands in the water, and she has necklaces, earrings, some rings, and her ribbons. She will have everything on the ground, together in one place. You get there and, when you come upon the maiden playing with her hands in the water and with soap in her eyes, she won't see you come, and you quickly snatch those earrings, her necklace, her ribbon, and her ring. And you put them into your pocket. And when it is time for the maiden to return to her senses, when she reaches with her hand to sprinkle water on her face to remove the soap, then she'll look for her necklace, which won't appear. Then she will say, 'Oh! my necklace! and Oh! my earrings! and Oh! my ribbon! and Oh! my ring! They're all worth thousands of pesos!' And you say, 'Aren't these here some of those things?' You take them out of your pocket and show them to her. And she'll say, 'Well yes. They are like those. They are the ones I lost.' From there, it will start, and you will talk to each other so the maiden will bring you back here. She will help you, and if it were not for that maiden, you would go to stay and would not return."

That man does exactly what the little old woman on earth told him. He does just what she advised him to do, and he and the maiden started talking to each other.

"Well now, I'll take you to my home," she says. "If you'll really take me away, then let's go."

"Why wouldn't I take you? I came; I'll take you. I didn't come just to see your face."

"Now, I won't have to go back home because you came. My father is going to give you work, but he's going to trick you because he only wants to eat you. But he won't do anything to you if you really take me away."

"No, I came to take you away," Juan insists.

"Good. Go see my father. Let's see what he says to you."

So then that boy arrives where that old man is.

"I've come now," he says.

"You've come."

"Yes, I've come."

"Well, you go rest. Come early tomorrow so we can work. There isn't a lot of work. You'll do four tasks."

"Good," Juan replies.

Juan goes to the maiden, who asks, "What did he say to you?"

"He told me to go early tomorrow."

"Good."

Juan sleeps that day and goes early the next day to see him.

"I've come now."

"Yes, you've come."

"Yes."

"Good, go eat and come back so I can tell you what you're going to do."

Juan returns to the maiden and says, "Feed me so I can eat."

He has lunch and returns.

"I've come now."

"Yes."

"Well, now you're going to do a job," he says. "You're going to clear a field. You'll begin at the base of the earth—where the earth begins—and you're going to finish in the center of the earth because I want to plant some chilies and I want you to give me a sack full tomorrow so I can go to the plaza tomorrow to sell chilies. I want to go to the plaza tomorrow. So give me those sacks of chilies."

"Well fine," says Juan.

"I want you to give me those sacks of chilies in a little while because tomorrow I'm going to market."

"Well good," he replies. "I'm going to see her," he says to himself.

He goes to her.

"What did he say to you?" she asks.

"He told me to begin where the earth begins and finish clearing to the center of the earth and plant chilies and give him a sack of chilies tomorrow when he wants to go to the plaza."

"Yes, and will you do it?"

"Well, even though I may not want to, he ordered me to do it," Juan explains. "Go and bring me an ax and a machete."

"Go and be over there until I catch up with you," she says.

That boy, the one whom the old man counseled, goes over and, because he is used to how one works here on earth with a machete, he arrives and starts to get up to go to work when the maiden catches up with him.

"Well, you got up already," she observes.

"Yes."

"And this is how you work on earth?"

"Yes."

"Oh, so that's why you are so miserable," she says. "Not that way. That's why you suffer so many hardships. No. One must work this way. When would you ever do the job that way? No. Right now you are going to work as we work. Do you love ants?"

"Yes."

"Those ants are fine people," she says. "Those pepehuani ants are fine people. Those tiny ants, we love all of them. They will do the work."

She starts making a smacking sound on the earth with her hand. Ants begin to come up: the large stinging ants [tzīcameh], the pepehuani ants, those little tiny ants. They start to clear, they begin clearing, those large stinging ants commence cutting. And some of those little tiny ants spread chili seeds, they cut the forest, they place the trees to one side, and they quickly stack all of the wood. Those ants, all of the ones that were there, quickly start in. Some plant chilies, some prune chili plants, some cut chilies, and some put the chilies into sacks. They transport them from different places. They line up the sacks. They do all of that work, and the maiden says to him, "Now you see it is done. Go tell my father it is ready."

So that boy goes to tell the old man.

"I've come now."

"Yes, and did you do the job?"

"Yes, I did it."

That boy goes over to where the girl is, and she counsels him, "I'm helping you and don't trick me. You really will take me away!" she insists.

"Yes, I won't trick you; I shall take you away."

"Well, good."

The sun comes up. That boy goes again to where the old man is.

"I've come now."

"Yes."

"What shall we do?"

"Well now, I want you to make a bridge from here to the other side of the sea. I want troops to meet and wage war in the middle. They'll strike each other with stones."

"Fine."

So then the boy returns to the maiden, who asks, "What did he say to you?"

"He says to make a bridge across the sea and place it horizontally where troops will stone [fight] each other. Yes, that is what he told me."

"Good, we're going to do it. Don't ponder how."

She takes him in her shadow, and they come to where she is going to make the bridge at the edge of the sea. There, they say, she beautifully places horizontally one rainbow and then others, she lines them up, and they become a bridge. Then the pepehuani and the tzīca ants line up and meet in the middle, a rainstorm starts, and it begins to thunder until bolts of lightning reach the old man sleeping.

"Enough already!" he shouts. "Stop the fighting!"

He begins saying obscene things. He starts cursing.

"Have them stop now!"

So it stops. Then the boy comes again.

"Well, did you do the job?"

"Yes, it is now well done."

Again it does not take a long time. Afterwards he goes once more in the early morning.

"Well, I've come again."

"Fine."

"What do I do now?"

"Now I want you to get a gold ring. I lost it in the middle of the sea. I went to the plaza yesterday and lost it there," he says to Juan.

"Oh yes."

"Yes. Get it for me. I want you to give it to me today. Now go eat and do it."

Then the boy goes back to the maiden, and she asks, "What did he say?"

"He says for me to bring him a ring. Yesterday he went to market and threw a gold ring into the middle of the sea."

"Not true! He wants to beat you," she says. "But so it won't turn out that way, we'll do it and we'll give it to him."

The maiden takes a knife and cuts the middle of her finger; she goes around it. And he sees her bleed, and the blood around her finger dries. Then she removes it and it turns into a gold ring.

"Here it is," she declares. "Go take it to him."

"Here is your ring," Juan says to the old man.

"You went to get it?"

"Yes, I went to get it."

"Well, that's fine. Now go rest and come early tomorrow. You will do one more task and then you'll rest."

"Good."

The sun shines the next day, and he goes to see him again.

"I've come."

"Good."

"What shall I do?"

"Now you're going to bring me a yearling that no one can catch. Go get it, and I want you to tame it. Give it to me tame. Go get the one that runs seven thousand leagues."

"Fine."

And Juan returns to the maiden, who asks, "Well, what did he say to you?"

"He told me I must get a horse from the pasture up there: a yearling no one can catch. I must go get it and tame it. It runs seven thousand leagues."

"Yes."

"That's what he told me."

"But it isn't that way. Will you really take me away?" she asks again.

"Yes, I'll take you away. I am not tricking you one bit."

"I'm going to help you, and going to get the horse will be our way of getting away," she explains.

"Well, good."

Then they go into the pasture, and the maiden says to the boy, "Go around it; you drive it in this direction from way over there."

The maiden intends to rope it, and so the boy goes to drive it toward her.

"And you also bring the other one: the mare that runs one thousand leagues."

"Good."

They go to the pasture to get the horse and rope it and the other one.

"Now you'll tame this beast. Hit it and squeeze the liquid out of its head. Tire it out a lot. When you know it's tamed, climb up on its head and come down on its haunches. And also climb up on its haunches and come down over its head. Then you'll see how it gives up. You'll see it's tame now."

He does as told.

"Now go saddle the mare and get everything ready and take the other horse to my father," she explains.

"Good."

He tames the yearling completely and it is fine.

"Now saddle the mare and deliver [the yearling] to my father," says the maiden.

"Fine."

He saddles the mare. He gets the mare ready. And from there, yes, he takes the yearling to the old man, telling him, "Here it is."

"Fine."

And the maiden, who told Juan to deliver the horse to her father and come back, is preparing herself to leave.

"What did he tell you?" she asks Juan.

"He said yes and for me to rest now. I am to rest and go see him early tomorrow. But I won't work anymore. I'm to rest."

"He isn't telling the truth. Right now is a good time for us to leave. Let's go now because, if we don't, he'll eat you tomorrow."

So they come from there on the mare. It runs, and they come from there. The moment they give her father the horse, the maiden knows.

"Right now my father looks for us. He looks for us. It's certain he'll come looking for us. My old man is now awake."

That little old man decides to call his girl. He calls her Blancaflor.

"Blancaflor."

"Sir," her saliva responds.

The maiden has put a cup of her saliva under her bed. After a while, he father calls her again, and she realizes somehow, while she and Juan are on the road, that her father remembers her and calls to her.

"My father is calling to me right now," she says.

"Blancaflor," he calls again.

"Sir," she replies.

It's her saliva that answers him.

"My father is calling to me," she declares.

He rests for a little while and calls to her again.

"Blancaflor."

"Sir," responds her saliva.

Then the old man pays close attention.

"She doesn't get up."

He thinks she is asleep.

"What is she doing?" he says to the old woman. "That Blancaflor of mine doesn't get up."

"Well, who knows why?"

"Blancaflor," he calls to her.

"Sir," she answers.

The maiden tells Juan, "My saliva is losing its strength because it's not being replenished. My saliva is running out."

Meanwhile, the old woman says to the old man, "What is she doing? My child isn't sick, is she? Why doesn't she get up?"

"Who knows?" he says. "Go see her."

So the old woman goes to see her.

"She has disappeared. Where did she go? Who knows? She's disappeared. Well, now we must eat our little pig."

That man—Juan—is known as the pig they are taking care of. The old man and the old woman go look for that man, that pig.

"He's disappeared. He's disappeared. Oh *cabrón,* they've gone. I'm going to find them," he says.

"Well, you know what you have to do."

The maiden realizes what is happening at that very moment. She knows right away.

"My father comes looking for us. Well, he won't catch us," she tells Juan. "He is coming to look for us or he soon will."

So then that old man really does leave on his horse. The maiden spits some of her saliva onto the road as she comes. Bubbling mud appears in the road, keeping her father's horse from coming after them. So it is that she spits, causing the mud to ooze, keeping him from reaching her. So the old man decides to go back. Blancaflor and Juan are running in this direction, and the girl says to the boy, "My father found us, and my saliva is weak because it's not replenished. He found us."

But she scatters her saliva on the road and her father goes back because he couldn't go farther on down the road; it really turns into a hole of water and mud. So then the old man goes back. He arrives home and says to the old woman, "I came back because I couldn't reach them."

"Why not?"

"It was impossible. I ran into a mud and water hole, but a really big mud and water hole," he explains.

"You really are a deadhead. That was my Blancaflor's saliva. She spit it onto the road," explains the old woman.

"Son of the bad woman, I should have continued on after her."

"Instead, you rested," the old woman says.

"But I'm going again," he vows.

So then that old man comes after them again.

"My father is coming to find us," Blancaflor says to Juan.

Again he comes in this direction, and the maiden knows he is about to catch them.

"He's about to grab us right now."

She resolves to throw down one of her mirrors. Well, the mirror looks like a lake to that old man. It was impossible for his horse to run; it splashed in the water. The old man cannot come after them. The harder his horse runs, the more it goes into the water. It is impossible. So he comes back from there. He comes back from where he had gone.

"Did you find her?" asks the old woman.

"How would I have found her? I ran into a lake, but a real one. However could I go on? The more I wanted to, the more my horse went into the lake."

"Oh, you deadhead, that was my Blancaflor who threw down her mirror."

"*Cabrón*, I'm going after her again."

He comes again.

"My father is coming again. Right now who knows if he'll catch us. I don't know what to do. My old man will come."

The maiden has to think; she has a lot of ideas. It turns out he does come, and the maiden senses he's about to catch them.

"My father is about to catch us."

She decides to throw down her comb. Yes, she tosses her comb.

It turns into a big wooden enclosure. However could a horse pass through it? The old man appears.

"How can anyone get through this?"

There is a big wooden fence—but some fence! The horse wants to run, but where, the old man asks. At that moment, he returns. Once more he comes back from where he had gone.

"Did you reach her?" asks the old woman.

"How could I when I reached a big wooden fence—but some wooden fence! However would I reach her?"

"Oh, you deadhead, that was my Blancaflor who threw down her comb."

"Oh, *cabrón*, I'll go again."

So then the old man comes once more.

"My father's coming again. He's determined to catch us," the maiden informs the boy.

The maiden thinks over, as he comes, what to do about her father.

"Well now, let's see what we'll do."

The maiden senses her father is about to catch her.

"He's about to catch us! Who knows what to do?"

She decides to throw down a lock of her hair. She throws it down as she comes. The lock of her hair becomes a big forest. It's a place with many vines, and since it turns into a place with many vines, a forest of vines, who can pass through it? From there, yes his horse will run into that place. It won't pass through it. It'll get caught. The old man arrives back home after returning from where the maiden is and asks the old woman, "Well, now what can I do? I didn't reach her. A lock of her hair and there is a big wilderness: a forest of vines but a real vineyard. Where could anyone get through? I wanted to run my horse; it simply got stuck."

"Oh yes. You really are a deadhead. That was she, it was also she, it was my Blancaflor's hair she threw."

"*Cabrón*, what shall I do now? I'll go again."

"Here he comes again; it's my father," the maiden exclaims. "Who knows what to do?"

The maiden senses he is about to catch them.

"Well, who knows what to do? He's going to catch us. Now we shall do it this way," she resolves. "You sit down in that place in the road, and I'll turn into fruit. And when you come out into the road, my father will ask you forcefully, he'll say to you, 'Have you seen a man and a maiden come by here?' You'll tell him, 'Two for five.' He'll say to you again, 'I'm asking you if you've seen a man and a maiden?' You'll say, 'Two for five.' And this time he'll be a lot angrier and he'll say to you, 'I'm telling you, not asking you, to tell me if you've seen a man, a boy who passed by here!' 'Ah, well, take one and eat it.' Then at that moment, he'll go back right away without taking it from you and he'll be gone."

Yes, he returns from that place and says to the old woman, "Well, I've come now."

"Did you find her?"

"Where would I have found her? I went to a town and found a man selling fruit. I asked him forcefully and he said to me, 'The fruit is two for five.' I asked him again, and he told me to eat one."

"Oh, you mudhead, why didn't you take it? Don't you see he offered you my Blancaflor who was the fruit?"

"Oh, *cabrón*, I should have taken it from him. I'll go again."

So then the old man comes after them again.

"My father is coming right now. Who knows what to do? He's going to catch us."

They are running away from there on that mare that runs one thousand leagues, but the old man's horse runs faster. He is about to catch them.

"My father is about to catch us. Who knows what we're going to do? Now I'm going to become a town, this mare is going to become a church, let its tail be the tower, and you be here ringing the bell. He'll come by and climb up the bell tower. He'll say to you, 'Maybe you saw a man or a woman pass by here?' You won't answer him. You just say, 'Three for four, three for four, three for four.' Again he'll ask. You won't answer him. You just say, 'Three for four, three for four, two for four, two for four.' You just answer him that way. And he'll ask you again. You'll say, 'There is going to be a mass.' He'll say, 'Oh, I'm asking you a question. Did a man or a girl pass by here?' Don't pay him any heed. You tell him, 'No. There comes the priest!' At that point, he'll go back and that's how he'll go back."

Then that old man really does show up.

"Maybe you've seen a man or a girl?" he asks.

Juan does not pay any attention to him. He starts ringing the bell and says, "Two for four, two for four, three for four, three for four."

The old man asks him again, "Perhaps you've seen a man or a maiden?"

"There is going to be a mass."

"No. Oh fuck! I'm not asking you that. I'm asking you to tell me if you've seen a man or a maiden."

"Well, there comes the priest."

Then, at that moment, he goes back. He goes home. And that's how he goes away. After that, the maiden says to Juan, "Now I've helped you and brought you, but right now you're going to arrive home, and now you've arrived, you'll forget about me."

"Why?"

"Yes, you'll forget about me."

"I won't forget about you."

"Yes, you'll arrive home and they'll smoke you with incense. You'll arrive and forget about me."

"I won't forget about you. You've helped me. I won't forget about you."

"Yes, you'll forget about me. You'll see now."

"No."

"Yes, I'm telling you."

They arrive. They really arrive now. And that boy's mother is very pleased he arrived now because she thought she wouldn't see him again, because, to her, he had worked for four years while he thought he had gone to work for four days. He arrives. They smoke him all over, and he does forget about the fine little woman. He does not realize where she is. The maiden is grief-stricken.

"You will leave me. You will abandon me in the street," she is the first to tell him.

"No."

But he does; from the moment they smoke him in greeting, he does not know about her because he is a deadhead. And he decides to get betrothed right away. He looks for a little old woman. The time comes to hold a marriage celebration, and the boy knows there is a woman, a fine woman. But he doesn't realize he was with her; he forgot she brought him fleeing from there. She helped him. Well, he does know she is among those who will prepare the meal.

"I know a girl who is over there," he tells his mother. "She prepares food well. She makes something and it is done right away—whatever she makes. She goes to do a little work and now it is done."

"Well, go get her if you know about her," says his mother.

He knows where the maiden is who brought him. He decides to go see her.

"I've come with this," he says to her. "Would you be interested in preparing the food for a celebration?"

"Yes, why wouldn't I go?"

And because he was already betrothed, she will go to his marriage celebration. He gets married and is preparing for the fiesta.

"I'll go and prepare the meals. Why not? Would you like me to make some dolls and would you like me to make them dance?"

"Why not?" he says to her.

"That's how the celebration is going to be done. That's why I ask you. I say this so you'll know what you will do and that your guests will take pleasure in the fiesta."

"Yes."

The fiesta comes. Juan and his betrothed are married and they dance. And the woman, the one who helped him, makes little dolls: one male doll and one female doll. That is to say, one is a boy and one is a woman. The fiesta comes, and they dance. And the maiden prepares all of the food. Now they begin to play the music. And the dolls decide they are going to dance too. The male and female dolls, made by Blancaflor, start dancing, and the female doll whips the male one's little behind with her shawl. Those same dolls are hitting each other. While they dance, the female doll says, "Are you remembering the day I helped you? It was when you arrived and took my ribbon and everything: my jewel necklace, my earrings, and my ring all worth thousands of pesos. And then you gave them back to me."

"I am remembering," answers the male doll.

They start dancing again; those dolls begin dancing. The music continues, they commence dancing again, and the woman, that is, the female doll, whips the little behind of the boy doll with her shawl.

"Don't hit me. I'm remembering. Don't hit me."

The girl doll resolves to say to him, "Do you recall the day I helped you do a job and kept my father from eating you? I helped you with everything."

"I'm remembering."

And she hits him again.

"Don't hit me. I remember."

They start to dance and, while they are dancing, she says, "Do you remember that day when the bridge was made and how my father wanted to beat you?"

"I remember."

She whips his little behind with her shawl still another time.

"Ah nāhueh [a term of endearment], don't hit me. I remember."

They begin dancing still another time. The dolls who are dancing are the same ones who are talking. That man, the one who just married, is standing there and is thinking as well. The dolls speak to him, and the boy doll is the same as the boy and the girl doll is the same as the woman who brought him. And so they commence dancing again.

"Are you remembering the day I gave you that ring because my father ordered you to get it out of the sea?"

"Yes, I am remembering."

She hits him once again with her shawl.

"Enough hitting, oh nāhueh, don't hit me. I'm remembering."

Then they begin dancing again.

"Do you remember that day my father ordered you to tame the horse we caught in the pasture?" she asks him still another time.

"Yes, I'm remembering."

And she hits him again on his little behind with her shawl.

"Don't hit me anymore now, nāhueh. Don't hit me. I'm remembering."

"Did you forget how I told you I would remain in the road, and you would forget about me?"

"No. I'm remembering you."

"No, I told you how you would forget about me."

"No, I didn't forget. I'm remembering."

She hits him again.

"Don't hit me."

She would have hit him again.

"Oh nāhueh, enough, don't hit me anymore. I'm remembering." And the man remembers and decides at once to put his arms around the maiden's neck.

"Now yes, I won't abandon this maiden because if it had not been for her, I would not have come back. She helped me with the work. She did all the work for me. I came back because of all the work she did. Even though I have to abandon this other one they pull to me, right now it cannot be, even though she is angry—no matter what. Because if it were not for this maiden, I would not have arrived back home. How can I abandon her?"

He took her, he took the one who helped him, and left the other one he married. Then the story ends.

"HERO COMES INTO OGRE'S POWER"

Nacho began his tale by drawing attention to the power of the spoken word, which, in his view, can seriously affect human relations by invoking the supernatural. His central character is a gambler who happened to mention God before the devil, whom Nacho identified with the euphemism "he who is not good" (ahmō cualli) to avoid invoking him as he narrated his story. Juan Barajero's destiny is entirely determined by this naming sequence. By pronouncing the name of God first, he will win when playing cards with the devil, secure the help of Blancaflor, return safely from the underworld, and regain his memory of his supernatural wife. Had Juan invoked the devil before God, his destiny would have been different. Nacho made clear he would have lost when playing cards with the devil and left the rest up to our imagination. Luciano Vega, another Nahuat narrator from Santiago Yaonáhuac, made clear what else would have happened in his telling of the same story. His gambler invoked the devil without mentioning God, he lost everything in the card game, and although he secured the help of Blancaflor to complete the incredible tasks and flee from the underworld, she returned him to the "mouth" of her father.

A concern with the power of the spoken word is a special case of Nacho's view of īlihuiz, which he also expressed when representing economic exchange. Nacho made clear, in "Blancaflor" as well as in other stories, that a man who makes an inconsiderate transaction with another man can destroy the precarious order in human relations. It was mentioned earlier that Nacho told a version of "The Rich and the Poor Peasant" (1535), in which he depicted the trickster as a sinister figure who took advantage of his luck or fate to take money from his gullible compadre who loved him. Concordant with his representation of economic exchange in other stories, Nacho depicted the male protagonist in his "Blancaflor" as a gambler who wins from the devil and then feels obligated to make restitution, to restore the precarious order in human relations disrupted when one man acquires wealth from another. Other narrators in Spain and Mexico depicted a different kind of economic exchange: their gamblers in "Blancaflor" stories lose to the devil or sell themselves to the devil for a pack of winning cards so that they can acquire money.[4] Nacho's representation of an economic transaction appears in stories told by other Nahuat narrators in Huitzilan who similarly described a man winning wealth in a competition and feeling uneasy and obliged to make restitution to the loser.[5] His image of exchange is part of his view of human relationships as more important than the acquisition of property. Nacho's view of exchange, which is shared by others in his village, made the Nahuat extremely vulnerable to the Spanish speakers who came from Tetela de Ocampo after the turn of the century with the specific aim of acquiring land to raise cattle and coffee. They set up stores and demanded land as security from Nahuat who purchased on credit medicine to cure their sick and supplies to honor their ritual kin, make offerings to their dead relatives, and maintain their relationship with the gods. When the Nahuat could not come up with the money to pay their bills, some store owners seized land as payment for the goods purchased on credit.

An awareness of the history of Spanish-speaking Mexican and Nahuat ethnic relations in Huitzilan is the commonly understood background to Nacho's use of repetition to drive home to his listeners the point that Juan Barajero made an exchange in the Nahuat manner with a man who will devour him, much as the Spanish speakers swallowed their land. Repetition occurs when Nacho described Juan Barajero passing through four towns looking for Deodan de Oro, who is the ahmō cualli living in Way Down Below the Earth (mictān). The ahmō cualli, to whom Juan feels obliged to make restitution, is unmistakably a Spanish-speaking Mexican. He is a ubiquitous figure in many folktales and is described as a well-dressed man (coyōt) mounted on a horse, carrying money to tempt his victims whom he intends to devour. No one in the many towns through which Juan passes can understand why he wants to work for the devil. The devil has no work, declares the old woman sitting all alone, and only wants to eat him. Nacho explained that the old woman is Mother Earth, who appears as a benevolent figure in many Nahuat folktales.

Juan Barajero's first meeting with Blancaflor sets the tone for their relationship, which Nacho represented according to his general view of power in human relationships. In all of his stories, Nacho represented different forms of power—masculine strength, economic power, the power of the spoken word—according to a view of the cosmic and human order as a fragile and precarious structure. His notion of power is the basis of his conviction that one should avoid any form of īlihuiz. Like many other narrators, Nacho described the first meeting with Blancaflor taking place near a body of water, where Juan finds her jewelry lying on the shore. Following the instructions of Mother Earth, Juan picks up the jewelry and puts it into his pocket. Juan develops a relationship with Blancaflor slowly and carefully, just as one should speak slowly and carefully, respecting the power of the spoken word. Juan does not steal jewelry to extract a promise of help or marriage; that would be acting with īlihuiz. Instead, he talks to Blancaflor, and they agree to an exchange: she will help him if he takes her away with him.

To provide a perspective on Nacho's representation of the first meeting between Blancaflor and the male protagonist, it is useful to consider how other narrators develop this part of their story. Florencio, as mentioned earlier, described the first meeting to set up and then show the limitations of patriarchal authority. He represented the devil as a father with seemingly so much power that he can command his daughters to draw straws to select who will be killed, chopped up, stuffed into a demijohn, and thrown into the sea. Obediently and with no agency, Ursula draws the lucky straw and undergoes her mutilation. Other Spanish and Mexican narrators offer different images of patriarchal power, which they usually locate in the man as husband-to-be, and they grant varying amounts of agency to Blancaflor when selecting and negotiating a relationship with her mate.

Blancaflor has a great deal of agency and seeks out the male protagonist in stories by Lorenza "la Capillona" and an unidentified narrator in Cuenca, Spain, and by an unidentified Spanish-speaking Mexican narrator and the Tepecano Eleno Aguilar in Mexico.[6] She and her husband have nearly equal agency, seeking out and falling in love with each other in tales by Rafael Curillo in Spain and an unidentified Spanish-speaking narrator in Jalisco, Mexico.[7] In other stories, Juan seeks out Blancaflor, just as a man is expected to initiate formally a courtship in Spain, Spanish-speaking Mexico, and among the Nahuat of Huitzilan. Juan seeks out Blancaflor in tales by Magdalena Frutos of Salamanca and José Díaz Sánchez of Cáceres, Spain, the Spanish-speaking Hortensia Herrera Guzmán of Mexico City, and the Zapotec Rosa Santiago of Mitla in Mexico.[8]

Blancaflor's agency decreases when her future husband snatches her clothing or jewelry and extracts a promise of help or marriage, as happens in thirteen out of the thirty-seven "Blancaflor" stories in the two countries.[9] Leavy suggests that the symbolism of stealing clothes or jewelry to extract a promise represents a man subjecting a woman to male domination.[10] Certainly some Spanish and Mexican stories are consistent with Leavy's interpretation. Men are particularly forceful in extracting a promise of help or marriage in stories by Adelino Blanco of Asturias, Gregoria Ramos of Piornal in Cáceres, and an unidentified narrator in Palencia, Spain, and by unidentified Spanish-speaking narrators in Jalisco, Oaxaca, and northern Mexico.[11] Gregoria Ramos used imagery that drew particular attention to Blancaflor's sexual vulnerability. Blancaflor is nude and alone as she bathes, separated from her sisters, and Juan takes her clothes and keeps them from her. She cannot easily defend herself against the sexual predator who abounds in many other stories circulating in the oral tradition of Piornal, Gregoria's village in Spain.

In versions among some Spanish-speaking and native Mexican narrators, men use more force with Blancaflor. A Spanish-speaking storyteller in Oaxaca told how a charcoal seller, working as a gardener, steals the heroine's clothing and refuses to return it despite her pleading. He follows her as she walks nude to her room in her house and "did what he wanted" (*hizo lo que quiso*). Paul Radin and Aurelio Espinosa, who collected this tale, told us nothing about the narrator.[12] At the very least, one would like to know the teller's gender to discover if the tale represents a woman's fear or a man's fantasy. The forceful abduction of the heroine appears to be a male fantasy in a masculine variant from Durango. The Nahua Bonifacio Natividad Gonzales told how the male protagonist carries away the heroine by force and then relies on her magic to elude her pursuing father.[13]

Rape is īlihuiz and can destroy the precarious order of any structure. Nacho, who may have inherited "Blancaflor" (313C) from Spanish-speaking Mexicans, treated his heroine with considerably more respect. Erotic imagery is toned down to remove the connotation of sexual vulnerability; Blancaflor is not a nude bather but is washing clothes in the river. To be sure, Juan steals her jewelry, but his motive is to initiate a conversation, following the instructions of Mother Earth. This Blancaflor has sufficient agency to set her own conditions for giving her promise of help; she demands that he take her away with him.

"THE OGRE'S TASKS"

Nacho's view of Blancaflor unfolds further in his account of the son-in-law tasks. This Blancaflor has the ability to utilize ants to plant and harvest a huge field, rainbows to build a bridge across the sea, animals to act as an army, and thunder to mimic the sound of battle. She calls the ants for the first task by smacking the earth with her hand, making a noise like a baby smacking its lips while nursing at the mother's breast: "she started to make a smacking noise on the earth with her hand" (pēhuac tālcocomotza imāi). The word tālcoco-motza is a compound of the noun tāl ("earth") and cocomotza, a verb describing a baby's "smacking noise nursing at the breast."[14] Nacho's symbolism is interesting considering that he and other Nahuat regard the earth as a woman.

Nacho stressed love (tazohtaliz) rather than power in human and cosmic relations as he described Blancaflor declaring her love for the ants and asking Juan if he loves them too. As the ants clear, plant, harvest, and sack the chilies, Juan has his first glimpse of life without toil. Blancaflor uses animal helpers in other Spanish and Mexican stories, but Nacho is the only narrator I know of who depicts Blancaflor declaring her love for her animal helpers and extracting a similar declaration from Juan. Her declaration of love for ants is one of many expressions of an intimate human-animal connection in Nahuat culture. Another is the belief that each man and woman has an animal companion in the wilderness whose destiny is identical to the human counterpart. Blancaflor's declaration of love for the ants as well as the belief in animal companions are further examples of an interconnected view of the universe. Forceful or inconsiderate behavior is bound to be damaging in unanticipated ways precisely because one is connected to so many things. Tazohtaliz is an emotion of connection that helps hold the precarious human and cosmic order together as long as it is not excessive and does not result in behavior that is īlihuiz.

A concern with the precarious order of things, which leads Nacho to represent the relationship between Juan and Blancaflor as developing slowly and carefully, also accounts for why he handled Blancaflor's mutilation differently than other narrators. As mentioned earlier, Florencio and nearly all of the Spanish storytellers—women as well as men—described Juan killing Blancaflor, chopping her up, and shedding her blood as she undergoes death and rebirth.[15] To be sure, Juan is often reluctant, but he is the one who wields the knife, makes the cuts, and stuffs the dismembered pieces of her body into a bottle that he tosses into the sea. For reasons that are not entirely clear, Blancaflor undergoes less mutilation in Mexico, shedding her blood in only one Spanish-speaking and three native Mexican variants.[16] Her mutilation appears to represent her participation in sexual relations and human reproduction. The knife is a phallus and the dismembering and reconstitution of her body stands for giving birth. Usually Juan does the cutting in the stories from Mexico as well as Spain, but in Nacho's tale Blancaflor handles the knife and mutilates herself. When commanded to recover a ring dropped into the sea, Juan goes to Blancaflor for help, and she cuts around her own finger and removes a ring of her dried blood that turns into gold. By making Blancaflor the agent of her own mutilation, Nacho represented his Blancaflor as a woman who maintains control over her own participation in sexual relations and human reproduction.

Relative to other Blancaflors in Spain and Mexico, Nacho's Blancaflor has agency to select her mate, assuming an autonomous role in human reproduction, and the ability to obtain the help of animals enabling a man to live without toil. As fantastic as Blancaflor is, it is nevertheless possible to identify some of the ways that Nacho's image of her is grounded in reality. As the mother of a man's sons, a woman actually does have the reproductive power to enable man to live with less toil because she provides sons whose labor contributes to filling a granary and a purse. She may, of course, give birth to daughters, who make their own contributions to the household economy by providing labor and bringing sons-in-law into their parents' domestic group. From Nacho's point of view, a man needs children to make a living, and he expressed none of the incompatibilities between man as father and man as provider that appeared in the stories of Florencio, Bernardo, Gregoria Ramos, and other narrators in Cáceres villages.

"THE FLIGHT"

When describing the flight, Nacho depicted Blancaflor as the object of her father's search and told how the devil as father "looked" for his

Fig. 8. "The maiden takes a knife and cuts the middle of her finger;
she goes around it."

daughter. He repeatedly used the verb tēmoā ("he or she looks for someone"),[17] which expresses love in ordinary Nahuat speech as well as in folktales. Unlike the devil in stories by Florencio and Gregoria, this father does not attempt to kill Blancaflor. Rather, he wants her to return because he loves her, even though he is the ahmō cualli and personifies all that is bad in the Nahuat human experience. Juan is an incidental object of the devil's search; he is just a pig to be eaten.

This Blancaflor, like the others, succeeds in eluding her pursuer by producing obstacles and making transformations. Consistent with Nacho's view of human relations where forceful and inconsiderate behavior can only disrupt the precarious order, Blancaflor's father has no power to affect his daughter and son-in-law after their escape from his clutches. As mentioned earlier, Florencio represented the patriarch's residual power with his curse that Ursula turn into a serpent for seven years. The ahmō cualli pronounces no curse in Nacho's story; he simply utters the Spanish obscenity chinga'o (chingado, or "fucked," as in "I am fucked") and returns home. This story provides some insight into Nahuat husband-wife relations when the devil's return is depicted after each failed attempt to find his daughter. His wife, who also desperately wants Blancaflor to come back home, says to her husband: "You're a deadhead" (Timihmiquilot) and "You're a mudhead" (Tizoquit) on the many repeated occasions he returns empty-handed. Her language reveals a woman wielding power in her family.

"THE FORGOTTEN FIANCÉE"

Nacho did not end his story with the usual poetic devices that explain why the hero forgets about the heroine in the final episode of "Blancaflor." The poetic devices are a curse and a prohibition, both of which appeared in Florencio's story. Ursula's father utters the curse that she will become a serpent for seven years, and Ursula tells Joaquín not to allow anyone to kiss him. However, Ursula's prohibition is broken when Joaquín's grandmother kisses him while he sleeps, making him forget about the woman who saved him from annihilation. While a curse is unusual, a prohibition appears in most Spanish and Mexican variants of "Blancaflor" that contain the episode of "The Forgotten Fiancée" (Tale Type 313C).[18] The curse, the prohibition, and the manner of its violation have several narrative effects: they represent the efforts of one character to control other characters, and they depict a man's difficulty in transferring his loyalties from the women in his family to his wife. It was mentioned that some Spanish narrators specifically direct the prohibition to a show of affection by a female member of the male protagonist's family.[19] Within Mexico, Nahuat narrator Luciano Vega specified that a kiss from the male protagonist's mother will erase his memory of Blancaflor.

Nacho took the unusual step of removing the prohibition entirely. Blancaflor makes no request; she simply tells Juan he will forget about her when his family bathes (or "smokes") him in incense upon his return. She gives Juan no directives because no one can turn a desire into a command. Moreover, no man or woman makes Juan forget about Blancaflor by showing him affection with a kiss or a hug. The narrative effect is to present a man's transition at marriage with less intense emotional conflict, as perhaps one would expect in a culture encouraging moderation and considerate behavior.

A LAST GLIMPSE OF BLANCAFLOR

Narrators offer a final and sometimes lasting glimpse of Blancaflor, telling what she means to them in their concluding episode of "The Forgotten Fiancée." Florencio represented Ursula, cast in his own image, as a nurturer who brings an unwanted, weak, and sickly calf back to robust health. Ursula is given the calf to raise for Joaquín's wedding banquet as he prepares to marry another woman. When its owners come for it, they have little hope of finding it alive but are astounded by the healthy animal they see before them. The calf refuses to stand up, and Joaquín is among those who hear Ursula say, "Get up, little calf, get up. Don't forget to walk [andar], like your master forgot me in the olive grove [olivar]." Joaquín recovers his memory, he and Ursula embrace, and they celebrate their wedding banquet in fine style.

For Gregoria Ramos Merchán of Piornal in Spain, Blancaflor is the desirable object of men's amorous intentions. No maiden is more beautiful than she, and her husband and his two friends decide to court her. She invites his friends to spend the night in her bed and pours a glass of water over one and places a door over the ribs of the other. The friends, who are only too eager to leave the next morning, nevertheless brag about their stupendous and divine experiences with Blancaflor, as men exaggerate and lie about their sexual conquests. When Juan takes his turn, Blancaflor talks to him through a glass of water, which speaks in her voice, and a glass of wine speaks in Juan's. Juan remembers, they marry, and have a good wedding.[20]

For Nacho, Blancaflor is a woman who can prepare food without toil. "She goes to do a little work and now it is done," says Juan Barajero. The adjective "little" is a typical form of understatement in Nahuat speech; it means, in this case, a great deal of work. This Blancaflor is the same woman who, in an earlier episode, called the animals she loves to perform incredible tasks and offered Juan a glimpse of life without toil. The female character with the supernatural power to provide vast quantities of food appears in many Nahuat stories.[21] Narrators usually identify her as a lightning-bolt woman who wears a pouch from which she takes a single kernel of corn to make a huge quantity of *nixtamal* for tortilla dough and a single bean to prepare a huge pot of bean soup. Like Blancaflor, she is connected intimately with animals and often appears as a serpent in her animal-companion form. She is a sexual being, but she is faithful to her husband and supportive of the Nahuat family order. She changes into her animal form to scare her adulterous husband back into monogamy and repel the sexual advances of men whose attentions she does not want.[22]

The principal difference between Florencio's Ursula and Nacho's Blancaflor is the source of their supernatural power. Although Ursula is a saint, she derived her power from a diabolical source. She used demons to plant the vineyard and cut the crooked pieces of wood, and she inherited her supernatural power from her diabolical parents, who acted like witches by transforming themselves into animals to harm others. Nacho's Blancaflor derives her supernatural power from her love of animals and her connection to the forces of nature. Nacho called her nāhueh, an affectionate kinship term of address that he applied to his mother and his nieces in his extended family. The term translates as "she who is close to all things" in the precarious human and cosmic order.[23]

Florencio's and Nacho's Blancaflors have husbands who need them, but they have different relationships with men. Ursula has very little sexual autonomy; she has no agency to choose her mate, and she passively undergoes brutal mutilation at the hands of her husband, who chops her up and puts the pieces of her body into a demijohn that he throws into the sea. Nacho's Blancaflor has more agency and sexual autonomy; she negotiates her relationship with her husband and carries out her own, much milder form of mutilation by picking up a knife and cutting around her finger to produce the gold ring her father claims he dropped in the sea. While both women have men who depend on them, Blancaflor uses her supernatural power less than Ursula, particularly to complete the impossible tasks demanded by her father. Taking all stories into account, Nacho depicted gender relations with less ambivalence and more autonomy in accord with his view of a man with more diffused relationships in his family. His male characters are connected not only to woman but also to their fathers, sons, and brothers.

Chapter 10

"ORPHEUS"

SO FAR, NACHO HAS EXPRESSED HIS NATIVE MEXICAN IDEN-
tity in stories adopted from Spanish oral tradition. Comparison with
similar tales told by Florencio reveals that Nacho expressed his masculinity by respecting the power of the spoken word, distancing himself from characters who personify inconsiderate behavior, holding a
connected view of a man's relationship with other men, and regarding
woman as "she who is close to all things." Nacho also presented his
masculine identity in two stories about a man searching for his wife
in the land of the dead, part of a native North American Orpheus tradition with no parallels in Spain.

Outside of Spain, Orpheus ballads and the related folktale "The
Man on a Quest for His Lost Wife" (Tale Type 400) are well known in
the folklore of other European countries.[1] Reidar Christiansen examined 285 variants of Tale Type 400, which he refers to as "The Supernatural Bride," collected from nineteenth- and twentieth-century oral
tradition in northern Europe alone. Included in this category are many
variants of "The Swan Maiden" in which the hero loses his wife because he breaks a promise and then searches for her in another realm,
which is usually not the land of the dead. Most stories have happy
endings as the husband successfully finds his wife, returns with her
to his home, and restores his marriage. The tales have considerable
antiquity; Christiansen found their traces, apparently borrowed from
folktales, in European literature dating from the ninth century.[2]

Colonialists from different parts of Europe brought this story to the
Americas, where it was incorporated into native North American oral
tradition.[3] However, it did not travel well across the Pyrenees into
Castilian-speaking Spain. For some reason, lost-wife tales are ex-
tremely rare in Spanish oral tradition, despite the popularity of Tale
Type 400 in other parts of Europe.[4]

Florencio and the other forty-one Cáceres narrators I knew did not tell a story of a man searching for his wife in any location. Spanish-speaking narrators in the United States and Mexico do tell lost-wife tales, as do Nahuat narrators in Santiago Yaonáhuac, perhaps because they are well known among American Indians as well as among settlers originating from parts of Europe other than Spain.[5]

While one certainly cannot rule out Old World origins, Nacho's tales appear to be part of an independent native North American Orpheus tradition distinguishable from the lost-wife tales derived from Europe and adopted by American Indians. Äke Hultkrantz defines that tradition as consisting of stories about a "man or woman who sets out for the realm of the dead to bring back a recently deceased loved one, only, as a rule, to fail."[6] Hultkrantz identified a number of characteristics of native North American Orpheus tales that justify his conclusion that the tradition is probably an indigenous development rather than an importation from Europe. The characteristics include accounts of the hero's desperate state of mind following the death of his loved one, the difficult journey to the land of the dead, and markers of difference between the hero and the dead; the dead eat another kind of food, notice human odor, and sometimes show hostility or emotional coldness to the hero.[7] Hultkrantz based his definition on 120 variants told by narrators in 78 native North American societies in the United States and Canada.[8] He did not include any examples from Mexico, but stories that fit his general description are told by native Mexican narrators who speak Tepecano, Tzotzil Maya, Yucatec Maya, Nahua of Durango, and Nahuat.[9]

Nacho's two tales, when taken as a whole, have four specific story elements that Hultkrantz considered important in the native Orpheus tradition north of Mexico: (1) the hero expresses a great deal of grief over the death of a loved one; (2) he passes into an unusual psychological state; (3) he makes a difficult journey to the land of the dead; (4) he is noticed by his smell.[10] Nacho's stories differ from many native North American Orpheus tales because they do not contain prohibitions which, if broken, mean the loved one will not return to the land of the living.[11] The wife's return on the condition of observing a prohibition is not a common feature of the Orpheus tales told by other native Mexicans.[12]

In his Orpheus tales, Nacho expressed a man's complicated feelings about women: a husband's horror of watching his wife make love with another man and bereavement for a woman who has left him. The image of a man watching his wife make love with another man expresses an Oedipal anxiety that Nacho and Florencio have in common. Florencio expressed similar Oedipal fears when he told how the companions stole the princess from the hero in "The Bear's Son" (Chapter 2). Using a narrative style that mimicked the exploits of his hero, Florencio revealed his close identification with the victim of the companions' treachery. Only Nacho told a story expressing a man's bereavement for a woman who has not been faithful.

NACHO'S FIRST ORPHEUS TALE

Native North American Orpheus stories differ according to the relationship between the hero or heroine and the object of his or her search in the land of the dead. Nacho's first story is about a husband who searches for his dead wife and is the most common type of tale in the North American Orpheus tradition.[13] Nacho used familiar storytelling conventions when telling his first narrative. Like Relajo's compadre, the mourning husband is a man who loves another to excess and consequently places himself in a position of possible annihilation. As in his "Blancaflor," to be annihilated means to be devoured by the ahmō cualli. Nacho's words convey the impression that the hero mourns the loss of his dead wife as lover. Unfortunately, she is "a woman who lived playing around" (cihuāt āhuilnemi), a phrase referring to a woman who makes love with many men. The husband's obsessive feelings of longing and loss for his wife, who he knows has been having sex with other men, compels him to make a difficult journey into a hollow mountain where he enters the land of the dead (mictān).

"The Woman Who Lived Playing Around"
by Nacho Ángel Hernández

One day there was a woman who went about playing around. Her husband never said anything to her because he really loved his wife. And the woman did it with whomever she wanted. Her husband did not frighten her. And he had a sister who told him, "Leave that woman. She plays around a lot. She plays around with men."

But he didn't pay his sister any heed. He wanted to be with his wife because he liked her and found pleasure in being with her. So that woman went on playing around as she wanted. And the day came when she went with her sister-in-law to do laundry. But her sister-in-law did not want to go with her.

"Let's go do the laundry."

"I won't go."

The sister-in-law didn't want to go because she knew her brother's wife spoke to many men, and many men detained her.

"I won't go because I don't like what she does and how they grab her in front of me."

"Let's go," implored the woman who played around.

So the husband's sister gave in, and they were doing the laundry. A man, that is to say a gentleman, appeared and spoke to her.

"Let's go to my house."

"No, I came here to do laundry."

"Yes? Well, I'll give you money."

He gave her the money and grabbed her. He grabbed her and put her on top of his horse and carried her off. Her sister-in-law went home.

"Where did she go?" asked her husband when he came home.

"I don't know. She went to wash clothes and a gentleman grabbed her and took her. He gave her money and took her."

And that man started to feel sad. He started to weep.

"But not for her. I had to take her, and she went away. No, leave her. You saw how she served you. She really lived playing around."

"Yes, but I have to go see her."

He set out looking for her. He went to look for her. He went on and on and found what was perhaps a hilly place, whatever it was, and there were some men; those men were black.

"Where are you going?" they asked.

"Well, nowhere. I'm looking for a woman. Maybe you saw her? Maybe you saw where they took her?"

"Sure. We saw her. She passed through here. They took her."

"I want to go see her."

"Why did you come? No one comes here."

"I came because I am looking for her."

"Well, how did you ever get through to here? You cannot go on through. Well, just this once we're going to drop you off, and you'll return right away. We're going to drop you off this one time."

"Good. I'm going to see where my wife is."

They left him down inside a dangerous place. But who goes where they passed him through a big hollow mountain, a dark place where it was getting thoroughly dark, where there was nothing? He was in a place where wind blew into his face. And

Fig. 9. "But who goes where they passed him through a big hollow
mountain, a dark place where it was getting thoroughly dark,
where there was nothing?"

they took him across. That one, who perhaps was a man, says to him where he dropped him off, "Your wife is hereabouts."

Then, they say, he went to find her sewing.

"You've come!" she exclaims.

"Yes. I ran into a lot of difficulty looking for you."

"It's good you came. Don't be angry. Why did you come? No Earth Christian comes here."

"I came because you left me."

"Yes, but don't be angry. I have another here."

And her husband heard him come shouting.

"Listen. He's coming. You're not going to be seen. Climb up into the loft."

She covered him inside a pot. He heard him shout closer.

"You're going to see him eat me, and you'll see what he does to me."

Yes, he saw that animal closing in on her.

"I've come now," the animal says.

"Yes, you've come," she replies.

"I smell you're keeping an Earth Christian."

"No! Whom do you know who comes here? No one comes here. What you smell is left over from when I was on earth and my husband fondled me."

That animal went over and hauled that woman toward him. Her husband saw him burrow into her bones. He ate all of her. He just left her heart. Her husband watched it all. He was very frightened. Afterwards, he who is not good left. Then the husband saw her heart slip and flip over backwards. It slipped and flipped over backwards. It slipped and flipped over backwards until she made herself whole again and she was as big as she was before, until she became a whole woman again. Yes. Her husband saw he who is not good.

"That is what you wanted. It would have been better if you had not seen your husband," said he who is not good.

Yes, after he finished eating her, he left her heart and went away. Then she started to make herself whole again. She made herself whole again, and then spoke to her husband.

"You saw what he did to me. Here. Take this money. Eat or buy clothes with it. And take these clothes. I sewed them for you. Take them and put them on."

That man came back again. The one who dropped him off waited for the husband, who passed through and arrived home.

Then he decided, "Well, I shouldn't feel sad because I won't be able to go again soon. I would like to go and I do feel sad, but I won't be able to go."

And he went up and reached his sister.

"Well, I've come."

"You've come. Did you find her?"

"Yes, I found her. I brought these clothes and this money. She told me to wear the clothes, and she told me to buy something to eat with the money."

"Yes, but don't wear the clothes and don't eat with the money."

That woman came to the conclusion that the man ought to show those things to a priest.

"I did this," he tells the priest. "I went looking for my wife until I found her. She always played around when she lived here. They took her away from me. I went to find her. She is down there. She gave me these clothes and this money to buy something to eat."

"I see," says the priest.

"Yes, and she has someone else there: he who is not good."

"Don't wear those clothes because, if you do, he'll eat you. The same with the money. He put them out so you would find him. Don't wear them. Then he won't take you. Now it would be better to burn the clothes and the money. You're free. Look for another woman and you'll have a better life."

That man really believed the priest. He looked for another woman to marry. The priest burned all of those clothes and the money for him.

"It's over. He wanted to eat you, but that's not the way it will be. We must burn these clothes and burn this money. You'd be better off looking for another woman and marrying her and you'll be better off with her."

And there it ended.

Nacho took particular care to describe how this husband loves his wife to excess and enjoys her particularly as a lover. He said the man "loved her a great deal" (cimi quitazohtaya), found happiness or pleasure (pāquiliz) in just being with her, ignored her frequent affairs with other men, and felt compelled to look for his wife (tēmoā) after the gentleman, who is unmistakably a Spanish-speaking Mexican, rides away with her on his horse. The husband's excessive love compels him to travel to a dangerous place (ohuihcān) where the custodians pass him through a big hollow mountain (huēi tepēcōnco) that is dark inside and where wind blows into his face. Nacho used conventional symbolism for his culture when he described his protagonist entering the land of the dead (mictān) by falling into a dark abyss. Death is a state of extreme disorder represented by the act of falling and the condition of darkness and cold. Nacho and other Nahuat walk slowly and carefully to avoid falling, by which they could break a bone and enter into an actual state of bodily disorder, and they identify the sources of order as heat and light. Children who fall on the cold ground are said to suffer soul loss, a frequently mentioned cause of death.

The impression Nacho conveyed in words and images is not anger and rage that a man might feel if the woman he loved left him for another man. Rather, the predominant emotions are longing, loss, and horror. The wife is a woman who lives "playing around" (cihuāt āhuil-nemi), an expression for having sex with many men but without the connotation of "slut" or "promiscuous woman" in American English. Rather, the Nahuat I knew used it to refer to a woman who put herself in danger by making herself a plaything for men. Nacho illustrated by dramatic example what the danger is for a woman who "plays around" by describing in graphic detail how she must endure sex as annihilation when the devil devours her and leaves her heart slipping and flipping over backwards on the floor of a cave. Annihilation as a devouring act is a very familiar theme in Nacho's stories, where characters come into contact with the ahmō cualli. The wife's painful sexual experiences, while in the clutches of her jealous demon lover, most assuredly warn women against marital infidelity. Nacho's tale performs a didactic function of restricting woman's sexual autonomy, and it could easily be a male fantasy of what happens to a woman who leaves her husband, thinking that she has found a better lover. Nevertheless, the image of a heart slipping and flipping over backwards until a woman reforms herself suggests that even the ahmō cualli cannot deprive a woman of the power of reproduction, even though she may "play around" with men.

The hero escapes annihilation because of his connection to his sister, who repeatedly tries to counsel her brother. His sister tells him to leave his wife, is reluctant to go with her sister-in-law to do laundry, and tries to persuade her brother not to look for his wife after she is taken by the devil. His sister eventually saves her brother from annihilation by telling him to see a priest after he returns with gifts of clothes and money. The brother-sister relationship can be very strong in the Nahuat families of Huitzilan. Brother and sister sometimes select each other to be the baptismal sponsors of their children, and brothers fiercely defend their sisters when mistreated by their husbands. One of the most dramatic examples of outrage I witnessed in Huitzilan took place when a Nahuat man yelled obscenities (in Spanish) and threw very large rocks at the house of his former brother-in-law, who had abandoned his sister for another woman.

NACHO'S SECOND ORPHEUS TALE

The mourner in Nacho's second tale is a younger brother who searches for his older sister, the two of whom lived together as husband and wife. A brother searching for his dead sister appears in a number of native North American Orpheus tales.[14] Nacho used repetition to convey how the mourner reaches a desperate psychological state from his intense feelings of longing and loss. The story supports the incest taboo and contains language and imagery representing the possible early childhood source of Nacho's anxieties about recapitulating the Oedipal triangle. Once again, the brother, who looks for his dead sister and lover, is a man who faces annihilation by being devoured when he encounters the ahmō cualli in the underworld.

"The Brother Who Looked for His Sister"

by Nacho Ángel Hernández

One day there were two siblings; one was a man and the other was a woman. And, they say, they loved each other: the woman as much as the man. The woman had never had a man, and the boy did not have a woman. They loved each other. They only served each other. And the day came, they say, when the sister died. She died, and from there on, he lived looking for her. He looked for that sister of his. She died. And so it was, he really looked for her. He did not know where she was. He cried as he lived. So he went to see a priest.

"I am really looking for my sister," he says. "Where can I find her?"

"Do you want to see her?"

"Yes, I want to see her."

So the priest opened where they passed. They say he opened it up, and the brother went to see her.

"You will find your sister sewing."

Then the man went, he went to see his sister. They say she was sewing a blanket.

"You came," she says.

"Yes, I came." I really looked for you until I don't know what. I really looked for you until I didn't know where I was."

"You shouldn't have come. You came only because you had to. No one comes here."

"I came and I was so desperate that I didn't know what I was doing. I really looked for you."

"But you shouldn't have come. I have a man here. I have a man

here who commands me. Well, now you're going to see him because he'll come. Don't you hear that man shouting? Listen to
him coming now. He's coming right away to see you. Climb up
into the loft."

He climbed up into the loft and went into a pot.

"You go in here, and I'm going to put a lid over you. You put it
on well. Just watch me with one eye. You'll be able to look down
and see the man come."

He was heard close by. Now he arrived. The brother heard him
shout again.

"He's coming now," says the sister.

That man came to stand in the corridor. They say her brother
saw that the man's mouth was down to here [Nacho gestured to
his waist]. They say he was a goat. They say he came sniffing in
the corridor.

"I smell that you're keeping meat here," he declares.

"No."

"Certainly you are. I smell you're keeping an Earth Christian."

"No, never!"

"Sure you are."

"My clothes still carry the scent of my crotch from when I
came. But there is no one here."

"Yes there is; you're keeping him."

"No, I'm not keeping him. I'm not keeping him. How can you
say that? There isn't anyone here."

Then, they say, he grabbed his wife and started to scare her. He
frightened her and started to eat her. He finished eating her and
left just a little of her. He just left her heart. He made a loud crack-
ing noise, finishing everything. He finished eating her. He just left
her heart. From there, that animal went away. Her brother saw everything. They say he was frightened. He was afraid. He watched
her heart as it slipped and flipped over backwards on the ground.
It slipped and flipped over backwards. It slipped and flipped over
backwards. They say she started to revive herself that way. She
began to slip and flip over backwards until she made herself
whole and reappeared as a woman.

"Come down," she says to her brother.

He came down.

"You saw clearly what happened to me. He is the man I am with
here. Now you saw what happened to me. Now it would be better
for you to work and look for a woman. Look for a woman so you
don't do to yourself what I did to myself. Look for a woman and
go work. And take some money I've been gleaning from him.
Now wait for me. I'm going there. I'll go there tomorrow, and
watch for me down by your feet. Watch for me."

Then, they say, her brother came. He arrived and was watching
and waiting for that soul to appear. He looked and saw a big fly—
one of those great big flies. He saw it come out. It started walking
around. He decided to hit it with his hat. The next day, they say,
he went to see his sister again.

"You didn't tell me the truth."

"I went, but you just hit me."

"That was you? But how could it have been?"

"I went."

That is how he realized a flying insect is a soul. Many are seen
about. There are many of those flying insects. They say that souls
are flying insects or flies.

As in the first story, Nacho set the plot of his second tale into motion by specifying that the brother and sister love each other to excess.
He repeated that they loved each other and implied that their love was
incestuous by saying they "served each other" (motequipanohuayah),
an expression restricted to the marital relationship. Neither the sister
nor her brother have ever left the nuclear family to live as husband
and wife with another. The moral message of the tale supports the
incest taboo by explaining why a man must look for another woman
as wife. Nacho indicated that the sister is older than her brother, referring to them respectively as a woman (cihuāt) and a boy (tēlpōch =
youth or young man). Had Nacho wished to express age symmetry, he
would have used parallel terms—cihuāt and tācat (man) or ichpōch
(maiden or young woman) and tēlpōch. In a culture where age is important in family life as well as in kinship terminology, the age asymmetry between this sister and brother suggests, by metaphorical extension, that Nacho is also describing the relationship between a
mother and her son.[15]

The graphic image of the ahmō cualli devouring the sister could then
be the representation of an early childhood memory of the primal
scene.[16] Nacho and other Nahuat have the opportunity to witness
their parents making love because of the sleeping arrangements in
cramped quarters. I could not reconstruct what actually happened in
Nacho's early childhood because he was twenty-four when I met him,
his father was dead, and his mother was sixty-five. To have asked his
mother if Nacho had seen her and her dead husband have sex would
have been extremely inconsiderate behavior (īlihuiz). One can infer
the probability that Nacho and his brothers may have witnessed their
parents having sex by examining their own sleeping behavior, which
they probably learned from their parents.

As mentioned earlier, Nacho, when I first met him, lived with his widowed mother, his two older brothers Miguel and Nicolás, and their wives and children in two dwellings consisting of three small rooms. Miguel and his wife María Agustina Ayance slept on separate mats placed on the earthen floor in a very small room, originally built to provide a sleeping space for some members of the extended family while the brothers were rebuilding the main dwelling. María Agustina slept with her newborn infant on one mat, and Miguel slept with his son Juan (age five) and daughter Jovita (age two) on another. Jovita had slept with her mother until the sixth month of the mother's next pregnancy. At that time, María Agustina had weaned Jovita by putting a bitter herb (chichicxihuit) on her nipples and passing Jovita over to Miguel's mat to keep the child from taking the breast at night. Nacho explained that married couples ordinarily abstain from sex for six months following the birth of a baby, after which the father visits the mother at night by discreetly moving over to her mat. At that time, a nursing infant could easily observe close at hand his or her parents making love. The sleeping arrangements of Nicolás and his wife María Gabriela and their children, who occupied the room next to Miguel and María Agustina, illustrate that some children sleep exclusively with the mother until they are twenty months old. Nicolás slept on one mat with his sons Francisco (age nine), Enrique (age five), and sometimes José Ramírez (age eleven) when José was not sleeping with his grandmother in the dwelling next door. His wife, María Gabriela, slept on a different mat with her twenty-month-old baby, who probably witnessed Nicolás making love to María on her mat. Older children who sleep with the father have opportunities to watch their parents having sex, but they witness the primal scene from a greater physical distance. Memories of what they saw while sleeping first with the mother and then with the father could easily appear in Nacho's second Orpheus tale.

Nacho represented the primal scene as the ahmō cualli violently grabbing the sister, burrowing into her bones, and devouring all of her body except for her heart, which he leaves on the ground. Freud observed that children who witness the primal scene see parental sex as subjugation and also as cannibalism, if they are still nursing and in the oral phase, because they have not yet separated sexual activity from the ingestion of food.[17]

Nacho represented the sister's subordination to her new lover by combining the Spanish verb *mandar* (to order, to command) with a Nahuat ending to make nechmandaroā ("he commands me") when telling how the sister depicted her relationship with the ahmō cualli as one of submission. The sister's near complete disappearance after the ahmō cualli devours most of her body could express a childhood memory of separation from the mother at weaning. A child might interpret the move from the mother's to the father's mat as the mother's disappearance.

As in a dream, several characters in this Orpheus story may represent different aspects of the same person. This ahmō cualli is no Spanish-speaking Mexican who rides a horse, offers money, and takes a woman to his underground abode. He is a grotesque but small animal—his head is waist high—that stands in the corridor shouting and could be the child's image of himself crying (screaming) when being weaned. He appears as a grotesque figure because, according to the omnipotence of his own thought, the child has caused his mother to wean him because of his own repulsiveness. The ahmō cualli devouring the sister could be a man's memory of his wish as an infant to devour the mother, a wish nourished in frustration following weaning. The brother hiding inside the pot in the loft may be the child, now older, who sleeps on the father's mat and witnesses his parents making love from a greater distance. Now the ahmō cualli, jealous of the mother's contact with an Earth Christian, resembles a jealous father. In our journey through the Nahuat poetic imagination, we have already found two expressions of Oedipal aggression between fathers and sons in other stories (Chapter 3). A son threatens his father in Nacho's "The Bear's Son," and a father brutally punishes his son in Juan Hernández' variant of the same tale. Both the bear and his son personify īlihuiz and are not models for a man to follow.

Nacho's Orpheus tales make the point that a man who loves an inaccessible woman must break his attachment to her and move on to another. The sister is an important instrumental agent in her brother's transference of affection from his mother to a woman outside the nuclear family in both stories. In the first tale, the sister acted out her role as intermediary agent by imploring her brother to leave his wife, and this sister eventually saved him from being devoured by the ahmō cualli by directing him to a priest before wearing the clothes and spending the money provided by the dead wife. The sister in the second tale plays a similar role as intermediary agent by encouraging her brother to find another woman in order to prevent what happens to her from happening to him. Again, the emotional tone in Nacho's tale is not anger, requiring that the brother as husband take aggressive action to bring his wife back from the land of the dead. There is no suggestion in this story that the sister, who suffers the same horrible fate as the wife in the first Orpheus tale, is getting what she deserves. Nacho's narrative style conveys only a sense of loss and longing and an awareness that the brother cannot have his sister, however much he loves her.

NACHO'S MASCULINITY

In telling the Orpheus story, Nacho represented his masculinity differently than Florencio for several reasons. To begin with the most obvious, Nacho had folktale models from the native North American Orpheus tradition with which to express his Oedipal anxieties and his bereavement over the loss of a woman as love object. Florencio lacked the same models because Orpheus tales do not circulate in Castilian-Spanish oral tradition. Scholars offer a number of explanations for the appeal of Orpheus tales in North America, and some of their ideas apply to the language and imagery of Nacho's stories, which stressed a man's bereavement for his dead wife.[18]

Äke Hultzkrantz offered the most useful theory, which serves as a point of departure for interpreting this native tradition. Noting the similarities between the imagery in the tales and in the accounts of shamans, he hypothesized that the stories originated in shamanistic trances. He was particularly struck by the similarities between the psychological states of the mourners in the Orpheus tales and shamans as they enter a trance and prepare to travel to the land of the dead "to fetch the soul" of someone who is seriously ill.[19] Nacho's tales, of course, support this hypothesis to the extent that he, like other narrators in the Orpheus tradition, stressed the desperate psychological state of the husband in one story and his shamanlike journey to the land of the dead in another. His account of the husband's descent into the land of the dead in his first Orpheus tale is remarkably similar to a description that the Nahuatl shaman Antonio Pérez gave of his descent into Popcatepetl when interrogated by colonial officials in 1761.[20]

Taking a historical approach, Hultkrantz nevertheless recognized that the conditions that may have given rise to the native North American Orpheus tradition are not necessarily the same as those accounting for its popularity. Hultkrantz understood that the story changed "to conform to new viewpoints" as it spread from its original source and shamans no longer were its primary tellers.[21] His origins hypothesis cannot account for the appeal of Orpheus tales to a man like Nacho, who is not a shaman but who nevertheless represented his own experiences when telling his stories.

One of the noticeable features of Nahuat culture contributing to the appeal of Orpheus tales is the important connection between the living and the dead. The dead are continually involved with the living, usually disrupting their lives, particularly when someone engages in inconsiderate speech and pronounces the name of the "owl man" (tācatecolōt), another term for the ruler of the underworld. As Alan and Pamela Sandstrom explain so clearly, the "owl man" can lead the dead against the living;[22] thus, to pronounce his name is an act of īlihuiz. The owl is a harbinger of death, and I have heard Nahuat in Huitzilan describe how they threw stones to chase away owls that appeared in trees near their homes at night. The owl as harbinger of death has a long history in the Nahua world. As Louise Burkhart notes, it was associated with sorcery and the underworld in the sixteenth century and the bird's call indicated "the imminent demise of the hearer or the hearer's child."[23] Like many native and Spanish-speaking Mexicans, the Nahuat placate the spirits of their dead relatives by offering food, sweets, and cigarettes during Todos Santos.[24]

Not all people in Mexico, holding similar beliefs and practicing the same rituals, necessarily tell Orpheus stories. Nacho's tales contain images that point to still other reasons for why he described men grieving the loss of women who are now with other men. Hultkrantz provides a useful hint for understanding the meaning of Nacho's tales when he noted that the native North American Orpheus tradition expresses "wish fulfillment for the desire to be reunited with a beloved dead person."[25] Nacho's tales anticipate a man's experience of losing the woman he loves. Nacho was still unmarried when he told the first Orpheus tale, but he knew many Nahuat men whose wives had left them for other men. Nahuat maidens in Huitzilan marry just after passing into puberty, and many early relationships are unstable, despite elaborate courtship rituals that ostensibly ensure a long and fruitful marriage. A young man (tēlpōch) initiates a courtship with a maiden (ichpōch) by announcing to his parents his intention to marry. His parents look for an intermediary (cihuātanqueh), an old and respected woman who makes several visits to the maiden's parents carrying the boy's proposal. If all parties agree to the match, the two families set a date for the betrothal celebration in the home of the maiden's parents, where the groom and his family deliver the bridewealth consisting of turkeys, spices, cigarettes, *aguardiente,* and some money. After the betrothal ceremony, the bride ordinarily lives with her hus-

Fig. 10. Nacho, Victoria, and their first child, a son.

band's parents and works under the direction of her mother-in-law.
Young couples have a difficult time adjusting to married life, and
many young brides return home or fall in love with other men. Some
young Nahuat women become involved with Spanish-speaking Mexican men, who offer them money in return for sex, as in Nacho's first
story.

NACHO'S "RELATIONAL CAPACITIES"

Nacho's Orpheus tales, which express a man's wish to be reunited
with the woman he loves, are part of his connected view of the human
condition and reveal another dimension of his relational masculinity.
With the help of Chodorow's revision of Freud's theory of gender, it is
possible to identify some of the ways in which Nacho's relational
masculinity may have developed in his extended family. Chodorow
points out that relationality originates in the mother-infant relationship during which the child develops empathy as an extension of self
and experiences reciprocal primary love, identification and sense of
oneness with the mother, orality, and mutual mother-infant attachment.[26] Ordinarily, in families where the mother primarily parents infant children, relationality becomes part of femininity but not masculinity because mothers experience sons as "a male opposite." They
"push the son out of the pre-Oedipal relationship," and boys consequently "curtail their primary love and sense of empathic tie with
their mother." The result is more pronounced "individuation" for
boys. The girl, however, remains more attached to the mother and
acquires a stronger basis for empathy, "experiencing another's needs
or feelings as one's own." Girls, in contrast to boys, "do not define
themselves in terms of the denial of pre-Oedipal relational modes."[27]

Nevertheless, we have found in our journey through Nacho's poetic
imagination many examples of his relational capacities when he represented characters as connected rather than autonomous. Relative to
Florencio, Nacho depicted an unusually connected view of human relations that probably developed in the crucible of his cohesive extended family. His connected view of human relations first appeared
in his version of "The Bear's Son," in which the hero had more solidarity with his male companions (Chapter 2). Nacho represented exchange by placing a higher value on human love than on the acquisition of wealth and property (Chapter 4), and he depicted how his ideas
of exchange differed from those of Spanish-speaking Mexicans, represented as the ahmō cualli (Chapter 9). He presented a picture of more

diffused family relations (Chapter 7), which gave him a different perspective on women, whom he described with comparatively less ambivalence and contradiction than did Florencio (Chapters 8 and 9). Nacho's accounts of a husband's bereavement and search for a beloved dead wife, even though she has not been faithful, are other expressions of his relational capacities because they extend his connected view of human relations from the living to the dead.

It is possible for relational capacities to develop in boys, particularly if the father is involved in the care of his infant son. The basis for relationality exists in the infant son's pre-Oedipal relationship with the mother. It is a reasonable deduction from psychoanalytic theory that the father can reproduce relationality by meeting his son's "attachment needs" immediately after weaning. Attachment needs refer to the "primary need for human contact itself" during the pre-Oedipal period in early infancy.[28] Attachment behavior is manifest when children demand a lot of body contact; it develops around six months, and it reaches its peak around one year to eighteen months.[29] It can be directed to anyone who has a strong relationship with the infant, and that person may or may not be the mother. According to Chodorow, this finding has crucial importance for those who think there are benefits for getting fathers involved in caring for young children because it can help develop relational capacities in men that are necessary for their success in parenting.[30]

Nacho and his brothers may have acquired relational capacities if their father parented them as Miguel and Nicolás are parenting their own children. On the basis of what he knew of his own extended family, Nacho explained that it is customary to move a child over to the father's sleeping mat when the child is weaned during the sixth month of the mother's next pregnancy. Nacho reported that at this point the father plays an important role, providing physical comfort to the recently weaned child by holding the child on his knee and sleeping with the child on his own mat—usually around the time the child's attachment needs are reaching a peak. I suspect that men like Nacho's father and brothers in this way reproduce the relational capacities in their sons that Nacho expressed in his stories.

At the same time, fathers may also help their sons separate from the mother with less anger toward women. Robert Stoller observed that for a boy to develop a masculine identity, he must move from the world of the mother to the world of the father. When his relationship with the mother is extraordinarily close, he may have to "erect intrapsychic barriers that ward off his blissful sense of being one with the mother."[31] Exclusive mother-infant sleeping arrangements, such as in

Nacho's family, might intensify a boy's connection with the mother and require the construction of what Stoller called a "protective shield," which originally takes the form of fantasy and may become the traits of "character" that include fear and deprecation of women.[32] It is a reasonable conclusion from Stoller's work that a father, who actively cares for his infant son, can contribute to reducing his son's need to build a protective shield by helping the son separate from the mother. The result is the reproduction of a masculine identity in which there is less fear and greater respect for the autonomy of women.

Nacho's stories express the psychological processes described by Chodorow and Stoller. His connected cosmovision, which includes his expression of a man's wish to be reunited with the woman he loves, reveals his relational capacities. His less ambivalent and contradictory image of "Blancaflor" (Chapter 9), relative to Florencio's, is attributable to his having more easily made the transition from the world of the mother to the world of the father because his father was heavily involved in his care as an infant. It is possible that Nacho, as the surviving youngest child, benefited from a particularly close relationship with his father. The Nahuat use the term taxocoyot for "youngest child," and the word is derived from the verb xocoya, which translates as "to sour, ferment, spoil."[33] Taxocoyot carries the connotation of "spoiled" or "indulged" because of the perception that parents lavish more affection on their youngest son or daughter.[34]

Chapter 11

CONCLUSIONS

THE HUSBAND MOURNING HIS LOST WIFE IN NACHO'S Or-
pheus tales reminds me of the Nahuat pouring out their grief at Victorio Cruz's funeral. Victorio died following a week of vomiting and
loss of appetite. His body lay inside an open pine coffin in his parent's
home and was covered with a white cloth. Mourners spent the night
near his coffin, and a steady stream of relatives and friends arrived
early the next day bearing flowers, corn, candles, and chicken. Women
were in the kitchen, and men were in the room with the coffin, talking, drinking *aguardiente*, and eating dishes of *mole*. At about one
o'clock in the afternoon, Nacho led us through the rosary.

The moment for burial had arrived and women joined the men in the
incense-filled room, sobbing with grief and uttering the word tepitzin
("the little thing") over and over. Each mourner bent down and kissed
the cloth over Victorio's face. His coffin was nailed shut and taken to
the cemetery in a solemn procession. Victorio's family preserved his
memory by holding nine nightly prayers after his funeral, by naming
Nacho as the godparent of the cross, and by making another procession to the cemetery on the ninth day after Victorio's death to place
the cross at the head of his grave. They put offerings of food on a special table covered with a white cloth and decorated with flowers and
an image of the Virgin Mary. They continued to place food on their
altar for the annual Day of the Dead because of their conviction that
Victorio would look (tēmoā) for them as the husband looked for his
wife in Nacho's Orpheus tales.

To look for another (tēmoā) is an expression of love and connection
in Nahuat culture. In our journey through Nacho's poetic imagination, we have come upon many other expressions of connection in
his stories, originally adopted from Spanish oral tradition. Nacho presented a fuller picture of the hero's father in "The Bear's Son" (AT 301)

and eliminated sexual competition between the hero and his companions. He presented brothers with interdependence in "The Master Thief" (AT 1525) and described a high degree of fraternal communality in "The Two Travelers" (AT 613). Nacho's connected view of male relationships is one of the reasons he used words carefully and avoided speaking with īlihuiz (inconsiderately). Nacho used language according to his conception of masculinity in which a man should act carefully lest he disrupt the fragile order of his body, his family, and his cosmos. Out of a desire to avoid īlihuiz, Nacho distanced himself from the bold and courageous Bear's Son, whom he sent into the periphery.[1]

Behavior that represents īlihuiz can occur in any encounter, but a Nahuat expects it when dealing with a Spanish-speaking Mexican. It occurred in a minor way when the *razón* (Spanish-speaking Mexican) asked me if I worked with the ahmō cualli (he who is not good). It took place in a major way when the same *razón* tried to extort livestock from Nacho and his brothers when their mother was ill. Nacho expressed his concept of īlihuiz in interethnic relations in two of his stories of Spanish origin. The first was the trickster in "The Rich and the Poor Peasant" (AT 1535), who personified īlihuiz and annihilated the man who loved him. The second was the devil in "Blancaflor" (AT 313C), who played cards with the hero, whom he threatened to devour just as Spanish-speaking Mexicans gobbled up Nahuat land in Nacho's community of Huitzilan de Serdán. In many of Nacho's stories, the devil, whom Nacho referred to with the euphemism "he who is not good" (ahmō cualli) to avoid speaking with īlihuiz, appeared as a Spanish-speaking Mexican.

It was Nacho's desire to avoid behaving with īlihuiz that made him look passive relative to Florencio, who used strong language to mimic his strong and courageous heroes. Florencio, like many men of his culture, used words assertively, employing blasphemous and scatological expressions, hyperbole, and plot inventions to give his heroes a personal stamp. Unlike Nacho, who distanced himself from the strong and fearless Bear's Son, Florencio described his hero as an extension of himself. Florencio's assertive style of narration, mimicking his strong and fearless heroes, was based on a view of male relationships in which autonomy was an important value. No man should be beholden to another man, not even God, so Florencio sprinkled his stories with liberal doses of "I shit on God" to express his independence from divine authority. Of course, to curse the divine was also to recognize the importance of divine (and human) authority in his affairs. Florencio had to earn his masculinity by establishing his independence from his father, from the wealthy in his community, and from his god. In his village of Navaconcejo, a man acquires autonomy from other men by making shrewd transactions to obtain property. Florencio's hero in "The Rich and the Poor Peasant" (AT 1535) was not tied to other men by love. Instead, he was an unpromising hero of entrepreneurial capitalism, capable of turning the tables on others who had an initial advantage. Florencio's trickster had the freedom to operate with autonomy in an amoral world.[2]

Florencio nevertheless painted a verbal portrait of male relationships that differed from those by other men in his culture. He was an unusual man because he nurtured his sons with food; consequently, he toned down sexual rivalry among the Bear's Son (AT 301) and his companions, and he inserted the father into the lives of his sons in "Blood Brothers" (AT 303). But Florencio was also encouraged by his culture to use words assertively to depict aggressive masculine heroes unrestrained by bonds of love to other men and unconcerned about disrupting the social order. Florencio still remained the autonomous Hispanic Man in his most daring departures from the storytelling conventions of his culture.

Nacho's and Florencio's perspectives on man's relationship with other men were directly related to their views of man's relationship with woman. Nacho's connected vision of a man's relationship with other men was related to his respect for a woman's reproductive power. His Blancaflor was nāhueh—"she who is close to all things," whose power provides a man with sons who can free him from a life of toil. Nacho's respect for the reproductive power of woman converted into his respect for a woman's reproductive and sexual autonomy. Florencio, who represented man as isolated from other men, depicted man as dependent on Blancaflor (or Ursula), who lacked sexual and reproductive autonomy and passed from one man to another in a marriage exchange. Yet despite man's efforts to possess and exchange woman, Florencio recognized that man was actually powerless to control woman. His Blancaflor emerged as far more powerful than her father and her husband. Because a man depends so heavily on a woman, he perceives her with ambivalence. Florencio's contradictory picture of woman was particularly evident in his depiction of Blancaflor's identity and her origins: she was a saint born of parents who were devils.

Florencio's autonomous and Nacho's connected or relational masculinities were molded by their cultures, their families, and their particular historical experiences. Florencio was the living example of the Hispanic Man who achieved his masculinity as he asserted his autonomy by accumulating private property. George Collier demonstrated the relationship between the value on male autonomy and private property for men in Florencio's generation, who came of age during the period of Spain's labor-intensive agrarian economy, which was based heavily on wage labor, or alienated labor.[3] Marx argued that alienated labor, according to which a worker is severed from the product of labor by being paid a wage, produces an alienated or estranged consciousness in which man sees himself as disconnected from other men.[4] Florencio represented and reproduced his comparatively but not absolutely disconnected consciousness when telling his folktales, depicting an absent father and brothers in the process of assuming their economic independence.

There is some reason to believe that capitalism produces an autonomous or disconnected masculinity because of its effects on the organization of parenting labor in the family. Without a thorough knowledge of the historical changes that have taken place in Florencio's village of Navaconcejo, it is difficult to determine the extent to which capitalism has changed the particular organization of parenting labor which may have reproduced his comparatively disconnected consciousness. A hypothetical connection between capitalism and the organization of parenting labor is found in syntheses of Marxist and Freudian theory. Chodorow argues that capitalism has made the home less a place of work, removed men from child care, and left women with the bulk of the responsibility for caring for children and for men.[5] Under such conditions, men spend their early childhood in the world of the mother and then make an abrupt transition to that of the father, who in Florencio's case was distant, autonomous, and demanding. Florencio consequently developed fewer relational capacities, which Chodorow defines as empathy as an extension of self, reciprocal primary love, orality, and mutual mother-infant attachment that becomes the pre-Oedipal foundation of femininity.[6] The father's remoteness means that a boy like Florencio must take assertive action to construct a protective shield so as not to slip back into what Robert Stoller called the comfortable mother-infant symbiosis and "regress" to the world of woman.[7]

David Gilmore argues that most cultures promote an assertive masculinity by preventing boys from regressing to the world of the mother.[8] However, Nacho's case suggests other possibilities. Nacho's connected view of the human condition was a product of another culture and a different family organization and personal history. His culture features a highly connected cosmovision in which humans are connected to animals, spirits interfere in human affairs, and death only transforms but does not sever ties among human beings. The differences between Florencio's and Nacho's cultures are matters of degree. Florencio also declared that humans can transform themselves into animals with diabolical intervention, and he recognized his neighbors' belief in supernaturalism; furthermore, the Nahua food offerings to dead relatives are a synthesis of native Mexican and Spanish traditions.[9] Nevertheless, Nacho expressed a more connected vision of human relationships than did Florencio in their common folktales that originated from Spain. Nacho's connected view was represented and reproduced in the extended family where he and his brothers shared the fruits of their labor, which filled the granary and purse from which everyone could draw according to need. The communal organization of their labor was one reason Nacho represented a more connected consciousness in his stories about fathers, sons, and brothers.

The Nahua family has changed in many ways since the Spanish conquest of Mexico. Susan Kellogg provides a glimpse of changes that took place during the first centuries of colonial rule in the Valley of Mexico.[10] The sibling-extended family began to disappear; women lost their status as sisters in the kin group and were reduced to wives in the conjugal family. Nacho, nevertheless, is the living example of a man raised in a cohesive extended family whose members resisted the effects of wage labor. When Nacho ventured outside his extended family, he had to participate in the world of alienated labor controlled by the Spanish-speaking Mexicans of his village. His stories express how he was able to dichotomize his experiences by personifying the world of modern capitalism as the ahmō cualli.

The communal organization of labor in Nacho's patrilineally extended family depended heavily on close ties among men, which were reproduced with an organization of parenting labor different from the one in Florencio's family. Nacho grew up in a household where men assume a great deal of responsibility in taking care of their young, recently weaned sons and daughters. The nurturing care of a Nahuat father appears to reproduce in his sons a preconsciously or unconsciously established sense of oneness with another. Relative to Florencio, Nacho represents a different confluence of Marxist and psychoanalytic principles. Nacho embodies the idea that the role of the father is important in helping a boy make the transition from the world of the mother to that of the father without developing a highly autonomous and assertive masculinity.[11]

Like many in his village, Nacho lived a precarious existence as he traveled between two worlds in his own Huitzilan de Serdán. One world was that of his extended family where men reproduced in their sons a relational masculinity. The other was the economy of alienated labor created when Spanish-speaking Mexicans moved into the Huitzilan and acquired Nahuat land. Nacho's existence was particularly precarious because Huitzilan's history is laced with episodes of violence and bloodshed brought about by landlessness, alienation, and male aggression. I spent most of my time with Nacho during a period of relative calm, but as I prepared to leave Huitzilan to do fieldwork in Spain, his community became the scene of political turmoil when members of two political factions, La Unión Campesina Independiente (The Independent Farmers' Union) and La Antorcha Campesina (The Torch of the Farmer), fought for political control of the village.

The history of their conflict sounds like one of Nacho's stories in which one act of īlihuiz sets into motion a chain of disastrous events. The initiating act of īlihuiz took place when Spanish-speaking Mexicans took Nahuat land once used for growing corn and beans and converted it to a cattle pasture. The heirs of the Spanish-speaking Mexicans fought over the land and tied it up in the courts. The leader of La Unión Campesina appeared in the village in 1977, and he hatched a plan to seize the intestate pasture and convert it back into a communally planted milpa. After several efforts to disband La Unión Campesina, the Mexican government allegedly responded to the crisis in Huitzilan by sending in La Antorcha Campesina to wrest control from La Unión and take over the village. Over two hundred men, women, and children died in the violent clashes between La Unión and La Antorcha. One of their stray bullets struck and killed Victoria, leaving Nacho without the woman he loved. It is a cruel irony that Nacho, whose culture and family encouraged considerate behavior, was the victim of masculine aggression. I remember Victoria with a great deal of warmth and sadness, and I am sure that Nacho looks for her as the men in his stories looked for their wives in the land of the dead.

Appendix

"THE BEAR'S SON"
IN SPANISH
AND NAHUAT

THIS BOOK DESCRIBES HOW FLORENCIO AND NACHO REPRE-
sented and reproduced their conceptions of masculinity in the way
they used language to narrate their stories. Their versions of the popular folktale "The Bear's Son" (Tale Type 301) illustrate how they each
used their languages differently to represent a strong and courageous
hero. Their respective ways of using words to represent their hero are
typical of the narrative styles they used to tell the other folktales in
their repertoires. This appendix contains the original language texts
of their variants of "The Bear's Son" so that interested readers can examine Florencio's and Nacho's words for themselves.

Florencio told his tale in Castilian Spanish, and his use of language is typical for Cáceres villagers of his generation in Spain. Isabel
García, who is also a native of Cáceres and was born and raised in the
town of Ahigal, helped me correct my transcription of Florencio's stories. Nacho told his story in Nahuat, a language that is known as the
Zacapoaxtla dialect of General Aztec, or Nahuatl.[1] Nacho's village of
Huitzilan de Serdán is fifteen miles from Zacapoaxtla in the northern
Sierra de Puebla. Nacho and I carefully went over all of his stories
and the tales I collected from the other Nahuat storytellers in his
village. He provided me with invaluable assistance in correcting my
transcriptions and explaining to me the meaning of his words.

Nacho's words closely resemble those described by Harold Key and
Mary Ritchie de Key in their dictionary of Zacapoaxtla Aztec.[2] Nacho
also used a word structure that accords with the grammar prepared

by Dow F. Robinson, who spent many years in Zacapoaxtla.[3] Frances Karttunen examined the dictionary prepared by Key and Ritchie de Key and concluded that Zacapoaxtla Aztec differs from Classical Aztec, or Nahuatl, because the former is "a T-dialect; it has lost the characteristic lateral release of Tl."[4] She devised an accessible way of writing Nahua languages that uses a minimum of diacritical markers, and she corrected some of the errors in the dictionary compiled by Key and Ritchie de Key. One error, for example, was Key and Ritchie de Key's placement of long vowels immediately before a glottal stop, which is an impossibility in Nahua languages.[5] Whenever possible, I have represented all Nahuat words in accord with the method for writing Nahua developed by Karttunen. I made necessary corrections to account for the loss of the lateral release of Tl in Nahuat and Nacho's particular use of words, which occasionally departed from what appears in Karttunen's dictionary.

Because Nahuat is a much less accessible language than Castilian Spanish, I provide an interlinear translation of Nacho's version of "The Bear's Son." Nacho's patient and thorough explanations of his own words, coupled with Karttunen's dictionary, provided the basis of my translations of his story. Translation is a complicated process by which the denotative and figurative meanings of words in one language are converted into those of another. I confronted a difficult and sometimes insurmountable problem of finding the right words in idiomatic English to represent the original meanings in Nacho's as well as Florencio's stories. My purpose in translation was to remain faithful to the original meanings and yet produce accessible stories for readers in English. I also wanted to provide specialists with a clear picture of how I interpreted Nacho's and Florencio's words. So I decided on the strategy of providing free translations in idiomatic English in the body of this book and more literal translations of the original Nahuat texts in this appendix (and in a companion document entitled "Original Language Texts for 'The Bear and His Sons'"). Florencio's stories appear only in Castilian Spanish, which is a much more familiar language. The free translations differ from the literal ones in several respects, one of the most notable being tense consistency. Nacho and Florencio tended to shift tense, particularly as they moved from their description of events to their accounts of characters' dialogue. Verb tense in the free translations is more consistent to conform to the expectations and requirements for readability of an English-reading audience.

"THE BEAR'S SON" BY FLORENCIO RAMOS

Bueno, pues ésto era una vez un señor que era muy rico y tenía una hija. Soltera claro. Y la hija, pues lo que pasa, sea ella novia de alguno tal o cual, la cosa es que ya la hija empezó a echar barriga. Y dijon [dijeron], "Pues ésto tal."

"Pues nada," dijo el padre. "¡Me cago en diez! Cuando le tengas a él, y tal y cual, que yo bueno pues bien."

La hija, como en efecto, pasar unos tiempos, pues tuvo un niño. Y como el padre la había metido el miedo de que la iba a hacer, la iba a acontecer, que tal, que cual, pues se le dió a un cazador y le dijo, dice, "Mire, te doy tanta cantidad para que no . . . y el niño le extravía o le lleva al monte, vamos lo que tú quieras. A que no le vuelva yo a ver."

Le dijo el padre de la moza. Fue el cazador, pues cogió el [al] niño, y claro por no matarle—porque daba pena matar [a] la criatura—pilló, le dejó en el bosque. Entonces pasó por ahí una osa que precisamente estaba criando también [a] un[os] oso[s]. Y al ver el [al] niño que era chiquitín, pues la osa le cogió con mucho cuidado, y se lo llevó a la cueva, donde tenía el otro oso suyo, al niño. Entonces el niño, pues claro, como había[n] quedado los osinos chicos, se agarraban a la osa a mamar. Fue el niño, pues también se agarraba a mamar de la osa. Y iban boca todos de la osa, los osos y el niño. Luego al quedar mayorcillo ya, pues retozaba él con los osinos, y los osinos con él, y luchaban ellos ya retozando como muchachos, mirar. Luego que el muchacho, ya se iba siendo olarguero [más largo]. Y fueron y le . . . la osa, pues ya se enreda a luchar con la osa. Algunos días como retozando. Y casí le podía él a la osa, el niño. Y la osa cuando se salía para buscar comida para ellos, pues ponía una lancha bastante grande en la puerta para que no se salieran. Pues un día ya Juanito el Oso—¡Me cago en diez!— pilló y pegó un empujón a la osa y la tumbó. Ya el muchacho ya iba olarguerillo. Tumbó a la puerta—¡Me cago en . . . !—vamos, a la lancha y pilló y se fue al pueblo, el pueblo que había por allí. Y— ¡Coño!—el muchacho apareció allí en el pueblo. Y le recogieron para allí una, un matrimonio, vel [ves] aquí, como usted con esta niña supongamos. ¡Bah! El muchacho ya tenía seis o siete años. Le puson en la escuela. Y le puson "Juanito." Y como le había criado la osa, pues le llamaban "Juanito el Oso" de apodo. ¡Beh! [¡Bah!] Pues fue el muchacho a la escuela. Y el maestro le llamaba Juan. Pero los muchachos tenían la costumbre [de] decir "Juanito el Oso" en vez de llamarle "Juan" solo. Le llaman con que "Juanito el Oso" los muchachos, les daba un puñetazo. Con el puñetazo que les daba, los muchachos quedaban volteados. ¡Me cago en diez! Sabe que el maestro se enfadó un poco con él, le pegó un puñetazo. Y le partió al maestro. ¡Me cago en diez! Ya trataron de aquel muchacho, le sujetaban, o [a] ver qué pasaba. Y con que se encaraba, le jodía. Tenía mucha paciencia. Como se había mamado la leche de la osa, pues el muchacho tenía mucha fuerza. Total que trataron una cosa. Dice, "Este muchacho, lo mejor es que se vaya del pueblo. Y así no hay compromiso. Pues este muchacho va a matar a cincuenta personas o todo el pueblo va a estar atemorizado con él." Y le dijeron, dice, "Mira Juan, hemos pensado una cosa. Pegaste al maestro. Pegaste a unos pocos de muchachos. Aquel Guardia Civil también le pegaste, y hemos pensado de que te largaras del pueblo porque si no, te vamos a tener que llevar a la carcel y tal y cual." "Ah pues sí. ¡Bah! Pues bien."

El muchacho la tragó. Dice, "Bueno, va a saber [que sea] ser con una condición."

Dice, "Tú dirás."

Dice, "Me va a hacer una porra que pese cien quintales de hierro."

"¡Ve! Pues sí."

Se aliaron los herreros. ¡Me cago en diez! Allí venga a "pegotonar" [pegar] allí al hierro. Pin pan, pin pan. ¡Me cago en diez! Hizo una porra gorda. ¡Pero gorda! Como va en una campana pero mucho más gordo, de hierro. Bueno pues, ya que tenían la porra preparada, le dijon [dijeron], "Mira, Juanito, ahí tiene la porra."

"Ah pues sí. Pues una cosa así es como yo quería. Pues muy bien. Bueno pues da. Mañana me largo del pueblo."

Se alargó el muchacho ya. Iba cada vez más grande, claro. Ya a lo mejor tenía diez y seis o diez y ocho él. Salió del pueblo con su porra. ¡Me cago en diez! Y va allí más allá ya una distancia del pueblo. A lo mejor de cuatro leguas o así. Y se encuentra [a] un hombre que estaba arrancando pinos.

"¡Me cago en diez! ¡Cómo va arrancando los pinos!"

Los agarraba la cogolla [corolla]. Le daba así una vuelta. ¡Pum! El pino afuera.

"¡Hostia! Aquel hombre les zumban los huevos para arrancar los pinos. ¡Qué los arranca de un tirón!"

Se acerca para allá. "¿Qué está haciendo amigo?"

"¡Beh! [¡Ve!]. Aquí me han contratado para arrancar todos estos pinos."

Y dice, "¿Cómo arranca usted?"

Dice, "Y pego un tirón—¡Vel [Ves] aquí!—yo los refuerzo un poco a modo como cuando saca la muela, un sacamuela a uno."

Dice, "¡Joder! Pues ¡Me cago en diez! ¿Cuánto gana usted?"

"Me da poco. Dos duros me dan todos los días."

"Yo le doy tres. Se venga usted conmigo."

"¡Ve! Pues ya está. Pues ¡Allá!"

Ya, bueno, ya los dos. Cuando van más allá ya los dos, y ve[n] a un tío que estaba juegando [jugando] a las caras con dos piedras de molino. A coger las dos piedras así juntas como nosotros juegamos [jugamos] una perra gorda. Y vsss las tiraba.

"¡Qúe la madre que le parió!" decía. "¡Mira a aquél!" Dice, "¿No le ve?"

Cogía las piedras y ¡Ve! "¡Me cago en diez! ¡Que aquél es más fuerte que nosotros!"

Se acercan para allá.

"¿Qué hace usted amigo?"

"¡Ve! Aquí me entretengo tirando aquí estas caras. Todo el día juegando [jugando] como las caras con estas piedras."

"¡Me cago en diez! ¿Pero usted . . . ?"

"¡Ve! Yo las cobro aquí. Las tiro por alto y caen otra vez. Y cuando cae . . ."

Y dice Juanito el Oso, dice, "¿Cuánto tardan?"

Dice, "Se suelen tardar cinco minutos, siete minutos, según lo alto que las tiro, claro."

Dice, "Traiga usted para acá para que las tiro yo."

Las cogió y vss. Todavía no han bajado.

Dice, "¿Cuánto gana usted con el ganado?"

Dice, "¡Ve! Pues cinco pesetas."

"Yo le doy diez. Se venga usted conmigo."

"¡Ve! Pues ya está dicho hecho."

¡Cago en diez! Salieron los tres ya por el camino. Más contentos que nada. Como eran tres hombres temerarios los tres porque hacían trabajos temerarios. Y llegan a una . . . Ya se les iba haciendo de noche. Veían un edificio.

Dice, "Ve coño, ahí hay como un edificio. Se ve como una luz."

Dice, "Pues hay que mirar a ver si ahí esta noche nos apañamos."

Total, llegan para allá. Allí no había nadie. Pero había de comer bastante. Entraron en una casa. ¡Bah! ¿Sabe qué es esto?

Dice Juanito el Oso, dice, "Aquí vamos a ser una cosa, eh, porque todos tenemos hambre. ¡Y qué comer hay aquí!"

Estuvon [estuvieron] comiendo bien.

"Bueno, pues ahora que hemos cenado, acostarnos."

Y ellos, como no tenían miedo, aquél nunca cerraba la puerta. Dejaba la puerta abierta. De modo que se acostaron. Nadie les dijo nada. Y nada, más bien, que nada. Por la mañana se levantaron los tres.

"¿Y qué tal? ¿Qué tal?"

"¡Ve! Yo más bien que nada."

"Mira nadie me ha molestado esta noche. Yo más bien y tal."

Bueno. Dice uno, dice, "Pues mira, nosotros nos damos para allí un paseo a ver para allí el campo, un poco eso. Tú te vas a quedar aquí." Dice, "Tú te vas a quedar aquí y preparas la comida. Cuando tenga la comida preparada, pones la bandera arriba en el tejado."

Le dijo al arrancapinos. Bueno, pues, en efecto, los otros se fueron para allí. Ya iba siendo como mediodía. ¡Cago en diez! No pone la bandera el otro. Pues no. ¡Cago en diez! Ya era hora que pusiera la bandera y tal. Fueron para allá, a comer ya. Llegan allí. Ni comida, ni hostia. Le van al otro.

Dice "¿Qué tal ha pasado aquí?"

"¡Coño! ¡Pues qué me ha pasado!" Dice, "Estaba haciendo la comida. Va ahí un hombre. Me ha pegado todo lo que quería."

Dice, "Y dónde está?"

Dice, "Uh. Me pegó y se fue otra vez. ¡Me cago en diez! Pues te digo que me ha quedado el hombre como [m]agullado."

Dice él de las piedras del molino, dice, "¡Me cago en diez! Mañana me quedo yo. A ver si a mí me pega también."

Se quedó. En efecto, cuando el hombre está haciendo la comida, le apreció. ¡Qué era el diablo! Le apareció otra vez el diablo. ¡Me cago en diez! Le metió otro sobeo. Todo lo que quiso y no más. Vinieron los otros para acá y le vieron lo que pasó al otro. Allí estaba tirado en el suelo el hombre.

"¡Cago en diez! Ahí vino. Y me ha dado peleando." Dice, "Pero nada. No he podido con él. Me ha pegado. Me ha quedado igual más magulladito y tal."

Bueno, bien. Dice Juanito el Oso, dice, "Pues mañana me voy a quedar yo. A ver si a mí también me pega."

En efecto por la mañana los otros le prepararon.

Dice, "Bueno, nos vamos nosotros por ahí. Luego pones la bandera."

Estaba haciendo la comida.

Dice el otro, dice, "Que bajo."

Dice, "¿Cómo dice esto?"

Dice, "Que bajo."

"Espérate un poco."

Va para allá. Se coge su cachiporra. Le dice Juanito, dice, "Baja ya cuando quiera."

Baja para abajo. Se tira desde arriba encima de Juanito el Oso. Le puede así la porra. ¡Pum! Pega la porra con el pecho. ¡Me cago en diez! Otra [Otro] cayó de costilla. Se quedó allí medio magullado el hombre, el diablo. Se liaron allí, pin pan, pin pan. ¡Me cago en diez! Torturazo va, torturazo viene. Vio él que le quedó ya, el diablo ya, vamos igual que cuando un perro mata una culebra. A todos los huesos ya cachapariado [cachado por la cachiporra] allí ya. Dice . . . Fue, le colgó allí detrás de la puerta.

Dice, "Para ti te he enseñado yo." Le dijo Juanito el Oso. Le cortó una oreja. ¡Me cago en diez! Se la metió en una bolsilla de la chaqueta. Y dice . . . Luego ya fue y puso la bandera. Cuando dice el otro, "¡Coño! Ya ha puesto la bandera Juanito. Ya ha puesto la bandera."

Pues en seguida se fueron para allá.

"¿Qué tal? ¿Qué tal?"

"¡Ve! Bien. Ya está la comida preparada. Vamos, si quiere comer y tal."

Dice, "¿Pero qué no había?"

Dice, "¡Coño! Menuda pelea hemos tenido." Dice, "Dicéis vosotros que pegaba el hombre de cojones. Ahora conmigo ha salido negra [negro]." Dice, "Ahí le tengo puesto detrás de la puerta. Le he pegado todo lo que he querido."

Van a mirar a la puerta y vissss . . . Se había escapado.

Dice el otro, "¡Me cago en diez! Es mentira y no sé que, no sé cual, y tal y qué sé yo."

Dice, "Mira." Sacó la oreja y empieza, "Vel aquí. Tengo un recuerdo. Aquí está la oreja. Así que tú verás." Dice, "Ve con el tiempo que te vaya."

De modo que Juanito el Oso, porque de ser más hombre todavía, dice, "¡Me cago en diez! Pues tengo que mirar de dar cazado al señor ese!"

En efecto, salió de allá a la puerta y vio un chorrito de sangre para allí, vamos, goteando a cada distante, claro de la oreja que le había cortado. Y ellos detrás de la sangre. Detrás de la sangre. Llegaron a un pozo. Y dijo, dice, "Pues éste aquí se ha tirado." Dice, "Llega hasta aquí. Éste se tiró aquel pozo."

Un pozo que estaba seco.

"¡Me cago en diez! Pues así que a lo mejor es verdad."

Dice, "¡Toma! Aquí no hay trampa. Llega la sangre hasta aquí. Es que se ha tirado aquí."

Pilló Juanito el Oso. "¡Me cago en diez! Dáme a mí la soga. Voy a bajar para abajo. Este tío que tengo yo [que] a ver con todos huevos."

En efecto, le [lo] ataron de la soga a Juanito [el] Oso. Tan, tan, tan, tan, tan, tan. Abajo. Llegó abajo y se encontró con una moza más guapa del copón. Que él la tenía allí ya, el diablito, allí como encantada. Y dice, "¡Hoy! ¿Cómo vino usted para aquí? Tal, hu, tal, y qué sé si cuanto."

Dice, "¡Bah! Usted no se apure. Usted no se apure." Le dice a ella, él a la moza.

Dice, "¡Hoy! Si éste [a] todo lo que viene aquí, lo mata. Este hombre, este hombre es el diablo. Este hombre mata a todo el mundo." Dice, "Este hombre, cuando venga, le va a oler de que está usted para aquí." Dice, "Le va a tratar de matar, claro. Le va a decir si quiere usted lo que él bebe. Que lo diga que no. Porque lo que bebe es veneno. Lo que come es veneno. Y fuma veneno." Dice, "Luego, si no le mata, le va a decir que si quiere usted luchar ahí con la espada, para matarle, claro."

Dice, "Allá a la entrada, a la izquierda hay una espada que como está como rañosa [ruinosa], fea. Y tiene allí toda la habitación está llena de espadas brillantes, bonitas. Y él ha de decir que usted coja lo que usted quiera. Pero usted, según entra a la izquierda, en un rincón que hay una que está como rañosa [ruinosa], fea. Usted coja aquella. Que con aquél pelea. Los otras son de lata y se doblan todas."

[La] moza le puso [al] corriente. En efecto, llega el tío a poco rato. Le tenía ya preparada la moza la comida.

Dice, "Rrr, a mí me huele para aquí a carne humana."

Dice, "Ay, pues mire usted, si hay un señor que hay, tal, que ha venido y tal."

Dice, "Uhhh. ¿Adónde está ese hombre? ¡Que salga!"

Con que ya pues el hombre se presentó.

Dice, "Muy bien. ¡Coño! ¡Amigo! ¡Me cago en diez! Hombre. Tal y qué sé yo. Tal."

Más contento el diablo con él, Juanito. Y Juanito con el hombre, claro.

Dice, "Bueno, muy bien. Tenga usted un cigarro hombre."

Dice, "Yo no fumo."

"Venga, coma usted."

Dice, "No. Yo he comido mucho. Vamos. No como."

"Pues beba usted. Tenga usted. Beba usted."

"No, no bebo."

"¡Caramba! Satisfecho está el señor. Ni come, ni bebe, ni fuma, ni nada. Bueno, bien."

Estuvo el otro comiendo y algo y tal.

"¿Bueno, pues le gustará también luchar un poquito con la espada? ¿A usted le gustará, tal?"

Dice, "¡Ve! Yo no es que a mi me gusta luchar, pero vamos. Si eso es, y tal." Dijo Juanito el Oso.

Dice, "Pues ahora vamos a luchar allí con la espada y tal. Usted coja lo que usted quiera."

Se puso el diablo así sobre la otra.

"Usted coja lo que usted quiera en [la] habitación. Aquí hay muchas. Vel aquí las."

Dice, "Ya . . ."

Mira así por atrás del diablo.

Dice, dice, "Yo veo aquí está."

Dice, "¡Bah! Esta, pues ésta está ya para aquí como abandonada. Nadie . . . Está tanto . . . . Ya no vale para nada."

Dice, "¡Bah! Yo con esta misma y tal . . ."

Dice, "Pues si hay ahí, vel allí brillantes más buenas que nada."

"Ay, que mal me da. Ya con esta misma me apaño."

¡Cago en diez! La coge allí. Claro el diablo tuvo que con una de las brillantes. Se liaron allí. La del diablo se doblaba primero tiro que pegaba. La otra—¡Me cago en diez!—a cazar al hombre. Le pega con [la] rañosa. ¡Me cago en diez! Hasta que le venció. Le venció al diablo.

Y entonces ya, para que le quedó vencido, pues dice la moza, dice, "¿Y qué hacemos ahora aquí?"

Dice, "Pues esto es muy sencillo." Dice, "Tú lo que querías."

"Yo soy la hija del rey."

Dice, "Tú lo que quieres."

Dice, "Hombre, pues lo que yo quiero es salir de aquí," dijo la moza.

Entonces dice Juanito el Oso, dice, "Pues, yo es lo que me voy a conseguir." Bueno, dice, "Lo vamos a conseguir. Yo creo que salimos."

Los otros pues estaban arriba. Y va. Dice. La ató a la moza. Y subió para arriba a la moza. Otros tiraron y a subir a la moza arriba. Vuelve y tiran otra vez la soga para abajo. Él en vez de atarse, le ató la porra. Los otros tiraron como a mitad del camino. Soltaron y ¡Pum! Para abajo.

Dice el otro, dice, "Ése ya no sube."

Bien. Ya se quedó solo abajo sin la moza al otro [y los otros]. Y—¡Me cago!—ya pues le entró hambre.

"¡Me cago en diez! ¿Aquí cómo se apaña uno? ¡Cago en la madre que le parió!" Coge, dice, "¡Cago en diez! Sí tengo yo una oreja yo aquí en la bolsilla de [la] chaqueta del otro día."

Echó la mano. Como orejea a la oreja cuando sale el otro.

"¿Qué me quieres? ¿Qué me mandas? Que estoy a tu disposición."

Dice, "Mira, nada más te voy a pedir una cosa. Que me saques de aquí y me pongas en el palacio del rey."

Dice, "Sí, está hecho."

Seguía. ¡Pum! Le sacó, a él y la porra. ¡Pum! Al palacio del rey. Le puso allí a Juanito el Oso. Entonces ya los otros ya tenían como embo-babucha [como boba] como la moza, de que ellos, ellos se habían hecho el papel con que aquellos habían sacado [a] la moza. El rey. ¡Bua! Se había puesto el hombre todo chito de que vio a la hija. Pero entonces al momento se presentó allí Juanito el Oso.

Y dice la moza, dice, "Papá. Éste es él que ha salvado a mí. Éste."

Dice, "¿Pues no me decías que el otro?"

Dice, "No. No. Éste, éste fue él que salvó a mi. Que este hombre fue él que estuvo abajo."

De modo que dice al [el] padre. "Pues entonces, tú vas a decir con quien te quieres casar."

Dice, "Yo con éste."

Y entonces dice la moza, dice la moza a Juanito . . . No dice Juanito a la moza, dice, "¿Qué quieres que hágamos con estos dos?"

Dice, "Pues estos dos, les hemos de dar de un castigo."

Y dijo Juanito el Oso, dice, "Lo que tú digas."

Dice, "Pero yo, como soy buena persona, no me gusta que nadie perezca por mí."

Dijo a la moza. Dice, "Pues entonces tú dirás que hacemos con ellos."

Dice, "Pues yo creo que lo que los hace, colocarlos para aquí en el palacio. Ya que no se casen conmigo pero tampoco quiero que los maltrate a los hombres aquellos."

De modo que ya Juanito se casó con ella y tuvon [tuvieron] una boda. ¡Bua! Allá por las nubes. Y claro, yo si hubiera estado también, me había tocado algo, a que se hubiera sido un hueso por ejemplo. Pero yo hago gracia que allí la tengo bien derecha. A me no me manda nunca con los huesos en las narices. ¿Entiende usted? Y colorín colorado, cuento terminado.

"THE BEAR'S SON" BY NACHO ÁNGEL HERNÁNDEZ

Yetoya cē tōnal, quihtoah, cē tāgat tequitiā itech in mila.
They say that one day there was a man who works in the milpa.

Huān mōztah in cihuāt quitamacati.
And every day his wife goes to feed him.

Huān panōhuaya cē cuauhtah, nohon huēi cuauhtah cāmpa panō[hu]aya.
And she passed through a wood, that wood was big through which she passed.

Huān nemiah cuauhtahocuilimeh.
And animals of the forest live [in the wood].

Mōztah, mōztah, quihtoah, nēn [nē in] tāgatzin tequiti, huān cihuāt mōztah quitamacati.
Every day, every day, they say, that little man works, and every day his wife goes to feed him.

Huān ehōc in tōnal non cihuāt yahqui nepantah quitamacato nihuēhueht.
And the day came when that woman went at noon to feed her old man.

Huān quit[quiliah] quītzquiā cē mono.
And they say that a monkey grabs her.

Huān cuiāc nē cāmpa in tepēt.
And he took her to where that mountain was.

Ōmpa, cāmpa tēpecoyoc, cochiā nohon mono ōmpa īhuān.
There, where the cave is, that monkey sleeps with her there.

Bueno, ōmpa mocāhuato.
Well, she went to stay there.

Ahmō teh quichīhuili.
He did not do anything to her.

Ahmō tēcuā.
He does not bite anyone.

Tā quichīhuati quemeh yazquiā.
It's that she goes to do whatever she might.

Ilamatzin yazquiā.
It was as if she were his wife.

Ōmpa quipiyac.
He kept her there.

Huehcāhuac ihcon.
She was that way for a long time.

Tāhcon [Tā ihcon].
That was how it was.

Quipixtoc de cuiāc nitilman cihuātzin ihcon.
He is seeing that the little woman brought clothes.

Yēc, bueno, cē panti zā.
To be sure, that is, just one set.

Ihcon, mōztah, mōztah, ōmpa nē, quitquiliah, mā yā quitequipanoā non.
So it is, every day, every day, in that place there, they say, he goes hunting to serve her.

Tā, quicuiliā in pan, nācat, pero xoxōhuic quicuāti ya.
Yes, he brings her bread, meat, but now she eats it raw.

Pos cān quicuizqueh tit?
Well, where will they obtain fire?

Canah mōztah yohui non tēcuāni.
Every day that beast goes somewhere.

Mōztah yohui quitēmoti toni cuāzqueh.
Every day he goes to find something for them to eat.

Cuālcuiliā zantemano.
He brings her whatever.

Pero melāuh in nacātzin xoxōhuic quicuāltiā.
But he really does make her eat raw meat.

Ahmō yoccic.
It is not cooked.

Pan pos yoccic quīncuiti pero nācat ahmō.
Bread, well, he brings it cooked but not the meat.

Huān ihcon.
And so it was.

Hasta quipiyahqueh cē pilli.
Until they had a child.

Non pilli quipiyahqueh, quihtoah, tahco tēcuāni huān tahco den no alaxtic como cristianos.

That child whom they had, they say, was half beast and half smooth [without fur] as Christians are.

Huān tahco ohuiyō [tzohmiyō] quemeh ocuilin.

And half was down as an animal.

Ihcon pēhuac mozcaltiā non pilli.

So that child started to grow.

Cē oquichpil quipiya in cihuāt.

The woman has a son.

Pues alegre in oquichpil.

Well, the boy was happy [high-spirited].

Huān ihcon, quit[quiliah], non de nēnquēn zā mozcaltiā quemeh ocuili[n], ahmō como cristianos.

And so it was, they say, that he grows up quickly like an animal, not as Christians do.

Ihcon, quit[quiliah], pēhuac mozcaltiā, mozcaltiā, mozcaltiā.

So it was, they say, he started to grow, grow, grow.

Ceppa, quit[quiliah], non oquichpil telnāmiquiā huān tahtohuāya.

Afterwards, they say, that boy reasons and spoke.

Quitquiliā ninan, "Pos āxcān," quitquiliā, "hueliz," quitquiliā, "tinechhuī-caz," quitquiliā, "cān," quitquiliā, "nēn tochān," quitquiliā.

He says to his mother, "Well now," he says, "it's possible," he says to her, "for you to go with me," he says to her, "to where," he says to her, "that house of ours is," he says to her.

"Nicnequi nimitzhuīcaz," quitquiliā, "cān," quitquiliā nin, "tyāzqueh cān," quitquiliā, "tihuālliuh."

"I want to go with you," he says to her, "where," he says to that one, "we shall go where," he says to her, "you came from."

Quitquiliā ninan, "Pero quēmman[i]yān tinechhuīcaz?

His mother replies to him, "But when [how] will you go with me?

260

Huān huehcapan nicān tiyetohqueh.
And here we are very high.

Cē tepēīxco cāmpa [ti]ahctoqueh."
It is a side of a mountain where we are up [here]."

Quitquiliā, "Ahmō."
She says to him, "No."

Quitquiliā, "Huān tet," quitquiliā, "huēi," quitquiliā, "nicān techtzactehua
motat."
She says to him, "And [with] a rock," she says to him, "[a] big [one],"
she says to him, "your father closed us in here."

"Quēmah," quitquiliā, "pero [nic]xīcoz," quitquiliā, "in tet."
"Yes," he replies, "but I shall endure," he says to her, "the rock."

Quipēhuac cahahcui in oquichpil cē huēi tet.
The boy started lifting a big rock.

Quīnpampachohltiā cuando yohui.
He covers them up when he goes [away].

Pos quixīcoā in oquichpil.
Well, the boy endures.

Cahahcuic non tet.
He lifted up that rock.

Quitquiliā, "Ahmō taxīcoz ya," quitquiliā.
She says to him, "You won't endure it now," she says to him.

Quiliā, "Ahmō, tā nimitzhuīcaz.
He replies, "No, I shall go with you.

A ver nechhuīcaz cān," quitquiliā, "tihuālliuh."
Let's see [you] take me to [the place from] where," he says to her, "you
had come."

Huān ihcon, quit[quiliah], panōc tōnal.
And so it was, they say, that the day[s] passed.

Ayamō quineltoquili non ninan.
That mother of his did not believe him.

Quiliā, "Ahmō.
She says, "No.

Que tipili oc," quitquiliā, "ahmō tacahahcuiz.
You are still a child," she says to him, "who will not lift [the rock].

Huān niman," quitquiliā, "ahmō tinechxīcoz para nechcuīcaz.
And right away," she says to him, "you will not last to go with me.

Huehcapan nin cāmpa tihuāllahqueh."
We came to this distant place."

Quiliā, "Ahmō.
He replies, "No.

Tā nimitzxīcoz ya," quitquiliā.
I shall support you," he says to her.

"Nimitzxīcoz, huān tiquittaz," quitquiliā.
"I shall support you, and you will see," he says to her.

Ihcon, quit[quiliah], panoā in tōnal.
So it is, they say, the day[s] pass.

Huān que yohui oquichpil telnāmiqui cachi.
And the boy goes on to think more.

Quitquiliā, "Pero ahmō nēncah," quitquiliā nin, "para tinechhuīcaz.
[His mother] says to him, "But it won't work," she says to this one, "for you to go with me.

Cualāniz in motat huān techmagaz.
Your father will be angry and he will hit us.

Mitzmagaz."
He will hit you."

"Ahmō," quitquiliā.
"No," he replies to her.

"Tā niquīxnāmiquiz," quitquiliā, "notat," quitquiliā.
"It's that I shall face," he says to her, "my father," he says to her.

"Nicmagaz," quitquiliā.
"I shall hit him," he says to her.

"Ahmō nechmagaz," quitquiliā.
"He will not hit me," he says to her.

Moyōlchicāhuac in oquichpil.
The boy became inspired.

Quihtoā que quimagaz mazqui yeh in itat, non ocuilin.
He says that he will hit him even though he is his father, that animal.

"Como cualāni, techtohca, nicmagaz," quitquiliā.
"If he gets angry, [and if] he chases us, I'll hit him," he says to her.

"Ahmō teh ximāhuili."
"Don't be afraid of anything."

Huān entonces ehōc in tōnal.
And then the day came.

Quīztiuh nohon mono cāmpa ahctoya.
That monkey left from where he was up [on the side of the mountain].

Bueno, cāmpa nē mā yā ichān.
That is, he goes hunting where his house is now.

Yahqui.
He went away.

Tatēmolito.
He went looking for [food].

Quīztiuh non mono.
That monkey left.

Huān oquichpil conēt pos moliztotālihtoc īhuan ninan.
And the little boy is being alert with his mother.

De yahqui, "Bueno," quitquiliā, "āxcān quēmah," quiliā, "yahqui."
After he left, "Well," he says to her, "yes now," he says, "he has gone."

Quitquiliā, "Tyohueh," quitquiliā.
He says to her, "Let's go," he says to her.

Quinemili non oquichpil, quit[quiliah], cahahcuic non tet.
That boy decided, they say, to lift up that rock.

Quīxquepac.
He turned it over on its face.

"Āxcān quēmah," quitquiliā.
"Now yes," he says to her.

"Ximopilo tahcuitapan.
"Hang on to [my] back.

Tyohueh," quitquiliā.
Let's go," he says to her.

"Mitzmāmalti."
"[I] am going to carry you."

Non cihuātzin, yeh yēc nochi tamic nitilman.
That little woman, all of her clothing had ended already.

Yēc tamic.
Really ended.

Yēc tequitzāntzauctoc [tequitzayāntzauctoc].
She is working very hard closing what is torn.

[Ī]ca tetepitzintzin zā nitilman, quemeh nohon, pos tēl tequitzān [tequit-zayān] [ī]ca tzitzicāutoc nohon tilmantzin.
With only the little tiny bit of her clothing, like that, well, she works very hard struggling to fasten that little bit of torn clothing of hers.

Quiyēctamito.
It had ended for her.

Huehcāhuato, quit[quitiliah], no yactoya cāmpa nē tēpecoyoc.
It was a long time, they say, that she too was there in that cave.

Quiliā, "Pos nimitzmāmalti," quitquiliā.
He says, "Well, I am going to carry you," he says to her.

"Ahmō teh ximā[hui]li."
"Don't you be afraid."

Quimāma non niconīuh.
That child of hers carries her.

Huān quitemōlti non taīxco.
And he lowered her down that surface [of the mountain].

Cuiāc.
He took her.

Ōmpa quēmah.
From there, yes.

Ahcic ya non pueblo.
He arrived at that town already.

Huān tons [entonces] non cihuātzin, quit[quiliah], niman quiteīxmatiti
īhuān cura.
And then that little woman, they say, goes right away to see the face
of a priest.

Ōmpa nē, quit[quiliah], cuiāc.
They say that she took him there.

Pos yeh quitapōhuito quēnin pasaro.
Well, she went to tell him what happened.

Ōmpa motepiyalti in cihuāt.
There the woman was taken care of.

Quiliā, "Huān āxcān," quiliā, "pos neh niquihtoā ya teh xinechhuīquili,"
quitiliā, "māmahhui nin noconīuh."
She says, "And now," she says, "well, I say now that you carry for me,"
she says to him, "[the burden of] governing this child of mine."

Entonces non padre, quit[quiliah], yeh itocay mocāu.
Then that priest, they say, became his godfather.

Monōtzac, quit[quiliah], "Juan" nohon pilli.
That boy, they say, was called "Juan."

Huān ihcon, quit[quiliah], mozcaltiā, mozcaltiā non pilli.
And so, they say, that child grows [and] grows.

Pēhuac m[o]āhuiltiā.
He started to play.

Pēhuac īhuān m[o]āhuiltiā nohon conēmeh.
He started to play with those children.

M[o]āhuiltiā den escuela.
He plays [with the children] from school.

Quitītani in escuela non nitocay yeh in non cura.
His godfather, who was that priest, sent him to school.

Quit[quiliah] nē momachtiti.
They say he is going to learn there.

Nō yohui ya non oquichpil.
That boy also goes now.

Huān ehōc tōnal quihtoā nitocay, "Neh," quitquiliā, "padrino nicnequi," quitiliā, "cē nopelota.
And the day came when he says to his godfather, "I," he says to him, "want," he says to him, "a ball.

Xinechchihchīhuili," quitquiliā.
Get one ready for me," he says to [his godfather].

Tatītani mā, "Nech[chih]chīhuilica nopelota," quitquiliā, "huān cē notopil."
He orders, "Have my ball made for me," he says to him, "and one of my club[s]."

Quitquiliā, "Que ye ōme ahijado?"
[His godfather] says to him, "Why the two [things], godson?"

266

"Nitatītaniz porque nē," quitquiliā, "nē m[o]āhuiltiah," quitquiliā, "nē pipil, ahmō nicuelitta," quitquiliā, "porque ahmō etic," quitquiliā.

"I shall order it because that one," he says to him, "that one they play with," he says to him, "those children, I don't like it," he says to him, "because it is not heavy," [Juan] says to him.

"Neh nicnequi," quitquiliā, "de cē arroba [ī]ca etic," quitquiliā, "nopelota huān cē arroba [ī]ca etic notopil."

"I want it," he says, "to weigh one *arroba*," he says to him, "my ball and my club to weigh one *arroba*," he says to him.

Quiliā, "Pos nitatītaniz," quiliā.

[The priest] says, "Well, I shall order it," he says to him.

Entonces, quit[quiliah], non tocay melāuh tatītanic non pelota qui-[chih]chīhuilican que cē arroba de etic.

Then, they say, that godfather of his really ordered [them] to make that ball, which weighed one *arroba*.

Cuālcuilihqueh.
They brought it.

Huān quēmah, quit[quiliah], non oquichpil pēhuac m[o]āhuiltiā.
And yes, they say, that boy started to play.

[Ī]ca hon [nohon] tamōta in pelota.
With that he throws the ball.

Cualli quixīcoā.
He endures well.

Pero in occequīn nicompañeros, non conēmeh ahmō quixīcoah.
But the other companions, those children do not endure it.

Quihtoah non, quit[quiliah], [ī]ca quīntamōta pos quīnmictiā.
Those [children] say, they say, that he kills them throwing it to them.

Ihcon ōmpa quēmah, quit[quiliah], mā yā cualāni non nitocay.
So it is that from there, yes, they say, he goes to hunt for that godson of his, getting angry.

Quiliā, "Huān yēquīntzin qué[nin] chīhuati," quitquiliā, "nē notocay?

He says, "And right now what [am I] going to do," he says, "with that godson of mine?

Huān ahmō teh quiyēccaqui."

And he does not listen very well."

Entonces quitquiliā nē, quiliā non itocay de nohon ocuilin, quiliā, "Pos āxcān," quitquiliā, quitmoiliā nohon sarcedote, quitquiliā nitocay, "Āxcān," quitquiliā, "neh," quitquiliā, "mōztah," quitquiliā, "nyo nēpa."

Then he says, that godfather of that animal says, he says, "Well now," he says to him, that priest thought, he says to his godson, "now," he says to him, "I," he says to him, "am going over there tomorrow," he says to him.

"Nechnōtza.

"[Someone] calls me.

Nechinvitaroā mā nicchīhuati cē misa.

[Someone] invits me to go and do a mass.

Teh xicochi," quitquiliā, "itech nocama.

You sleep," he says to him, "in my bed.

Tahpihpiya," quitquiliā, "mā ahmō acah motoqui.

Stand watch," he says to him, "so that no one comes close.

Neh," quitquiliā, "nyo.

I," he says to him, "go.

Como niehcō," quitquiliā, "niehcō.

If I arrive," he says to him, "I arrive.

Huān in hora nechhuihhuintiah," quitquiliā, "achah nihuintiehcōz," quitquiliā.

And the moment they get me drunk," he says to him, "perhaps I shall arrive drunk," he says to him.

"Ahmō nicmati toni hora niehcōz, pero nyo."

"I do not know when I shall arrive, but I go."

Den quichīhuac nohon cura, quit[quiliah], ahmō melāuh yahqui.

As for what that priest did, they say, he did not really go.

Mocalaqui in cama tampa.
He goes under the bed.

Ōmpa nē, quit[quiliah], mocalaqui.
There that one, they say, goes in.

Quimaquiti cē cuchullo.
He goes to give [his godson] a knife.

Quiliā, "Pos āxcān," quitquiliā, "nimitzmaca nin cuchillo huān neh nyo,"
quitquiliā.
He says, "Well now," he says to him, "I give you this knife and I'm
going," he says to him.

Huān tahc [tahcah] calānquīza in oquichpil.
And at midday the boy goes outside.

Ahmō momac cuenta cān nicān . . . cox yahqui o ahmō yahqui.
He did not realize where here . . . if he went or did not go.

Entonces non cura mocalaqui in cama tampa.
Then that priest comes in under the bed.

Non teōtaquito, motēcato in telpōch cāmpa no nicama in cura.
Enter the night, the boy went to lie down on where the priest's bed
also was.

Huān ōmpa quēmah.
And there yes.

Non yohuac, quit[quiliah], pēhuac tena.
That night, they say, he [the priest] started to complain of discomfort
[groan].

Yeh quimauhti, quit[quiliah], quimauhti nitocay.
He frightened, they say, [he] frightened his godson.

Ihcon, quit[quiliah], pēhuac tena.
So it was, they say, he started groaning.

Huān īxpetāni non oquichpil.
And that boy awoke.

"Huān teh hijo de la chingada," quitquiliā.
"And you son of the fucked one," he says to him.

"Toni," quitquiliā, "teh," quitquiliā, "toni quichīutoc?
"What," he says to him, "are you," he says to him, "doing?

Āconi teha?" quitquiliā.
Who are you?" he says to him.

"Nicān," quitquiliā, "ahmō īca neha nim(o)āhuiltiā," quitquiliā.
"Here," he says to him, "I do not play around," he says to him.

"Nicān nechcāuti nopadrino mā nitahpiya," quitquiliā.
"My godfather left me here to take care [of things]," he says to him.

Ihcon cachi tena.
So it was that he groans more.

"Nimitzili," quitquiliā, "hijo de la chingada, āconi teha?" quitquiliā.
"I told you," he says to him, "son of the fucked one, who are you?" he
says to him.

Huān cahahcuic, quit[quiliah], nē sābana den tech in cama huān quināl-
quechilihtoc in chuchillo.
And he lifted up, they say, that sheet from the bed, and he is putting
the knife toward his neck.

"Ay ahijado," quitquiliā, "neh," quitquiliā, "nicān nihuetztoc.
"Oh godson," he says to him, "I," he says to him, "am fallen here.

Nihuinti," quitquiliā.
I am drunk," he says to him.

"Ahmō nicmati," quitquiliā, "ihcuāc niehoc," quitquiliā.
"I do not know," he says to him, "when I arrived," he says to him.

"Nechtapohpolui," quitquiliā.
"Forgive me," he says to him.

"Nihuintic," quitquiliā.
"I got drunk," he says to him.

"Ahmō nicmati."
"I don't know."

"Pos [xi]calānquīza niman porque tā neh," quitquiliā, "nimitzmictiāya," quitquiliā.
"Well, get out right know because I," he says to him, "would have killed you," he said to him.

"Que ye," quitquiliā, "ōmpon ticalaquihqui?
"Why," he asks him, "did you come in there?

Nechnahuati," quitquiliā, "mā nicān nitahpiya," quitquiliā.
[You] advised me," he says to him, "to take care of here," he says to him.

"Pos neh nitahpixtoc."
"Well, I am taking care."

"Pero nihuintic," quitquiliā.
"But I got drunk," he says to him.

"Ahmō nicmatic," quitquiliā.
"I did not know," he says to him.

Tons [Entonces] quīzac non itocay.
So then he removed that godfather of his.

Ōmpa quēmah.
From there, yes.

Quicencui tamilihtoc non cura quēnin quichīhuaz non nitocay.
That priest continued thinking about what he will do with that godson of his.

Ōmpa quēmah, quit[quiliah], nēn [nē in] quinemili, quitmoliā, "Pos āxcān, nēpa cē quimatoc yetoc cē cuauhtah telnemi tēcuānimeh.
From there yes, they say, that one decided, he says to himself, "Well now, one knows that there is a forest where many wild beasts live.

Huān mā quicuācan in tēcuānimeh.
And may the wild beasts eat him.

271

"Mā yā, mā yohui cuauhtah," quitquiliā.
"May they catch [him], may he go to the forest," he says.

"Huān āxcān," quitquiliā, "neh niquihtoā que xyo cuauhtah, xicuiti cuauhuit."
"And now," he says, "I tell him to go into the forest to bring me [fire]wood."

"Que ticuīca [ti-qui-huīca] nē burrito," quitquiliā.
"You take that donkey," he says to him.

"Xūn," quitquiliā, "xinechcuālcuauhuiti [xi-nech-qui-huāl-cuauh-cuiti]," quitquiliā.
"Be sure," he says to him, "to go bring me some [fire]wood," he said to him.

Tons quīztiuh non tēlpōch īhuān non niburritos.
So then that boy left with those donkeys of his.

Yahqui cuālcuauhuito.
He went to bring [fire]wood.

Mientras non tēlpōch pēhuac tētequi in cuauhuit.
Meanwhile, that boy started to cut the wood.

Huān iburritos quīntzītzihco.
And [something] came to detain [grab] his donkeys.

Cuāc ceppa quīnahcito, quit[quiliah], niburritos, quit[quiliah], īpa quīncuahqueh non tēcuānimeh.
When he went to find, they say, his donkeys, they say, those wild beasts had eaten them.

Zātēpan, quit[quiliah], cualāncamiqui in tēlpōch.
Afterwards, they say, the boy dies [shakes] with anger.

Quit[quiliah] pēhua quīntēmoā non tēcuānimeh, cān yahqueh den āquin quīncuahqueh in burritos.
They say he begins to look for those human-eating beasts, where they went after they ate the donkeys.

Quīnahcic.
He found them.

272

Huān yeh, quit[quiliah], quī[n]māmalti in cuauhuit.
And he, they say, loaded them with the [fire]wood.

Quīnmāmalti.
He loaded them.

Huān ōmpa quēmah, cuāc quittac non nipadrino, quit[quiliah], ōmpa hu-
itzeh tēcuānimeh.
From there, yes, that is when that godfather of his saw, they say, the
wild beasts coming from there.

Tāzah tehctenatihuitzeh [ī]ca in cuauhuit.
They fling themselves really complaining as they come climbing up
with the [fire]wood.

"Huān teha, ahijado," quitquiliā, "que ye," quitquiliā, "ticuālcui nohon
tēcuānimeh?
"And you, godson," [the priest] says to him, "why," he says to him,
"do you bring those wild beasts?

[Ī]ca non," quitquiliā, "cimi malos."
Because they," he says to him, "are very bad."

Quitquiliā, "Tēcuah," quitquiliā.
He says to him, "They bite," he says to him.

"Ahmō xicuālcuini."
"You should not have brought them."

"Pero padrino," quitquiliā, "que ahmō ni[quīn]cuālcuiz [ni-quīn-qui-huāl-
cuiz]."
"But godfather," he says to him, "I did not bring them."

Quitquiliā, "Huān nechīncuālcuiqueh noburritos," quitquiliā.
He says to him, "And they are my donkeys that brought [the pieces of
wood] for me," he says to him.

"Por eso, neha," quitquiliā, "niquīncuālcuiti," quitquiliā.
"For that reason, I," he says to him, "go to bring them," he says to him.

"Nin ahmō tēcuah," quitquiliā.
"These do not bite," he says to him.

Quitquiliā, "Yēc mancitos," quitquiliā.
He says to him, "They are thoroughly tame," he says to him.

"Ahmō tēcuah.
"They do not bite.

Que ye," quitquiliā, "nēn tēcuah?"
Why," he says to him, "do these bite?"

"Quēmah," quitquiliā, "ahmō nēncah," quitquiliā, "para nicān gentes quīncuāzqueh zā."
"Yes," [the priest] says to [Juan], "it won't work," he says to him, "because here they will just eat people."

"Pero nin," quitquiliā, "ahmō nechchīhuilihqueh."
"But these," [Juan] says to [the priest], "did not do anything to me."

"Pero quēmah," quitquiliā, "xiquīntemohuili," quitquiliā.
"But yes," he says to him, "take [the wood] down from them [unload them]," he says to him.

"Ahora niman xiquīncāhuati," quitquiliā, "cān tiquīncuito."
"Now go leave them right away," he says to him, "where you went to get them."

Quīntemohuili, quit[quiliah], cuauhuit huān quīncāhuato in cuauhtah.
He unloaded, they say, the wood from them and went to leave them in the forest.

Ōmpa quēmah.
From there, yes.

Quit[quiliah], non nitocay, quitmoliā, "Huān que nicchīhuati, huān ahmō teh quineltoca oc?
He says to him, that godfather of his, he says to himself, "And what am I going to do to him, and he still does not believe anything?

Bueno," quitmoliā, "pos āxcān, āxcān," quitmoliā, "ihcuīn nicchīhuati."
Good," he says to himself, "well now, now," he says to himself, "I am going to do it this way."

Quinemili, quit[quiliah] nēn, quipiya . . .
He decided, they say, he has . . .

Quiliā non nipadrino, "Āxcān," quiliā ahijado, "cuāntzin," quitquiliā, "cualcān nicchīhuaz misa."
That godfather of his says, "Now," he tells his godson, "early," he says to him, "is the proper time for me to do a mass."

Quinemili non sarcedote quicuito cequīn non ānimas tzontecomameh cacahuameh ya.
That priest decided to go take some empty skulls of dead persons.

Mā yā omimeh ya non quīnololoto.
So he goes hunting to gather some of those bones.

Huān, quit[quiliah], cada ōme escalera, bueno escalon, tech in torre, quit[quiliah], quitālihto nohon ānimas tzontecomat.
And, they say, every other step, that is, stair, in the tower, they say, he went to place one of those skulls.

Hasta panhuetzito, quit[quiliah], quitālihto.
He even went to the top, they say, to leave [one].

Quitquiliā, bueno nēpa ahmō quili nē nitocay.
He says to him, . . . that is, he did not tell his godson about [them] there.

Quiliā, "Cuāntzin, ahijado, [ih]cuāc titatzilīniti."
He says, "Early, godson, that is when you are going to ring the bell."

Entonces non oquichpil pēhuac non cuāntzin yahqui tatzilīnito ya.
Then that boy started that early morning to go to ring the bell.

Yeh quimatoc, quit[quiliah], quimahmahmauhtiti [ī]ca non ānimas tzontecomameh.
He [the priest] is knowing, they say, he is going to frighten him a lot with those skulls of the dead.

No, quit[quiliah], tēlpōch quittac panoti ya, ihcon quittac yetohqueh tzontecomameh.
He too, they say, the boy saw [when] he goes to pass, so it was that he saw that there were skulls.

Ahcic ahco.
He arrived above.

Tatzilīniā.
He rings the bell.

Ōmpa quēmah, huālliuh, quit[quiliah], huān pēhuac quīnololoā tzontecomameh [ī]ca icuexān.
From there, yes, he came, they say, and he started to gather up the skulls in his clothes.

Quīzac, quit[quiliah], cāmpa nipadrino.
He went out, they say, to where his godfather was.

"Padrino," quitquiliā, "ahmō tīncuāz [tiquīncuāz] cequīn calabacitas den nicuālic?" quitquiliā.
"Godfather," he says to him, "won't you eat some squash that I brought?" he says to him.

"Mā mitzīnchihchīhuilihcan," quitquiliā, "tiquīncuāz.
"Have [your cooks] prepare them for you," he says to him, "so you will eat them.

Para niquīnahci," quitquiliā.
For [that reason] I found them," he says to him.

Quitquiliā, "Ay ahijado," quitquiliā, "non," quitquiliā, "ahmō calabasas," quitquiliā.
[The priest] says to [Juan], "Oh, godson," he says to him, "those," he says to him, "are not squashes," he says to him.

"Non," quitquiliā, "calaveras."
"Those," he says to him, "are skulls."

"Neh nicmatiā calabacitas."
"I know them to be squashes."

"Ahmō, tā in calaveras.
"No, they are skulls.

Cā[n]," quitquiliā, "tiquīncuic?"
Where," he says to him, "did you get them?"

276

Quitquiliā, "Pos ōmpa nē," quitquiliā, "yetoya cāmpa escalones."
[Juan] says to [the priest], "Well, over there," he says to him, "where the stairs are."

Ōmpa quēmah.
From there, yes.

Quitmoliā nohon teōpixcāt, bueno quitmoliā nin, "Quēnin quichīhuati notocay, huān ahmō quēmman caquiti?
That priest says to himself, well this one says to himself, "What am [I] going to do with my godson, and he is never going to listen?

Ahmō hueli nictacaquiltiā.
I cannot complain to him.

Nimilitoc huān ahmō nicmati quēn quichīhuaz.
I am thinking and I do not know what to do.

Ahmō hueli quimahmauhtiā."
It is not possible to scare him."

Entonces quinemili quimatoc cē calli que yetoc huehca.
So then he remembered there is a house that is far away.

Ongac tā cēltican non calli cāmpa yetoc.
There is a lonely place where that house is.

Huān quiteltamahui.
And it frightened him very much.

Quitmoliā, "Pos āxcān," quitquiliā, "nēpa cē calli nicpiya.
He says to himself [He says], "Well now," he says to him, "I have a house there.

Ahmō hueli acah quimotoquiā.
No one can go near it.

Huān ōmpa nicpiya nēn . . .
And there I take care of them . . .

Nicnequi ōmpa xitahpiyati."
I want you to go and take care of it."

"Que ye ahmō," quitquiliā, "padrino?
"Why not," he says to him, "godfather?

Nyaz."
I shall go."

No non teōtaquito, quit[quiliah], yahqui.
That same afternoon, they say, he went.

Quimac in taxcal, huān yahqui.
He gave him tortillas, and [Juan] went off.

Ōmpa cochito.
He went there to sleep.

Non teōtaquito, quit[quiliah], non tēlpōch tā zōhui.
That evening, they say, that boy stretched out.

Huān motēac ya.
And he lay down already.

Ōmpa quēmah, non yohuac, quit[quiliah], caqui, quit[quiliah], tapanco huetzico.
From there yes, that night, they say, he heard, they say, it come falling from the loft.

Ahmō quichīhuac cuenta.
He did not realize [what it was].

Tā mō quit[quiliah], caqui occeppa huetzico.
There is no doubt, they say, he heard it come fall again.

Huān ihcon huetzi huān huetzi.
And so it fell and it fell.

Quiliā, "Āconi teh hijo de la chingada?
He says, "Who are you, son of the fucked one?

Neh," quitquiliā, "neh," quitquiliā, "nicān ahmō canah nechmauhtiā.
I," he says, "I . . ." he says, "nothing frightens me here.

278

Nicān nechcāuhuili nopadrino mā nitahpiya nicān que yeh ichān.
My godfather left me here so that I might watch over here [this place],
which is his house.

Ahmō acah hueli nechmahmauhtiz."
No one can frighten me."

Ihcon cachi huetzic toni chīuqueh tapanco.
So it was that more fell from what [they] were doing in the loft.

Cachi caquiztic, huān pēhuac es que nehnemi.
He heard more, and it started to wander about.

"Nimitziliā," quitquiliā, "āconi teha hijo de la chingada," quitquiliā.
"I tell you," he says, "who are you, son of the fucked one?" he said.

"Xinechnānquili."
"Answer me."

Quihtoah ahmō quinānquiliā.
They say that it did not answer him.

Entonces quihtoā nohon ton quichīuqueh, "Me caigo o no me caigo."
So then [one of] those, whoever were doing it, says, "I fall or I don't
fall."

Huān ihcon.
And so it was.

"Por eso," quitquiliā, "nimitziliā xihuāltemō."
"For that reason," [Juan] says to it, "I tell you to come down."

Quitquiliā, "Āconi teha?"
[Juan] says to it, "Who are you?"

Ōmpa quēmah nohon tāc melāhua yeh in ānima.
From there, yes, it was really a spirit.

Entonces quitemō.
So then he lowered it.

Quitquiliā, "Neha," quitquiliā, "nicān niyetoc," quitquiliā.
[He] says [to Juan], "I," he says to him, "am here," he says to him.

"Nicān," quitquiliā, "ahmō yeha mopadrino ichān," quitquiliā.
"Here," he says to him, "is not the house of your godfather," he says
to him.

"Tā nicān nochān," quitquiliā.
"It is my house," he says to him.

"Pero ahmō," quitquiliā.
"But no," he says to him.

"Quihtoā," quitquiliā, "tā yeh ichān!"
"He says," [Juan] says to him, "it is his house!"

Quitquiliā, "Ahmō," quitquiliā, "tā nin nochān nicān.
He says to him, "No," he says to him, "this is my house.

Huān ticmatiz que ye nicān tā niyetoc?" Quitquiliā.
And will you know why I am here?" he says to him.

"Ahmō por tamahmauhtiā," quitquiliā.
"Not to scare anyone," he says to him.

"Tā nechcohcocohtoc," quitquiliā, "nictēmo cequīn tomin.
"It is hurting me [making me sad]," he says to him, "to look for some
money.

Cequīn tomin nicpiya nicān," quitquiliā, "huān ahmō nihueli nipanōhuaya
īxpan Dios."
I have some money here," he says to him, "and I cannot pass in front
of God."

"Cān," quitquiliā, "yetoc?"
"Where," [Juan] says to him, "is it?"

"Nicān," quitquiliā, "yetoc calihtic.
"It is here," he says to him, "inside the house.

Por eso," quitquiliā, "yetoc neh non," quitquiliā.
That is why," he says to him, "I am this [way]," he says to him.

"Pero ahmō yeh ichān," quitquiliā, "mopadrino.
"But it is not the house of," he says to him, "your godfather.

Neh nochān."
It is my house."

Ōmpa quēmah.
From there, yes.

"Āxcān," quitquiliā, "xiquiliti mopadrino mā xinechnēxīti cān yetoc in tomin," quitquiliā.
"Now," he says to him, "go tell your godfather to show me where the money is," he says to him.

"Huān ticnōtzati mopadrino," quitquiliā, "huān xiquīxtican," quitquiliā, "in tomin.
"And you are going to call your godfather," he says to him, "and [you two] remove," he says to him, "the money.

Xiquīxtican," quitquiliā, "porque miac yetoc."
Remove it," he says to him, "because there is a lot."

Cox yeh quihtoā cox doce toneles de nohon tomin yetoya.
He says that there are twelve barrels of money.

Miac tomin, quit[quiliah], quipiya
non āconi.
A lot of money, they say, that one has.

Ōmpa quēmah.
From there, yes.

Quit[quiliah], huālliuh no [ī]ca yohual non tēlpōch.
They say, that boy came back with the night.

Tā mō, quit[quiliah], caqui in padrino ehōc ya.
There is no doubt that, they say, his godfather hears him return now.

Quiliā, "Padrino," quitquiliā, "que nihuāla," quiliā.
[Juan] says, "Godfather," he says to him, "I have come," he says to him.

281

Ahmō quināngili [quinānquili].
[His godfather] did not answer him.

Quiliā nē, "Tiquihtoā teh mochān," quitquiliā, "nē cāmpa nechtītantoc.
[Juan] says to that one, "You said it is your house," he says to him, "where you are sending me.

Ahmō teh mochān," quitquiliā.
It is not your house," he says to him.

"Tā cā[n] yetoc," quitquiliā, "ōmpa ichān," quitquiliā, "ōmpa nechnohnōtz.
"Because there is [someone]," he says to him, "whose house it is there," he says to him, "who spoke to me there.

Huān quihtoā," quitquiliā, "que ahmō teh mochān.
And he says," he says to him, "that it is not your house.

Tā ichān.
It is his house.

Huān quihtoā quēmah, mā xiquīxti cequīn tomin.
And he said that, yes, you must to go remove some money.

Ōmpa yetoc.
There it is.

Quihtoā mā niman tyaca tiquīxtiti.
He says for you to go right away to remove it.

Miac yetoc non tomin."
There is a lot of that money."

Quiliā, "Pos melāuh?"
[The priest] says, "Well, really?"

Quitquiliā, "Quēmah!
[Juan] says to him, "Yes!

Ihcon nechili.
So he told me.

Tyohueh niman," quitquiliā.
Let's go right now," he said to him.

Quīncuitēhua, quit[quiliah], non burritos occeppa, āquin quitamāltilih-
queh non tomin.
He gets up to get those donkeys again, who carried that money.

Quīxtihqueh huān moquepqueh.
They removed it and returned.

Den moquepqueh, molitoc nohon tē padrino, "Pero nin," quitmoliā,
"ahmō quēmman nictacaquiliti noahijado.
After returning, that godfather is thinking, "But this one," he says to
himself, "I am never going to teach my godson a lesson.

Āxcān," quitmoliā, "mejor nāmictiti ohti."
Now," he says to himself, "it will be better for him to go meet the
road."

Ōmpa quēmah.
From there, yes.

Non moquepqueh.
Those [two] returned.

Huān non tanēcic, quiliā non ahijado, "Āxcān mejor xyo," quitquiliā.
It dawned, and [the priest] says to that godson of his, "It would be
better now if you go," he said to him.

"Xyo," quitquiliā, "huehca."
"Go," he says to him, "far."

Den quichīhuac non tēlpōch, toni quicactoz, pos yahqui.
As for what that boy did, hearing that, well, he went.

Quicencui in ohti.
He follows the road.

Cuiāc, quit[quiliah], non ipelota huān non igordon.
He took, they say, that ball and that club of his.

Huān quiahci cē amigo.
And he finds a friend.

Quiahcito.
He went to find him.

Tāhuāntohqueh.
They were getting drunk.

Huān no, quit[quiliah], nēn mā yā quiinvitarohque mā tahtani nohon Juan del Oso.
And also, they say, that one goes to catch him to invite him, so that he may ask John the Bear a question.

Quiliā, "Huān teha amigo," quitquiliā, "cānachi [ī]ca tihuinti?"
He says, "And you, friend," he says to him, "with how much do you get drunk?"

"Pos neh," quitquiliā, "nihuinti," quitquiliā, "nitaxīcoā cē tina."
"Well, I," he says to him, "get drunk," he says to him, "I endure one tub [tubful of alcohol]."

Quitēliā nohon tēlpōch, nē ihcon taxīcoā.
That boy tells him, he so endures with that [much].

Tons [Entonces] quitēliā nohon Juan del Oso, "Ticompañeros."
So then John the Bear tells that one, "We are companions."

Quitquiliā, "Quēmah, ticompañeros."
[John the Bear] says, "Yes, we are companions."

"Entonces," quitquiliā, "tyohueh."
"So then," he says to him, "let's go."

Quīztenquīzteuhqueh non ōme amigos.
Those two friends left together.

Yahqueh.
They went.

Huān occeppa cē q[ui]ahcitoh.
And they went to find another one.

Q[ui]ahcitoh.
They went to find him.

Quit[quiliah] motatāhuāntohqueh.
They say they were getting drunk.

Tons occeppa no, quit[quiliah], ōmpa no quīntacmohuāntihque tepiztin non nitrago huān occeppa quitahtōltiā, "Teh," quitquiliā, "cānachi [ī]ca tihuinti?"
So then again, they say, there he also invited them for a little of his drink, and again [John the Bear] questions him, "You," he said to him, "with how much do you get drunk?"

Tēliā, "Pos neh," quitēliā, "nihuinti [ī]ca cē tina."
He says to them, "Well I," he says to them, "get drunk with one tub [tubful of alcohol]."

Taxīcoā cē tina.
He endures one tub.

Quitēliā, "Pos tehhān no titaxīcoah [ī]ca tina tihuintih . . .
He says to him, "Well, we also endure a tubful to get drunk . . .

Bueno, taxīcoā no cē tina no taī.
That is, he also endures drinking one tubful.

"Bueno," tēliā, "pos tons ticompañeros."
"Good," he says to him, "well then, we are companions."

Quitquiliā, "Quēmah.
He says to him, "Yes.

Tons tyohueh.
So then let's go.

Ticompañeros."
We are companions."

Quīncuitic non ōme compañeros.
He took those two companions [with him].

Ōmpa quēmah, ihcon quitquiliā, "Tyohueh."
From there, yes, so he says to him, "Let's go."

Huān yohueh.
And they went.

Ahcihqueh cē tēchān.
They arrived at someone's house.

Tēliā nohon Juan del Oso, quitēliā non compañeros, "Āxcān," quitēliā, "āxcān ticpiyah titequititih.
That John the Bear says, he says to those companions of his, "Now," he says, "now we have to go to work.

Tequititih.
Go to work.

Huān que chīhuaz huān ahmō ticpiyah cihuāt.
And what will one do, and we do not have a woman.

Tocēlti[n].
We are alone.

Tehhān mā tequitican," quitquiliā.
We must work," he says.

"Ahcmō ticchīhuatih cuenta."
"We did not realize."

Tons, quit[quiliah], nē, quinemili non Juan del Oso, quitēliā in compañero, "Āxcān teh ximocāhua.
So then, they say, that one, that John the Bear decided, he says to the companion, "Now you stay.

Tehhān titequitith, huān teha ximocāhua.
We go to work, and you stay.

Huān xitechtacua[l]chīhua huān xitechtamacati[uh]."
And you make dinner for us and you go to feed us."

Mocāu non compañero cē tōnal.
That companion stayed there for a day.

Quitacualchīhua, quit[quiliah].
He makes the meal, they say.

Huān ahcic non nepantah.
And that noon arrived.

Huān quīzaqui āqui[n] non ichān non tepēcoyoc.
And that one whose house it is comes out of that cave.

Quīzaqui in ahmō cualli.
He who is not good comes out.

Nochi quicuāli, quit[quiliah], non tacual den chihchīhuac ya huān quixixīxili.
He ate everything from him, they say, that food he prepared, and he urinated on it for him.

Ōmpa quēmah.
From there, yes.

Den quichīhuac, pos quihtoah que īhuān motehui.
After he did that, well, they say that he fought with him.

Pero quemeh ahmō mā [mā ahmō] ya ahmō quipiya chicāhualiz, ahmō hueli quitānitiz.
But since it is to be that he already does not have strength, he will not defeat him.

Tons [Entonces] occeppa cē tōnal quichīhuac in tacual huān quī[n]tamacato siempre.
So then again another day he made the meal and went to feed them as usual.

Quitēliā non, . . .
He says to them, . . .

Quitquiliah non compañeros, "Que ye," quitquiliah, "teōtac tihuālla?"
Those companions say to him, "Why," they say, "did you come in the afternoon?"

"Huān quēn[in] nicchīhuac?
"And what did I do?

Tā [ī]ca huālla," quihtoā, "cē tāgat," quitquiliā, "huān nechcuālic," quitquiliā, "notacual huān nechixīxili.

287

It is that he came," he says, "a man," he says, "and ate from me," he says to him, "my dinner and urinated on it for me.

Ceppa nicchīhua occē taman," quitquiliā, "para namechcuā[l]cuiliaya."
I make another one again," he says to him, "to bring to you."

"Hījole," quitmoliā, "pos . . ."
"Son of the," he says to himself, "well . . ."

Quitēliā occē, "Pos āxcān," quitēliā, "mōzta nimocāhuaz."
The other one said to him, "Well now," he says to them, "tomorrow I shall stay."

Non, quit[quiliah], mocāuhqueh non teōtac huān cochqueh huān occeppa cuāntzin, ōmpa mocāu occeppa occē.
Those, they say, stayed that afternoon and slept, and early the next morning, another one stayed again.

"Āxcān," quitēliā, "neh nimocāhua."
"Now," he says to them, "I stay."

Huān ceppa cē mā tequititih.
And again they have to go to work.

Ceppa yahqueh.
They went off again.

Tayacānqueh non Juan del Oso.
That John the Bear was the boss.

Tonces occeppa ihcon, quit[quiliah], pasaro.
So then again, they say, it happened.

Ahcic nepantah, huān quichīchiuh nitacual.
Noon came, and he made his meal.

Huān quitāliti in taxcal, huān quīzati in ahmō cualli.
And he put on the tortillas, and he who is not good goes out [he appears].

Ceppa, quit[quiliah], quicuālic non itacual ya.
Again, they say, he ate that meal already.

Huān quixixīxili huān occeppa yahqui.
And he urinated on it for him and went away again.

Motehuihqueh, quihtoā, huān ceppa yahqui.
They pounded each other, he says, and he went away again.

Tons teōtac no occeppa quī[n]tamacati.
So then again in the afternoon he goes to feed them.

Quitēliā, "Pos teōtac ya pero quēn quichīhuaz huān melāuh," quitēliā, "huāllaca non tāgat.
He tells them, "Well, it was afternoon already but what will [would] one do and it is true," he says to them, "that man had come.

Huāllaca non niman motehuiā," quitēliā, "cualli.
That one had come to fight," he tells them, "well.

Por eso," quitēliā, "in teōtac nihuālla."
That is why," he says to them, "I came in the afternoon."

"Hījole," quitēliā in Juan del Oso.
"Son of the," John the Bear says to them.

"Āxcān neh nimocāhuaz pos."
"Now I shall stay."

Tons non cuāntzin quīniliā nicompañeros, "Āxcān xitequiti[can] huān nicān nimocāhuati."
So that morning he says to his companions, "Now go to work, and I am going to stay here."

Ahcic, quitēliā [quitquiliah], in nepantah huān niman quittac que ahmō ahcic.
Noon came, they say, and soon [John the Bear] saw that [the devil] did not arrive.

Tons quitēliā, "Xihuālehuāca niman.
So then he says to him, "Come from there right now.

Neh," quitēliā, "īhuān neh," quitēliā, "huān no melāuh," quitēliā, "in tāgat, non āconi, huitza?"

289

I," he says to him, "am by myself," he says to him, "and is it really
true," he says, "the man, whoever he is, comes?"

Entonces quit[ē]ēhuac nohon.
So then he roused that one.

Ahcic nepantah huān, que ehōc occeppa in ahmō cualli.
Noon came, and he who is not good arrived again.

Quicuālic, quit[quiliah], non tacual.
He ate [He tried to eat], they say, that meal.

Yeh, quit[quiliah], ahmō quitacāhuili.
[John the Bear], they say, did not let him.

Mocuītilihqueh.
They called each other names.

Pēuqueh motehuiah.
They started pounding each other.

Entonces panōc in nepantah huān quittah, quit[quiliah], non compañeros,
pos ahmō ahci.
So then noon passed, and those companions, they say, see that he does
not arrive.

Huālleuqueh cāmpa tequitih.
They came from where they worked.

Quittah ehōqueh.
They see him [when they] arrived.

Quiahcitoh.
They went to find him.

Quit[quiliah], melāuh īhuān motehuitoc.
They say, he is really fighting with him.

Quitēhuītectiuh īca non itopil.
He shed his blood with that club of his.

Melāuh pōxonitohqueh, quihtoah.
They were really lying out on their stomachs [fighting], they say.

Huān quimagati, quit[quiliah], [ī]ca non nitopil.
And he goes to hit him, they say, with that club of his.

Occeppa, quit[quiliah], [mo]cuitequizqueh motehuiah.
Again, they say, they grabbed each other to cut one another fighting.

Quimaga, quimaga hasta quitoh[to]caqueh hasta cāhuato, quit[quiliah], ichān nohon Juan del Oso.
He hits him, he hits him until they [he] chased him away so that he went to leave, they say, that house of John the Bear.

Cuiāc, quit[quiliah], huehca, quit[quiliah], non tē coyoc.
He took him, they say, far, they say, into that cave of his.

Quitoh[to]cac.
He chased him away.

Huān quīnpiya ēyi non ichpōchhuan, quit[quiliah], quīncuilito.
And he has three of those maidens, they say, whom he went to fetch.

Entonces quī[n]zaco, quit[quiliah], huān quī[n]zaco huān quīncuālcui non ichpōchhuan.
Then he came to remove them, they say, and he came to remove them and he brought those maidens.

Quitquiliā nohon nicompañero, "Āxcān," quitēliā, "niq[uīn]cuālcui nihin, nihin ichpōchhuan," quitēliā.
He says to those companions of his, "Now," he says to them, "I brought these, these maidens," he says to them.

"Āxcān," quitēliā, "cada quien ninamechmacati cē cē huān neh no cē," quitēliā.
"Now," he says to them, "I am going to give one to each of you and there is one for me," he says to them.

"Huān cada quien yohui tequiti ya."
"And each goes to work now."

291

De ōmpa, quihtoa[h], nohon Juan del Oso, cuiahqueh nē tech in Cozōltepēt.
From there, they say, that John the Bear, they took him to Cozōltepēt.

Ōmpa quinequi mochāntāliz.
He wanted to make his home there.

Ōmpa yetoya cē tiempo.
He was there for a time.

Huān, quihtoa[h], quinemilihqueh nohon quiyahteōmeh, "Pos ahmō hueliz ōmpa yetoz porque techpolozquiā īca in āt."
And, they say, those rain gods decided, "Well, he cannot be there because he will lose [drown] us with water."

Ōmpa quēmah, quihtoa[h], quinemilihqueh mejor quicuicatih nē cāmpa in huēiāt.
From there, yes, they say, they decided it will be better to take him to the river.

Quihtoa[h] quicuāltachihchīhuitoh.
They say that they were going to take him to adorn it.

Quihtoa[h] nē tani, nē tani ihcuīn.
They say below there, thereabouts below.

Quihtoa[h] nē Cempōhuala, quit[quiliah], para tani.
They say the Cempōhuala River, they say, down below.

Cuāltachi[h]chīhuah, quit[quiliah] nochi [ī]ca xōchiarcos.
They bring [him] to adorn [it], they say, all with arcs of flowers.

Tachi[h]chīuh.
It was something adorned.

"Āxcān," quitquilia[h], "tyohueh," quitquilia[h].
"Now," they say to him, "let's go," they say.

"Tyohueh," quitquilia[h], "nēpa," quitquilia[h], "mochīhuatih ilhuit."
"Let's go," they say to him, "there," they say to him, "to hold a fiesta."

Yeh, quit[quiliah], ahmō quinequiā yaz.
He, they say, did not want to go.

Quitēliā, "Ahmō," quitquiliā, "cualli nicān niyetoc," quitquiliā.
He says to them, "No," he says, "I am fine here," he says.

"Ahmō.
"No.

Tā tyohueh.
Let's go.

Mā mochīhuati," quitēliah, "in ilhuit."
It is necessary to hold," they say to him, "the fiesta."

Huān quihtoa[h] de nē Cempōhuala ihcuīn tech huēiāt quitachi[h]chī-huihqueh nochi [ī]ca xōchiarcos.
And they say they decorated the Cempōhuala River all with arcs of flowers.

Cualtzin quīntachi[h]chīhuac.
He adored them beautifully.

Ōmpa tachixtoc.
He is gazing at it there.

Ōmpa cē xōchiarco [ī]ca yē, quit[quiliah], non cōzamālōmeh.
There was an arc of flowers by means, they say, of those rainbows.

Quīncuāltepētquetzqueh.
They placed them from one side of the mountain to the other.

Quitēliā, "Bueno," quitquiliā, "tyohueh," quitēliā.
He says to them, "Good," he says, "let's go," he tells them.

"Pero nin," quitēliā, "neh ahmō nimoquepati."
"But to this [place]," he tells them, "I am not going to return."

Quitēliā, "Nicuicati," quitēliā, "cē no cuāpech."
He tells them, "I am going to take," he says to them, "one of my pillows."

Entonces quitzicohtiuh [ī]ca ilpica, quit[quiliah], cē pedazo in tepēt quicuitiuh.
So he fastened it by tying, they say, he took a piece of the mountain.

Entonces non, quit[quiliah].
So then it was, they say.

Huān, quit[quiliah], cotōnito nohon ilpica.
And, they say, it cut that rope.

Zoquiapan tani mocāuhuitiquiz non cē tepēt ihcatoc.
He passed, leaving a mountain standing below Zoquiapan.

Quemeh Cozōlin.
It is like Mount Cozōlin.

Cē tepēt chiquititzin.
It is a small mountain.

Entonces ōmpa, quit[quiliah], ahmō hueli quicuiāc.
So then, they say, he could not take it [farther].

Ihcon yahqui ya.
So he went on now.

Entonces ahciqueh ya, quit[quiliah], nē cāmpa tech mar.
So then they arrived now, they say, there by the sea.

Pero ahmō quittac cān ahcic huān ahmō moquepac oc.
But he did not see where he arrived, and he did not return anymore.

Ōmpa quēmah non quitquiliah [ih]cuāc talhuitih; yeh quinequiā mā quimati quēmman[i]yān quiyahuiz.
From there, yes, those [rain gods] tell him when they are going to summon [him]; he wants to know when it will rain.

Quinequiā quimatiz quēmman[i]yān ilhuit tech dīa San Juan.
He wants to know when the fiesta is on the day of Saint John.

Pero ahmō quilitih quēmman[i]yān.
But they are not going to tell him when.

Quiliā, yeh quiliā, "Todavīa huitza oc," quitquiliā, "huān timitzilizqueh [ih]cuāc talhuitiz.
[One of the rain gods] says, he says, "It still comes," he says to him, "and we shall tell you when to summon you [for the fiesta].

294

Timitzilizqueh."
We shall tell you."

Quihtoā como ahmō taīxmatic nohon Juan del Oso.
He tells him because that John the Bear did not know how to read.

Ahmō taīxmatic.
He did not read.

Ihcon ya hueli quitahtātilihqueh in ilhuit.
So it was possible for them to hide the fiesta [from him].

Huān ahmō quimatic.
And [John the Bear] did not know.

Quihtoā que cada vez que ehcōz in ilhuit.
[One of the rain gods] tells him every time that the fiesta will arrive.

Pos ahmō teh quilihqueh quēmman[i]yān.
Well, they did not tell him when.

Mā ta[h]tani.
He must ask.

Quiliah, "Todavía huehca huitza oc."
They say, "It still comes in a long time."

Ihcuāc panoz in ilhuit, ahmō teh quiliah.
When the fiesta will pass, they do not tell him anything.

Huān ihcon.
And that is how it was.

Huān ōmpa tamic.
And there it ended.

NOTES

Chapter 1

1. Nahuat is an Aztec language (W. Miller 1983:121) that Dow F. Robinson (1966:iii) estimated is spoken by 50,000 people living "within a triangle having Cuetzalán on the north, Chignahuapan on the west, and Teziutlán on the east."

2. Lewis (1961 [1963]).

3. Lewis (1964 [1967]:xxxvii). Judith Friedlander (1975) also emphasized how the villagers in another Morelos community of Hueyapan had no interest in their "Indian" background, and she criticized anthropologists for attempting to find "Indians" in Mexico.

4. Lewis interpreted the stories of Jesús Sánchez and Pedro Martínez in the introductions to his books on both men (1961 [1963], 1964 [1967]). He stressed how both men live in "cultures of poverty" created by low wages and high unemployment, and he focused on the psychological effects of an absent or remote father on the development of the son's masculinity.

5. Village studies in Mexico and Spain that represent a man as distant from his father, close to his mother, estranged from his wife, and alienated from his sons are very numerous. The Mexican studies include Oscar Lewis's (1949, 1951) account of Tepoztlán, Judith Friedlander's (1975) study of Hueyapan, and John Ingham's (1986) ethnography of Tlayacapan, all of which are or were Nahuatl-speaking villages in the state of Morelos. Ethnographers working in Spain also allude to a remote relationship between the father and his adult sons by specifying a preference for matrilocality over patrilocality (Pitt-Rivers 1966:101–102), male fears of anal penetration by other men (Brandes 1980:95–96), and a competitive worldview (Gilmore 1987). Michael D. Murphy (1983b) offered an interesting and convincing account of the estrangement between fathers and sons that explains the preference for matrilocality over patrilocality. With respect to the Spanish man's relationship to woman, Brandes (1975) provided a vivid and complete picture of family life in southern Ávila and represented a man as very dependent on a woman, first as mother and then as wife. Richard and Sally Price (1966: 314–315) presented a more estranged picture of the marital relationship. They declared that the long and formal courtships during the early decades

of the Franco regime perpetuated rather than removed the barriers to marital intimacy in Los Olivos, a village in southern Spain. Courted maidens, who felt constrained to guard their premarital chastity in the eyes of their community, never really knew their sweethearts. After marriage, recently married husbands spent their leisure time with men and had sex with other partners before their wife's first pregnancy. David Gilmore (1990) placed the Hispanic man in a broad cross-cultural perspective and concluded that he has a similar but not identical masculine identity to men in many cultures because men are generally socialized to be progenitors, providers, and protectors in their society. See José Limón (1989) and Michael Herzfeld (1980, 1984, 1985) for other interesting views of masculinity.

6. See Alan Dundes (1989:57–82) for an excellent account of the comparative method in folklore and anthropology. James Clifford (1988) argues for multivocal representation to correct for the excesses of writing ethnography with an unwarranted and unsubstantiated authority.

7. Frances Karttunen (1983:127) defined macēhual as "subject, commoner, indigenous person, speaker of Nahuatl."

8. Karttunen (1983:104) defined īlihuiz as "inconsiderately, sin consideración, y desvariadamente, fuerte, fuertemente."

9. Darbord (1984:31, 97–101).

10. Behar (1993:16–18).

11. Freud (1900 [1978]).

12. Dundes (1987:1–46).

13. Boas (1912).

14. There are several accounts of the traces of sixteenth-century Nahua mythic themes in twentieth-century Nahua oral narratives. They include Elsa Ziehm's (1982:9–40) discussion of the texts collected by Konrad Preuss (1982:74–225) in Durango in 1907, and my description (Taggart 1983:85–113) of Nahuat myths apparently derived from stories like those which appeared in Sahagún (1953:3–8), Paso y Troncoso (1903:14, 30), Lehmann (1906:245–257), Feliciano Velázquez (1975:119–121), and Bierhorst (1992:146–147, 147–149). See Miguel León-Portilla (1986:136–141) for an excellent anthology of contemporary Nahua texts with ancient mythic themes.

15. López Austin (1990).

16. It is difficult to be exact about the historical connections between villages in Cáceres, Spain, and the northern Sierra de Puebla, Mexico. One method is to correlate the approximate date that Spanish colonialists arrived in the northern Sierra de Puebla with the periods during which waves of emigrants departed from different regions in Spain. The first colonialists probably arrived in the northern Sierra de Puebla in the late 1700s, when, according to Foster's (1952) calculations, the majority of Spanish emigrants left from provinces in northern Extremadura and southern Old Castile. Navaconcejo and the other Cáceres villages where I collected Spanish folktales are near the border between Old Castile and Extremadura.

17. Wolf (1959).

18. Dundes (1989:57–82).

19. Clifford (1988:21–54).
20. Dundes (1989:63).
21. Dundes (1989:63).
22. Dundes (1989:64).
23. Dundes (1989:73).
24. Friedrich Panzer (1910) recognized the similarities between the Grendel episode of the Old English epic *Beowulf* and a folktale he called "The Bear's Son" (Tale Type 301). J. Michael Stitt (1992) reconsidered the relationship between the two stories and presented a strong case against arguing that the literary story is the source of the oral folktales.
25. Thompson (1946 [1977]:165).
26. Darbord (1984:31).
27. Aarne and Thompson (1961 [1987]:104–107). Leavy (1994:213) describes the similarities between "The Girl as Helper in the Hero's Flight" and the classical Greek tragedy of "Jason and Medea."
28. Gayton (1935) and Hultkrantz (1957).
29. Wheeler (1943) and Robe (1970). See also Stanley Robe's collections of folktales from Narayit (Robe 1972) and Veracruz (Robe 1971).
30. Alan Sandstrom very generously gave me the texts of stories he recorded and painstakingly transcribed from Nahuatl storytellers in the Huasteca region of Veracruz. I have not used those stories because I prefer to co-author articles on folktales with him to recognize his contribution to the collection, transcription, and translations of the tales.
31. Laughlin (1977). In contrast, see, for example, folktales in Spanish collected by Mason (1914, 1956) and Parsons (1932b) from narrators who may be native Mexicans.
32. Róheim (1992:9–10).
33. Sherzer (1987).
34. Fernandez (1986:vii–xv, 140–142) offers a very useful account of the importance of words in anthropological fieldwork. See Tedlock (1983) on written representions of the spoken word and Dundes (1986:259) for what happens to an oral tale when converted to type or print.
35. Interested readers can contact me to request additional, unpublished original language texts for "The Bear and His Sons."
36. Lacan (1977:151–152) illustrated his theory of language and gender with the anecdote of a brother and sister seated facing each other in the compartment of a train arriving at a station. The compartment window passes restroom doors marked "Ladies" and "Gentlemen." The brother exclaims, "We're at Ladies!" "Idiot!" replies the sister. "We're at Gentlemen." The labels on the restroom doors are phonemes that are combined "according to the laws of a closed order," which Lacan called a "signifying chain" (1977:153). See Jane Gallop (1982:9–11) for her explication of the meaning of Lacan's anecdote.
37. Lacan (1977:147).
38. See Gallop (1982:19–20) for an account of how Lacan used the term "castration" to refer to "the general relation of subject to signifier."

39. Gallop (1982:11).
40. Róheim (1992:5).
41. See Freud (1900 [1978]; 1940 [1989]:29–44).
42. Drawing on Freud's theory (1900 [1978]), Róheim (1992:44–57) hypothesized that oral narratives originate as dreams.
43. Róheim (1992:9).
44. Some of the most vehement criticisms are directed toward Freud's theory of femininity. See Bernheimer and Kahane's (1985 [1990]) volume, which critically evaluated Freud's handling of Dora (Freud 1963).
45. Freud (1905 [1975]:85–86).
46. Freud (1905 [1975], 1930 [1961]:62–83, 1931 [1959], 1932 [1933]: 112–136).
47. Freud (1923–1925a:173–179, 1923–1925b:248–258).
48. Freud (1932 [1933]:112–135).
49. Freud (1923–1925a:173–179, 1923–1925b:248–258).
50. Freud (1932 [1933]:130–131).
51. Freud (1932 [1933]:112–135).
52. Freud (1932 [1933]:128–130).
53. Kardiner (1939:382–385). See Dundes' (1987:1–46) interesting discussion of the value of Kardiner's work for interpreting folklore. See also Shweder's (1979a, 1979b, 1980) critique of the culture and personality school for which Kardiner laid the foundation.
54. Kardiner (1939:387–388).
55. Kardiner (1939:387–388).
56. Kardiner (1945:23–26).
57. Kardiner (1945:24).
58. Sydow (1948:44–59).
59. Kardiner (1939:317).
60. Kardiner (1939:328).
61. Freud (1905 [1975]:8–11).
62. Kardiner (1945:23).
63. Mead (1935). See David Gilmore (1990) for a more recent summary of the variation in gender roles across selected cultures. L. L. Langness (1990) provides an interesting account of fathers who are emotionally closer to their children than mothers among the Bena Bena of New Guinea.
64. Stoller (1985:11).
65. Stoller (1985).
66. Stoller (1985:171–180, 181–199). See also Herdt (1981).
67. Chodorow (1978).
68. Chodorow (1978:3–6).
69. Chodorow (1978:87).
70. Barry and Paxson (1971) summarize the cross-cultural variation in fathering, Hewlett (1991, 1992) provides a rich picture of fathering among the Aka Pygmies and in other cultures, and Peggy Sanday (1981) and Scott Coltrane (1988, 1992) describe the broad cross-cultural relationship between fathering and culture.

Chapter 2

1. Panzer (1910).

2. Stitt (1992:11, 193).

3. Thompson (1946 [1977]:33).

4. Aurelio Espinosa (1924:275–283) collected three versions of "The Bear's Son" (AT 301) from unidentified narrators in Soria, Santander, and Toledo. I know of at least five masculine and four feminine variants collected from storytellers in Cáceres and provinces to the north and south in Spain. Marciano Curiel Merchán (1944:324–327) reported one from Isidro Lurengo of Trujillo in southern Cáceres. I heard three others from Juan Julián Recuero in Serradilla, Julio López Curiel in Garganta la Olla, and Florencio Ramos of Navaconcejo; Luis Cortés Vázquez (1979:II:142–147) published a fifth by Rafael Curillo of Saucelle in Salamanca.

The feminine variants are by Angela Cuadrado of Trujillo in Cáceres (Curiel Merchán 1944:210–214), Manuela Martín Cuadrado of Vilvestre and Manuela Hoyos of La Alberca in Salamanca (Cortés Vázquez 1979:II:130–141, 147–154), and a twelve-year-old girl in Cádiz who probably heard it from her grandmother (Larrea Palacín 1959:16–18, 141–147).

5. Robe (1972:124).

6. Christian (1972 [1989]); Pitt-Rivers (1966).

7. Christian (1972 [1989]).

8. Behar (1990).

9. George Collier (1987:5, 88–118) provided a very clear definition of the cultural meaning of *autonomía* and described a fascinating challenge to the *autonomía* of landowners during the Second Republic.

10. Murphy (1983a, 1983b).

11. I collected statistics on household social composition in Garganta la Olla and discovered a strong preference for matrilocality over patrilocality (Taggart 1990:25–28).

12. Dundes (1984 [1989]) and personal communication.

13. Curiel Merchán (1944:324–327).

14. Cortés Vázquez (1979:II:142–147).

15. Curiel Merchán (1944:324–327).

16. Isidro Lurengo Porras from Trujillo in Cáceres (Curiel Merchán 1944:324–327) and Rafael Currillo of Saucelle in Salamanca (Cortés Vázquez 1979:II:142–147) did not make comparisons of relative strength when they described the companions' first meeting. However, all Spanish narrators established the hero's superior fearlessness (or courage) in the following episode.

17. Brandes (1980:95–96).

18. Lison-Tolosana (1983:316–334) described the concept of gallantry in relation to masculine honor. His description fits accounts by other anthropologists of manliness, especially that of Pitt-Rivers (1966), and applies to the construction of masculinity in Navaconcejo and other northern and central Cáceres villages.

19. Julio López Curiel, Juan Julián Recuero, Isidro Lurengo Porras (Curiel

301

Merchán 1944:324–327), and Rafael Currillo (Cortés Vázquez 1979:II:142–147) are narrators who developed the episode in this way.

20. The companions steal the maidens in a story by Rafael Currillo of Saucelle (Cortés Vázquez 1979:II:142–147), but in a variant by Juan Julián Recuero of Serradilla, the hero does not permit his companions to marry the maidens even though there is no theft. In the variant by Isidro Lurengo Porras of Trujillo, the hero marries one of three maidens recovered from the underworld, but the narrator did not say whether the companions marry the other two (Curiel Merchán 1944:324–327).

21. Pitt-Rivers (1966:36, 61).

22. Pitt-Rivers (1966:96).

23. See George Collier (1987) for an account of an extreme chastity code during the uncontested reign of private property and Jane Collier (1986) on changes in the chastity code after the collapse of the land-based and labor-intensive rural economy in the village of Los Olivos in Andalusia.

24. Cortés Vázquez (1979:II:147–154, 130–141); Larrea Palacín (1959:141–147); Curiel Merchán (1944:210–214).

25. Cortés Vázquez (1979:II:147–154).

26. Cortés Vázquez (1979:II:130–141); Larrea Palacín (1959:141–147). It is interesting that Angela Cuadrado from Trujillo described her hero as having a widowed father (Curiel Merchán 1944:210–214).

27. Cortés Vázquez (1979:II:130–141, 147–154); Larrea Palacín (1959:141–147).

28. Cortés Vázquez (1979:II:147–154, 130–141); Curiel Merchán (1944:210–214); Larrea Palacín (1959:141–147).

29. Cortés Vázquez (1979:II:147–154).

30. Cortés Vázquez (1979:II:147–154, 130–141).

31. Cortés Vázquez (1979:II:147–154).

32. Taggart (1990:93–115).

33. Gilmore and Uhl (1987).

34. Cortés Vázquez (1979:II:147–154, 130–141).

35. Cortés Vázquez (1979:II:147–154).

36. Cortés Vázquez (1979:II:130–141).

37. Cortés Vázquez (1979:II:147–154).

38. Cortés Vázquez (1979:II:130–141).

39. Taggart (1990:93–115).

40. Cortés Vázquez (1979:II:130–141).

Chapter 3

1. Thompson (1946 [1977]:33).

2. Folklorists have found "The Bear's Son" among Spanish-speaking narrators in Mexico and the southwestern United States (Robe 1972:44–47). Within the modern boundaries of Mexico, Howard T. Wheeler (1943:239–240, 240–246, 247–259, 259–271) collected four interesting variants from unidentified Spanish-speaking narrators in Jalisco. Stanley Robe (1970:114–116)

heard two more from women living in the same part of Mexico. Paul Radin and Aurelio Espinosa (1917:211–212, 212–216, 216–220) included three by unidentified narrators in Oaxaca. In northern Mexico, Robert A. Barakat (1965:331–332, 333–334, 336) found two by Spanish-speaking men, and Frank J. Dobie (1935 [1947]:xii, 201, 211, 212–227) published a third he collected from a cowboy known as Ismaél. When Stith Thompson did his study of native North American folktales, he found "The Bear's Son" in collections of stories by the Loucheux, Chilcotin, Thompson River, Kwakiutl, Shoshoni, Assiniboin, Ojibwa, Micmac, and Malecite in the United States and Canada, and by the Tehuano and Tepecano in Mexico (1929 [1966]:205–207, 359).

3. In addition to Nacho's story, I also recorded versions of "The Bear's Son" by the Nahuat-speaking narrators Juan Hernández in Huitzilan and Mariano Isidro in Santiago Yaonáhuac.

4. Outside of the Huitzilan and Yaonáhuac, at least ten other speakers of native Mexican languages have told versions of "The Bear's Son" appearing in published collections. Nine of the ten are men who speak Toztzil Maya (Laughlin 1977:401–404), Mochó (Maya) (Martin 1987), Popolucan (Foster 1945:229–230), Zapotec (Boas 1912:241–245; Radin 1943:22–30), Tepehua (Mason 1956:385–388), and Tepecano (Mason 1914:176–179), and a dialect of Nahua in Durango (Preuss 1982:560–583, 583–587). Matilde de Jesús, also a speaker of Nahua from Durango, told a truncated version of this tale focusing on the hero's origins as the product of a union between a woman and jaguar (Preuss 1982:324–333). Laura Martin (1987) offers an interesting comparison of Mochó (Mayan) and Spanish variants by the same storyteller. I did not have access to the complete Mochó text, which was collected by Terrence Kaufman. The preponderance of masculine variants of this and other popular folktales in published collections may not be a true reflection of gender patterns in storytelling. There is a great deal of gender segregation in native Mexican communities, and men, who have been the main collectors, might not have had access to women storytellers. Brenda Rosenbaum (1993:64–87) found a fascinating Tzotil Mayan storytelling tradition in Chamula and presents a very useful account of gender patterns in male and female narratives.

5. Thompson (1946 [1977]:85).

6. A. Espinosa (1923:80–81).

7. Wheeler (1943:73–75); Laughlin (1977:81–84, 370–372).

8. Robe (1970:114–116); Boas (1912:241–245) and Radin (1943:22–30).

9. Sydow (1948:44–59).

10. Paso y Troncoso (1903:30) and Sahagún (1953:3–8); Paso y Troncoso (1903), Lehmann (1906), Feliciano Velázquez (1975), and Bierhorst (1992: 147–149).

11. I discussed these and other aspects of Nahuat mythology elsewhere (Taggart 1983). For another interesting account of native Mexican identity in folktales, see Gossen (1974).

12. The three Nahuat-speaking communities are Huitzilan, Santiago Yaonáhuac (Taggart 1983:60–61, 91–92, 212, 214–216, 264–265), and Hueyapan (Díaz Hernández 1945).

13. Louise Burkhart (1989:61) drew my attention to the importance of slipping and falling in Nahua moral discourse.

14. Karttunen (1983:104).

15. Burkhart (1989:40–42, 64–65) described the use of the term tācatecolōtl in sixteenth-century Nahua documents.

16. Garibay (1953–1954:I:19). See also Garibay (1940[1961]). León-Portilla (1963 [1982]:75, 102–103; 1985:19) provides interesting examples of difrasimos in Nahuatl.

17. Readers can find the difrasimos (diaphrasis) for "town" as two separate words (in ātl, in tepētl) in León-Portilla (1963 [1982]:102) and as the compound noun āltepētl in Karttunen (1983:9).

18. León-Portilla (1963 [1982]:102).

19. Karttunen (1983:148).

20. Lévi-Strauss (1969).

21. Sandstrom (1991).

22. Burkhart (1989:58) from Launey (1979).

23. Lüthi (1970 [1976], 1975 [1984]:13, 28, 37).

24. Wheeler (1943:271, 282).

25. Boas (1912:241–245), Laughlin (1977:401–404), Mason (1956:385–388), and Radin (1943:22–30).

26. Radin (1943:22–30); Boas (1912:241–245); Mason (1914:176–179, 1956:385–388).

27. See the stories by Rito Villa and Doroteo Jesús (Preuss 1982:560–583, 583–587). Sometimes no father is mentioned because the narrator did not describe the hero's origins (see Foster 1945:229–230).

28. Lewis (1961 [1963]).

29. Dobie (1935 [1947]:212–227).

30. Dobie (1935 [1947]:212–227); Barakat (1965:333–334).

31. Dobie (1935 [1947]:212–227).

32. Barakat (1965:333–334).

33. Wheeler (1943:240–246).

34. Robe (1970:116–125, 114–116).

35. Murphy (1983b), Brandes (1975:112–117), Gilmore and Uhl (1987), and Lison-Tolosana (1966 [1983]:151).

36. Brandes (1975:112–117), Gilmore (1987:145–146), Gilmore and Uhl (1987), and Lison-Tolosana (1966 [1983]:151).

37. Lewis (1961 [1963]).

38. Gutmann (1993, 1996).

39. Dundes (1987:1–46).

40. See Taggart (1983:47) for the frequencies of patrilocality and matrilocality in Huitzilan and Yaonáhuac.

41. Nutini (1967).

42. Laughlin (1977:401–404); Foster (1945:229–230); Mason (1914:176–179); Mason (1956:385–388); Radin (1943:22–30).

43. Boas (1912:241–245).

44. See the story by Rito Villa (Preuss 1982:560–583).
45. Barakat (1965:333–334); Dobie (1935 [1947]:212–227).
46. Barakat (1965:331–332).
47. Robe (1970:114–116, 116–125).
48. Wheeler (1943:239–240, 247–259, 259–271, 240–246).
49. Boas (1912:241–245), Foster (1945:229–230), Laughlin (1977:401–404), Mason (1914:176–179), and Radin (1943:22–30).
50. Preuss (1982:560–583).
51. Foster (1945:229–230); Boas (1912:241–245).
52. Wheeler (1943:240–246, 247–259, 259–271).
53. Wheeler (1943:247–259).
54. Barakat (1965:333–334).
55. Dobie (1935 [1947]:212–227).
56. Robe (1970:116–125, 114–116).

Chapter 4

1. Thompson (1946 [1977]:165–167).
2. Thompson (1946 [1977]:165); Aarne and Thompson (1961 [1987]:440).
3. Aarne and Thompson (1961 [1987]:440–441).
4. Thompson (1946 [1977]:166, 174).
5. Thompson (1946 [1977]:167) noted that there are 253 version of "Cleverness and Gullibility" (Tale Type 1539) in Finland alone and that the tale is popular in the Baltic region and in Russia. See Aarne and Thompson (1961 [1987]:443) for a more complete and updated list of the geographical distribution and frequencies of this tale.
6. Thompson (1946 [1977]:167) also observed that "The Rich and the Poor Peasant" and "Cleverness and Gullibility" are "little more than a loose series of single anecdotes. Types of this kind have a natural ability to be very baffling to the investigator of folktale origins and dissemination."
7. Aurelio Espinosa collected folktales in many Spanish provinces in 1920 and 1921 (Espinosa 1921; Espinosa and Espinosa 1985:35–49), and Aurelio de Llano Roza de Ampudia carried out his project in Asturias between 1919 and 1923 (Llano Roza de Ampudia 1975:339–347).
8. "Juanito Malastrampas" from Burgos, "Los dos compadres" and "Juan Bobo" from Santander, and "Los dos compadres" from Granada (A. Espinosa 1926:381–383, 377–378, 415–417, 379–381); "Los tres hermanos" by Mercedes Morán and "El anduvinón" by Serafín Pérez (Llano Roza de Ampudia 1975:142–145, 340, 183–185, 342); and "El compadre rico y el pobre" by Victoria Coca and "El compadre rico y el pobre" by Magdalena Frutos (Cortés Vázquez 1979:I:255–260, 252–255).
9. Variants by unidentified narrators in Santander and Granada (A. Espinosa 1926:377–378, 379–381), Victoria Coca and Magdalena Frutos in Salamanca (Cortés Vázquez 1979:I:255–260, 252–255), Serafín Pérez in Asturias (Llano Roza de Ampudia 1975:183–185), and Román Santo in Navaconcejo,

Leandro Jiménez and Felipa Sánchez in El Guijo de Santa Bárbara, Maximina Castaño and Santos López in Garganta la Olla, and Victoria Díaz and Zacaria Iglesias in Piornal.

10. Variants by unidentified narrators in Santander and Burgos (A. Espinosa 1926:415–417, 381–383), Mercedes Morán in Asturias (Llano Roza de Ampudia 1975:142–145, 340), and two Cáceres storytellers: Florencio Ramos in Navaconcejo and Felisa Sánchez Martín in Serradilla.

11. A. Espinosa (1926:415–417).

12. Variants by Román Santo in Navaconcejo, Leandro Jiménez and Felipa Sánchez in El Guijo de Santa Bárbara, Maximina Castaño in Garganta la Olla, and Victoria Díaz in Piornal. See also stories by an unidentified narrator in Granada (A. Espinosa 1926:379–381) and by Magdalena Frutos and Victoria Coca in Salamanca (Cortés Vázquez 1979:I:252–255, 255–260).

13. Dundes (1984 [1989]:80–84) provided examples in German folklore of the symbolic association between excrement and money that Freud (1908 [1959]) observed in his German-speaking patients.

14. This episode in Felisa Sánchez Martín's version of "The Rich and the Poor Peasant" (AT 1535) may be derived from the related trickster tale known as "Old Hildebrand" (AT 1360C); see Aarne and Thompson (1961 [1987]: 404–405).

15. Llano Roza de Ampudia (1975:183–185, 342).

16. The only exception within Spain once again comes from a narrator in Asturias who told a tale that Ralph Boggs (1930:130) classified as "The Rich and the Poor Peasant" (AT 1535). However, it actually resembles another folktale known as "Crop Division" (AT 1030); see Aarne and Thompson (1961 [1987]:350–351). The narrator is Mercedes Morán from La Riera, and she also called her tale "The Three Brothers." Mercedes told of Juan, Pedro, and Manuel, whose mother dies and leaves an inheritance of a bed, a garden with some cabbage, and a small plot of land for growing corn. The brothers have only a single blanket on their bed, and Pedro, who sleeps on the edge and is frequently uncovered, strikes a deal with Juan and Manuel. He offers to sell them his portion of the cabbage and the corn if they will allow him to sleep in the middle of the bed. He asks his brothers if they want the stalks or the leaves of the cabbage, and they choose the leaves. Of course, by keeping the stalk, Pedro has the part of the cabbage plant that reproduces the leaves he sells to his brothers. He asks them if they would like the stalk or the ears of corn, and this time they choose the stalks, which of course have little value. Trickery among the brothers does not appear in subsequent episodes of this long story (Llano Roza de Ampudia 1975:142–145. 340).

17. Llano Roza de Ampudia (1975:142–143, 340).

18. Thompson (1946 [1977]:73). Folklorists and anthropologists collected seven variants of Tale Type 566 from the time of Aurelio Espinosa's and Aurelio de Llano Roza de Ampudia's folklore projects. The seven variants are by an unidentified narrator in Rio Tuerto, Santander (A. Espinosa 1924:314–316), Pilar Díaz from Villanueva in Asturias (Llano Roza de Ampudia 1975:

44–48), and five storytellers from villages in Cáceres: Ángel García, María Alfonsa García Gil, and the schoolboy Juan Antonio Sánchez Ávila from Madroñera (Curiel Merchán 1944:177–184, 144–148, 57–62), and Leandro Jiménez of El Guijo de Santa Bárbara and Florencio Ramos of Navaconcejo.

19. Thompson (1946 [1977]:73).

20. Curiel Merchán (1944:177–184) and Llano Roza de Ampudia (1975: 44–48).

21. Curiel Merchán (1944:177–184).

22. Llano Roza de Ampudia (1975:44–48).

23. Variants by María Alfonsa García Gil and the schoolboy Juan Antonio Sánchez Ávila in Madroñera (Curiel Merchán 1944:144–148, 57–62) and Leandro Jiménez of El Guijo de Santa Bárbara and Florencio Ramos of Navaconcejo.

24. The episode of "The Wonderful Fruits" appears in variants by an unknown narrator from Río Tuerto (A. Espinosa 1924:314–316), Pilar Díaz from Villanueva in Asturias (Llano Roza de Ampudia 1975:44–48), and three Cáceres storytellers: the schoolboy Juan Antonio Sánchez Ávila and María Alfonsa García Gil from Madroñera (Curiel Merchán 1944:57–62, 144–148) and Leandro Jiménez of El Guijo de Santa Bárbara. Heroes successfully recover the objects and marry the princess in most variants. The exceptions are stories by Angel García of Madroñera in Cáceres, in which three companions fail to recover the objects and end up imprisoned by the king (Curiel Merchán 1944: 177–184), and by an unidentified narrator from Río Tuerto in Santander, in which the hero fails to recover the objects but succeeds in marrying the princess (A. Espinosa 1924:314–316).

25. Thompson (1946 [1977]:74).

26. Curiel Merchán (1944:177–184).

27. In all variants in which heroes recover the magic objects with the wonderful fruits, the companions drop out of the plot for most or all of the tale. See note 24 for a list of the stories with "The Wonderful Fruits" episode.

28. Brothers appear in variants by the unidentified narrator from Río Tuerto in Santander (A. Espinosa 1924:314–316), Pilar Díaz from Villanueva in Asturias (Llano Roza de Ampudia 1975:44–48), and four Cáceres narrators: María Alfonsa García Gil and the schoolboy Juan Antonio Sánchez Ávila in Madroñera (Curiel Merchán 1944:144–148, 57–62) and Leandro Jiménez of El Guijo de Santa Bárbara and Florencio Ramos in Navaconcejo.

29. A. Espinosa (1924:314–316).

30. Llano Roza de Ampudia (1975:44–48).

31. Curiel Merchán (1944:57–62, 144–148).

Chapter 5

1. See Thompson (1946 [1977]:165–167) for a general description of "The Rich and the Poor Peasant" (1535) and its relationship to "Cleverness and Gullibility" (1539).

2. Thompson (1946 [1977]: 166–167) listed the motif of "The magic hat pays all bills" (K111.2) as part of "Cleverness and Gullibility" (1539). However, he also noted the frequent transfer of motifs between "Cleverness and Gullibility" and "The Rich and the Poor Peasant" (1535). The motif of "The resuscitating horn" (K113.7) is generally part of "The Rich and the Poor Peasant" (1535), according to Thompson.

3. Cortés Vázquez (1979:I:255–260); Robe (1970:429–434).

4. A. Espinosa (1926:377–378, 381–383, 379–381); variants by Magdalena Frutos of Hinojosa de Duero and Victoria Coca of Miranda del Castañar (Cortés Vázquez 1979:I:252–255, 255–260).

5. Robe (1970:429–434).

6. Cortés Vázquez (1979:I:255–260).

7. Robe (1970:429–434).

8. Spanish variants are by Magdalena Frutos and Victoria Coca in Salamanca (Cortés Vázquez 1979:I:252–255, 255–260), unidentified narrators in Santander, Burgos, and Granada (A. Espinosa 1926:377–378, 381–383, 379–381), and Cáceres narrators Santos López and Maximina Castaño of Garganta la Olla, Román Santo of Navaconcejo, Felipa Sánchez and Leandro Jiménez of El Guijo de Santa Bárbara, and Zacaria Iglesia of Piornal. Mexican variants are by Augustina Gómez of Jalisco (Robe 1970:429–434) and Fernando Vega of Santiago Yaonáhuac.

9. Karttunen (1983:20).

10. Lockhart (1992).

11. Lockhart (1992:153–155, 163–170).

12. Lockhart (1992:299–303). The shift in exchange experienced by the Nahua under colonialism is like that which Marcel Mauss (1927 [1967]) theorized for economies moving from gift to commodity exchange. See Annette Weiner (1992) for a recent discussion of Mauss's theory.

13. Kardiner and Ovesey (1951).

14. I thank Alan Dundes for this insight.

15. A. Espinosa (1926:415–417).

16. Llano Roza de Ampudia (1975:142–145).

17. Variants by Salvador Esparza Guerrero from Acatic and José Mora of Tepatitlán (Robe 1970:436–441, 444–449), two unidentified narrators from Tuxpan in Jalisco and from Ixtlán in Oaxaca (Wheeler 1943:458–459, Radin and Espinosa 1917:198–199), and the Tepecano Felipe Aguilar (Mason 1914:189–195).

18. Thompson (1946 [1977]:174–175).

19. Thompson (1946 [1977]:174). See Thompson (1946 [1977]:174–175) for a fuller description of the nucleus and the subtypes of "The Master Thief" (1525) and Moser-Rath (1981:646–650) for a more recent bibliography of published variants of this story in collections of folktales from around the world.

20. Thompson (1946 [1977]:174) mentioned that literary variants are common since Pauli's *Schimpf und Ernst* in the sixteenth century. In addition to variants of "The Master Thief" (1525) listed in Boggs (1930:129–130),

Luis Cortés Vázquez (1979:I:134–135) reported one from a woman in southern Salamanca, Curiel Merchán (1944:39–42) heard another from a man in Madroñera in southern Cáceres, and I collected a third from Abundio Sánchez Sánchez in Cabezuela.

21. Boggs (1930:129–130); Hansen (1957:133–134); Robe (1973:176–180).

22. Curiel Merchán (1944:39–42); Cortés Vázquez (1979:I:134–135).

23. Robe (1970:428–429; 1972:62–80) and Wheeler (1943:62–65, 435–441, 496–499); Radin and Espinosa (1917:130–131, 225–229).

24. Paredes (1970:144–148, 222).

25. Cortés Vázquez (1979:I:134–135). I thank Alan Dundes for pointing out that the image of a thief's decapitated body appears in the folktale "Rhampsinitus" (AT 950), an ancient narrative found in Herodotus (Aarne and Thompson 1961 [1987]:335–336).

26. Robe (1972:63–80).

27. Spanish-speaking Mexican variants of "The Master Thief" (1525) that begin with brothers and continue with one brother acting independently of his other brothers include stories by unidentified narrators from Juanactlán and Guadalajara in Jalisco (Wheeler 1943:62–65, 435–441) and Mitla in Oaxaca (Radin and Espinosa 1917:225–227).

28. Thompson (1946 [1977]:275) defined subtype 1525D of "The Master Thief" as a thief who steals animals by placing shoes in the road or pretending to be hanged to divert the attention of the owner.

29. Variants of "The Master Thief" (1525D) that involve the thief acting alone and stealing animals with the ruse of placing a shoe in the road or pretending to be hanged include Spanish stories by Antonio Sánchez Ávila of Madroñera (Curiel Merchán 1944:39–42) and Abundio Sánchez Sánchez of Cabezuela and Mexican tales by unidentified narrators from Tizapan in Jalisco (Wheeler 1943:496–499) and from Talea and Mitla in Oaxaca (Radin and Espinosa 1917:130–131, 225–227). The hero has confederates who are like employees and feign their hanging to steal cattle in a story by the Spanish-speaking Mexican narrator Camilo Villegas from Jalisco (Robe 1972:63–80). María de Jesús Navarro de Aceves, from Tepatitlán, Jalisco, told "The Master Thief" (1525D) from the point of view of the victim who loses his animals to an unidentified group of thieves (Robe 1970:428–429).

30. Paredes (1970:144–148).

Chapter 6

1. Thompson (1946 [1977]:24–32) and Aarne and Thompson (1961 [1987]: 95–98). Ranke (1979:912–919) provided a more recent list of some of the folktale collections containing "Die zwei Brüder" ("The Two Brothers").

2. Hollis (1990).

3. Ranke (1934). See Thompson (1946 [1977]:32, 24–32) on the relationship between "Blood Brothers" and "Saint George and the Dragon" and for his summary in English of Ranke's study, which is based on an examination of

770 variants of "Blood Brothers" and 368 of "The Dragon Slayer." The published Spanish variants of "Blood Brothers" are by unknown narrators in Burgos, Zamora, and Salamanca (A. Espinosa 1924:319–320, 289–292; Cortés Vázquez 1979:II:21–28) and by Adela Romero Cuesta of Herrera del Duque in Badajoz (Curiel Merchán 1944:279–281), Francisca Borrallo of Trujillo in Cáceres (Curiel Merchán 1944:352–358), and Manuela Martín Cuadrado of Vilvestre, Magdalena Frutos of Hinojosa de Duero, and Beatriz Mancebo of La Alberca in Salamanca (Cortés Vázquez 1979:II:28–32, 32–34, 34–40). Llano Roza de Ampudia (1918 [1975]:74–76) collected a masculine variant from Pandon Caso of Caravia in Asturias.

4. Gehrts (1967); see Ward (1968:110) for a summary in English.

5. Ward (1968:85).

6. Curiel Merchán (1944:352–358); Cortés Vázquez (1979:II:32–34, 34–40).

7. Cortés Vázquez (1979:II:28–32).

8. See Curiel Merchán (1944:352–358) for "The Blood Brothers" tale by Francisca Borrallo of Trujillo.

9. Variant by Julia Lobato Gil of Serradilla; variants by Estrella Iglesias of Navaconcejo, José Díaz Sánchez of Serradilla, Florencio Ramos and Bernardo Ramos of Navaconcejo, Julio López Curiel of Garganta la Olla in Cáceres, and Manuela Martín Cuadrado of Vilvestre and Beatriz Mancebo of La Alberca in Salamanca (Cortés Vázquez 1979:II:28–32, 34–40); variant by Miguel Chorro Hernández of Navaconcejo; variant by an unknown narrator from Vilvestre (Cortés Vázquez 1979:II:21–28).

10. Thompson (1946 [1977]:29).

11. Curiel Merchán (1944:279–281); Cortés Vázquez (1979:II:32–34, 34–40).

12. Cortés Vázquez (1979:II:28–32).

13. Curiel Merchán (1944:352–358).

14. Lockhart (1992:72–85).

15. Radin and Espinosa (1917:202–203, 236–237).

16. See Robe (1973:49–50), Rael (1957:170–181), and J. M. Espinosa (1937 [1969]:53–56).

17. Adela Romero Cuesta from Herrera del Duque in northern Badajoz (Curiel Merchán 1944:279–281), Manuela Martín Cuadrado of Vilvestre (Cortés Vázquez 1979:II:28–32), and Beatriz Mancebo of La Alberca in Salamanca (Cortés Vázquez 1979:II:34–40) described the brothers' origins without representing an exchange of future economic prosperity for children in their variants of "Blood Brothers" (303).

18. Karttunen (1983:242).

19. The phrase in ancient Nahuatl is I(h)tic motlāliā in piltzintli, which López Austin (1980 [1988]:297) translated as "The infant is seated in the womb."

20. Cortés Vázquez (1979:II:28–32, 34–40).

21. Curiel Merchán (1944:279–281).

22. Radin and Espinosa (1917:236–237).

23. It is difficult to determine precisely why Nahuat narrators in Yaoná-

huac have adopted the image of the brothers' origins that prevails in Spain and probably expresses the strong filial loyalties between a mother and her daughters as well as her sons. The rates of patrilocality and patrilineal extended family household formation, which depend heavily on the filial ties between a father and his sons, are nearly the same in Yaonáhuac and Huitzilan. One major difference is that Yaonáhuac women inherit much more land than their Huitzilan sisters and consequently have more economic power to influence the images of procreation represented in stories like "Blood Brothers." Yaonáhuac women acquire land because inheritance is more bilateral—parents bequeath more land to their daughters as well as to their sons—and thus is more like inheritance among Hispanicized rural Mexicans (Lewis 1951) and Spaniards, particularly in Castilian-speaking Spain, which, of course, includes all of Cáceres (Pitt-Rivers 1966:103–104; Freeman 1970: 67–72; Brandes 1975:120–123; Behar 1986:68–88; Taggart 1990:214–215). Emmanuel Todd (1988) argued that inheritance expresses sentiments and deeply ingrained models of family relations. If so, then sentiments within the Yaonáhuac family favor a strong position of women, manifest in more symmetrical images of procreation in stories like "Blood Brothers." In short, the popularity of the eating-as-procreation image of the brothers' origins may have a relationship to similar sentiments and models of family relations reproduced in the Yaonáhuac, Spanish-speaking Mexican, and Cáceres Spanish family.

24. Karttunen (1983:163).

25. Karttunen (1983:208, 104).

26. Ranke (1934).

27. Spanish storytellers who combined "The Dragon Slayer" and "Blood Brothers" are Julio López Curiel of Garganta la Olla, Adela Romero Cuesta of Herrera del Duque in northern Badajoz (Curiel Merchán 1944:279–281), and Manuela Martín Cuadrado of Vilvestre and Beatriz Mancebo of La Alberca in Salamanca (Cortés Vázquez 1979:II:28–32, 34–40). Paul Radin and Aurelio Espinosa (1917:202–203) heard a variant mixing the two stories from a Mexican narrator in Oaxaca. See Gossen (1964:238–239, 242, 245) on the charcoal-seller impostor as one of the distinguishing traits of the Spanish variants of "The Dragon Slayer."

28. Freud (1900 [1978]:52).

29. See Spiro (1982:98–101) on the Oedipus complex recast as male sibling rivalry in oral narratives.

Chapter 7

1. Thompson (1946 [1977]:80–81) and Aarne and Thompson (1961 [1987]: 222–223) provide a list of the literary versions and the geographical distribution of the oral folktale variants of "The Two Travelers" (Tale Type 613). See also Christiansen's (1916) study of the derivation of the oral tales from their apparent Asian origin. Aarne and Thompson (1961 [1987]:222) identify "The Two Travelers" as story number 107 in the Grimms' *Nursery and Household*

Tales, also known as *Grimms' Fairy Tales, The Household Tales, Grimms' Tales for Young and Old,* and *Gammer Grethel's Tales* (Bottigheimer 1987:4).

2. Darbord (1984:31). The story that folklorists call "The Two Travelers" is chapter 28 in the *Libro de los gatos* (Darbord 1984:97–101) and is entitled "Enxienplo [Ejemplo] de los dos compañeros" ("The Example of the Two Companions").

3. Cortés Vázquez (1979:I:260–266). See also Bolte and Polívka (1963:II: 473) and Christiansen (1916:18).

4. J. M. Espinosa (1937 [1969]:107–109), Huning and Fisher (1937:125–129), E. K. Miller (1973:275–279, 287–292), Rael (1957:II:203–211), Parsons (1932a:350–352, 1932b:299–300), Radin and Espinosa (1917:256–258), Robe (1970:444–449), Wheeler (1943:393–394, 395–397, 397–398), and Mason and Espinosa (1914:189–195). See also Dobie (1935 [1947]:8–18) for a variant that is probably substantially revised from the original narrator's version.

5. Darbord (1984:97–101).

6. Lüthi (1970 [1976]:21, 24, 50–51, 135–146).

7. Lüthi (1975 [1984]:13–20).

8. Cortés Vázquez (1979:I:260–266).

9. Thompson (1946 [1977]:68–69) argued that oral variants of "Open Sesame" (Tale Type 676) are probably derived from Galland's translation of *Thousand and One Nights.*

10. Thompson (1946 [1977]:72) noted that this tale "has a very extensive distribution, and is present in almost every collection of stories in Europe and Asia."

11. Robe (1970:444–449), Radin and Espinosa (1917:256–258), Parsons (1932a:350–352), and Wheeler (1943:393–394).

12. Parsons (1932a:350–352) and Wheeler (1943:393–394).

13. Wheeler (1943:395–397).

14. See Spanish-speaking Mexican variants of "John the Bear" (Tale Type 301) with a humanized portrayal of the father in Barakat (1965:333–334), Dobie (1935 [1947]:212–227), Robe (1970:114–116), and Wheeler (1943: 240–246).

15. Wheeler published four variants of "John the Bear" (Tale Type 301) (1943:239–240, 240–246, 247–259, 259–271) and three of "The Two Travelers" (Tale Type 613) (1943:393–394, 395–396, 397–398).

16. Mason and Espinosa (1914:189–195); Parsons (1932b:299–300); Croft (1957:318–320).

17. Mason and Espinosa (1914:189–195).

18. Parsons (1932b:299–300). See Aarne and Thompson (1961 [1987]:28) for a description of "Claw in Split Tree" (AT 38).

19. Thompson (1929 [1966]:xix–xx) referred primarily to trickster and animal bride and groom stories. Lüthi (1970 [1976]:96) also noted the close association with animals in North American Indian tales in which "heroes are animals and stars, not human beings, as in the European fairy tale."

20. Croft (1957:318–320).

21. The ancient Nahua formed fraternally extended family households

consisting of married brothers, sisters, and sisters and brothers on a more frequent basis than do the contemporary Nahuat. See Carrasco (1964, 1976) on the social composition of Nahua households in the sixteenth century.

22. Burkhart (1989) described the representations of good and evil by the Spanish friars, who introduced Christianity to the Nahua of Mexico.

23. The Nahuat of Huitzilan use the term "Chichimeco" to refer to the demon who dances with the St. Michael dancers. However, the ancient Aztecs used the same word to refer to the "barbarians" who lived to the north of Tenochtitlan in the Valley of Mexico (Burkhart 1989:59).

24. Karttunen (1983:93–94).

25. Wheeler (1943:395–397).

26. Croft (1957:319–320).

27. The original parental dwelling was a small house with a thatch or *zacate* roof that eventually became too small for the family after Miguel married María Agustina and she gave birth to the couple's first children. The brothers (the father had died) built a second house with a corrugated tar-paper roof within a few feet of the first. Miguel and María Agustina moved into the new structure, leaving the rest of the family in the original dwelling. The wooden plank walls and the *zacate* of the parental house deteriorated in the humid climate of Huitzilan, and so the brothers decided to tear it down and put a new one in its place. They built a small room attached to the house, now occupied by Miguel and Agustina, so the other members of the household would have a place to sleep while the brothers rebuilt the original dwelling. Nicolás, who is younger than Miguel, was the second brother to marry, and he brought his wife María Gabriela Sánchez to live in the original house with his widowed mother and his other brothers. Nicolás, his wife, his mother, and Nacho all moved into the provisional structure and then moved back to the rebuilt house. Soon, the elements took their toll on the corrugated tar-paper room of Miguel and Agustina's dwelling, so Miguel and Agustina and their children moved into the original parental house and into a new, temporary room that was built against the wall of the house whose tar-paper roof had fallen into disrepair. At that time, María Agustina Ayance (Miguel's wife) and María Gabriela Sánchez (Nicolás's wife) decided to split their kitchens when the original kitchen, a small room attached to the parental dwelling with the *zacate* roof, fell apart. María Agustina eventually put her kitchen in the room attached to the dwelling with the corrugated tar-paper roof. Here she, her daughter, and her mother-in-law now prepared meals for their families. María Gabriela Sánchez placed her kitchen in the main room of the house with the tar-paper roof after the brothers completed its renovation. The renovated dwelling became a single room with a new but as yet unoccupied hearth.

Chapter 8

1. Aarne and Thompson (1961 [1987]:104–107).
2. Leavy (1994:28–38).
3. Aarne and Thompson (1961 [1987]:128–131).

4. See Leavy's interpretation of "Blancaflor" (1994:208–211, 291), "The Swan Maiden" (1994:50, 227–232), ambivalent masculine images in both stories (1994:57, 253–260, 265, 268, 272–273, 276), and the psychological origins of the patterns she believes are universal in gender relations (1994: 267–269, 272–276).

5. Published "Blancaflor" stories of Tale Type 313A or 313C collected in Spain were told by the following: Adelino Blanco of Asturias (Llano Roza de Ampudia 1975:97–103), Agripino Domínguez of Lubián, Zamora (Cortés Vázquez 1976:62–66), and Rafael Curillo of Saucelle in Salamanca, Manuela Martín Cuadrado of Vilvestre, Magdalena Frutos of Hinojosa de Duero, Lorenza "la Capillona" of Pereña in Salamanca (Cortés Vázquez 1979:II:83–89, 70–83, 90–96, 96–99), and unidentified narrators in Granada, Cuenca, Soria, and Palencia (A. Espinosa 1924:240–245, 245–248, 248–252, 245–248). I collected "Blancaflor" stories (313A and 313C) from Florencio Ramos in Navaconcejo (Taggart 1990:174–180), José Díaz Sánchez and Eugenio Real Vázquez in Serradilla, Leandro Jiménez in El Guijo de Santa Bárbara, Gregoria Ramos Merchán in Piornal (Taggart 1990:190–194), and Evarista Moreno in Cabezuela, Cáceres.

6. Cortés Vázquez (1979:II:265).

7. See Aarne and Thompson (1961 [1987]:107) for the geographical distribution of "The Girl as Helper in the Hero's Flight" (AT 313C). Aarne and Thompson (1961 [1987]:106) credit Grace Knapp with tracing this folktale to the ancient Greek story of "Jason and Medea" in her dissertation for Stanford University.

8. The male protagonist's dependence on the heroine fits Leavy's (1994: 208–211, 291) interpretation of the "Blancaflor" story (AT 313C) as a tale about a man clinging to woman as wife as he once clung to woman as mother.

9. Taggart (1990:165).

10. Aarne and Thompson (1961 [1987]:104–105).

11. A different English translation of Florencio's "Blancaflor" (Tale Type 313C) appeared in Taggart (1990:174–180).

12. Taggart (1990:190–194).

13. A gambler appears in "Blancaflor" stories by Spanish narrators Adelino Blanco of Asturias (Llano Roza de Ampudia 1975:97–103), Manuela Martín Cuadrado of Vilvestre in Salamanca (Cortés Vázquez 1979:II:70–83), Gregoria Ramos Merchán of Piornal in Cáceres (Taggart 1990:190–194), by unidentified narrators in Granada and Palencia (A. Espinosa 1924:240–245, 252–255), and by Mexican narrators Rosa Santiago of Mitla (Parsons 1932b: 312–314), Nacho Ángel of Huitzilan, and unidentified narrators in Jalisco and northern Mexico (Wheeler 1943:310–314; Aiken 1935:61–66).

14. The male protagonist meets the heroine bathing and steals her clothes or jewelry in stories by Eugenio Real Vázquez in Serradilla, Leandro Jiménez in El Guijo de Santa Bárbara, Evarista Moreno in Cabezuela, and Manuela Martín Cuadrado in Salamanca (Cortés Vázquez 1979:II:70–83). Thefts of clothing and jewelry to extract a promise appear in tales by Ade-

lino Blanco of Asturias (Llano Roza de Ampudia 1975:97–103), Gregoria Ramos of Piornal in Cáceres (Taggart 1990:190–194), and an unidentified narrator from Palencia (A. Espinosa 1924:252).

15. Blancaflor undergoes mutilation to recover a ring in stories by José Díaz Sánchez and Eugenio Real Vázquez of Serradilla, Leandro Jiménez of El Guijo de Santa Bárbara, Rafael Curillo of Saucelle in Salamanca (Cortés Vázquez 1979:II:83–89), Adelino Blanco of Asturias (Llano Roza de Ampudia 1975: 97–103), Agripino Domínguez of Lubián, Zamora (Cortés Vázquez 1976:62– 66), Gregoria Ramos of Piornal (Taggart 1990:190–194), Evarista Moreno of Cabezuela in Cáceres, Manuela Martín Cuadrado of Vilvestre (Cortés Vázquez 1979:II:70–83), Lorenza "la Capillona" in Pereña, Salamanca (Cortés Vázquez 1979:II:96–99), and unidentified narrators in Granada, Cuenca, Soria, and Palencia (A. Espinosa 1924:240–245, 245–248, 248–252, 252–255).

16. Most but not all Blancaflors who shed their blood are physically changed, permitting their husbands to recognize them. They appear in stories by Rafael Curillo of Saucelle in Salamanca (Cortés Vázquez 1979:II:83–90), Adelino Blanco of Asturias (Llano Roza de Ampudia 1975:97–103), Agripino Domínguez of Lubián, Zamora (Cortés Vázquez 1976:62–66), Florencio Ramos of Navaconcejo (Taggart 1990:174–180), José Díaz and Eugenio Real Vázquez of Serradilla, and Leandro Jiménez of El Guijo de Santa Bárbara in Cáceres, and Manuela Martín Cuadrado of Vilvestre (Cortés Vázquez 1979:II: 70–83), Lorenza "la Capillona" of Pereña of Salamanca (Cortés Vázquez 1979:II:96–99), Gregoria Ramos Merchán of Piornal (Taggart 1990:190– 194), and Evarista Morena of Cabezuela in Cáceres, and unidentified narrators in Granada, Cuenca, Soria, and Palencia (A. Espinosa 1924:240–245, 245– 248, 248–252, 252–255).

17. Leavy's argument (1994:267–269, 272–276) that folktales express man's heavy dependence on woman as wife and mother rests on the premise that a man retains a memory, in his unconscious, of an omnipotent mother.

18. Florencio's story consequently could be the fulfillment of wishes from his conscious as well as unconscious. See Róheim (1992:4–5), who interpreted folktales as wish fulfillment.

19. Taggart (1990:184–185).

20. A. Espinosa (1924:240–245).

21. Llano Roza de Ampudia (1975:97–103); Cortés Vázquez (1979:II: 70–83).

22. Broken prohibitions appear in stories by Florencio, Eugenio Real Vázquez of Serradilla, Adelino Blanco of Asturias (Llano Roza de Ampudia 1975: 97–103), Rafael Curillo of Saucelle in Salamanca (Cortés Vázquez 1979:II: 83–89), Gregoria Ramos Merchán of Piornal (Taggart 1990:190–194), Magdalena Frutos of Hinojosa de Duero (Cortés Vázquez 1979:II:90–96), and Lorenza "la Capillona" of Pereña in Salamanca (Cortés Vázquez 1979:II:96–99), and unidentified narrators in Granada, Palencia, and Cuenca (A. Espinosa 1924:240–245, 252–255, 245–248).

23. These Spanish narrators include Adelino Blanco of Asturias, who simply indicated "a woman" (Llano Roza de Ampudia 1975:97–103), and an unidentified narrator from Cuenca who named the grandmother (A. Espinosa 1924:245–248).

24. See Taggart (1990:146–164) and an unpublished "Cupid and Psyche" (Tale Type 425) collected from Nahuat narrator Mariano Isidro in Santiago Yaonáhuac.

Chapter 9

1. Aarne and Thompson (1961 [1987]:104–105).

2. Mexican "Blancaflor" stories come from unidentified Spanish-speaking narrators in Jalisco (Wheeler 1943:302–307, 307–310, 310–314), Oaxaca (Radin and Espinosa 1917:220–221, 222–223), northern Mexico (Aiken 1935: 61–66), and Mexico City (Reid 1935:110–112), and from Spanish-speaking Hortensia Herrera Guzmán, also from Mexico City (Mendoza and R. R. de Mendoza 1952:416–418). The native Mexican tales are by the Tepecano Eleno Aguilar (Mason and Espinosa 1914:174–175), the Zapotec Rosa Santiago (Parsons 1932b:312–314), the Nahua Bonifacio Natividad Gonzales of Durango (Preuss 1982:528–535), and the Nahuat Luciano Vega of Santiago Yaonáhuac and Nacho Ángel Hernández of Huitzilan de Serdán. Angélica Quero, a Zapotec in Mitla (Parsons 1932b:312), told a fragment consisting of "The Obstacle Flight" (Motif D672), and an unidentified Nahuatl speaker from Milpa Alta, in the Federal District, told "The Transformation Flight" (D671) (Casanova 1920:25–27). One variant was unavailable for analysis at the time of this writing (Huning and Fisher 1937:121–130).

3. See note 2 for a list of the Spanish-speaking Mexican versions of "Blancaflor."

4. Gamblers who lose or sell themselves to the devil are in stories by unidentified Spanish speakers in Jalisco and northern Mexico (Wheeler 1943: 310–314; Aiken 1935:61–66) and by the Nahuat Luciano Vega of Santiago Yaonáhuac. Rosa Santiago, a Zapotec in Mitla (Parsons 1932b:312–314), told an interesting variant in which Juan Pelotera plays ball with and beats the devil, who gives him permission to marry his daughter. Juan makes a journey to Hell to obtain his bride.

5. Juan Hernández told a radically reworked version of "Hansel and Gretel" (327A) in which a man wins wealth in a donkey race and then feels uneasy and obliged to make some restitution to the loser.

6. Cortés Vázquez (1979:II:96–99); A. Espinosa (1924:245–248); Reid (1935:110–112); Mason and Espinosa (1914:174–175).

7. Cortés Vázquez (1979:II:83–89); Wheeler (1943:302–307).

8. Cortés Vázquez (1979:II:90–96); Mendoza and R. R. de Mendoza (1952: 416–418); Parsons (1932b:312–314).

9. See note 14 in Chapter 8 for a list of the Spanish "Blancaflor" stories in which the male protagonist steals the heroine's clothes or jewelry and, in

some cases, extracts a promise. Among Mexican narrators, Nahuat Nacho Ángel Hernández of Huitzilan told how the male protagonist snatches Blancaflor's jewelry to initiate a conversation through which he might obtain her help. Most of those who described the male protagonist stealing clothes or jewelry or both to extract a promise of help or marriage are unidentified Spanish-speaking narrators in Jalisco (Wheeler 1943:307–310, 310–314), Oaxaca (Radin and Espinosa 1917:222–223), and northern Mexico (Aiken 1935:61–63).

10. Leavy (1994:227).

11. Llano Roza de Ampudia (1975:97–103); Taggart (1990:190–194); A. Espinosa (1924:245–248); Wheeler (1943:307–310, 310–314); Radin and Espinosa (1917:222–223); Aiken (1935:61–66).

12. Radin and Espinosa (1917:222–223).

13. Preuss (1982:528–535).

14. Karttunen (1983:39).

15. See notes 15 and 16 in Chapter 8.

16. The three additional Mexican variants of "Blancaflor" in which the heroine undergoes mutilation are by an unknown narrator in Jalisco (Wheeler 1943:310–314), the Zapotec Rosa Santiago of Mitla (Parsons 1932b:312–314), and the Nahuat Luciano Vega of Yaonáhuac. The heroine's mutilation is not linked to her recognition in the story from Jalisco.

17. Karttunen (1983:223).

18. Spanish "Blancaflor" stories that contain a prohibition are by Florencio Ramos of Navaconcejo, Eugenio Real Vázquez of Serradilla in Cáceres, Adelino Blanco of Asturias (Llano Roza de Ampudia 1975:97–103), Rafael Curillo of Saucelle in Salamanca (Cortés Vázquez 1979:II:83–89), Gregoria Ramos Merchán of Piornal in Cáceres (Taggart 1990:190–194), Lorenza "la Capillona" of Pereña in Salamanca (Cortés Vázquez 1979:II:96–99), and unidentified storytellers in Granada, Palencia, and Cuenca (A. Espinosa 1924:240–245, 252–255, 245–248). Manuela Martín Cuadrado of Vilvestre in Salamanca (Cortés Vázquez 1979:II:70–83) and Leandro Jiménez of El Guijo de Santa Bárbara combined a curse with a prohibition. José Díaz Sánchez of Serradilla included a mother's curse—this Blancaflor will become a frog for seven years—but no prohibition. The curse does not explain why Juan forgets about Blancaflor. Mexican "Blancaflor" stories with prohibitions are by unidentified Spanish-speaking narrators from Jalisco (Wheeler 1943:310–314), Oaxaca (Radin and Espinosa 1917:220–221), and northern Mexico (Aiken 1935:61–66), and by the Nahuat Luciano Vega from Santiago Yaonáhuac. The heroine's mother or father pronounces a curse, saying that Blancaflor will be forgotten, in a story by the Spanish-speaking Hortensia Herrera Guzmán (Mendoza and R. R. de Mendoza 1952:416–418) and an unidentified Spanish-speaking narrator in Mexico City (Reid 1935:110–112). A mother's curse turns her wedding banquet into *zacate* in a tale consisting of "The Obstacle Flight" (Motif D672) by the Zapotec Angélica Quero of Mitla (Parsons 1932b:312). In a variant of Tale Type 313C by the Tepecano Eleno Aguilar (Mason

and Espinosa 1914:174–175), there is no curse or prohibition; the male protagonist's father tries to make him marry another woman.

19. See note 23 in Chapter 8 for a list of the Spanish narrators who direct the prohibition to the male protagonist's female family members.

20. Taggart (1990:190–194).

21. Taggart (1983:114–160).

22. Taggart (1983:169–171, 130–133).

23. The term nāhueh is closely related to the noun nāhuaqueh, defined as "the one that is close to all things, god." It is also related to nāhuahtequ(i), a reflexive and transitive verb meaning "to hug oneself, to embrace someone," and the postposition -nāhuac, translated as "near to." See Karttunen (1983:157).

Chapter 10

1. The Orpheus story is both a ballad and a folktale in European oral tradition (see Leavy 1994:246–255, 259, 273–275). It appears in Scandinavian ballad and folklore (Jacobsen and Leavy 1988) and in collections of folktales from the British Isles (Briggs 1978:2 : 372–375), Alsace-Lorraine (Henderson and Calvert 1925:229–232), the former Yugoslavia (Curčija-Prodanovic 1957:155–164), Czechoslovakia (Baudis 1917:71–97), and Hungary (Jones and Kropf 1889:95–110, 362–373).

2. Christiansen (1959:126–153) examined variants of "The Supernatural Bride" or "The Man on a Quest for His Lost Wife" (AT 400), collected in Norway (60 variants), Denmark (90), Sweden (20), Finland (76), Ireland (30), and Scotland (10). See Aarne and Thompson (1961 [1987]:128–131) for a more complete listing of this tale type in other parts of Europe.

3. Thompson (1946 [1977]:289).

4. Aurelio de Llano Roza de Ampudia (1975:53–58, 339) reported the only true example of Tale Type 400 I know of from Spain. Leavy (1994:327, 335) regards a story that Charles Sellers (1888:133–149) reported from Asturias as an example of a lost-wife or "Swan Maiden" tale. However, this particular Asturian narrative is not really an example of Tale Type 400 because it is about a hero who disenchants a princess who does not become his wife until the story's conclusion.

5. Many variants of Tale Type 400 appear in collections of folktales from Spanish-speaking narrators in the United States and Mexico (Robe 1973:51–55, 68–70). Within the boundaries of modern Mexico, the story is told by unidentified Spanish-speaking Mexicans in Jalisco (Mason 1912:196–198; Wheeler 1943:295–302, 416–421), the Nahua Cruz Reyes of Durango (Preuss 1982:464–481), and the Nahuat Luciano Vega of Yaonáhuac in the northern Sierra de Puebla (Taggart 1983:133–135).

6. Hultkrantz (1957:60–115). See also Gayton (1935).

7. Hultkrantz (1957:60–61, 69–70, 91–117).

8. Hultkrantz (1957:313–315).

9. Mason and Espinosa (1914:182–185); Laughlin (1962:228–231); Burns (1983:121–134); and Preuss (1982:438–451, 450–463, 464–481, and 481–487).

10. Hultkrantz (1957:60–115).

11. Hultkrantz (1957:115–137). See also Dundes (1964:76–77), who likewise considers the prohibition and its violation important structural characteristics of the native North American Orpheus tales.

12. The wife's return on the condition of observing a prohibition does not appear in the variants by Tepecano, Tzotzil Mayan, and Yucatec Mayan narrators (Mason and Espinosa 1914:182–185; Laughlin 1962:228–231; Burns 1983:121–134). It is quite possible that anthropologists and folklorists will discover native Mexican variants where the prohibition is an important part of this tale.

13. Hultkrantz (1957:57–58).

14. Hultkrantz (1957:57–58).

15. Spiro (1982:21–29) noted that many anthropologists from Tylor to Claude Lévi-Strauss have brought up the erotic attraction between a brother and a sister in their theories of incest. Freud (1913 [1946]) made the brother-sister relationship one of the cornerstones of his theory of culture. Spiro (1982:21–29) explains that the age difference between a mother and son and imagined or real castration threats from the father create defense mechanisms that block a son from acknowledging his erotic urges toward the mother.

16. See Róheim (1992:7–8, 67–71, 74–75, 77, 83) for many examples of the primal scene in folklore.

17. Freud (1905 [1975]:62, 64–65).

18. Explanations of the appeal of the native North American Orpheus tradition differ in their treatment of the mourner and the dead relative as allegory. Guy Swanson (1976:117–118) categorically rejects the argument that the tale is "a sweet, sad story of bereavement" in marital love. Instead, he argues that Orpheus represents task-leadership roles in society and his dead wife personifies emotional leadership. Ignoring the specific language and imagery of particular tales, Swanson conducts a statistical comparison based on gender roles that are applicable to his own society but not necessarily fitting to the cultures of those who actually tell the tales. The native North American Orpheus tradition thrives, concludes Swanson, when task and emotional leadership roles are divided in the social structure. Barbara Fass Leavy (1994: 245–276) takes a different approach and considers native North American and other Orpheus tales as very much about gender relations, although she too rejects the interpretation that the story is about romantic or conjugal love. The wife is the heroine in a woman's fantasy of escaping domestic toil and male domination and of regaining her female autonomy and her status lost in marriage. Her husband's search is man's effort to restore patriarchal control over woman as well as the male-centered cultural order by preventing her from reverting to animal type. She and her husband are protagonists in the politics of married life. Leavy's interpretation is likewise grounded in assump-

319

tions about masculine and feminine roles and constructions of masculinity and femininity that are part of her own culture.

19. Hultkrantz (1957:226, 310).

20. Gruzinski (1989:105–172).

21. Hultkrantz (1957:310–311).

22. Sandstrom and Sandstrom (1986:79–80).

23. Burkhart (1989:64–65).

24. See Nutini (1988). Alan and Pamela Sandstrom (1986:70–129) described in rich detail Nahua shamanistic rituals to manipulate the spirits of the dead in the Huasteca region of Veracruz.

25. Hultkrantz (1957:225).

26. Chodorow (1978:87).

27. Chodorow (1978:166–167).

28. Chodorow (1978:63–64) bases her observation on the work of the object-relations theorists Michael and Alice Balint (M. Balint 1965, 1968).

29. Chodorow (1978:72) mentioned Bowlby (1969 [1982]), Kotelchuck (1972), Schaffer (1971), and Schaffer and Emerson (1964).

30. Chodorow (1978:72). See Diane Ehrensaft (1987 [1990]) for a description of the experience of co-parenting couples in modern capitalism who are attempting to put into practice Chodorow's theory of the reproduction of relational capacities in all children.

31. Stoller (1985:182).

32. Stoller (1985:183).

33. Karttunen (1983:329–330).

34. See Benjamin Paul's (1950) very interesting account of the last-born son in another native Mesoamerican culture.

Chapter 11

1. Ilihuiz is the link in Lacan's (1977:153) "signifying chain" that placed Nacho in his gender.

2. Florencio and Nacho are subjects in a "signifying chain" or culture (Lacan 1977:153; Gallop 1982:9–11) they cannot see. The configuration of their culture and their place in their culture become apparent through the comparison of their versions of the same stories.

3. G. Collier (1987).

4. Marx (1964:106–119).

5. Chodorow (1978:3–7). See also Herbert Marcuse's (1955) synthesis of Marx's (1964:106–119, 132–146) theory of alienated labor and Freud's (1930 [1961]) theory of instincts to argue that modern capitalism promotes an aggressive masculinity. Chodorow (1989:114–153) offered a critique of Marcuse's argument.

6. Chodorow (1978:87).

7. Stoller (1985:40, 182–183).

8. Gilmore (1990).

9. See Hugo Nutini (1988) for an account of the Mexican Day of the Dead in Tlaxcala as a synthesis of pre-Hispanic Nahua and Spanish practices.

10. Kellogg (1995).

11. Florencio and Nacho illustrate the role of culture and social experience rather than biology in the construction of masculinity. Freud appears to have moved away from biological determinism in his final essay on gender where he expressed his grave doubts about masculine activity and feminine passivity (1932 [1933]: 114–115). Psychological anthropologists, many of whom owe a debt of intellectual gratitude to Freud, have consistently stressed the role of cultural conditioning and contributed to moving psychoanalytic theory farther away from biological determinism and essentialism. However, recent members of this school have argued even more forcefully for the importance of culture rather than biology. After his thorough review of the literature, Richard Shweder (1980) argues that culture should be taken more seriously, and Michele Rosaldo (1984) stressed how affect is constructed through intersubjective experience. Catherine Lutz (1989: 114–153) declared that Western theories, stressing how emotions develop from within according to biological determinism, are products of an individualistic construction of identity. Marxists (see Marcuse 1955) have argued that radical individualism is a form of estrangement that results from alienated labor. It is interesting but not surprising that anthropologists, who embrace Marxist theory, also argue against essentialistic theories of gender (see Sacks 1975).

Appendix

1. W. Miller (1983:121).
2. Key and Ritchie de Key (1953).
3. Robinson (1966).
4. Karttunen (1983:xxi).
5. Ibid.

REFERENCES

Aarne, Antti, and Stith Thompson. 1961 [1987]. *The Types of the Folktale: A Classification and Bibliography.* Helsinki: Academia Scientiarum.

Aiken, Riley. 1935. "A Pack Load of Mexican Tales." In *Puro Mexicano,* ed. J. Frank Dobie, pp. 1–87. Texas Folk-Lore Society Publications, No. 12. Austin: Texas Folk-Lore Society.

Balint, Michael. 1965. *Primary Love and Psycho-Analytic Technique.* London: Tavistock Publications.

———. 1968. *The Basic Fault: Therapeutic Aspects of Regression.* London: Tavistock Publications.

Barakat, Robert A. 1965. "The Bear's Son Tale in Northern Mexico." *Journal of American Folklore* 78:330–336.

Barry, Herbert, III, and Leonora A. Paxson. 1971. "Infancy and Early Childhood: Cross-Cultural Codes." *Ethnology* 10:466–508.

Baudis, Josef. 1917. *Czech Folk Tales.* London: Allan and Unwin.

Behar, Ruth. 1986. *Santa María del Monte: The Presence of the Past in a Spanish Village.* Princeton: Princeton University Press.

———. 1990. "The Struggle for the Church: Popular Anticlericalism and Religiosity in Post-Franco Spain." In *Religious Orthodoxy and Popular Faith in European Society,* ed. Ellen Badone, pp. 76–112. Princeton: Princeton University Press.

———. 1993. *Translated Woman: Crossing the Border with Esperanza's Story.* Boston: Beacon Press.

Bernheimer, Charles, and Claire Kahane, eds. 1985 [1990]. *In Dora's Case: Freud—Hysteria—Feminism.* New York: Columbia University Press.

Bierhorst, John, ed. and trans. 1992. *History and Mythology of the Aztecs: The Codex Chimalpopoca.* Tucson: University of Arizona Press.

Boas, Franz. 1912. "Notes of Mexican Folk-lore." *Journal of American Folklore* 25:204–260.

Boggs, Ralph S. 1930. *Index of Spanish Folktales.* Folklore Fellows Communication, no. 90. Helsinki: Suomalainen Tiedeakatemia.

REFERENCES

Bolte, Johannes, and Gerog Polívka. 1963. *Anmerkungen zu den Kinder- u. Hausmärchen der Brüder Grimm.* 5 vols. Hildesheim: George Olms Verlagsbuchhandlung.

Bottigheimer, Ruth B. 1987. *Grimms' Bad Girls and Bold Boys: The Moral and Social Vision of the Tales.* New Haven: Yale University Press.

Bowlby, John. 1969 [1982]. *Attachment and Loss.* Vol. 1, *Attachment.* London: Hogarth Press.

Brandes, Stanley H. 1975. *Migration, Kinship, and Community: Tradition and Transition in a Spanish Village.* New York: Academic Press.

———. 1980. *Metaphors of Masculinity: Sex and Status in Andalusian Folklore.* Philadelphia: University of Pennsylvania Press.

Briggs, Katherine. 1978. *The Vanishing People: Fairy Lore and Legends.* 2 vols. New York: Pantheon.

Burkhart, Louise. 1989. *The Slippery Earth: Nahua-Christian Moral Dialogue in Sixteenth-Century Mexico.* Tuscon: University of Arizona Press.

Burns, Allan F. 1983. *An Epoch of Miracles: Oral Literature of the Yucatec Maya.* Austin: University of Texas Press.

Carrasco, Pedro. 1964. "Family Structure in Sixteenth-Century Tepoztlán." In *Process and Pattern in Culture: Essays in Honor of Julian H. Steward,* ed. Robert J. Manners, pp. 185–210. Chicago: Aldine.

———. 1976. "The Joint Family in Ancient Mexico: The Case of Molotla." In *Essays on Mexican Kinship,* ed. Hugo G. Nutini, Pedro Carrasco, and James M. Taggart, pp. 45–64. Pittsburgh: Pittsburgh University Press.

Casanova, Pablo Gonzales. 1920. "Cuento en Mexicano de Milpa Alta, D.R." *Journal of American Folklore* 33:25–27.

Chodorow, Nancy. 1978. *The Reproduction of Mothering: Psychoanalysis and the Sociology of Gender.* Berkeley: University of California Press.

———. 1989. *Feminism and Psychoanalytic Theory.* New Haven: Yale University Press.

Christian, William A. 1972 [1989]. *Person and God in a Spanish Valley.* Princeton: Princeton University Press.

Christiansen, Reidar Th. 1916. *The Tale of the Two Travelers or The Blinded Man: A Comparative Study.* Folklore Fellows Communications, no. 24. Hamina: Soumalainen Tiedeakatemian Kustantama.

———. 1959. *Studies in Irish and Scandinavian Folktales.* Copenhagen: Rosenkilde and Bagger.

Clifford, James. 1988. *The Predicament of Culture: Twentieth-Century Ethnography, Literature, and Art.* Cambridge, Mass.: Harvard University Press.

Collier, George. 1987. *Socialists of Rural Andalusia: Unacknowledged Revolutionaries of the Second Republic.* Stanford: Stanford University Press.

Collier, Jane. 1986. "From Mary to Modern Woman: The Material Basis of Marianismo and Its Transformation in a Spanish Village." *American Ethnologist* 13:100–107.

Coltrane, Scott. 1988. "Father-Child Relationships and the Status of Women: A Cross-Cultural Study." *American Journal of Sociology* 93:1060–1096.

———. 1992. "The Micropolitics of Gender in Non-Industrial Societies." *Gender and Society* 6:82–107.

Cortés Vázquez, Luis. 1976. *Leyendas, cuentos y romances de Sanadria: Textos leoneses y gallegos.* Salamanca: Gráficas Cervantes.

———. 1979. *Cuentos populares salmantinos.* 2 vols. Salamanca: Librería Cervantes.

Croft, Kenneth. 1957. "Nahuatl Texts of Matlapa, S.L.P." *Tlalocan* 3:317–333.

Curcija-Prodanovic, Nada. 1957. *Yugoslav Folk-Tales.* London: Oxford University Press.

Curiel Merchán, Marciano. 1944. *Cuentos extremeños.* Madrid: Consejo Superior de Investigaciones Científicas Instituto Antonio de Negrija.

Darbord, Bernard. 1984. *Libro de los gatos: Édition avec introduction et notes.* Paris: Klincksieck.

Díaz Hernández, Vicente. 1945. "Nanawatzin, Hueyapan Puebla." *Tlalocan* 2:64.

Dobie, J. Frank. 1935 [1947]. *Tongues of the Monte.* Boston: Little Brown.

Dundes, Alan. 1964. *The Morphology of North American Indian Folktales.* Helsinki: Academia Scientiarum Fennica.

———. 1984 [1989]. *Life Is Like a Chicken Coop Ladder: A Study of German National Character through Folklore.* Detroit: Wayne State University Press.

———. 1986. "Fairy Tales from a Folkloristic Perspective." In *Fairy Tales and Society: Illusion, Allusion, and Paradigm,* ed. Ruth B. Bottigheimer, pp. 259–269. Philadelphia: University of Pennsylvania Press.

———. 1987. *Parsing through Customs.* Madison: University of Wisconsin Press.

———. 1989. *Folklore Matters.* Knoxville: University of Tennessee Press.

Ehrensaft, Diane. 1987 [1990]. *Parenting Together: Men and Women Sharing the Care of Their Children.* Urbana: University of Illinois Press.

Espinosa, Aurelio M. 1921. "A Folk-lore Expedition to Spain." *Journal of American Folklore* 34 (132): 127–142.

———. 1923. *Cuentos populares españoles.* Vol. 1. Stanford: Stanford University Press.

——. 1924. *Cuentos populares españoles.* Vol. 2. Stanford: Stanford University Press.

——. 1926. *Cuentos populares españoles.* Vol. 3. Stanford: Stanford University Press.

Espinosa, Aurelio, and José Manuel Espinosa. 1985. *The Folklore of Spain and the American Southwest: Traditional Spanish Folk Literature in Northern New Mexico and Southern Colorado.* Norman: University of Oklahoma Press.

Espinosa, José Manuel. 1937 [1969]. *Spanish Folk-Tales from New Mexico.* New York: Kraus Reprint.

Feliciano Velázquez, Primo, ed. and trans. 1975. *Códice Chimalpopoca: Anales de Cuauhtitlan y Leyenda de los Soles.* Mexico City: Universidad Nacional Autónoma de México.

Fernandez, James W. 1986. *Persuasions and Performances: The Play of Tropes in Culture.* Bloomington: Indiana University Press.

Foster, George M. 1945. "Sierra Popoluca Folklore and Beliefs." *University of California Publications in American Archaeology and Ethnology* 42: 177–249.

——. 1952. "The Significance to Anthropological Studies of the Places of Origin of Spanish Emigrants to the New World." In *Selected Papers of the XXIXth International Congress of Americanists,* ed. Sol Tax, pp. 292–298. Chicago: University of Chicago Press.

Freeman, Susan Tax. 1970. *The Social Contract in a Castilian Hamlet.* Chicago: University of Chicago Press.

Freud, Sigmund. 1900 [1978]. *The Interpretation of Dreams.* New York: Random House.

——. 1905 [1975]. *Three Essays on the Theory of Sexuality.* New York: Basic Books.

——. 1908 [1959]. "Character and Anal Erotism." In *Sigmund Freud: Collected Papers,* ed. James Strachey, pp. 45–50. New York: Basic Books.

——. 1913 [1946]. *Totem and Taboo.* New York: Vintage.

——. 1923–1925a. "The Dissolution of the Oedipus Complex." In *Standard Edition of the Complete Psychological Works of Sigmund Freud.* Vol. 19. Ed. James Strachey, pp. 173–179. London: Hogarth Press.

——. 1923–1925b. "Some Psychical Consequences of the Anatomical Distinction between the Sexes." In *Standard Edition of the Complete Psychological Works of Sigmund Freud.* Vol. 19. Ed. James Strachey, pp. 248–258. London: Hogarth Press.

——. 1930 [1961]. *Civilization and Its Discontents.* New York: W. W. Norton.

———. 1931 [1959]. "Female Sexuality." In *Sigmund Freud: Collected Papers*, ed. James Strachey, pp. 252–272. New York: Basic Books.

———. 1932 [1933]. "Femininity." In *Standard Edition of the Complete Psychological Works of Sigmund Freud.* Vol. 22. Ed. James Strachey, pp. 112–135. London: Hogarth Press.

———. 1940 [1989]. *Outline of Psycho-Analysis.* New York: W. W. Norton.

———. 1963. *Dora: An Analysis of a Case of Hysteria.* New York: Collier.

Friedlander, Judith. 1975. *Being Indian in Hueyapan: A Study of Forced Identity in Contemporary Mexico.* New York: St. Martin's Press.

Gallop, Jane. 1982. *The Daughter's Seduction: Feminism and Psychoanalysis.* Ithaca: Cornell University Press.

Garibay K., Ángel María. 1940 [1961]. *Llave del náhuatl: Colección de trozos clásicos con gramática y vocabulario, para utilidad de los principiantes.* Mexico City: Otumba.

———. 1953–1954. *Historia de la literatura náhuatl.* 2 vols. Mexico City: Porrúa.

Gayton, A. H. 1935. "The Orpheus Myth in North America." *Journal of American Folk-Lore* 48:263–293.

Gehrts, Heino. 1967. *Das Märchen und das Opfer: Untersuchungen zum europäischen Brüdermärchen.* Bonn: Bouview.

Gilmore, David D. 1987. *Aggression and Community: Paradoxes of Andalusian Culture.* New Haven: Yale University Press.

———. 1990. *Manhood in the Making: Cultural Concepts of Masculinity.* New Haven: Yale University Press.

Gilmore, David D., and Sarah C. Uhl. 1987. "Further Notes on Andalusian Machismo." *Journal of Psychoanalytic Anthropology* 10:341–360.

Gossen, Gary H. 1964. "The Dragon Slayer in Costa Rica: A Version of Aarne-Thompson Tale Type 300." *Southern Folklore Quarterly* 28:237–250.

———. 1974. *Chamulas in the World of the Sun: Time and Space in a Maya Oral Tradition.* Cambridge, Mass.: Harvard University Press.

Gruzinski, Serge. 1989. *Man-Gods in the Mexican Highlands: Indian Power and Colonial Society, 1520–1800.* Stanford: Stanford University Press.

Gutmann, Matthew C. 1993. "Los hombres cambiantes. Los machos impenitentes y las relaciones de género en México en los noventa." *Estudios Sociológicos* 11 (33): 727–742.

———. 1996. *The Meanings of Macho: Being a Man in Mexico City.* Berkeley: University of California Press.

Hansen, Terrence Leslie. 1957. *The Types of the Folktale in Cuba, Puerto Rico, the Dominican Republic, and Spanish South America.* Folklore Studies No. 8. Berkeley: University of California Press.

Henderson, Bernard, and C. V. Calbert. 1925. *Wonder Tales of Alsace-Lorraine*. London: Allan.

Herdt, Gilbert H. 1981. *Guardians of the Flutes*. New York: McGraw-Hill.

Herzfeld, Michael. 1980. "Honour and Shame: Some Problems in the Comparative Analysis of Moral Systems." *Man* 15:339–351.

———. 1984. "The Horns of the Mediterreanist Dilemma." *American Ethnologist* 11:439–454.

———. 1985. *The Poetics of Manhood: Contest and Identity in a Cretan Mountain Village*. Princeton: Princeton University Press.

Hewlett, Barry S. 1991. *Intimate Fathers: The Nature and Context of Aka Pygmy Paternal Infant Care*. Ann Arbor: University of Michigan Press.

Hewlett, Barry S., ed. 1992. *Father-Child Relations: Cultural and Biosocial Contexts*. New York: Aldine de Gruyter.

Hollis, Susan Tower. 1990. *The Ancient Egyptian "Tale of Two Brothers": The Oldest Fairy Tale in the World*. Norman: University of Oklahoma Press.

Hultkrantz, Äke. 1957. *The North American Indian Orpheus Tradition: A Contribution to Comparative Religion*. Publication no. 8. Stockholm: Statens Etnografiska Museum.

Huning, Dolores, and Irene Fisher. 1937. "Folk Tales from the Spanish." *New Mexico Quarterly* 7: 121–130.

Ingham, John. 1986. *Mary, Michael, and Lucifer: Folk Catholicism in Central Mexico*. Austin: University of Texas Press.

Jacobson, Per Schelde, and Barbara Fass Leavy. 1988. *Ibsen's Forsaken Merman: Folklore in the Late Plays*. New York: New York University Press.

Jones, W. Henry, and Lewis L. Kropf. 1989. *Folktales of the Magyars*. London: Stock.

Kardiner, Abram. 1939. *The Individual and His Society: The Psychodynamics of Primitive Social Organization*. New York: Columbia University Press.

———. 1945. *The Psychological Frontiers of Society*. New York: Columbia University Press.

Kardiner, Abram, and Lionel Ovesey. 1951. *The Mark of Oppression: A Psychosocial Study of the American Negro*. New York: W. W. Norton.

Karttunen, Frances. 1983. *An Analytical Dictionary of Nahuatl*. Austin: University of Texas Press. Reprint, Norman: University of Oklahoma Press, 1992.

Kellogg, Susan. 1995. *Law and the Transformation of Aztec Culture, 1500–1700*. Norman: University of Oklahoma Press.

Key, Harold, and Mary Ritchie de Key. 1953. *Vocabulario mejicano de la Sierra de Zacapoaxtla, Puebla*. Mexico City: Instituto Lingüístico de Verano/la Dirección General de Asuntos Indígenas de la Secretaría de Educación Pública.

Kotelchuck, Milton. 1972. "The Nature of the Child's Tie to His Father." Ph.D. diss., Harvard University.

Lacan, Jacques. 1977. *Écrits: A Selection.* New York: W. W. Norton.

Langness, L. L. 1990. "Oedipus in the New Guinea Highlands?" *Ethos* 18: 387–406.

Larrea Palacín, Arcadio de. 1959. *Cuentos gaditanos.* Vol. I, *Cuentos populares de Andalucía.* Madrid: Consejo Superior de Investigaciones Científicas.

Laughlin, Robert. 1962. "Through the Looking Glass: Reflections on Zinacantán Courtship and Marriage." Ph.D. Diss. Harvard University.

———. 1977. *Of Cabbages and Kings: Tales from Zinacantán.* Smithsonian Contributions to Anthropology, no. 23. Washington, D.C.: Smithsonian Institution.

Launey, Michel. 1979. *Introduction à la langue et à la littérature aztéques.* 2 vols. Paris: L'Harmattan.

Leavy, Barbara Fass. 1994. *In Search of the Swan Maiden: A Narrative on Folklore and Gender.* New York: New York University Press.

Lehmann, Walter, ed. and trans. 1906. "Traditions des anciens Mexicains: Texte inédit et original en langue náhuatl avec traduction en latin." *Journal de la Société des Américanistes de Paris,* n.s., 3: 239–297.

León-Portilla, Miguel. 1963 [1982]. *Aztec Thought and Culture.* Norman: University of Oklahoma Press.

———. 1985. "Nahuatl Literature." In *Handbook of Middle American Indians. Supplement 3, Literatures,* ed. Victoria Reifler and Munro S. Edmondson, pp. 7–43. Austin: University of Texas Press.

———. 1986. "Yancuic tlahtolli: palabra nueva. Una antología de la literatura náhuatl contemporánea." *Estudios de Cultura Náhuatl* 18:123–169.

Lévi-Strauss, Claude. 1969. *The Raw and the Cooked: Introduction to a Science of Mythology.* Vol. 1. New York: Harper and Row.

Lewis, Oscar. 1949. "Husbands and Wives in a Mexican Village: A Study of Role Conflict." *American Anthropologist* 51:602–611.

———. 1951. *Life in a Mexican Village: Tepoztlán Restudied.* Urbana: University of Illinois Press.

———. 1961 [1963]. *The Children of Sánchez: Autobiography of a Mexican Family.* New York: Vintage.

———. 1964 [1967]. *Pedro Martínez: A Mexican Peasant and His Family.* New York: Vintage.

References

Limón, José. 1989. "*Carne, Carnales,* and the Carnivalesque: Bakhtinian *Batos,* Disorder, and Narrative Discourses." *American Ethnologist* 16: 471–486.

Lison-Tolosana, Carmelo. 1966 [1983]. *Belmonte de los Caballeros: Anthropology and History in an Aragonese Community.* Princeton: Princeton University Press.

Llano Roza de Ampudia, Aurelio de. 1975. *Cuentos asturianos: Recogidos de la tradición oral.* Oviedo: Editorial la Nueva España.

Lockhart, James. 1992. *The Nahuas after the Conquest: A Social and Cultural History of the Indians of Central Mexico, Sixteenth through Eighteenth Centuries.* Stanford: Stanford University Press.

López Austin, Alfredo. 1980 [1988]. *The Human Body and Ideology: Concepts of the Ancient Nahuas.* Vol. 1. Trans. Thelma Ortiz de Montellano and Bernard Ortiz de Montellano. Salt Lake City: University of Utah Press.

———. 1990. *The Myths of the Opossum: Pathways of Mesoamerican Mythology.* Trans. Bernard R. Ortiz de Montellano and Thelma Ortiz de Montellano. Albuquerque: University of New Mexico Press.

Lüthi, Max. 1970 [1976]. *Once Upon a Time: On the Nature of Fairy Tales.* Bloomington: Indiana University Press.

———. 1975 [1984]. *The Fairytale as Art Form and Portrait of Man.* Bloomington: Indiana University Press.

Lutz, Catherine. 1988. *Unnatural Emotions: Everyday Sentiments on a Micronesian Atoll and Their Challenge to Western Theory.* Chicago: University of Chicago Press.

Marcuse, Herbert. 1955. *Eros and Civilization: A Philosophical Inquiry into Freud.* New York: Vintage Books.

Martin, Laura. 1987. "The Interdependence of Language and Culture in the Bear Story in Spanish and Mochó." *Anthropoloigal Linguistics* 29:533–548.

Marx, Karl. 1964. *The Economic and Philosophical Manuscripts of 1844.* New York: International Publishers.

Mason, J. Alden. 1912. "Four Mexican-Spanish Fairy Tales from Azqueltán, Jalisco." *Journal of American Folklore* 25:191–198.

———. 1956. "Juan el Oso." In *Estudios antropológicos publicados en homenaje al doctor Manuel Gamio,* ed. Walter W. Taylor, pp. 383–389. Mexico City: Universidad Nacional Autónoma de México.

Mason, J. Alden, and Aurelio Espinosa, eds. 1914. "Folk-Tales of the Tepecanos." *Journal of American Folklore* 27:148–210.

Mauss, Marcel. 1927 [1967]. *The Gift: Forms and Functions of Exchange in Archaic Societies.* New York: W. W. Norton.

References

Mead, Margaret. 1935. *Sex and Temperament in Three Primitive Societies.* New York: New American Library.

Mendoza, Vicente T., and Virginia R. R. de Mendoza. 1952. *Folklore de San Pedro Piedra Gorda Zacatecas.* Mexico City: Instituto Nacional de Bellas Artes, Secretaría de Educación Pública.

Miller, Elaine K. 1973. *Mexican Folk Narrative from the Los Angeles Area.* Austin: University of Texas Press.

Miller, Wick. 1983. "Uto-Aztecan Languages." In *Handbook of North American Indians.* Vol. 10. Ed. William C. Sturtevant, pp. 113–124. Washington, D.C.: Smithsonian Institution.

Moser-Rath, Elfriede. 1981. "Diebes Ausrede." In *Enzyklopädie des Märchens.* Vol. 3, Ed. Kurt Ranke, pp. 646–650. Berlin: Walter de Gruyter.

Murphy, Michael D. 1983a. "Coming of Age in Sevilla: The Structuring of a Riteless Passage to Manhood." *Journal of Anthropological Research* 39: 376–392.

———. 1983b. "Emotional Confrontations between Sevillano Fathers and Sons: Cultural Foundations and Social Consequences." *American Ethnologist* 10:650–664.

Nutini, Hugo G. 1967. "A Synoptic Comparison of Mesoamerican Marriage and Family Structure." *Southwestern Journal of Anthropology* 23:383–404.

———. 1988. *Todos Santos in Rural Tlaxcala: A Syncretic, Expressive, and Symbolic Analysis of the Cult of the Dead.* Princeton: Princeton University Press.

Panzer, Friedrich. 1910. *Studien zur germanischen Sagengeschichte.* Vol.1, *Beowulf.* Munich: C. H. Beck.

Paredes, Américo. 1970. *Folktales of Mexico.* Chicago: University of Chicago Press.

Parsons, Elsie Clews. 1932a. "Folklore of Santa Ana Xalmimilulco, Puebla, Mexico." *Journal of American Folklore* 45:318–362.

———. 1932b. "Zapoteca and Spanish Tales of Mitla, Oaxaca." *Journal of American Folklore* 45:277–317.

Paso y Troncoso, Francisco del, ed. and trans. 1903. *Leyenda de los soles.* Florence: Tipografía de Salvador Landi.

Paul, Benjamin D. 1950. "Symbolic Sibling Rivalry in a Guatemalan Indian Village." *American Anthropologist* 52:205–218.

Pitt-Rivers, J. A. 1966. *The People of the Sierra.* Chicago: University of Chicago Press.

Preuss, Konrad T. 1983. *Mitos y cuentos nahuas de la sierra madre occidental.* Ed. Elsa Ziehm. Mexico City: Instituto Nacional Indigenista.

REFERENCES

Price, Richard, and Sally Price. 1966. "Noviazgo in an Andalusian Pueblo." *Southwestern Journal of Anthropology* 22:302–322.

Radin, Paul. 1943. "Cuentos y leyendas de los Zapotecos." *Tlalocan* 1:3–30.

Radin, Paul, and Aurelio M. Espinosa. 1917. *El folklore de Oaxaca.* Mexico City: Escuela Internacional de Arqueología y Etnología Americana.

Rael, Juan B. 1957. *Cuentos españoles de Colorado y Nuevo Méjico.* Vol. 2. Stanford: Stanford University Press.

Ranke, Kurt. 1934. *Die zwei Brüder, eine Studie zur vergleichenden Märchenforschung.* Folklore Fellows Communication no. 114. Helsinki: Suomalainen Tiedekatemia.

———. 1979. "Brüder: Die zwei B. (AaTh 303)." In *Enzyklopädie des Märchens.* Vol. 2. Ed. Kurt Ranke, pp. 912–919. Berlin: Walter de Gruyter.

Reid, John Turner. 1935. "Seven Folktales from Mexico." *Journal of American Folklore* 48:109–124.

Robe, Stanley L. 1970. *Mexican Tales and Legends from Los Altos.* Folklore Studies, no. 20. Berkeley: University of California Press.

———. 1971. *Mexican Tales and Legends from Veracruz.* Folklore Studies, no. 23. Berkeley: University of California Press.

———. 1972. *Amapa Storytellers.* Folklore Studies, no. 24. Berkeley: University of California Press.

———. 1973. *Index of Mexican Folktales.* Folklore Studies, no. 26. Berkeley: University of California Press.

Robinson, Dow F. 1966. *Sierra Nahuat Word Structure.* Hartford Studies in Linguistics, no. 18. Santa Ana, Calif.: Dow F. Robinson.

Róheim, Géza. 1992. *Fire in the Dragon.* Princeton: Princeton University Press.

Rosaldo, Michelle. 1984. "Toward an Anthropology of Self and Feelings." In *Culture and Theory: Essays on Mind, Self, and Emotion,* ed. Richard A. Shweder and Robert A. Levine, pp. 137–157. Cambridge: Cambridge University Press.

Rosenbaum, Brenda. 1993. *With Our Heads Bowed: The Dynamics of Gender in a Maya Community.* Albany: Institute for Mesoamerican Studies.

Sacks, Karen. 1975. *Sisters and Wives: The Past and Future of Sexual Inequality.* Urbana: University of Illinois Press.

Sahagún, Fray Bernardino de. 1953. *Florentine Codex: General History of the Things of New Spain, Book 7 — The Sun, Moon, and Stars, and the Binding of the Years.* Trans. Arthur J. O. Anderson and Charles E. Dibble. Santa Fe, N.M.: School of American Research/the University of Utah.

Sanday, Peggy Reeves. 1981. *Female Power and Male Dominance: On the Origins of Sexual Inequality.* Cambridge: Cambridge University Press.

Sandstrom, Alan R. 1991. *Corn Is Our Blood: Culture and Ethnic Identity in a Contemporary Aztec Indian Village.* Norman: University of Oklahoma Press.

Sandstrom, Alan R., and Pamela Efrein Sandstrom. 1986. *Traditional Papermaking and Paper Cult Figures of Mexico.* Norman: University of Oklahoma Press.

Schaffer, H. Rudolph. 1971. *The Growth of Sociability.* Baltimore: Penguin Books.

Schaffer, H. Rudolph, and Peggy Emerson. 1964. "The Development of Social Attachments in Infancy." *Monographs of the Society for Research in Child Development* 29 (3):1–77.

Sellers, Charles. 1888. *Tales from the Lands of Nuts and Grapes.* London: Field and Tuer, the Leadenhall Press and Company.

Sherzer, Joel. 1987. "A Discourse-Centered Approach to Language and Culture." *American Anthropologist* 89 (2):295–309.

Shweder, Richard. 1979. "Rethinking Culture and Personality Theory, Part I: A Critical Examination of Two Classic Postulates." *Ethos* 7:255–278.

———. 1979b. "Rethinking Culture and Personality Theory, Part II: A Critical Examination of Two More Classic Postulates." *Ethos* 7:279–311.

———. 1980. "Rethinking Culture and Personality Theory, Part III: From Genesis and Typology to Hermeneutics and Dynamics." *Ethos* 8:60–94.

Spiro, Melford E. 1982. *Oedipus in the Trobriands.* Chicago: University of Chicago Press.

Stitt, J. Michael. 1992. *Beowulf and the Bear's Son: Epic, Saga, and Fairytale in Northern Germanic Tradition.* New York: Garland Publishing.

Stoller, Robert J. 1985. *Presentations of Gender.* New Haven: Yale University Press.

Swanson, Guy E. 1976. "Orpheus and Star Husband: Meaning and the Structure of Myth." *Ethnology* 15:115–133.

Sydow, C. W. von. 1948. *Selected Papers on Folklore.* Copenhagen: Rosenkilde and Bagger.

Taggart, James M. n.d. "Original Language Texts for 'The Bear and His Sons.'" Unpublished ms.

———. 1983. *Nahuat Myth and Social Structure.* Austin: University of Texas Press.

———. 1990. *Enchanted Maidens: Gender Relations in Spanish Folktales of Courtship and Marriage.* Princeton: Princeton University Press.

333

Tedlock, Dennis. 1983. *The Spoken Word and the Work of Interpretation.* Philadelphia: University of Pennsylvania Press.

Thompson, Stith. 1929 [1966]. *Tales of the North American Indians.* Bloomington: University of Indiana Press.

———. 1946 [1977]. *The Folktale.* Berkeley: University of California Press.

Todd, Emmanuel. 1988. *The Explanation of Ideology: Family Structures and Social Systems.* Oxford: Basil Blackwell.

Ward, Donald. 1968. *The Divine Twins: An Indo-European Myth in Germanic Tradition.* Folklore Studies, no. 19. Berkeley: University of California Press.

Weiner, Annette B. 1992. *Inalienable Possessions: The Paradox of Keeping-While-Giving.* Berkeley: University of California Press.

Wheeler, Howard T. 1943. *Tales from Jalisco Mexico.* Philadelphia: American Folk-Lore Society.

Wolf, Eric. 1959. *Sons of the Shaking Earth.* Chicago: University of Chicago Press.

Ziehm, Elsa. 1982. "Introducción." In *Mitos y cuentos nahuas de la sierra madre occidental,* by Konrad T. Preuss, pp. 9–72. Mexico City: Instituto Nacional Indigenista.

Index

Aarne, Antti, 175, 196, 299 n.27, 305 nn.2–3, 5, 306 nn.14, 16, 309 nn.1, 25, 311 n.1, 313 nn.1–3, 314 nn.7, 10, 316 n.1, 318 n.2

Aarne-Thompson (AT) tale types:
—AT 38 "The Claw in Split Tree," 153–154
—AT 300 "The Dragon Slayer": and AT 301 "The Bear's Son," 23; and AT 303 "Blood Brothers," 142
—AT 301 "The Bear's Son": and AT 650 "Strong John," 46–47; and *Beowulf*, 12, 23; and Christian redemption, 166; and *difrasismo* (diaphrasis) 57; distribution of, 23, 46; and dragon slayer, 23; English translation of Nahuat story of, 48–56; English translation of Spanish story of, 24–31; father in, 63–67; feminine narrative style of, 40–41; feminine variants of, 39–44; filial loyalties in, 44, 69; food symbolism in, 38, 43, 59–60; formulaic endings of, 61–62; human-animal relationship in, 154; and literature, 23; masculine narrative style of, 31–35; masculine variants of, 36–39; Nahuat text of, 257–295; Nānāhuatl as Nāhuēhueht in, 63–65; native American language groups where collected, 303 n.2; native Mexican language groups where collected, 302 nn.2–4; nursing in, 36, 66; Oedipal struggle in, 6; oicotype of, 47; peer relations in, 67–69; rain gods (quiyahteōmeh) in, 47–48; repetition as poetic device in, 57–60; sexual competition in, 38, 43–44, 69–70; Spanish text of, 250–257; as

"The Three Stolen Princesses," 13
—AT 303 "Blood Brothers," 154; adultery in, 141; and ancient Egypt, 119; and AT 300 "The Dragon Slayer," 119, 142; and AT 313C "Blancaflor," 189–190; compared to AT 676 "Open Sesame," 151; conception in, 135–138; connections among brothers in, 139–143; dreaming in, 140; English translation of Nahuat story of, 130–134; English translation of Spanish story of, 120–125; father's image in, 125–127, 134–139, 190; by gender of storyteller, 125–127; honor and shame in, 125, 127, 141; masculine autonomy in, 126; origins of, 119; recasting aggression in, 142; repetition as poetic device in, 134, 139; and "Saint George and the Dragon," 303 n.3; sexual competition in, 127–128; and sibling terminology, 129–130
—AT 313A and 313C "Blancaflor," 174; agency of women in, 214–216; ambivalence toward women in, 192; and AT 303 "Blood Brothers," 189–190; and AT 425 "Cupid and Psyche," 194; charcoal seller in, 215; contrasting images of women in, 220–222; and courtship and marriage, 174–175; curse as poetic device in, 219–220; Earth Mother in, 214; English translation of Nahuat story of, 197–212; English translation of Spanish story of, 175–189; episodes of, 175; erotic imagery in, 216; exchange in, 213–214; father's image in, 189–190;

gambler in, 190, 212–213; gender and ethnic relations in, 197; and gender relations, 13, 196; as "The Girl as Helper in the Hero's Flight," 13; heroine's mutilation in, 190–191, 216–217; human-animal relationship in, 216; irony in, 191, 193–194; and Jason and Medea, 13, 174; kinship terminology in, 221; love for animals in, 216; power of words in, 212–213; prohibition as poetic device in, 194, 219–220; repetition in, 213–214; sexual reproduction in, 217; Ursula Andress as heroine in, 175; witchcraft in, 192; and woman's predicament, 173–174

—AT 327A "Hansel and Gretel," 316 n.5

—AT 400 "The Man on a Quest for His Lost Wife," 13; antiquity of, 223; distribution of, 223–224; and literature, 223, and native American Orpheus tradition, 13; and "The Swan Maiden," 173, 223. *See also* Orpheus

—AT 425 "Cupid and Psyche": and AT 313C "Blancaflor," 194;

—AT 510 "Cinderella": beauty and ugliness in, 44; food symbolism in, 43

—AT 563 "The Table, the Ass, and the Stick," 82; brothers in, 150–151

—AT 566 "The Three Magic Objects and the Wonderful Fruits," 84; brothers in, 93–94; English translation of Spanish story of, 85–93

—AT 613 "The Two Travelers," 82; and AT 38 "The Claw in Split Tree," 153–154; and AT 301 "The Bear's Son," 152–153; distribution of, 144; English translation of Nahuat story of, 156–163; English translation of Spanish story of, 146–150; father in, 152–153; food sharing in, 155; and Grimms, 144; history of, 144; and *Libro de los Gatos*, 144–145; linear plot of, 145–146, 153; and literature, 144; non-linear plot of, 154–166; origin of, 4

—AT 650 "Strong John," 117; and AT 301 "The Bear's Son," 46–47

—AT 676 "Open Sesame," 82; brothers in, 150; and literature, 150

—AT 759 "God's Justice Vindicated": blasphemy in, 32; scatology in, 32

—AT 1525 "The Master Thief": distribution of, 113; English translation of Nahuat story of, 114–115; fraternal interdependence in, 115–117; Nahuat origins of, 113; relational masculinity in, 113, 115–117; and Renaissance literature, 113; and *Schimpf und Ernst*, 308 n.20

—AT 1535 "The Rich and the Poor Peasant," 71, 82; and "Big Claus and Little Claus," 71; *compadrazgo* in, 102–107, 112; critique of capitalism in, 77–78; English translations of Nahuat story of, 97–102, 109–111; English translation of Spanish story of, 73–77; and ethnic stratification, 105–107; exchange in, 104; greed in, 112–113; and Hans Christian Andersen, 71; love between men in, 96, 102; number of variants of, 71; relational masculinity in, 113; scatology in, 73; and Unibos, 12, 71. *See also* motif K111.2 "The hat that pays everything"; motif K113.7 "The resuscitating horn"

—AT 1539 "Cleverness and Gullibility," 71, 82

—AT 1737 "The Parson in the Sack to Heaven," 71

adultery, 141, 154

aggression, recasting of in stories, 142

Aiken, Riley, 314 n.3, 316 nn.2,4, 317 nn.9,11,18

Andersen, Hans Christian, 71

Andress, Ursula, 175

animal companion spirits (tōnalmeh), 154

annihilation, image of, 230

anthropomorphized image, 66

autonomía (autonomy), 2, 33–44; definition of, 33. *See also* masculinity

avoidance relationship, 67

Aztecs, 47: language of, 1. *See also* Nahua; Nahuat; Nahuatl

Balint, Alice, 320 n.8
Balint, Michael, 320 n.28
Barakat, Robert A., 66, 302 n.2,
  304 nn.30,32, 305 nn.45–46,54
Barry, Herbert III, 300 n.70
basic personality structure, 19. *See
  also* Kardiner, Abram
Baudis, Josef, 318 n.1
Behar, Ruth, 4, 298 n.10, 301 n.8,
  311 n.23
Beidelman, Thomas, 11
Beowulf, 23. *See also* AT 301 "The
  Bear's Son"
Bernheimer, Charles, 300 n.44
betrothal ceremony, 165
Bierhorst, John, 298 n.14, 303 n.10
Big Claus and Little Claus, 71. *See
  also* AT 1535 "The Rich and the
  Poor Peasant"
birth. *See* procreation
blasphemy, 31. *See also* masculinity
Boas, Franz, 298 n.13, 303 nn.4,8,
  304 nn.25–26,43, 305 nn.49,51
Boggs, Ralph S., 113, 306 n.16,
  308 n.20, 309 n.21
Bolte, Johannes, 312 n.3
Bottigheimer, Ruth B., 312 n.1
Bowlby, John, 320 n.29
Brandes, Stanley, 7, 37, 297 n.5,
  301 n.17, 304 nn.35–36, 311 n.23
Briggs, Katherine, 318 n.1
brother and sister, 230–231. *See also*
  Orpheus
brothers. *See* AT 301 "Blood Broth-
  ers," AT 566 "The Three Magic
  Objects and the Wonderful Fruits,"
  AT 613 "The Two Travelers," AT
  1525 "The Master Thief," and AT
  1535 "The Rich and the Poor
  Peasant"
Burkhart, Louise, 61, 237,
  304 nn.13,15,22, 313 nn.22–23,
  320 n.23
Burns, Allan F., 319 nn.9,12

Calbert, C. V., 318 n.1
capitalism: critique of in Spanish stories, 77; Nahuat personification of,
  246; and parenting labor, 245. *See
  also* labor
Carrasco, Pedro, 313 n.21
Cassanova, Pablo Gonzales, 316 n.2

censorship, 141–143
charcoal seller, 215, 311 n.27
chastity, 39. *See also* honor and
  shame
children: and father, 134–135, care
  of, 165; sleeping arrangements of,
  234; weaning of, 234
Chodorow, Nancy, 239–240,
  300 nn.67–69, 320 nn.26–30,5–6;
  gender theory of 21–22; and relationality, 22;
Christian, William A., 301 nn.6–7;
  and religious authority, 32–33
Christian dualism, 165–166
Christiansen, Reidar Th., 223, 318 n.2
Clifford, James, 11, 298 n.6, 299 n.19
cognate folktales, 10
Collier, George, 320 n.3; and *autonomía* and masculinity, 301 n.9;
  and changing chastity code,
  302 n.23; and chastity code and private property, 39
Collier, Jane: and changing chastity
  code, 302 n.23; and chastity code, 39
Coltrane, Scott, 300 n.70
communalism, 166–167
compadrazgo, 102; in folktales, 112;
  and naming, 105; obligations of,
  105; selection of *compadres* in, 105
comparative method: and Alan Dundes, 10–12; and Archer Taylor, 12;
  and cognate folktales, 10, 12; and
  cultural relativism, 10–12; and
  Finnish method, 12; and Géza Róheim, 15; and Grimm brothers, 12;
  and Stith Thompson, 12; and stories compared, 13–14
conception: images of, 135–138. *See
  also* procreation
consciousness, 245
Cortés Vázquez, Luis, 40, 113, 144,
  146, 174, 301 nn.4,14,16,
  302 nn.19–20,24–31,34–38,40,
  305 nn.8–9, 306 n.12,
  308 nn.3,4,6,8, 309 nn.20,22,25,
  310 nn.3,6–7,9,11–12,17,20,
  311 n.27, 312 nn.3,8, 314 nn.5–
  6,13–14, 315 nn.15–16,21–22,
  316 nn.6–8, 317 n.18
cosmovision: and connected consciousness, 245–246; and relationality, 241

creation, Nahuat eras of, 48
Croft, Kenneth, 312 nn.16,20, 313 n.26
cuckold: and masculinity, 38; in retrospect, 38–39
cultural relativism, 10–12; and Abram Kardiner, 19; and Margaret Mead, 21
culture of poverty, 297 n.4
Curcija-Prodanovic, Nada, 318 n.1
Curiel Marchán, Marciano, 113, 301 nn.4, 13, 15–16, 19, 302 nn.19–20,24,26,28, 307 nn.18,20–24,26,31, 309 nn.20,22,29, 310 nn.3,6,8,11,13,17,21, 311 n.27
curse as poetic device, 219–220

Darbord, Bernard, 298 n.9, 299 n.26, 312 nn.2,5
dead: and funerals, 242; journey to land of, 229–230; land of, 225
death, Nahuat conception of, 229–230
Deutsch, Helen, 18
devil: Nahuat word for, 3; as Spanish-speaking Mexican, 165
Díaz Hernández, Vicente, 303 n.12
difrasismo (diaphrasis), 57, 304 n.17; and compound words, 57; definition of, 57; examples of, 57
division of labor, 164–165
Dobie, Frank J., 66, 303 n.2, 304 nn.29–31, 305 nn.45,55, 312 nn.4,14
dreaming in folktales, 140
Dundes, Alan, 10–12, 67, 298 nn.6,12,18, 299 nn.20–23,34, 300 n.53, 301 n.12, 304 n.39, 306 n.13, 308 n.14, 309 n.25, 319 n.11; and comparative method, 10–12; and Freud, 5; and scatology in folklore, 34

earth, personification of, 135, 214
Ehrensaft, Diane, 320 n.30
Emerson, Peggy, 320 n.29
Espinosa, Aurelio M., 72, 129, 136, 215, 301 n.4, 303 nn.2,6, 305 nn.7–9, 307 nn.24,28–29, 308 nn.4,8,15,16, 309 nn.23,27,29, 310 nn.3,15,22, 311 n.27, 312 nn.4,11,16–17, 314 nn.5,13, 315 nn.14–16,20,22,

316 nn.2,3,23, 317 nn.9,11–12,18, 318 n.18, 319 nn.9,12
Espinosa, José Manuel, 310 n.16, 312 n.4
estranged labor, 245. See also labor
ethnic relations, 105–107; and Christian dualism, 165–166; and exchange, 197
ethnic stratification, 105–107; and AT 1535 "The Rich and the Poor Peasant," 105–107; and fatalism, 105–108
exchange: in AT 313C "Blancaflor," 213–214; and ethnic relations, 197; and greed, 112–113; historical changes in, 104; and masculinity, 117–118; partners in, 104; power asymmetry in, 105–108; as theme in folktales, 104; and transactions, 77–84
extended family, communal organization of, 167–171. See also family

family: brothers' relations in, 164–167; communal organization of, 167–171; organization of labor in, 108; patrilineally extended, 67, 167–171; sleeping arrangements in, 233–234
fatalism: and ethnic stratification, 105–108; and family structure, 108
father: in AT 301 "The Bear's Son," 36, 63–67; in AT 303 "Blood Brothers," 125–127, 134–139, 190; denial of by Spanish men, 36; focus on, 22; image and family life of, 67; image and parenting role of, 67; and reproduction of masculinity, 240, 246; Spanish women's image of in AT 301 "The Bear's Son," 41–42
Feliciano Velázquez, Primo, 298 n.14, 303 n.10
femininity, 18. See also gender theory
Fernandez, James, 299 n.34
Fifth Sun, 47
filial loyalties, 69; women's expression of, 44
Finnish method, 12. See also comparative method
Fisher, Irene, 312 n.4, 316 n.2
folktales. See stories

food: and AT 301 "The Bear's Son,"
38, 43, 59–60; and AT 520 and
510B "Cinderella," 43; and conception, 135–138; consumption of in
folktales, 105; and Nahuat ethnic
identity, 60; and repetition, 59–60;
sharing of, 32, 155, 166; in women's
stories, 43
Foster, George M., 298 n.16, 303 n.4,
305 nn.49,51
Freeman, Susan Tax, 311 n.23
Freud, Sigmund, 70, 77, 234, 239,
300 nn.41,42,44–52,61, 306 n.13,
311 n.28, 319 nn.15,17, 320 n.5,
321 n.11; and Abram Kardiner,
19–20; and censorship, 142; criticisms of, 18; and dreams, 5; and
femininity, 18; gender theory of,
18–19; and Helen Deutsch, 18; and
Jeanne Lampl-de Groot, 18; and
Marxist theory, 245; and masculinity, 18; and Oedipus complex,
18; revisions of, 21–22; and unconscious, 17
Friedlander, Judith, 297 n.5

gallantry, 38
Gallop, Jane, 299 nn.36,38, 300 n.39,
320 n.2; and Jacques Lacan, 16
gamblers, 190, 212–213
Garibay K., Ángel María, 304 n.16;
and *difrasismo* (diaphrasis), 57
Gayton, A. H., 299 n.28, 318 n.6
Gehrts, Heino, 119, 310 n.4
gender relations, 197
gender theory: and Abram Kardiner,
19; and David Gilmore, 245; and
Helen Deutsch, 18; and Jacques La-
can, 16; and Jane Gallop, 16; and
Jeanne Lampl-de Groot, 18; and
Margaret Mead, 21; and Nancy
Chodorow, 21; and Robert Stoller,
21; and Sigmund Freud, 18; and
Stanley Brandes, 37
Gilmore, David, 43, 245, 297 n.5,
298 n.5, 300 n.63, 302 n.33,
304 nn.35–36, 320 n.8
Gossen, Gary H., 303 n.11, 311 n.27
greed, 73, 112–113
Grimm brothers, 12
Gruzinski, Serge, 320 n.20
Gutmann, Matthew, 67, 304 n.38

Hansen, Terrense Leslie, 113,
309 n.21
Henderson, Bernard, 318 n.1
Herzfeld, Michael, 298 n.5
Hewlett, Barry S., 300 n.70
Hispanic. *See* Spanish-speaking
Mexican
Hispanic culture, 10
Hispanic Man, 1–2, 20
Hollis, Susan Tower, 119
honor and shame, 125, 127
Hueyapan, 297 n.5
Hultkrantz, Åke, 236–237, 299 n.28,
318 nn.6–8, 319 nn.10–11,13–14,
320 nn.12,21,25
human-animal relationship, 216
Huning, Dolores, 312 n.4, 316 n.2

īlihuiz: definition of, 4; personification of, 60
Ingham, John, 297 n.5
inheritance, 79–80; in folktales, 84–85
irony, 191, 193–194

Jacobsen, Per Schelde, 318 n.1
Jason and Medea, 174, 314 n.7
Jones, W. Henry, 318 n.1

Kaguru, 11
Kahane, Claire, 300 n.44
Kardiner, Abram, 105, 300 nn.53–
57,59–60,62, 308 n.13; and basic
personality structure, 19; criticisms of, 20; masculinity theory of,
20; and Ralph Linton, 20; and Sigmund Freud, 19–20
Karttunen, Frances, 57, 249,
298 nn.7–8, 304 nn.14,17,19,
308 n.9, 310 n.18, 311 nn.24–25,
313 n.24, 318 n.23, 319 nn.14,17,
320 n.33, 321 nn.4–5
Kellogg, Susan, 246, 321 n.10
Key, Harold, 248–249, 312 n.2
Kinder- und Hausmärchen, 144
kinship terminology, 129, 221. *See
also* sibling terminology
Knapp, Grace, 314 n.7
Kotelchuck, Milton, 320 n.29
Kropf, Lewis L., 318 n.1

La Antorcha Campesina (The Torch
of the Farmer), 246

labor: alienated (wage), 107, 245–246; migrant, 107; organization of in Nahuat family, 108, 167–171; and parenting, 245

Lacan, Jacques, 299 nn.36–37, 320 nn.1–2; and gender theory, 16

Lampl-de Groot, Jeanne, 18

land: and changing ownership conceptions of, 104; obtaining for *milpas*, 107

Langness, L. L., 300 n.63

language and culture: and AT 301 "The Bear's Son," 16; and blasphemy, 31–35; and *difrasismo* (diaphrasis), 57; and disorderly speech, 57; and *īlihuiz* in speech, 16; and Jacques Lacan, 16; and Jane Gallop, 16; and linguistic change, 104; and masculine speech in Spain, 31–35; and narrative style, 31–35, 56–62; and power of spoken words, 196, 212–213; and repetition as a poetic device, 57–60, 139; and use of language in storytelling, 15–16

Larrea Palacín, Arcadio de, 301 n.4, 302 nn.24,26–28

Laughlin, Robert, 299 n.31, 303 nn.4,7, 304 nn.25,42, 305 n.49, 319 nn.9,12; and Tzotzil Mayan folktales, 14

Launey, Michael, 304 n.22

La Unión Campesina Independiente (The Independent Farmers' Union), 247

Leavy, Barbara Fass, 173–174, 215, 313 n.2, 314 nn.4,8, 315 n.17, 317 n.10, 318 nn.1,4, 319 n.18

Lehmann, Walter, 298 n.14, 303 n.10

León-Portilla, Miguel, 298 n.14, 304 nn.16–18; and *difrasismo* (diaphrasis), 57

Lévi-Strauss, Claude, 304 n.20

Lewis, Oscar, 67, 297 nn.2–5, 304 nn.28,37, 311 n.23; and Hispanic Man stereotype, 1

Libro de los Gatos, 144, 153

lightning bolts. *See* rain gods (quiyahteōmeh)

Limón, José, 298 n.5

linear plots, 165–166

Lison-Tolosana, Carmelo, 301 n.18, 304 nn.35–36

Llano Roza de Ampudia, Aurelio de, 72, 305 nn.7–9, 306 nn.10,15–18, 307 nn.18,22,24,28,30, 308 n.16, 310 n.3, 314 nn.5,13, 315 nn.14,15–16,21–22, 316 n.23, 317 nn.11,18, 318 n.4

Lockhart, James, 104, 129, 308 nn.10–12, 310 n.14

López Austin, Alfredo, 5, 298 n.15, 310 n.19

love (tazohtaliz): between humans and animals, 216; between man and woman, 225, 229; between men, 96, 102; incestuous, 233; Nahuat expression of, 219, 242

Lüthi, Max, 61, 145, 304 n.23, 312 nn.6–7,19

Lutz, Catherine, 320 n.11

Malinowski, Bronislaw, 11

Marcuse, Herbert, 320 n.5, 321 n.11

marital chastity, 141. *See also* honor and shame

marriage, 237–239

Martin, Laura, 303 n.4

Marx, Karl, 245, 329 nn.4–5; and Freud, 245; and Nancy Chodorow, 21

masculinity, 1; and Abram Kardiner, 20; and assertiveness, 245; and *autonomía* (autonomy), 2, 33–34, 126, 128, 151, 244; and *autonomía* and capitalism, 245; and *autonomía* and private property, 245; and blasphemy, 31–35; and cuckold, 38; and denial of the father, 36; and exchange, 117–118; and fathering, 240, 246; and gallantry, 38; and male connection, 2; and matrilocality, 34; and relationality, 113, 115–117, 244; and religious authority, 32–33; and scatology, 31–35. *See also* gender theory

Mason, J. Alden, 299 n.31, 303 n.4, 304 nn.25–26,42, 305 n.49, 308 n.17, 312 nn.4,16–17, 316 nn.2,6, 317–318 n.18, 318 n.5, 319 nn.9,12

matrilocality, 34. *See also* post-marital residence

Mauss, Marcel, 308 n.12

Maya. *See* Tzotzil Maya; Yucatec Maya

Mead, Margaret, 300n.63; and gender, 21
Mendoza, Vicente T., 316nn.2, 8, 317n.18
Mendoza, Virginia R. R. de, 316nn.2,8, 317n.18
mestizo, 10. *See also* Spanish-speaking Mexican migrant labor, 107. *See also* labor
Miller, Elaine K., 312n.4
Miller, Wick, 297n.1, 321n.1
moral discourse, 141–143
Moser-Rath, Elfriede, 308n.19
Mother Earth, 216. *See also* earth motifs: and castration, 106; D671 "The Transformation Flight," 316n.2; D672 "The Obstacle Flight," 316n.2, 317n.18; by gender of the storyteller, 127–128; K111.2 "The hat that pays everything," 96, 102–103; K113.7 "The resuscitating horn," 96–97, 102–104, 106; N342.3 "The jealous brother" or "Jealous and overhasty man kills his rescuing brothers," 127–128, 140, 142–143; and Oedipal anxieties, 106
Murphy, Michael D., 67, 297n.5, 301n.10, 304n.35; and matrilocality, 34

Nahua, 215, 224
Nahuat, 153; number and location of, 297n.1
Nahuatl, 153
Nahuat language, 1; and Classical Aztec or Nahuatl, 249; definition of, 248–249; and *mexicano*, 3; and Zacapoaxtla dialect of Classical Aztec, 248
Nānānhuatl: as Nāhuēhueht, 63–65, 154; as Nānāhuatzin in At 301 "The Bear's Son," 47–48, 154
narratives. *See* stories
narrative style: *difrasismo* (diaphrasis), 57; gender differences in, 41; Nahuat and Spanish, 56–62; Nahuat art of, 56–57
narrators. *See* storytellers
Nursery and Household Tales, 311–312n.1
nursing in folktales, 36, 66

Nutini, Hugo G., 2, 67, 304n.41, 320n.24, 321n.9

Oedipal themes, 45, 70, 117; and AT 301 "The Bear's Son," 66; and Orpheus, 225, 235
Oedipus complex, 66
oicotype, 19
Orpheus, 223; annihilation in, 230; brother and sister in, 230–231; cannibalism in, 234; death in, 229–230; distribution of in Mexico, 224; English translation of Nahuat stories of, 225–229, 231–233; incestuous love in, 233; journey to land of the dead in, 229, 230; land of dead in, 229–230; in native North America, 224; Oedipal themes in, 224; primal scene in, 233–235; prohibition in, 224; and shamanism, 236–237; sister in, 230, 235; theories of, 236–237, 319–320n.18; types of in native North America, 225; weaning memory in, 235; women's reproductive autonomy in, 230
Ovesey, Lionel, 105, 308n.13
owl man (tācatecolōt): and devil, 57; as harbinger of death, 237

Panzer, Friedrich, 299n.24, 301n.1
Paredes, Américo, 113, 116, 309nn.24,30
parenting labor: and capitalism, 245; and masculine *autonomía* (autonomy), 245
Parsons, Elsie Clews, 299n.31, 312nn.4,11–12,16,18,314n.13, 316nn.2,4,8, 317nn.16,18
Paso y Troncoso, Francisco de, 298n.14, 303n.10
patron-client, 115
Paul, Benjamin D., 320n.34
Paxson, Leonore, A., 300n.70
Pentameron, 144
Pitt-Rivers, Julian A., 297n.5, 301nn.6,18, 302nn.21–22, 311n.23; and cuckold in retrospect, 38–39; and religious authority, 32
plots: and European folktales, 145–146; linear form of, 145–146, 153; and Max Lüthi, 145–146; nonlinear form of, 154–166

poetic devices: and AT 313C "Blanca-flor," 219–220; and repetition, 213–214. *See also* language and culture
Polívka, Georg, 324 n.3
Popolucan, 68, 69
positional identity, 37
postmarital residence, 67; and matri-locality in Spain, 9, 34; and patrilo-cality among Nahuat, 9; and rates, 138; and sibling terminology, 129
power, 221
Preuss, Konrad T., 298 n.14, 303 n.4, 304 n.27, 305 nn.44,50, 316 n.2, 317 n.13, 318 n.5, 319 n.9
Price, Richard, 297 n.5
Price, Sally, 297 n.5
primal scene: as cannibalism, 234; and Orpheus, 233–235; as subjuga-tion, 234–235
private property, 39, 104. *See also* land
procreation, images of: as eating, 135–138; and family loyalties, 136–137; and gender division of la-bor, 136; as planting, 134–138
prohibition as poetic device, 194, 219–220

Radin, Paul, 130, 136, 215, 303 nn.2,4,8, 304 nn.25–26,42, 305 n.49, 308 n.17, 309 nn.23,27,29, 310 n.15, 311 n.27, 312 nn.4,11, 316 n.2, 317 nn.9,11–12,18
Rael, Juan B., 310 n.16, 312 n.4
rain gods (quiyahteōmeh), 47–48
raising animals by halves, 80, 107
Ranke, Kurt, 119, 142, 309 nn.1,3, 310 n.3, 311 n.26
rape, 215–216
reduplication. *See* language and cul-ture; repetition as poetic device
Reid, John Turner, 316 nn.2,6, 317 n.18
relational capacities, 95
relationality: and attachment needs, 240, and boys, 22; conditions for in men, 230–240; and cosmovision, 241; definition of, 22; expression of in stories, 67–68; and father, 240; and femininity, 239; and girls, 22; and masculinity, 239; and Nancy Chodorow, 22

relational masculinity, 239
repetition as poetic device, 57–60, 134; in ritual 60
Ritchie de Key, Mary, 248–249, 321 n.2
ritual kinship, 102, 105. *See also* compadrazgo
robbers, 113
Robe, Stanley L., 96–97, 115, 299 n.29, 301 n.5, 302 n.2, 303 n.8, 304 n.34, 305 nn.47,56, 308 nn.3,5,7–8,17, 309 nn.21,23,26,29, 312 nn.4,11,14, 318 n.5
Robinson, Dow F., 249, 297 n.1, 321 n.3
Róheim, Géza, 199 n.32, 300 nn.40,42–43, 315 n.18, 319 n.16; and approach to the study of folktales, 14–15; and compara-tive method, 15; and folktales and dreams, 17; and repression, 17
Rosaldo, Michele, 321 n.11
Rosenbaum, Brenda, 303 n.4

Sacks, Karen, 321 n.11
Sahagún, Bernardino de, 5, 298 n.14, 303 n.10
Saint George and the Dragon, 309 n.3
Sanday, Peggy R., 300 n.70
Sandstrom, Alan R., 60, 237, 299 n.30, 304 n.21, 320 nn.22,24
Sandstrom, Pamela, 237, 320 nn.22,24
scatology: men's use of, 31; women's use of, 40. *See also* language and culture
Schaffer, H. Rudolph, 320 n.29
Schimpf und Ernst, 308 n.20
Sellers, Charles, 318 n.4
sexual abstinence, 234
sexual competition: and AT 301 "The Bear's Son," 38; and brothers, 127–128; in stories by native Mexicans, 69–70; in stories by women, 43–44. *See also* AT 303 "Blood Broth-ers;" motif N342.3 "The jealous brother"
sexual reproduction, 217. *See also* procreation
shamanism, 236–237
sharecropping, 80, 107. *See also* rais-ing animals by halves

Sherzer, Joel, 299n.33
Shweder, Richard, 300n.53, 321n.11
sibling terminology: and family life, 129; and folktales, 129–130; and matrilocality, 129; and patrilocality, 129
sister, 230, 235
sorcery, 4
Spanish-speaking Mexican: as *gente de razón*, 3; in Jalisco, 14; as storytellers, 9–10; taking Nahuat land, 107. *See also* ethnic relations
Spiro, Melford E., 311n.29, 319n.15
spoken word, 212–213. *See also* language and culture
Stitt, J. Michael, 23, 299n.24, 301n.2
Stoller, Robert, 240–241, 300nn.64–66, 320nn.7,31–32; and Freud, 21; and transsexual men, 21
stories: and Nahuat narrators learning, 6–7; and Spanish narrators learning, 8; and transcription of, 15; and types of compared, 13–14
story, Nahuat term for, 141
storytellers: number of Nahuat, 5; number of Spanish, 7; Spanish-speaking Mexican, 9–10; women as, 8–9
storytelling: censorship in, 141–143; didactic function of, 105, 113, 116, 141, 230; differences between Spanish and Nahuat in, 8–9; as discursive act, 15; gender differences in, 41; and moral discourse, 141–143; Nahuat occasions for, 6–7; performance of, 41; Spanish occasions for, 8
style: and European folktales, 145–146
Sustenance Mountain, 47
Swan Maiden, 223: *See also* AT 400 "The Man on a Quest for His Lost Wife"
Swanson, Guy E., 319n.18
Sydow, C. W. von, 300n.58, 303n.9; and oicotype, 19
symbiosis anxiety, 240–241

Taggart, James M., 298n.14, 301n.11, 302nn.32,39, 303nn.11–12, 304n.40, 311n.23, 314nn.5,9,11–13, 315nn.14–16,19,22, 316n.24, 317n.18, 318nn.5,20–22

Tanala, 20
Taylor, Archer, 12
Tedlock, Dennis, 299n.34
Teotihuacan, 47
Tepecano, 68, 153, 214, 224
Tepehua, 68
Tepoztlán, 297n.5
Thompson, Stith, 23, 46–47, 85, 113, 127, 154, 175, 196, 299nn.25,27, 301n.3, 302n.1, 303nn.2,5, 305nn.1–6, 306nn.14,16,18, 307nn.1,19,25, 308nn.2,18–20, 309nn.1,3,25,28, 310n.10, 311n.1, 312nn.9–10,18–19, 313nn.1,3, 314nn.7,10, 316n.1, 318nn.2–3; and cognate folktales, 12; and comparative method, 12
Thousand and One Nights, 150, 312n.9
Tlayacapan, 297n.5
Todd, Emmanuel, 311n.23
Todos Santos, 237
Totonacs, 129
transcription of stories, 248
translation of stories, 249
transsexuals, 21
Trobriands, 11
Tzotzil Maya, 14, 68–69, 224

Uhl, Sarah C., 43, 302n.33, 304nn.35–36
Unibos, 12

wage labor, 245. *See also* labor
Ward, Donald, 119, 310nn.4–5
weaning, 234, 235
Weiner, Annette B., 308n.12
Wheeler, Howard T., 68, 69, 152–153, 299n.29, 302n.2, 303n.7, 304nn.24,33, 305nn.48,52–53, 308n.17, 309nn.23,27,29, 312nn.4,11–15, 314n.13, 316nn.2,4,7, 317nn.9,11,16,18, 318n.5
witchcraft, 192
Wolf, Eric, 10, 298n.17
women: agency of in AT "Blancaflor," 214–216; and chastity, 39; contrasting images of in AT 313C "Blancaflor," 220–222; depicting violence in AT 301 "The Bear's Son," 42; father's image by, 66–67;

and food symbolism, 43; interdependence among, 40; men's ambivalence toward, 192; moral reputation of, 39; reproductive autonomy of, 217, 230; reproductive power of, 217, 230; sexual autonomy of, 221–222; sexual competition depicted by, 43–44, 128; speech of in AT 301 "The Bear's Son," 40; as storytellers, 8–9; and supernatural power, 221

words. *See* language and culture

Yucatec Maya, 224

Zapotec, 68–69, 153, 215
Ziehm, Elsa, 298n.14